Straight from the Heart

ALSO BY DOTTIE LAMM

Daddy on Board (2007)

Choice Concerns (1996)

Second Banana (1983)

Straight from the Heart

Dottie Lamm

Colorado's former first lady shares her insights on family,
friends, feminism, politics, and the fine art of growing older
through 25 years of her newspaper columns

ISBN: 978-0-578-64677-0 (print)

Also available in ebook

Edited by Joan Sherman

Cover and book designed by Sue Campbell Book Design

Author photo by Katy Tartakoff

Contact the author: dolamm59@gmail.com

Typeset in Adobe Garamond Pro

This book is dedicated to my late parents
John King Vennard
and
Dorothy Walton Vennard
for their love, for their trust, and
for their unwavering encouragement
of my ambitions

CONTENTS

PREFACE

So why, you might wonder, would I publish a third book of columns? Didn't my first one—*Second Banana* (1983), which described my life as a feminist woman married to a "Top Banana" man—and my second one—*Choice Concerns* (1996), which put forth the most politically controversial columns of my career—say it all? No, they did not, I decided—and for two reasons. First, they didn't encompass the columns I've done since or those I'd left out earlier. And second, this time I wanted to select columns that emphasized heart over head, feelings over analysis and give them their own special place.

Now retired at 83, I'm hoping to reach back to family, friends, special readers, and occasional "fans"—those of you who responded more passionately to my personal articles that touched your lives than to my blatantly political ones that touched the sometimes troubled world. So even the political columns included here come mostly from a sense of exploration, not from a need to prescribe.

Through this book, I want to reach the women who came up to me in airports and asked how my "consciousness raising" group got started and how they could start their own. The wife who approached me in a theater line to tell me that my column on "male entitlement" was still taped to her fridge. The mother who walked beside me as we exited the grocery store struggling with multiple bags and exclaimed with a laugh, "Your column on how women always have to 'schlep' has made my load lighter." And the man who confided to me at a cocktail party, "Your piece on marriage just may have saved mine."

You are the special ones who touched my heart when asking, oh so gently, if I really had survived breast cancer and inquiring, oh so cautiously, how my children could possibly survive the media glare of their parents' public lives.

This book is also a legacy for those very children, now grown and parents themselves, to whom I want to reveal a fuller picture of myself as a writer and a person, as a woman who deals with more than politics and policy and had the good fortune to be their mother, something that has informed much of my work. When I do fight for political causes, it is with them in mind.

Advice to readers: Take this book one section or one column at a time. Read what appeals to you and leave the rest. No column collection book is meant to be read straight through. So consider this ...

an airplane book
a park bench book
a waiting-in-line book
a just-before-sleep book

And thank you for joining me on my life's journey over the past decades. Your own heartfelt journeys have dramatically infused and enriched mine.

Straight from my heart ...

—Dottie Lamm, 2020

Family, Child Rearing, Marriage:
From Whence My Energy Springs

For the Joy of Children:
They Come, They Cry, They Grow, They Go

Fortune Smiled on Yuletide Child

Denver Post
DECEMBER 25, 1984

IN MY 47 YEARS OF CHRISTMASES — SOME remembered fondly, some forgotten — the one I loved the most was the one I almost missed. In fact, I did miss dinner that Christmas, but that gets ahead of the story.

The year was 1967. Dick and I had planned the birth of our first child for somewhere between its paternal grandmother's birthday (Dec. 1) and its maternal grandmother's birthday (Dec. 7). But somehow we suspected the birth might be closer to Christmas.

That fall, in a state of exhilarated expectancy, each time the two of us climbed into our Volvo station wagon, we would burst into our favorite song, "Fortune Smiles on the Christmas Child" from the Broadway play "Irma La Douce."

And ours *was* a Christmas child — almost. I entered the hospital Dec. 18, two hours after getting home from work. Our son was born at 6 a.m. on the 19th, with Dick in the delivery room.

Attentive, but anxious. Hiding behind his surgical mask and his clicking camera.

People have told me I would be treated like a "Queen for a Day" with the birth of my first child, so be sure to take advantage of it. I was. And I did.

Doting grandparents

My mother and father arrived from California, beaming over my bed and cooing through the nursery window. My friends came, or called, or sent gifts. My husband came each day and each evening and was *always* on time. I "reigned" at the hospital.

But domestic turmoil reigned at home. On Dec. 23, the water pipes in the basement of our "new" house broke, keeping Dick and our just-met next door neighbors up all night mopping the floor and wrestling with backed up sewage lines.

On the morning of the 24th, my brother-in-law arrived from New Mexico with his black Lab puppy "Bruno," who found his way out of the basement, promptly tore all the wrapping off the Christmas gifts, devoured three Christmas fruitcakes and regurgitated them on the rug.

Then while my parents tried to clean up the mess, the vacuum cleaner broke.

My mother told me later that my father, anxious that the house be immaculate for my arrival, had gotten down on his hands and knees and had picked the remaining shreds of lint, cotton and tissue out of the dark green carpet with his fingers.

And the house *was* immaculate. No, not so much immaculate, but sparkling. Sparkling is the only word that describes the radiance of the day as Dick and I pulled into the driveway with our firstborn.

Sparkling is the only term I can think of as I remember the sun on the snow surrounding the house — our house. And the smile on the face of my mother as she opened the door. And the light in my father's eyes as he came from the living room to greet us. Of the tinselly Christmas song on the radio. Of the blinking lights of the Christmas tree. Of the fuzz on the light blue blanket which wrapped the only Christmas "gift" that would matter that year.

> *"Sparkling is the only word that describes the radiance of the day ..."*

Luxurious dual role

That day, Dec. 24, and the few days that followed, l experienced that once-in-a-lifetime luxurious state of being new mother to my child and at the same time still child to my parents, who kept lunch on the table, dinner cooking in the oven and snow shoveled off the steps.

I was 30 when our son was born. And I remember telling someone later that if I'd been younger, I might have had to prove my "independence."

But with a first child arriving at *semi-maturity*, how easy it was to be dependent. To revel in as long a period of convalescence as possible. Knowing that as the holidays dwindled, my parents left and my responsibilities and work load resumed, I'd have to *really* mature, once and for all.

I don't remember much about Christmas Eve or Christmas morning. I didn't mind staying home from the huge Christmas dinner at my sister-in-law's house, and I looked forward to the Christmas platter Dick would bring me that I could consume at my own pace.

There would be other Christmases, I knew, packed with family, growing kids and newer babies. Raucous Christmases full of childhood glee and sibling fights. Ones in which I could never again get by without either cooking or clearing up, or both. And there were.

But that Christmas of 1967 I was content to rock in the easy chair by the glowing Christmas tree, nursing my new baby and softly singing, "Fortune Smiles on the Christmas Child."

For it had.

And on his parents and grandparents, too.

School's Never Out for Summer When You're Active Tribe's Mom

Denver Post
JUNE 11, 1979

SCHOOL IS OUT. SUMMER IS IN. THE MIXED blessings feel a little like the Christmas when Santa brought great presents and the chicken pox, too. At least the bombardment of messages from the school will stop temporarily: Those wrinkled yellow sheets brought home late by the children informing me that the paper drive, for which we had towering stacks of dust and moth-infested newspapers, was held yesterday.

But the anticipation of the thundering steps (there are always at least four pre-adolescent boys at a time) of not-so-little feet up and down three flights of stairs eight hours a day for 11½ weeks is enough to send my eyes rolling skyward. And the thundering says nothing of daily requests: "Can the whole gang stay for dinner? Spend the night? Watch the 1:30 a.m. horror show? But why not?"

Just as urgent pleas will emit from athletic little girls in one-piece playsuits: "Can we build the dog a playhouse on the roof of the veranda? Why can't we walk to the store for the fourth time? We forgot the crayons the third time. And besides, walking conserves energy!" By age eight children can be seductively logical and most aware of which arguments will hit a proud parental nerve.

Last summer was different. It was a campaign year. We were gone. They were gone. The house was so empty that when I did return home my own footsteps echoed on the back stairs.

But this year, following a togetherness-promoting plan conceived in January, we are all to be around more. I look forward to the togetherness. I'm glad I'm not out campaigning; I'm glad that instead I have a part-time job and I work at home.

Working at home has many little advantages. No bus fare, no parking, no carpools. My office is close to the hearth from which many of my writing ideas spring. During the school year, I slip easily from writer-researcher to mother when the clock strikes 3:30 p.m. No rush-hour hassles impede me; no anxiety lurks in the back of my mind about whether I will arrive home before the kids hit the door.

Yet, writing and research take concentration. And I worry that the periods of concentration, which the winter provided, are what the summer may lack. I am reminded of a 19th-century poet whose name I cannot recall and whose words rise only vaguely from my subconscious. She wrote a couplet that went something like this:

"When one continually must tie a bonnet,
It is much more difficult to write a sonnet."

Some people have enormous powers of concentration: "She can sit right down amid the piles of dirty laundry and write the weekly newsletter with the TV going all the time," said a friend of mine enviously describing the productivity of a mutual friend, a mother of four. "That's how she manages all of these high-powered, volunteer projects!"

Other people are exceptionally bright. Take Richard Valeriani's description of Henry Kissinger:

"I once gave him a three-page paper in his office. He took off his glasses, held the paper about 4 inches from his eyes and zipped through them without ever missing a beat of my conversation. He responded to what I was saying and then went on to discuss the contents of the paper."

Of course, my energetic friend was sitting amongst the laundry, not the children, as the latter were in school. And Henry Kissinger never has been a mother.

Ah! There's the rub! Suddenly, I realize that constant interruptions aren't the real problem. I can arrange for sitters at certain regular intervals. I can insist on quiet and solitude from my children at other special times.

Yet, the arrangements and the negotiated agreements don't solve the basic issue: It isn't that the children take over my life, but rather that my mothering instincts seem to engulf me when the children are present! They may be in the charge of a super surrogate, but when the children are around, I am a mother first — whether by instinct, habit, or commitment.

I can sit in my office and block out the laughter of 200 people at a party downstairs. I can turn a cold, deaf ear to the plaintive whines of the family dog. I can pretend the phone is off the hook. But the noise of the children, or even their quietness, rings a different bell.

It isn't only their actual need, but the mere anticipation of their possible need, that interferes with my concentration. "That's not very logical," I tell a friend, thinking I might be able to change.

"Change? Forget it! Your anticipation is what insures the survival of the species," she quips.

So it's cosmic?

I don't know.

What I do know is that my whole state of consciousness is altered, sometimes wrenchingly, but more often willingly, when that side door opens and someone yells, "Mom!"

> *"My whole state of consciousness is altered, sometimes wrenchingly, but more often willingly, when that side door opens and someone yells, 'Mom!'"*

"Walls," "Doors" Channel Youth

Denver Post
SEPTEMBER 13, 1983

EACH YEAR IN THE DOG-DAYS OF MID-AUGUST, I count the days, the hours and the minutes until the opening of school. Each year when it finally comes, I get goosebumps and butterflies. As the kids, outwardly cool and collected, go back through those doors that say "Welcome" in diagonal letters, my desire for days of squabble-free solitude is gone. Instead, I want to follow.

Brick Walls/Welcome Doors
Take good care of my kids
I sit in the car and watch her
Join her group, giggling,
Hesitating, they approach the steps
I sit in the car, but my heart is on her shoulder
as the fall sun streaks her hair

Wasn't it just last year that I like her was entering seventh grade, hair short, shirt baggy, riding my bike to school? We wore white bucks and skirts; no jeans and backpacks. Thirty-four years ago — just a grain in the sands of time.

Brick Walls/Welcome Doors
Take good care of my kids
I sit in the car and watch him
solitary, striding across the esplanade.

He does not look back, but I know, he knows
I have not yet driven away

Wasn't it just yesterday that I grabbed his chubby hand and walked him through that first Welcome Door? He already had been to day camp. Kindergarten would be nothing, I told myself. He took his place in the circle. I waved "bye-bye." His eyes clouded, his hand reached out. I fled.

We ask the impossible of our schools. They must provide our children all that we received as children. They must also provide them all that we missed. They must equal our fulfillment and make up for our lost dreams. We worry: She goes, mind alert, inquisitive, will she be challenged or bored? He goes feet dragging, thoughts still on summer adventures, will they get him to work hard or let him slip by?

"A rising tide of mediocrity plagues our schools," the presidents' commission said. A rising tide of voices echoes back: A longer day is needed. A longer year is needed. More sciences and math are needed. More homework is needed. The schools have become soft.

Toward the 21st century

Cogs in the wheel of our future rotate in and out of those Welcome Doors. My kids, your kids, our kids. Imprint the wisdom of past ages on their brains. Give them the tools to make the 21st century work. Teach them to question, but also to accept. To fight, but also to fit in. Teach them to love (I know that's my job, but please help), as well as

> *"We ask the impossible of our schools."*

to learn. Teach them to tolerate, "to walk a mile in another's moccasins," to understand.

The only treasures which matter in our lives we entrust to you, year after year. Do not be fooled by their "cool." They are vulnerable, ripe for learning, turned on by excellence, crying for usefulness. Despite their shrugs and their "no-sweat" stance, they are desperate to find meaning in their brittle, noisy, self-centered world.

Brick Walls/Welcome Doors
Take good care of my kids
They are on loan to you as
The minutes and years tick by
K-3, 4-6, 7-8, 9-12
Do not waste their time.

Job of Parent Lasts Lifetime

Denver Post
AUGUST 2, 1983

SUZANNE IS HAVING A BABY AND SHE'S ONLY 19. Kay and Mark are having a baby, and they're at least 40.

Overall fertility rates are not increasing in the United States. But fertility talk proliferates this summer. Personal conversations and the media are pregnant with the subject of pregnancy.

In front of me are five articles from The Denver Post and The New York Times. All deal with the subject of having babies.

One reports that while the fertility rate of American women — ages 18 to 24 — is declining, that of women over 40 is increasing. That of women between 30 and 34 is booming. Another compares the medical advantages and disadvantages of giving birth at various ages.

The third tells working pregnant women of all ages how to fight for, prepare for, and best use maternity leave while having that baby. The fourth promotes paternity leave.

The fifth quotes author Herb Goldberg as he eulogizes the ideal couples of tomorrow who will have it so "altogether" personally that they will only conceive and have babies when "they (the babies) enhance their parents' lives ...."

What it really means

"Having a baby." A concise term meaning to be pregnant and eventually to give birth. Yet the media and prospective parents seem to dwell on the timing and convenience of that act, that stage of parenting that takes hours at the most, while neglecting what that act may mean to the rest of their lives. *Becoming* a parent is something one can plan for; *being* a parent is less easy to anticipate.

I was one of those "older" mothers a decade-and-a-half before it became common. We were finally ready to have that baby! At age 30 I knew about mother/infant bonding before the term became fashionable. La Leche League pamphlets were teaching me about breast-feeding.

Changing a diaper didn't intimidate me or my husband. And if our baby cried all night, I'd just sleep in the morning and arrange afternoon appointments for my clients at work. We "had it together" in true Herb Goldberg style. It would be easy.

Then a month before I was to deliver, I visited my friend Janet who was lending me some infant equipment. To Janet, "having a baby" had turned into having babies. Her second pregnancy scarcely two years after her daughter was born had produced twin boys.

The "babies" were now 4, 2 and 2.

Janet and I tried to talk politics; the 4-year-old spun in airplane turns and crashed into the coffee table. We talked comparisons of preschools in the Denver area, but the twins were strangely quiet.

"In short, we were 'having a person.'"

"I'd better go check on them," said Janet, exiting swiftly to the music room. "Oh, no!" she moaned from around the corner. The boys, it seems, were seated on the piano bench, calmly spreading peanut butter and jelly on the piano keys.

'Having a Person'

A rude awakening, that visit. On leaving, I patted my stomach in awe and with some trepidation. We weren't having a baby, we were having a child. We were ready for a baby, but would we ever be ready for a child? We really were having more than a child, we learned in the next short 15 years. We were having a baby, a toddler, a preschooler, a child, a teen-ager — and projecting to the future, a college student, a young adult, and an older adult — all wrapped into one.

In short, we were "having a person." A person who, the order of things being as they should, will be our "person" till the end of our lives.

Changing the colloquial, societal phrase "having a baby" to "having a person" would be awkward. Can you imagine being asked: "How old is your person?" "How many people do you have?" Or being told: "My person just entered junior high." "Help! All of our people will be in college next year!"

No, it will never happen. But "having a baby" is such an inadequate phrase. Because having that baby is not just the end product of a pregnancy, but God willing, the beginning of a 30- to 50-year relationship. And how many prospective parents (be they 20 or 40) really think about that?

Mom Finding It Tough to Let Go

Denver Post
AUGUST 21, 1984

THIS MORNING I WOKE UP THINKING ABOUT A conversation I had with a mother of three boys who joined us for a weekend holiday last month.

"I don't know if I'm abnormal but I just don't miss my kids when I'm gone," said the mother, whose boys are all under 7. "It's not that I don't think about them — I do — and I have to feel they are going to be well-cared for, but once I'm gone, I just don't miss them."

Well, I don't miss my kids when I'm gone either. Correction. I didn't miss them when they were that age.

I remember when Scott was exactly 1. Dick and I left him with the grandparents and went to Mexico for a week. Our first holiday sans child. I was ecstatic. Dick was depressed. "Suppose he takes his first step?" he worried. "He won't — that's at least a month away," I answered, eager to be gone.

Now, when the babies were tiny, it was different. The infant/mother bonding process is a physical as well as emotional need. It pulls each with the force of gravity.

When my babies were really babies I breastfed them, cuddled them in a Snugli while doing light chores, and seldom went out nights on the three days I worked outside the home. But after that mutually dependent and divinely nourishing period of infancy, I found I could leave them without compunction.

Maybe it was the feeling of "never ending-ness" that allowed me my physical distance and emotional space without guilt. I knew that when I came back from whatever trip, the tears to dry, the noses to blow, the hugs to give, the games to play, the "no's" to say would still be there. Day after day. Year after year. Never stopping. Never ending. Forever. Or so it seemed.

School would start in the fall and stop in the spring. Family ski trips — while respites from the weekend workathon — would structure the winter. A special family vacation excursion would mold the summer. Halloween would follow Halloween. Christmas follow Christmas with cyclical regularity. And wherever we spent the latter, we would spend it intact, together.

But suddenly, things changed. Our two dependably predictable kids became teen-agers, quickly and decisively, in one month's time. The 14th birthday marked the change for him, the 11th for her.

All at once, family vacations were resisted. Ski weekends tolerated only if friends could come, too. Even Christmas mildly scorned. Early this summer, one of our offspring announced plans to earn the money to go visit an East Coast friend next Christmas. Gulp. "Well maybe after Christmas," I say.

And they distance themselves from us not only in their absences, but even in their presence. With adolescents, if tears are shed they are likely to be hidden behind closed doors. If joys are experienced they are shared, not with us, but over the phone, with friends.

Our "no's" are defied no longer with one loud wail or two stamped feet, but with the seasoned, reasoned verbosity of a trial attorney. Anger and scorn seem the only emotions worth wasting on parents, or the "Oldies" as they call us in their more affectionate moments.

Now on trips away from home I do miss my kids. I find myself thinking: Wouldn't Scott have like this seafood restaurant? Wouldn't Heather have loved this beach?

The "never endingness" of parenting seems in fact to be ending sooner than I'd ever dreamed. So I want to clutch tighter when I should gradually be letting go. All of a sudden:

I miss my kids when *I'm* gone.

I miss my kids when *they're* gone.

And, I miss them even more when they're home.

After-Dinner Enlightenment

Denver Post
JULY 30, 1985

WHILE WRITING LAST SUNDAY'S COLUMN ON the psychological benefits derived when families sit down together for dinner, I came across an unpublished column I wrote three summers ago. My kids had protested: "No more columns on us for awhile! Please Mom!" So I substituted another column.

Three years later, here goes:

My husband and I cherish family dinners. In our midlife wisdom we know how precious and fleeting are the years our children will be home.

Our children do not cherish family dinners. In their youthful lack of wisdom they are not cognizant of how each moment with their devoted and enlightened parents should count.

One-way dialogues

At dinner we come eagerly hoping to catch a glimpse of our offsprings' growing lives. At dinner they come defensively, fending off our questions like gladiators with impenetrable shields.

A typical Lamm dinner table conversation:

Father: (brightly) "What did you do in school today, Scott?"

Son: (slowly) "Huh?"

Father: (still trying) "Did you learn anything new in school today?"

Son: (rebelliously) "No, I never learn anything I don't have to."

Mother: (annoyed) "You must have had to have learned something."

Son: (indifferently) "Nope."

Mother: (brightly) "How was your day, Heather?"

Daughter: (daydreaming) "Huh? Oh, fine."

Father: (enthusiastically) "What did you do at school?"

Daughter: (shrugging) "Nothing."

Son: (yawning) "Can I be excused? I'm bored."

Mother: (more annoyed) "You wouldn't be if you would contribute …"

Daughter: (jumping up and down) "I want to be excused, too!"

Father: (coming on strong) "Not till you've each shared something intelligent about your day …."

Surprise switch

But this summer on a family houseboat trip with the kids' uncle, aunt, and 11-year-old cousin, something happened. Each of the three children began to open up. Each night after dinner we would talk.

One night, my brother-in-law's new wife, Peggy, suggested a more personal area of conversation. "Let's each person tell what we think our best and worst traits are," said Peggy with enthusiasm. "Let's start with you, Scott."

My husband and I exchanged glances. We had tried this kind of "personal revelation" tack before, with zero results.

But this time it worked. Scott shuffled his feet, hemmed and hawed, but eventually he talked. Each child unfolded slowly and tentatively like a flower — finding their worst traits easier to reveal than their best. The adults joined, too, and soon the still Lake Powell air was filled with shared warmth and understanding laughter.

"You can't think you're as bad as that!"

"That's a good trait, but here's one you have I think is better."

Consider the source

Did the breakthrough come from the intimacy of the houseboat? The getting away from Denver? The letting go of the normal daily schedule? The temporary relief from politics? Maybe.

But I suspect it was something more. The subject of conversation had been suggested by a non-parent. What was accepted from Peggy (who is family, but mother of no child present) probably would have been rejected from any of the rest of us.

So, if you are parents with retentive children, don't despair. Invite a non-parent to dinner. It might work wonders for familial communication.

And if our kids complain about the "three years later" publication of this column? We'll simply invite a non-parent to dinner, and "communicate" about it while dining.

Peggy, are you free?

Name Change
Daughter Asserts Her Independence

Denver Post
NOVEMBER 3, 1991

The Denver Post

ENOUGH IS ENOUGH.

It's all happening too fast.

Our daughter, Heather, has almost grown up. The aura of independence she used to wear around her shoulders now radiates from her inner being.

As a college sophomore she chose a foreign study program with no input from us. That program involves a full year in Bristol, England, rather than the traditional semester abroad. She will even celebrate her 21st birthday 7,000 miles from home!

Isn't all that enough?

No. Our daughter is now going to commit a supreme act of independence. She's going to change her name.

It's not that she hasn't done it before. Once, when she was 8, like countless other little girls who assert their independence by renaming themselves, she solemnly announced that henceforth she would be called: Heather Elizabeth Susan Cindy Wendy Olivia Laura Linda Lamm.

Then, as a teenager she stretched Susan, her given middle name, to the more beguiling Suzanne.

But now she wants to do it legally. She wants to drop the Susan/Suzanne completely and become Heather Elizabeth.

Elizabeth! One of the names we consciously avoided.

Elizabeth, you see, is a family name. And my husband and I, first-time parents in the late '60s, rejected, out of hand, all family names.

Our children would not be hindered by tradition, ours or anyone else's. *Our children* would be themselves, no juniors among them. No family monogrammed saddlebags to weigh them down on their journey through life. No burdening ancestors they would have to live up to or escape from. No predestination of any kind, period.

So we picked names we like: neutral names; predominately Scottish names; we, with no Scottish ancestors on either side.

Scott Hunter was the first in 1967.

Heather Susan was the second in 1970.

I did toy with the name Elizabeth briefly. It was tempting to use the middle name of my only sister, Jane Elizabeth Vennard. She was named after her great Aunt Beth, an artist, whose vibrant watercolors of New England scenes still grace the walls of our mother's home.

Elizabeth, in some small way, would carry on my side of the family.

But what parent in her right mind would want to give a young girl the initials H.E.L.! It wouldn't take much imagination for the school yard and bullies to change H.E.L. to Hell: "Nah, nah, nah, here comes Heather, the girl from Hell."

Furthermore, in those days it was still assumed that a woman would renounce even her father's surname when she married. Why, then, did she need to carry on anything of her mother's?

So, Heather Susan she became and Heather Susan she remained, until now.

I'm not sure why I feel so WEIRD about this whole thing.

Occasionally, over the years, I have intimated to Heather that I wish we had given her the family name of Elizabeth; that her father's and my idea of independence just might have been spelled s-t-u-p-i-d-i-t-y.

So, on one hand, I'm warmed and gratified that my only daughter wants to reconnect with the women in my family, and, not incidentally, with her cousin Harmony Elizabeth, and her great Aunt Libby on her father's side.

On the other hand, I'm apprehensive and mildly threatened. By reclaiming the family name she is rejecting the name we gave her. And shouldn't naming one's offspring be the last bastion of parents' rights?

It has long been a tradition of some Native American tribes for children to choose new names for themselves as they reach adolescence. Do they then become not just mature people, but new people with whole new destinies?

I have women friends in midlife who have renamed themselves as they have shed former identities. For one friend the rejecting of her given name, her married name, and the careful claiming of a new name signaled the start of a personality metamorphosis that was almost total.

Is this, then, my real fear? That in changing her name to Heather Elizabeth, our Heather will no longer be "our" Heather?

Nonsense. Of course, she will still be our Heather. Yet, just bordering on 21, she will change. Again. And again. And again. Just like we all do, name change or not.

The fact is, it's our daughter's right to rename herself. It's her right to claim her independence by reuniting with tradition, just as it was our right to claim our independence by rejecting it.

So, Heather Susan Lamm becomes Heather Elizabeth Lamm. Legally. Finally. Officially.

And I'm glad. And I'm proud.

And someday, the watercolors of her great, great Aunt Beth will grace the walls of her home, reminding her of her New England heritage.

And I'm glad of that, too.

How Much We Can Learn from Our Children

Denver Post
JULY 5, 1992

OUR SON'S PRESENCE FILLED HIS END OF THE table of 16 guests, the perfect host at the dinner celebrating his college graduation. His warmth seemed to radiate to all in the restaurant.

I sat in a euphoria of maternal pride.

When did this rebellious, self-centered man/child metamorphose into a person more concerned with the comfort of his grandparents than with the celebration of his own moment in the sun?

And what did we all — his family — have to do with his step-up, step-back ascent up the mountain of maturity?

Was it that we are an "intact" family with "family values"? Perhaps.

Yet, I know single mothers whose sons have also grown to accomplished personhood. As Post columnist Tomás Romero writes, "Two-parent households may be an ideal, but one motivated parent can do much more than two laid-back elders."

"A home is the place where, when you go there, they have to take you in," wrote Robert Frost. And our Scott was "taken in" by far more than his home-centered nuclear family. While growing up he was blessed with:

A grandmother who loved and lectured.

A grandmother who loved and listened.

A grandfather who taught him to fish and drive a motorboat, and who did not deride his "manhood" when he rejected hunting.

A grandfather who died when Scott was 2, but whose legend as a great teacher was kept alive for him by his family.

Uncles and aunts who cared.

Suddenly, as I reflect on our son's childhood and upbringing, the whole Murphy Brown/Dan Quayle "family values" debate seems like so much polemic blather.

If home and family is the place that has to take you in, what kind of a "family value" is it to not take in one's own gay son or lesbian daughter? What kind of a "family value" is it to reject a daughter who becomes an unwed mother?

My parents' message to my sister and me was, "I may not always love what you do, but I will always love you."

Ditto to my kids. And what our son sometimes did was not always easy to love. But I'll spare him and you a litany of his youthful "excursions."

Instead, I'll follow the example of Marian Wright Edelman, founder of the Children's Defense Fund, who, in her new book, "The Measure of Our Success: A Letter to My Children and Yours," asks her three sons' forgiveness for her mistakes and tells them how much she has learned from them.

As I read Edelman's wise, sensitive book, it occurs to me that nudging a growing kid into a responsible adult takes not only good, solid family values, but one heck of a lot of good luck.

And family dinners. Yes, I mean it. If there is any tip I would pass on to other families still raising their kids, it would be to sit down to a meal together at least four times a week. Whether you are a two-parent family, a one-parent family, a foster-parent family or a grandparent family, just do it! And turn the TV *off*.

I'll admit, there were those family dinner times I was tempted to throw in the spaghetti-smudged, tear-stained towel. The phone always rings and the kids do nothing but fight, I complained to a friend.

It doesn't matter, said this older and wiser confidante, that family dinners *work*. It matters that you *do* them. It's not quality time, it's not even quantity time; it's repetitive time.

It's the same with parental advice that so often seems to fall on deaf ears. It matters not that your advice isn't always taken, but that you give it. Advising is caring, and kids can even learn by rejecting it.

Which brings me back to Scott. He rejected everyone's advice — his parents, his counsellors, his peers — that he not take a major in business, the second-hardest major at Lewis and Clark College.

But he took it, passed it, and graduated.

We're proud of you, Scott.

And thanks for all you have taught us.

A World Full of "Ifs" at Graduation Time

Denver Post
JUNE 6, 1993

PURE RADIANCE.

I can't think of another way to describe the moment our daughter, Heather — auburn hair gleaming in the sunlight — stepped through the majestic Van Wickle Gate as a member of Brown University's graduating class of 1993.

Four years ago, as Brown tradition dictates, she had walked through this gate with her class to begin her studies. And poof! As of this Memorial Day weekend, she's out:

Facing the "'Real World,'" the numerous graduation speakers pronounce.

Facing the "Worst Employment Year For College Graduates Since The Great Depression," the newspaper headlines announce.

Facing, in short, a world full of "If's."

My heart swells with pride, then pounds with anxiety.

What can I tell my only daughter at this milestone in her life? I have always wanted to rewrite Rudyard Kipling's poem, "If," for girls and for women.

Why not for *my* girl, *my* young woman?

And so, dear Heather, as your feet wind down College Street from the gate and up through your continuing journey of life, remember:

If you can feel, and not let feelings overwhelm you,
If you can think, and not make thought your only
    aim,
If you can meet with Triumph or Disaster,
And still, in equilibrium, remain the same;
If you can bear the slights you'll receive as a female,
And rise above 4,000 years of bias against your sex,
Knowing that a Goddess wisdom resounds within you.
Exulting: Fight! Keep going! One more time! You'll
    make it! Or: Let go. Mourn. Move on, with grace,
    to what is next.

If you can honor the "mother" side of your psyche
Whether or not you have children of your own,
Yet give freedom to any being's growth you nurture,
As true grit is never attained till one leaves "home";
If you can "father" your own ambition,
Hone your natural skills to the nth degree.
If you can delight in doing and succeeding,
Yet take time, also, just to be;

If you can stretch your heart, soul, mind and muscle
Beyond what caring advisers think is common sense;
For others' praise can keep you "good" forever,
But only you can strive for excellence.
If you can talk with crowds and keep your virtue,
Or walk with royalty, yet keep the common touch
If you can love, still knowing love can hurt you,
Trust your intuition, then not fear caring "too much."

If you can fill the unrelenting minute
With sixty seconds' worth of distance run,
The Earth will be yours to enjoy, protect and cherish,
From baby whales to the ozone layer that screens
    the sun.
If you can weave a net of solid oak and fragile lace
To encompass all things living, tame and wild
Then you will make the world a better place,
And doing so, this moment as you graduate,
You are becoming a woman, my child.

Letting Go
My Protective Wings Are Still Flapping, but I'm Getting Better

Denver Post
OCTOBER 5, 1986

The Denver Post / Bonnie Timmons

EVERY TIME I USED TO BACK THE CAR DOWN the long narrow driveway of our old family home in California, my mother would call out the same three words: "Bye. Drive carefully."

Usually I answered her cautionary send-off. Sometimes I didn't. But almost always I felt a prick of annoyance. I could understand her admonitions back when I had just been licensed to drive at age 16. But at 18, then 19, and even 22? Come on!

By then, I had driven six years without even a "fender bender." And, as a college student, I had mastered the insane freeways of Los Angeles. Had her predictable send-off become a mere habit? Or was it her way of remaining ever vigilant and therefore "protective" of me?

Most likely the latter.

But was she also being protective of herself? Was she, in a sense, making sure that if I did have an accident, she would not be to blame? That she had worked her "magic" and tried to warn me?

If so, I now understand.

Our son graduated from high school in June. Many readers asked me why I didn't write about this milestone in his life, the beginning of the "empty nest" in my life, etc.

I didn't, I said, because it's difficult to write about my empty nest when it's not yet empty (our son lives in town; our daughter at home). And it's not fair to issue "progress reports" on one's adolescent kids in the Sunday newspaper their friends' families read. So I won't write about our son and what he's doing and feeling, but I will write about what I felt about his [high school] graduation.

First, I felt joyous. I didn't even cry!

In fact, I smiled the whole time. And waved at him. And he smiled back and waved at us. I thrilled to the playing of "Pomp and Circumstance" and to the undulating sea of red and white as the 335 East High School graduates rose and sat and rose and sat, and, finally, flung their caps to the acoustical disks which hang high from the ceiling of Boettcher Hall. In short, I had fun; we *all* had fun.

But the next day I began to feel something else: fear.

And through the summer the fear grew and made me a little crazy. Males age 18 to 25 think they are immortal. They walk the edge incessantly, intrepidly — confident that if they should fall off, they will, of course, land flat on their feet on the opposite side of trauma. They don't learn from others' mistakes. They are at highest risk for accidents and other unnamed disasters.

High-school graduation marks a time when you let your kids go out into the world, knowing full well they don't know half what they should know. And you can't do a blasted thing about it.

Except worry. So I began to worry. Continually. Neurotically. At times I began to wonder if "Pre-Empty Nest Syndrome" would soon be classified with "Pre-Menstrual Syndrome" as one of those mysterious, weird "diseases" afflicting women.

I didn't worry so much about the real risks. (Somehow I was confident both my husband and my son would survive unscathed the perils of their recent wild river trek in Peru.) I worried, instead, that some specific direction from me or, on the other hand, some *lack* of cautionary advice on my part would make me responsible for my son's fate.

"I fear for them," said a friend of mine, uneasily, when we had lunch last June. Her boy is in his second year of college. Her vague, unnamed anxiety fueled my own fears. I had thought getting a kid settled in college would help. Yet, clearly being "settled" in college is not really "settled." Nothing is "settled" at that age.

There were times this summer I became practically immobilized by my fears. Twice, I almost didn't advise our son on the *least* risky way to do something, out of the fear that if he took my advice, and something went wrong anyway, I would be to blame.

At other times, I *over*-warned him. One night, when I reminded him to be sure to call us for a ride home if the kids he was with began mixing drinking with driving, he looked at me as if I were demented or senile. "You already told me that," he said, shaking his head. "*Twice* in the last hour!"

The nest may be emptying, but the protective wings keep on flapping. It's as if we momma birds want to return to the age of infancy when getting references for a baby sitter, closing the gate to the driveway, and putting the cover on the mini-pool will guarantee our fledglings' survival.

But, as a psychiatrist friend to whom I finally went to discuss all this, said to me, "The only way to let them grow is to let them go, Dottie."

I know that, but I don't want anything to go wrong. And just at the time I should be letting go of my parental power I am acting as if it were omnipotent. I want it to work its magic.

I'm getting better. This fall, the protective wings flap less vigorously. I'm not as crazy as I was in June and July. Now I look at the odds and call it as I see it. He takes my advice or he doesn't, and that's the way it will be.

But there's one "protective" thing I still do when I'm home, and he's home, and I happen to hear him start the car in the driveway.

I call out in a voice not unlike my mother's: "Bye. Drive carefully."

> *"Was she also being protective of herself? Was she, in a sense, making sure that if I did have an accident, she would not be to blame?"*

Different Years, Changing Fears

Denver Post
MARCH 31, 1996

PARENTAL PANIC.

We weren't that nervous when, early last month, our 25-year-old daughter headed to Costa Rica to travel on her own. But then, right after she left, we heard that two young American women had been raped and murdered there recently.

The chill of quiet panic crept into my heart. Its icy grip has been thawed somewhat by two warm, exuberant "I'm OK" phone calls from south of the border.

Yet, just the worrying makes me think of three other trips taken by three generations of women in my family, and the very *different* kinds of parental fears each trip evoked.

This "three generation saga" began in 1932.

My mother, Dorothy Walton, a 24-year-old school teacher two years out of Wellesley College, had just planned a cross-country car trip in a two-seater convertible with a female teacher friend.

They would journey from Portsmouth, N.H., south through New Mexico to the summer Olympic games in Los Angeles, up the West Coast and back again through Yellowstone and the Great Lakes.

Her father — my grandfather — was horrified. In fact he tried to "buy her off" from the trip for which she had saved her meager Depression dollars by sending her to Europe on his own dollar.

His worry: The roads were bad (a U.S. map of the year resembles an ancient person's face with tiny lines running randomly everywhere); their car might break down; they would become stranded and burn up in the heat of the desert by day or freeze to death in the Rockies by night.

My mother was adamant. She was now an adult. She would go. And go she did, encountering none of the predicted catastrophes.

Flash forward 30 years. 1962. My sister, Jane Vennard, at 21 is now an adult. After her own graduation from Wellesley College, she decides to grab a ride across country, back to our family home in Palo Alto, Calif., with a girlfriend and two boys.

Her parents — my parents — are horrified. Their fears are not of road conditions, desert strandings or car breakdowns. Their fears are societal.

A three-day trip across the country with two boys! What will the neighbors think? My sister argues that the boys are merely friends, that she will room with her girlfriend, so what does it matter what the neighbors think? Didn't they bring her up to think for herself? Her cool logic prevails; our parents relent. But the point remains. *Their* overriding fears were society's sanctions.

Flash forward 30 more years. 1992. Our daughter, Heather Lamm, now also 21, is returning from Denver to Brown University in Rhode Island for her senior year. She will drive her car across country alone. We are terrified!

Our fears are not of bad roads, flat tires, sunstroke or societal sanctions. Our fears conjure up visions of rapists, carjackers, kidnappers and murderers. Our worries are justified.

Since 1960 there had been a 560 percent increase in violent crimes. Carjacking, a relatively new offense, had been on the rise for two years. In 1991, "the bloodiest year on record," 24,703 Americans were murdered, a 5.4 percent increase from 1990. In addition, forcible rapes had increased by 3 percent. Young women between the ages of 18 and 24 are *three times* more likely to be victims of rape than other women.

Terrified? "Catatonic" would be a more accurate description.

Then a miracle appears. A friend from high-school (male) needs a ride back to his East Coast college, too. They will drive together. We are "weak kneed" with relief.

Is it sexist in this day and age to say that our strong-willed independent daughter needs a man to "protect" her? Perhaps. But the truth remains: No matter the degree of acceleration of the liberation of women, the crime rate has accelerated faster.

> *"Our fears conjure up visions of rapists, carjackers, kidnappers and murderers. Our worries are justified."*

Is this male friend of hers truly a friend who happens to be a boy, or is he a secret "boy-friend?" The thought hardly crosses our minds. What will the neighbors say? Who knows. How will the two travelers arrange their camping out or their motel stays? Frankly, we don't care.

He's a male she knows well.

A male we know, too.

And he is going.

In 1990s America, that's all that matters.

To the Mother I Was …

Denver Post
MAY 13, 2012

MY 6-MONTH-OLD GRANDDAUGHTER LIES ON her back in the grass on a partly cloudy day. Intermittent sparkles of sunshine dance on her face as, with her left hand, she twists to reach for a dandelion growing by her right shoulder.

Stretch, stretch, stretch and … suddenly she has rolled over from back to front for the first time.

"Atta girl," I croon and clap my hands, elated.

Not a remarkable moment, really. A common occurrence for a mother or grandmother — watching a child physically develop right before one's eyes.

But the mother/grandmother contrast jumps out at me. It is not where my granddaughter is in her state of development, but where I am in my state of mind.

The contrast is so strong that a little "lecture" starts forming in my brain — a message from the grandmother I am now to the mother I was then.

I am here. Truly present. As the grandmother I am now, I am not thinking of my next deadline (though I still have them) or what my next big career or political move will be.

I'm no longer torn by the tension of personal ambition and the desire for a child's perfect trajectory toward the next stage. For this moment, the nitty gritty of everyday life simply disappears.

The news of the world, bad as usual, drifts from the radio and I ignore it. My cellphone rings. I glance at the number and shut it off.

This interlude with my granddaughter is mine alone, not even to be shared with my dearest friend.

It is the same sense of "presence" I feel with my three grandsons. One, age 5, wants to play endless "Wizard of Oz" games. He, of course, is the wizard and, thrilled that my real name is "Dorothy," has renamed my dog Toto. Up and down the stairs the three of us bound, from "Kansas" on the first floor to "Oz" in the basement.

Another, age 7, climbs every tree in sight while I stand below, forbidding him certain unsafe branches, but then patiently going on to the next tree, and the next, and the next …. The sun starts to set in the West, but I don't look at my watch.

The third, age 4, is no longer satisfied with books being read, but wants stories being told. "Chapter stories," he says. So each time we meet, we go on to another chapter in the monster-chasing adventures of his "gang of four" playmates. We are now on Chapter 10.

It has become cliché, but still true, to say that one of the best things about grandkids is that you can send them home, then viola! Responsibility over. What is less often said but even more true is that the purity of uncluttered moments we have with them is the real joy.

So from the grandmother I am now to the mother I was then, I start to say, "Why didn't you enjoy your own kids this much?"

But the mother I was interrupts, "Give me a break! How could I? Parenting is about being a parent, not a playmate. And parenting is rude enough to come at the same time as career-building, marriage-sustaining, financial obsessing, schedule-jockeying, other family and friends demanding …. What was I supposed to do?"

The grandmother I am retorts, "Give *me* a break! I'm not criticizing you for the decisions you made — going to work, taking on politics, going off on an occasional solo trip. It's not the physical absences from your kids when you were gone that makes me sad; it's the mental absences when you were there.

"Your kids didn't suffer much from your mind clutter, but *you* did! Unless there was a crisis, you often weren't paying attention, and you missed so much of the *fun*!"

"Yes," says the mother I was. Then a wistful, almost pleading look comes into her eyes.

"And my time with them went so fast…."

> *"It's not the physical absences from your kids when you were gone that makes me sad; it's the mental absences when you were there."*

Extended Family Tributes:
Bles't Be the Ties That Bind

Mother's Day
Syrupy, but I Like It

Denver Post
May 12, 1985

It's Mother's Day again. And this year we have finally pulled it off. My mother will be here, and so will our children's cousin, Joshua, and his mother, Barbara. In former years it has been either my mother joining us, or Barb and Josh, never both.

As I wake up leisurely this morning, I will remember that the plans for the day will have been totally marshaled by Dick and the three kids. We three mothers will merely luxuriate in whatever the four of them choose to bestow upon us.

I laugh as I think of this, and recall, a few years ago, that what the three kids chose to "bestow" upon Barb and me, after they let us "sleep in," was a homemade chocolate cake, iced with chocolate frosting, and decorated with two packs of M&M's. For a 7:30 breakfast no less!

But that's OK. Whatever they do is fine, as long as *they* do it!

I can be a real cynic about Mother's Day when it's not Mother's Day. And with good reason.

It's hard to stomach its hyped commercialism; its syrupy, sanctifying of motherhood for one day, when the other 364 it's considered OK both for society and for grown kids to neglect Mom and take her for granted.

OK to leave working-outside-the-home moms with inadequate child care and still less than equal pay. OK to leave working-inside-the-home moms without adequate financial compensation or appreciation. OK to subtly eliminate career ladder opportunities for the professional "mom" as soon as her pregnancy starts to show under her three-piece business suit. OK to relegate 75 percent of household tasks to mom, even those moms who have husbands and able-bodied teenage kids.

When it's not Mother's Day, I can even build a case for the fact that Mother's Day is not really for mothers at all. Instead it is a cathartic guilt-reliever that allows everyone — business leaders, politicians, government officials, and wayward children — to "make up" for the cumulative "neglects" of the year and thus feel good about themselves.

But that's how I feel about Mother's Day when it's not Mother's Day. On Mother's Day, I think about things like this:

My mother telling me gently a few years back, "You know, since your father died I've gotten more and more casual about holidays like Thanksgiving and Christmas, but I only have two children and I need to be with one of you on Mother's Day."

That same mother telling of how over the years, well after the adulthood of both, that she always had to be the one to remind her younger brother of Mother's Day, Father's Day and her parent's birthday each year.

"One year, shortly after I got out of college, I got angry and resentful at my role of constant prodder," said my mother. "I just sent my own present off on my mother's birthday, and didn't remind Bill. I never, never did it again! The only one who paid for that was my mother, devastated that her 'beloved and constantly thoughtful' son had forgotten her."

And I think of these things on Mother's Day, partially because I realize that our family is close to the time when we will not be able to hold Mother's Day — or Father's Day, or Easter, or Christmas — as a kind of inviolate family day that everyone marks on his/her calendar way ahead of time.

The fact is that I like Mother's Day! I like the one day of the year that I don't have to arrange, balance and dovetail. That my enjoyment rules supreme, whether this enjoyment is brought about by a chocolate cake, a nightgown or a new 10-speed bike. That I am appreciated just for the fact that I have given birth and am raising two kids, period!

And I wonder how I'll feel when my kids are gone from home. Will I simply fold Mother's Day into the parade of other spring Sundays — each one of which gets longer and lovelier with the heightened, wider arch of the sun — and not make a big deal about it? I doubt it.

I already find myself hoping my grown kids will remember. Not only because I want my day of gratification, but because I want the wider satisfaction of knowing that this remembrance symbolizes that they just may remember other things: Father's Day, thank-you notes to friends' families, apology letters to people they have wronged.

In short, I want them to remember Mother's Day, with a card, a silly gift, even a phone call that ends with an apologetic "By the way, I also need money," not only because it will make me feel praised, but because it will reflect on how they were raised.

Oh, bull! That's too sanctimonious, and not quite true.

What I really hope is that they'll remember *me* on Mother's Day — and the fun we all had on those days when they were young.

And if they don't that someone will think to remind them.

And even if I suspect that someone reminded them, that I'll never know for sure.

> *"I already find myself hoping my grown kids will remember."*

Remembering Dad
No One Knew That Special Man Like I Did

Denver Post
DECEMBER 1989

MY FATHER WOULD HAVE BEEN 80 THIS MONTH. Instead, he died 20 years ago of a massive heart attack when our son was 2 and our daughter not yet born.

A few years back, I obtained his autopsy report to forewarn myself of any potential heart disease that my children might have inherited. I thought I was far enough away from his death to be objective.

But the "Patient Description" section hit me like a cold shower. It consisted simply of the hastily scribbled words "Caucasian male, aged 60."

But didn't they *know*?

Didn't they know he was *my* father? The special father who built my baby sister and me a gazebo playhouse in the backyard of my grandparents' New Hampshire home where we spent our early childhood summers.

The young, athletic father, who, as a former track man, constructed a "high-jump" bar for us when we moved from a New York City apartment to our own California house in 1946.

"Of course, girls can be track stars," he said, as we watched wide-eyed.

The funny, whimsical father who sang "One Fish Ball" and "Smoke Gets In Your Eyes" each morning in the shower. Who read aloud "The

The Denver Post / Maureen Scance

Cremation of Sam McGee" and "Casey at the Bat" on Sunday nights by the fire.

Who would stare delightedly at the boyish reflection in the hall mirror, and then bellow to his all-female family, "Oh you lucky people!" as he rode off to work on his bicycle.

Didn't they know my father was an eminent engineering professor and textbook author who loved his teaching so much that he would never move into the higher-paid world of department heads and deanships, because he wanted all of his energy to go into the classroom.

That he was a registered Republican with a democratic heart who treated all at his prestigious university — from the president to the janitor who scrubbed the floors of his hydraulic laboratory — with the same respect. Whose tennis partners were ministers and bartenders.

Whose own father had been a store clerk, his mother a seamstress. Who worked his way through M.I.T., and never could have gone to college at all if he had not been able to live with his maiden aunt across the river in Brookline and commute to class each day.

That when this aunt, who made his education possible, retired at age 82, he moved her to California, found her an apartment, then a nursing home, included her in our family activities, and cared for her financially, without asking for any public assistance until her last illness at age 94.

Didn't they know that he was a "conservative thinker" who encouraged his two girls to be all they could be in an age when "liberal thinkers," such as Adlai Stevenson, held forth that the main reason for educating women at all was to make them more enlightened housewives.

That my mother, now 80, still gets letters from his former students 20, 30, even 40 years back.

My father was moral, and sometimes moralistic. He believed in Christian forgiveness, but not so much that "forgiving others' sins could make it easier for you to sin yourself."

Strong in his idea of what was good and what bad, he chastised my sister, by then a college student, for wasting her time reading such "trash" as "Lady Chatterley's Lover."

"Have you read it?" Jane retorted, and tossed him the book. Two days later, he told her he'd thrown it out. "I've read it, and it's still trash," he said.

Caucasian male, aged 60?

How could the doctor or hospital official who scribbled those stark words know of the hundreds of little favors my father did for my childhood girlfriends, many of whom had lost their own fathers in World War II.

Or of the letters he wrote my sister and me in camp, in college, continuing after we were married, meticulously keeping a carbon of each for "posterity."

Or of the way he proudly showed off his grandson's picture. Or of how he would have loved his granddaughter, had he known her.

Or of the long weeks in which, every day, he visited a colleague with a debilitating nerve disease; slowly, patiently loading him into his car, driving him to the hospital for his treatments and back again.

Shortly after my father's death, in April of 1970, my husband, Dick, and I went "spring skiing." The weather raged back and forth from bad to horrible, and the day inched toward disaster.

Two months pregnant with Heather, I fell off the chairlift flat on my stomach. Three minutes later Dick, who had started cautiously down the hill with 2-year-old Scott between his knees, was hit by a recklessly skiing teenager, all three landing in a twisted, snowy heap of skis, poles and back packs.

I screamed every profanity I knew at the teenager, and after depositing Scott in the day nursery, I cried the entire ride up the slope.

Dick tried to console me. No one was hurt; Scott was safe; and my short, though hard, fall from the lift was not going to dislodge a 2-month-old fetus, he said. He was right, and I agreed, but I kept on crying.

"I miss my father," I finally blurted out.

The loss is no longer so intense. And my days seldom so trauma-filled.

But 20 years later, I still miss him.

> *"Of course, girls can be track stars,' he said, as we watched wide-eyed."*

Character Is Made From Persistence — Not Compulsion

Denver Post
APRIL 7, 1980

"PERSISTENCE BUILDS CHARACTER," SAID MY father when I complained that typing his civil engineering references on file cards was just plain boring!

"Then why don't you do it?" I asked impertinently.

"Because I already have character." He grinned, took a long draw on his cigar, blew three smoke rings, and settled down in his favorite chair with a copy of Time magazine.

I sighed and made a face. At least he paid me 2 cents a card. At one card per minute I could make $1.20 an hour. Not too bad for a 14-year-old in 1951.

Character. How is it really built? Is character created by constructing a philosophical tolerance for tedious work? Do we develop character in ourselves like a carefully tended plant, nurturing it with compliance to assignments we don't like, because such compliance keeps us ever prepared for the inevitable tedium we will meet in later life?

Or is character built simply by providing children with reasonably good role models, then allowing them to pick their own challenges, find their own way, thus learning from each success and failure?

Actually we bought the "persistence trip" back then, my sister and me. We teased our father unmercifully: "Persistence builds character!" we

would chant, if he were working on a frustrating project at his work bench or couldn't get the checkbook to balance.

Yet, in our own lives we pursued our A's in boring subjects. We ironed the clothes, did the dishes every night, raked the yard summer after summer, often grumbling and grousing but never really challenging the "character building" value of persistence in routine jobs.

We built our "character" and our "character" built us. Both of us entered top colleges and were accepted at top graduate schools. Success was its own reward.

Yet a choice which presented itself to me in the graduate school of social work pulled me up short and challenged my old assumptions. My passionate interest was in psychotherapy with preschool children. But, my wish to pursue this passion to the near exclusion of all other subjects was sacrificed. To have become expert in this endeavor alone would have meant occasional C's in other subjects. Unthinkable.

So there my compulsive character building was outliving its purpose. At age 30 I was still an overachiever, seeking perfection in too many areas. The knee-jerk "character building" response was no longer serving my goals but getting in their way.

Then the rude awakening of parenthood, combined with an accelerating political life, quickly brought home a frightening but strangely liberating reality.

As a governor's wife and the mother of two young children, doing "it all" to perfection became impossible. Doing it all, at all, frequently looked doubtful. Through this rude but welcome jolt, I learned to set my own priorities.

Now at the mellow age of 42, I wonder: Is always doing one's best, no matter what the worth of the task, crucial to a child's development? Is it really necessary for a youngster to try to do everything well, so that he/she will know his/her own specific talents and limitations? Can character only be "built" young and "mellowed" at middle age? Or, can so much character building only serve to limit spontaneity in later life? I'm not sure. But with my own children, I'll go a little lighter on the "persistence" message I think.

Recent events have again brought the issue to the surface.

"I figure I can get a C in math now that I'm in the high group," says our sixth-grader flippantly and confidently at dinner.

"What?" reply my husband and I simultaneously.

"Well, I can't get an A," replies our son.

"Well maybe you can't, but you've got to try!" I admonish.

"Persistence builds character," I find myself repeating with total assurance. No one in the room is smoking, but the complacent rings of smoke from my father's cigar seem to pervade the air.

Creativity or Perfection? "Job Worth Doing Is Worth Doing Badly"

Denver Post
OCTOBER 15, 1979

"A THING WORTH DOING IS WORTH DOING WELL," my paternal grandmother used to sing as she carefully inspected each dish my sister and I had dried, and placed it gingerly on a cupboard shelf too high for us to reach. Silently and guiltily I wondered just what was so well worth doing about dishes. Nana, I thought, was a little over-fussy. But I kept quiet.

"A Thing Worth Doing Is Worth Doing Well."

Nana, in fact, lived her whole life by that well-worn phrase. As a girl in England she had been trained as a seamstress. When she came to this country in 1905 and married the manager of a small grocery in New Hampshire, she was able to perfect the art of both her professions, sewing for extra money and homemaking for love. She excelled in the details of her small world with a zeal and agility admired by all who knew her.

I admired Nana, too. As a small child I played with her button box and watched with wonder as her needle flashed back and forth, always coming up precisely in the tiny hole of the button. I appreciated her painstaking patience as she taught me to sew. By age 12 I had emulated her perfection in this area, learning quickly that an item less than perfectly made would not be worn but instead would gather dust in the closet.

"But is everything worth doing, worth doing well?" I once asked my mother, having heard the phrase a few times too often from Nana.

"Well," my mother said, and she paused a moment. (Nana lived with us, and my mother probably did not want to appear too contradictory.) "My mother used to say some things are worth doing well, others only worth doing quickly." So, my maternal grandmother, dead but by no means forgotten, added another dimension.

As I have grown older, I've thought even more of the contrast between my two grandmothers. My maternal grandmother was a Latin teacher for 18 years before her marriage. "The best teacher in New England," my grandfather used to say.

Married at 39, delivered of my mother at 40, and my uncle at 41, she suddenly found herself the wife of a banker in his prime, the mother of two small babies, the mistress and protector of a large home and garden, and the caretaker of her husband's two elderly parents.

"Prioritizing" is what we call it today. And how she must have had to do it! She did have a live-in nurse for the babies, but most of the homemaking and gardening she did alone. Her world was a little larger than Nana's. Perfection (though it might have been bred in her New England character) was simply not an option.

I'll bet Grandma was a crackerjack Latin teacher; I know she was a marvelous cook; New England clam chowder, lobster, and fresh corn from the garden are my remembered favorites. But I imagine that her dishes, although clean, did not sparkle. And I know that her cellar

was a musty, messy collection of junk; that's why I loved it!

The air of perfection seems to serve different needs of different people at different times. Once I spent almost an entire day wood-staining the back porch of a mountain cabin.

"What are you doing, painting the Taj Mahal?!" exclaimed my exasperated husband who had finished the larger front porch in half the time.

I couldn't explain to him that after a winter of little children with runny noses and endless diapers, this outdoor spring chore was more than a chore to me. It was something that had an end and a beginning; it was a gratifying, clean-smelling task, the aroma of which blended with the warm, spring air. To me its performance with perfection epitomized an offering to the Gods, a way to thank them for a final end to the long, cold winter. Perhaps, symbolically, it was my Taj Mahal.

The desire to do things perfectly can enhance or hinder. For a surgeon or an architect, an obsession with perfection is a mandatory trait. For a mother or a politician, it can be the undoing of potential success.

"The desire to do things perfectly can enhance or hinder."

A year ago, I glimpsed another dimension of the perfection question. The new insight came from a member of a large women's convention to which I was speaking about new options for women.

The woman, probably a generation younger than my two grandmothers, suddenly stood up.

"Heck!" she said in a response to a part of my speech. "I think a job worth doing is worth doing badly!" There was a shocked silence. Qualifying

her statement somewhat, the woman continued, "Now, I have my fussy, perfect areas; in fact my kitchen is one of them. But what I mean is, we must be willing to do things we love, even if we do them poorly. I love playing the piano everyday and I play it badly, but I don't care. Heck! I have a friend who won't take painting lessons with me because he's convinced he'll never be a Rembrandt. Now really!"

Really, indeed! How many of us must cut off certain unexplored creative parts of ourselves out of fear of failure or the pride of unattainable perfection? I thought again with fondness of my two grandmothers. I hoped this woman of adventurous spirit was the grandmother of some lucky child today.

Treasures
Certain Ones Last

Denver Post
April 7, 1985

WHEN MY SISTER AND I WERE GROWING UP, our family owned one camera. The camera, operated usually — but not exclusively — by our father, was the only camera in the family until I was a teenager.

Our family also owned: one pair of binoculars. One flashlight. One jack knife. One canteen.

And one car. First a 1937 Chevy, second a 1947 Chevy, third a 1952 Chevy. But never more than one car at once. And never to last less than five years.

In fact, I don't remember any young kid I grew up with whose family had more than one car. Conspicuous consumption simply was not the style of the World War II years or even the early 1950s.

When I was in London two weeks ago, I was reminded of this "non-consumption" ethic through the words of a British economist:

"The problem with the British economy is our lack of boosterism and consumerism," he said. "If something lasts, we don't replace it."

A London tour guide corroborated the economist's view: "British education trains us for the life of the mind; for a life with durable goods and enduring friendships — not for planned obsolescence of either."

Perhaps that's what's wrong with the British economy, but it could be what's right with the British character.

Sometimes I feel inundated, almost drowned by sheer force of "goods" I have collected, bought, been given. Every six months, I clear out, reorganize, give away, throw away, but at best I stay even — treading water in a vast sea of accumulations.

Yet, at the same time I'm sorting out and throwing out, I'm wondering: Is there something here I'll want later? And the indecision sharply reminds me of certain childhood possessions I wish I had kept:

- The wooden Noah's Ark, replete with hand-carved pairs of animals that my sister and I used to decorate with my paternal grandmother's dressmaking scraps.
- The doll house constructed for us by a family friend, a father of boys who had been dying to try his carpentry skills on a miniature house and accompanying furniture.
- The mechanical train that worked — really worked — no matter the smoothness of the floor boards, the lint on the tracks, or the awkwardness of small and eager hands.

I did save some things and I'm glad:

- An ice-skating doll with blue eyes, blinking eyelids, and brown braids. (The fact that the tiny leather and metal ice skates were chewed up years ago by our family

basset hound only slightly diminishes the doll's sentimental value.)

- And the two sets of multicolored design blocks, with which I used to play at my maternal grandparents' house; that my kids played with at their grandparents' house; and, hopefully, that their kids will play with at their grandparents' house.

Our children, as they grew, adored the few toy treasures saved for them in their grandparents' homes. Whereas, in their own home even a new and much clamored-for toy soon became devalued by the mere volume of junk surrounding it.

Yet a parent cannot always judge what is "junk" to a child.

Today, being Easter, I am reminded of a traumatic episode with my daughter a few years back when we couldn't find the special Easter basket she had saved from year to year in which to collect her dyed eggs on our family Easter egg hunt.

It was just a dime store basket, and I'm sure I had thrown it out in one of those twice yearly reorganization binges. But dime store or not, the basket did mean something to her. A bit of durability, a bit of a tradition saved. Something symbolic of happy Easter mornings.

In a New York Times essay on the "throw-away society," Anne Farrer Scott writes:

"I wear my grandmother's wedding ring. In my daughter's bedroom are two oak chests from my grandmother's summer cottage. When I make chocolate pudding, I use my grandmother's recipe.

> *"Every six months, I clear out, reorganize, give away, throw away, but at best I stay even—treading water in a vast sea of accumulations."*

These things are important to me, but, all together, it's not exactly what you'd call a history, a heritage … you work with what you have, but not much has been made to last."

A couple of years after the Easter basket episode, my daughter and I were redecorating her room and I suggested she pick out some special toys — those she felt she had outgrown but wanted to save — and put them in a special handmade trunk her father had bought her. She did not pick a lot, but she chose carefully. And one of the things she chose was "my" ice-skating doll.

Design blocks from the 1930s. A skateless ice-skating doll from the 1940s. A hand-carved trunk from the 1970s. Not exactly a heritage, but you work with what you have …

Solemn Spring
For the First Time, Molly Won't Be Here to Share It

Denver Post
April 5, 1992

I'M RESISTING SPRING THIS YEAR, NOT EVEN looking for that first crocus, not wanting to plant the annuals. I think it's because my mother-in-law, who passed away last Thanksgiving, will not be here to share it.

My tiny garden, tended awkwardly with my decidedly non-green thumb, was such a joy to her. Something she always found "right." Something in which she often discovered surprises — a blossom I had not seen or a perennial, long thought lost, reappearing.

How big a part Mary Townsend played in our lives! So much a part that I still measure myself by her standards, projecting what she will think. Sometimes I accept her thoughts, sometimes I reject them, but consistently I use her as my benchmark.

"She sounds like she's saying goodbye," said our daughter tearfully when we talked by phone after her grandmother's first heart attack. Perhaps she was. But she lived another nine months, good months, even joyous months.

When I wrote the following tribute to my mother-in-law for the Women's Foundation's 1991 Honor a Woman in Your Life dinner, she was unable to attend.

Not because she was ill, but because she and her husband of nearly 60 years had joined a tour of the Rockies to view the fall colors. This is my tribute:

My mother-in-law, Mary Townsend Lamm, has been the heart of the steadfast Lamm family since long before I knew her.

A "can do" person since her own childhood, she has taught our children lessons that will last them all their lives.

One time at the Governor's Mansion gazebo with our then 12-year-old son Scott, she spotted a young man propelling himself in a wheelchair around Governor's Park. "Scott," she said, "let's go invite him to tour the mansion grounds with us."

Scott hesitated, shy and embarrassed. "Come on," his grandmother said firmly, in a tone that would countenance no argument. The young man accepted eagerly, and Scott not only made a friend but conquered a little of his shyness.

Once when our 5-year-old daughter Heather burst into tears over some minor frustration, tears that stubbornly refused to recede to any of her mother's sympathetic murmuring, her grandmother stepped in.

"Heather," she said firmly but kindly, "save your tears for the important losses in life; this is not one of them."

"Oh!" said Heather, satisfied, and gradually resumed her sunny disposition.

As mother-in-law and daughter-in-law, Molly — as I affectionately call her — and I have had our inevitable moments of tension. I remember one argument beginning on some aspect of child-rearing. But Molly defused it: "That was my way of loving my kids," she said with a smile and a shrug. "You

Mary Townsend Lamm with her son, Dick Lamm, in the 1930s. / Dottie Lamm

have your ways. It doesn't matter as long as we truly love them."

Mary Lamm's three sons, her daughters-in-law and her six grandchildren have a wide variety of personalities, passions, lifestyles, and values. But there is one prime value we all share and that is our emphasis on family. Much of that attention to, and joy in, comes straight from the loving example set by Mary Lamm.

Mom to her sons, Molly to me and Gammy to her grandchildren, she is exceptional in her own way to all of us. Tonight, it is both my pleasure and

privilege to salute, honor and cherish my very special mother-in-law: Mary Townsend Lamm.
To Molly, my love and my thanks.

In the old days, my mother-in-law and I had more disagreements than this tribute indicates. She was strong and often judgmental. I was strong, too, often defensive, sometimes snappish.

But as my children, her grandchildren, approached adolescence and I was stricken by breast cancer, our relationship took a richer, more generative turn. No one in our family had ever been seriously ill. It was as if we suddenly looked at each other and knew our own mortality, knew that we had only now to become fast friends. And we did so.

Last May when my husband and I returned from a three-month trip, and his mother was still "recovering" from her February heart attack, I warned him about how she might look. "You will probably find a very aged and changed woman," I said.

Hardly! We weren't home five minutes when their car drove up. Out stepped Pop and Mom beaming welcoming smiles — she looking fitter and healthier than when we'd left and carrying a bag of groceries to stock our empty refrigerator.

In fact, she always came up that driveway carrying goodies.

Since I began this column, that first green daffodil shoot has broken through the sodden ground and dirty snow despite my resistance.

I simply cannot believe that Molly will not be here to see it bloom.

Mother's Christmas Gift
(A Tale of Two Sisters)

Rocky Mountain News
DECEMBER 25, 1996

IT WAS CHRISTMAS EVE IN 1947.

My sister, Jane, looked like an angel as she slept. Overcome with tenderness, I kissed her lightly on the cheek, but then withdrew in terror.

Suppose she wasn't really sleeping? Suppose she now knew that I really did love her despite all our fights?

And fight we did! All throughout our childhood. It drove our mother crazy. She could not stand the thought of malice or envy between us. But it was there and we both had our "reasons."

Jane was prettier than I, and I knew it from the day that, as a kindergartner, she came home with a cute new haircut which perfectly framed her face and accented her large blue eyes. I was more outgoing and "popular," a hard act for Jane to follow through grade school and junior high. I was a tease. She was a tattletale. And we played our roles to the hilt.

Our father told us to stop "wrangling." Our grandmother told us to stop "squabbling." Our mother told us just to STOP.

One year in a brief burst of sisterly togetherness, we asked our mother what she would like for Christmas.

She paused.

> *"Christmas came wrapped in sadness that year."*

"What I would like more than anything else in the world would be for you girls to get along," she said finally with a quiet intensity we had never before heard.

We were stunned, shamed. Yet somehow, each of us knew that gift was beyond our ability to deliver at that time. In fact "we girls" didn't really begin to get along until I went off to college in 1955.

Jane was seven the year she "slept like an angel," and I was ten. Now, almost 50 years later our competitiveness has ebbed; our love and friendship has deepened through the family joys and losses we have shared.

And our mother lived to see it.

But the one special time of generosity between us that I wish she had seen, she could not have seen, because only her absence made it possible.

The year was 1993, and after our mother's sudden death in October, Jane and I had divided her household goods amicably and easily except for two disappointments we each tried to hide.

I had very much wanted a small tile with a hand painted drawing of the California house in which we had grown up.

"Sorry," said Jane. "That was painted by a friend of mine and I think she would have wanted me to have it."

"Of course," I said.

She had wanted a small angel figurine. "Why not," I said, thinking of how it resembled how she had looked at age seven. "Besides, mother had another one just like it and I have it at home."

Later, a dear friend of our family's dropped over, and Jane, in her affection for this friend, told her to take any memento from our mother's apartment that she wanted. But she had forgotten to remove the angel from its perch.

"I'll take that," said the friend, pointing to the angel.

Seeing Jane swallow hard, I started to protest, but she signaled "no."

Christmas came wrapped in sadness that year. But it also came with our two families' memories and stories of the happy times our mother, our "Gamma-dot," our Dorothy had shared with us.

But what we wished our mother could have still shared was this:

When Jane opened her present from me, there was my angel figurine. I had decided she loved it more than I did.

She threw down the wrappings, jumped up and hugged me as we both cried and laughed.

Then, as I started to open her gift to me, I could feel the outline of a hard flat square object through the tissue. I looked up through more tears, as I did not have to look down to know it was the tile painting.

"The Gift of the Magi," said my husband.

"Gamma-dot lives," said my son.

Yes. And "we girls" get along, even when it's not Christmas.

Absence Can't Diminish Mother's Spirit

Denver Post
May 12, 1996

MOTHER'S DAY SWIRLS AROUND ME EARLY THIS year.

It's April 19, and I sit by myself in a tiny restaurant in the Mexican town of San Miguel de Allende.

Suddenly the restaurant erupts with shouts of *"Feliz cumpleaños,"* and the heretofore quiet family of seven in the corner begins serenading their 75-year-old mother with birthday songs.

My mother could have made this trip when she was 75. Why didn't we bring her here? I am sad. Then I laugh. We had a fabulous party for her when she turned 75 — just what she wanted. So what am I regretting? Just that she is no longer here for any birthdays, and I miss her.

I also regret that I wasn't there for her emotionally as much as I could have been in 1993, the last year that she lived. It isn't that I neglected her in any practical, tangible way. But I didn't (couldn't? wouldn't?) sense that her psychological needs were changing as she neared the end of her life. Yet, with her typical generosity of spirit, she never complained.

By the end of my own life, will I have attained her generosity of spirit?

Enough! I am here in Mexico for two weeks with my daughter — carrying on the mother/daughter friendship tradition that my mother and I shared. That's what I should be thinking about.

Tonight my daughter is practicing her Mexican cooking skills for a group of young people in a friend's apartment. She invited me for dinner. But I needed some "space." And I sensed a "tentativeness" in the invitation.

I am smug and self-congratulatory. I don't resent that tentativeness from my daughter and vow that I never will. "Oh yeah?" nags a little voice. *Vamos a ver.* We will see.

Suddenly I'm with my mother again, 33 years ago, taking a horse and buggy ride on a balmy night in Central Park. It's two weeks before my marriage, and I have flown to New York on one of my last trips as a United Airlines flight attendant. She is there visiting friends "from her youth." She is only 54.

We laugh like schoolgirls at the antics of the people, their pets, our driver. We talk over my early childhood days living in that city and what it was like for her as a young married woman coming to New York from a small New England town. I am just the age my daughter is now.

Mariachi music snaps me back to the present. How proud my mother would be of her grand-daughter, who is here learning Spanish, partially because of the fund for "special educational pur-poses" left to her in her grandmother's will.

My daughter has an ear for the language, a self-confidence, yet a relaxed attitude, which allows her to absorb the rhythm. As I watch her learn, respond, innovate so easily, I try not to beam that universally recognizable smile of pure, indulgent motherly pride.

Why didn't my mother and I take some trips, like this, together?

Central Park was a happy coincidence. But a planned trip?

At 25, would I have invited my mother to join me in Mexico and to live with the same Mexican family with whom I was residing? Probably not, as I was still too busy "separating" from my parents to risk that much closeness.

And if I had invited her, I'll bet my invitation would have exuded "tentativeness," and she would have understood and found a reason to decline.

Our true adult relationship came later.

But come it did, and as the mariachi music fades in the distance, the happy recollections of our times together overwhelm me: walking and talking among the tulips at the Governor's Mansion; clinking the ice cubes in our gin and tonics as we make fun of the "idiots" on McLaughlin and Co.; clothes shopping for her trips or my "events."

This year is the first year I will be neither with my mother, my sister nor my two kids on Mother's Day. No matter. Memories of my two weeks in Mexico with my daughter feed my soul; two long exchanges by phone with my son in California fill my heart.

My own tulips are blooming.

And my mother's generous spirit permeates the day.

Descansa en paz, Mamá. Rest in peace.

Parenting:
We Did the Best We Knew How at the Time

Parent Phobia
Mothers Get a Lot of Unwarranted Blame

The Denver Post / Maureen Scance

Denver Post
AUGUST 5, 1990

THE SOCIAL WORKER HAS JUST HAD HER FIRST baby and her professional experience isn't helping her cope with motherhood one bit.

Her name is Janna Malamud Smith. In a June 10, 1990, New York Times Magazine story Smith writes:

"In the dozen years I have worked in an outpatient psychiatric service at a hospital, I do not once remember ever having heard a clinician suggest that a patient had a really terrific mother … mothers have been made the cause of everything … from colic to mass murder."

My defenses sharpen.

Colic? My second child had colic. Did this make *me* a bad mother?

Mass murder? Ted Bundy didn't have a bad mother — insecure, embarrassed by her son's illegitimacy, but not *bad* …

No matter. The fact my defenses arise so quickly and that I, a new social worker/mother back in the late 1960s, identify so readily with the late 1980s "replica," demonstrates that my own motherhood anxieties have only to be gently ignited to come back full blast.

I don't ever remember a clinician exuding the virtues of any mother during my years of social work practice either. Mothers were either "over-attached," "under-attached," "dominating" or "rejecting." And there I was, suddenly, one of the "them."

So overwhelmed with the potential for evil in the mother/child relationship, I became mildly "catatonic." Once while bathing my newborn son, I caught my reflection in the bathroom mirror; my mouth was frozen into a superficially sweet "sorority rushing" type smile.

My God! I burst out. Did I honestly think that good mothering not only required the acts of feeding, bonding and bathing, but that I must *enjoy* each act every second?

But wait. This "parenthood panic" is hardly a disease exclusive to female social workers mothering infants. Any mother, and, increasingly, any father, of any age child can be immobilized by it. Remember Steve Martin's projected fantasies about his son in the movie "Parenthood"?

First fantasy: Grown son graduates No. 1 in his college class and publicly acknowledges his father's role in his success from his valedictory podium. Thousands applaud.

"Did I honestly think that good mothering not only required the acts of feeding, bonding and bathing, but that I must enjoy each act every second?"

Second fantasy: Grown son shoots people in random violence from the campus clock tower. Shots ring out in staccato bursts, sirens roar, police run around, and fingers point at DAD.

But mothers still take the worst childbearing rap even though many illnesses that once were traced directly to the mother/child bond have been found to have other origins. Childhood autism, schizophrenia and manic-depressive illness all have at least some genetic or neurological roots.

So why do mothers get and take so much blame? For a multiplicity of reasons, the following of which may be prime:

Time. Mothers still spend the most time tending children of all ages. Those on the longest "watch" will make the most mistakes.

Expectation. We have an almost "holy" expectation of what mothers should be. So our abuses stand out. It's like organized religion. Over the years religion has done more quiet good than blatant harm. Yet, when the church inflicts witch hunts and holy wars on its "children" we are shocked and then blame or discount the whole institution. Why? Simply because we hold what is "holy" to a higher standard.

Denial. It's easier to blame mothers as a species than to consider some of the factors in their lives that might take enormous personal or societal sacrifice on our part to change. Smith writes of her visits to poor women in housing projects:

"I witnessed the obstacles these mothers must overcome to arrange a day's worth of juice and Pampers for their toddlers." As an AFDC social worker, I, too, witnessed these obstacles: hunger, poor housing, no transportation, limited medical care, crime. (And some did far better overcoming them than I would have under the same circumstances!) But when such mothers are psychologically evaluated, these paralyzing obstacles are often disregarded.

Singularity. We forget that many others, besides mothers, influence a child's growth pattern, adult mental health and value systems. We also forget the "gestalt" of the times. The late, great University of Colorado Professor Morris Massey gave a classic speech titled, "What You Are Is When You Were." Did you come of age when Eisenhower was first elected, or when Kennedy was assassinated? Did your child attend Kent State in 1970 or Metro State in 1980? It makes a difference.

Sexism. Pure and simple. Conscious and unconscious. Let's face it. Mothers are women. And until very recently most of the people writing about their role and diagnosing their "illnesses" have been men.

Omnipotence. Love of assigning it. And love of accepting it! And we mothers — and we fathers, too — *are* omnipotent aren't we? Listen to what the character Mel says about parenthood in Ann Beattie's recent novel, "Picturing Will":

"Do everything right, all the time, and the child will prosper. It's as simple as that … except for fate, luck, heredity, chance, the astrological sign under which the child was born, his order of birth, his first encounter with evil, the girl who jilts him in spite of his excellent qualities, the war that is being fought when he is a young man, the drugs he may try once or too many times, the friends he makes, how he scores on tests, how well he endures kidding about his shortcomings, how ambitious he becomes, how far he falls behind, circumstantial evidence, ironic perspective, danger when it is least expected, difficulty in triumphing over circumstance, people with hidden agendas, and animals with rabies."

Amen.

Self-Flagellation Can Hurt Your Kids

Denver Post
MARCH 21, 1983

OUR FIVE-YEAR-OLD DID NOT SEEM SAD WHEN he left on the bus for day camp in 1972. Rather, he appeared in a daze. He hoisted his little pack and joined the rest of the kids without looking back. He hadn't even started kindergarten, but for eight weeks of the summer he would be gone from his home six to eight hours a day.

Around the middle of the camp term I received a call from the counselor: "Scott doesn't seem to be involved in what we are doing; he goes on his own track and seems to be waiting to come home each day, even though we have arranged many fun activities."

As she spoke, my repressed guilt at sending him away resurfaced. I was no longer working outside the home, yet our daughter was a year and a half old and I had hardly spent a moment with her alone. Heather needed time to blossom without a dominant older brother. Certainly, I thought, a good day camp was better than sending Scott to a daily sitter in town. I had wanted it to work out for everybody. But it didn't. Now, when our son shows the normal insecurities of adolescence, I sometimes reach back to that summer and blame myself.

Heather was ready to go to nursery school by age 2 ½. But the bus ride was a problem. We had two cars, but the gubernatorial campaign staff in

1973 needed one of them; my husband needed the other. Every Tuesday and Thursday I would wait for Heather on the corner to make sure the bus driver let her off safely. Each time she would fall into my arms exhausted. An hour's bus ride each way was simply too much for a 2 ½ year old. But we didn't have the means to change the system.

Between the ages of 6 and 8 Heather developed extreme fears about leaving home overnight without me. I agonized over the past. Was it the bus ride? The episodes were years before, but the guilt was as sharp as if her school bus were still rounding the corner twice a week.

I write about these happenings now because, irrational as it may be, I'm not entirely over the guilt. I still wake up in the night and think of these and other incidents. I would like to stop. Guilt is a useful tool if it hits one immediately and can be used as a mobilizing force to change a current circumstance.

Yet guilt can be a negative, self-deprecating blinder on one's creativity when it goes on for years.

Many parents I have talked to have struggled with similar guilt issues. One young woman I knew years ago set a good example when she admitted, "I now *own* the fact that I may have damaged my two boys by staying in a destructive marriage too long. Now that I own that fact and have stopped agonizing over it, I'm a better mom today."

Fathers are just as likely to suffer from parental guilt and anger as mothers, comments family relations authority Joseph Procaccini in a March 7 U.S. News and World Report article. Men are just less likely to talk about it.

Two years ago I discussed the sometimes crippling effect of parental guilt with a sensitive older friend. When, in speaking of my early child-rearing years, I said, "I tried to do the best I could but …" she interrupted me kindly and said:

"You don't do the best you can. You do the best you know how — the best you know how at the time. Just because you learn more later, you shouldn't blame yourself for not knowing it then. And sometimes things don't work out for every member of the family, even when you're doing the best you know how."

In the August 1982 edition of Ms. Magazine, author Gabrielle Burton illuminates my friend's advice: "I was guilty all the time; that made me mad too. It took a long time for me to give myself permission to work and to parent. To do my best and not feel one hand was robbing the other." And speaking of the relationship between herself and her husband, she wrote: "Looking back, I think we grew too isolated, turned to one another too much. But we were doing the best we knew how."

Arthur Gordon, in an essay called the "Secret of Self Renewal," tells of advice he received from a Denver psychiatrist:

"Step out of your own shadow," said the psychiatrist. "Stop judging yourself so harshly …. Stop focusing on your shortcomings and give yourself credit for a few virtues now and then …. People need to be kinder to themselves because very often self kindness reduces the

> *"Step out of your own shadow,' said the psychiatrist. 'Stop judging yourself so harshly.'"*

feelings of guilt and inferiority that are blocking the flow of power from the unconscious."

And when that power is released from the unconscious, perhaps "the best we know how" may indeed become "the very best we can," even in child rearing.

Give "Tiger Mom" Some Credit
She Learned in the End

Denver Post
JANUARY 22, 2011

GIVE AMY CHUA CREDIT. NOT FOR THE HARSH ways in which she is raising her daughters. Not for calling them "garbage" if they don't get straight A's. Not for threatening to burn up their stuffed animals if they don't practice on the piano long enough to get that piece just right.

Give her credit for her eventual flexibility.

Yes, I read the excerpt from Chua's book, "Battle Hymn of the Tiger Mother," in the Feb. 8 Wall Street Journal and was appalled by her punitive parenting methods.

But then I read more. First, Denver Post writer Claire Martin's Jan. 18 report of hearing Chua at the Tattered Cover. Then to Chua's own follow-up account in the Wall Street Journal on Jan. 15.

Although Chua's strict Chinese immigrant philosophy of child-rearing worked with her older daughter, Sophia — who, after years of piano practice, played at Carnegie Hall — they failed with her younger daughter, Lulu. Chua recalls the "darkest day of my life" was when Lulu, 13, rebelling against years of coerced violin practice, screamed and hurled a glass on the floor of a Moscow restaurant.

Chua did not make Lulu leave the restaurant, but left herself in order to calm down. When she returned, she told Lulu she would no longer be forced to practice.

She admits: "I certainly made mistakes and have regrets …. I got my comeuppance; much of my book is about my decision to retreat — but only partially — from the strict (Chinese) immigrant model."

One of the biggest challenges in parenting is to know when to be tough and when to back off; to understand that your children are individuals; and that a method that will bring out genius in one could cause a mental breakdown in another.

At least Chua eventually learned from her mistakes.

On Being Aware
I Want My Kids to See the Poor's Plight

Denver Post
DECEMBER 25, 1983

WHEN I WAS A LITTLE GIRL, MY SUNDAY School class was told the girlhood story of Jane Addams, the 19th century socialworker who in her later life pioneered the settlement house movement by establishing Hull House in the slums of Chicago.

Young Jane, it appears, had received a new coat for Christmas, a coat of fine wool, replete with fur collar, cuffs, and muff in the latest fashion of the day. Preening and proud, Jane donned her coat to go to church.

Her girlish joy, however, was cut short by a directive from her father. On Christmas day Jane could not wear her fine new coat. The family would be passing through the poorer sections of town on their way to church, he explained. And, naturally, Jane would not want the misery of people who had only rags to ward off the winter to be increased by envy of her finery.

Jane went to church.

The new coat stayed home.

Whether this episode was the beginning of the awakening of one of the greatest social consciences of history, or whether the tale itself is apocryphal, I don't know.

I do know that story's symbolic message has stuck with me over the years. This fall it was brought into sharp focus by a *Contemporary* article on children's fashion which showed well-scrubbed members of Denver's pre-teen set cavorting in their back-to-school finery, one outfit of Ralph Lauren's totaling $136.50.

It is not my purpose to deride the expensive clothes of other people's children. Although my daughter and her friends distain labels, there is no question that, compared to many, their snappy skirts and smart snow boots render them as "well-turned-out" as the kids featured in the fall fashion spread. And I *like* how our daughter looks. I *like* it when our son dons a coat and tie.

But as Christmas approaches, I read a newspaper article that says: "Americans are starving in Oakland, Calif. Relief officials are feeding over 20,000 people a day, but 40,000 go hungry."

And I hear from a Colorado Parole Board member of a female parolee in western Colorado who "came to her hearing with her four children — none of them wearing shoes, all having walked through the snow to get there."

And then I read of a highly placed presidential assistant who categorizes the poor who stand in the soup lines as not *really* poor, but cheap — "just looking for a free meal." And suddenly the pile of Christmas gifts under our tree, some of them containing new clothes, loses a little of its sparkle and luster.

Over the years our children voluntarily have sent money to their favorite charities. They have participated eagerly in the school canned food drives; they have given away their last year's ski parkas. One year they even rang bells and collected money for the Salvation Army from the mansion Christmas party guests!

Yet this Christmas season, as they reach the milestones of 13 and 16, I am suddenly aware of how naive, how ignorant they are about the immense suffering in their world. Abruptly I want to shout at them, "Do you kids know, *really* know, how lucky you are!" Yet, something stops me short, catching the words in my throat.

Another mother, one whom I've never met, expresses my feeling exactly in her poem, "One Mother's Paradox":

> *"Yet this Christmas season, as they reach the milestones of 13 and 16, I am suddenly aware of how naive, how ignorant they are about the immense suffering in their world."*

I bought my 9-year-old daughter roller skates today
They cost me twenty dollars
Two miles away children eat cereal for dinner
It's all their family can afford
My daughter doesn't understand why I'm upset
She's heard me describe the poverty and suffering I've seen
She's shared dinner table talks about human misery
She's even sent money to help the starving overseas
But she doesn't really understand
She's never missed school on a snowy day ...
Because she had no boots
She's never been evicted ...
Because there was no money to pay the rent
She's never gone to bed hungry ...
Because cash to buy groceries had run out

And, she's never known a dejected mother …
Drained of hope and riddled by guilt
Of being unable to provide the basics of life to her
  children
I want so desperately to teach my daughter
To be sensitive to inequities
To reach out to help others
But I also want her to enjoy the roller skates
            —Miriam Stein, Christian Science Monitor

A Hike
More Than Just an Outing

Denver Post
JULY 21, 1985

I STAND ON THE WIND-SWEPT POINT, A THOUSAND feet above the blue lagoons and white waves of the Pacific. The wind dries the tears to my face as I turn this way, then that way looking, groping for some geological sign that will tell me the worst is over.

Maybe if I just look hard enough I'll see that the red sandy trail, a 9-inch ribbon inclining precipitously toward the seas, will wind back into the safe lush forest valleys of the Na Pali coast and, this time, stay there until we reach Kalalau Beach.

Just two week previous to our Hawaii trip, I had never heard of this Northern Coast trail on the island of Kauai. But then a friend gave us an enticing account of the 11-mile backpack to Kalalau Beach. We looked at a map of Kauai, and the lure of the coast grew stronger. We decided we'd do it.

And here I am, frozen with fear.

Just one misstep.

That's all it would take.

My kelty pack lilts precariously with its top-heavy load. My head swims. I feel disoriented, head disconnected from body. In a sheer panic, I hug the inside edge of the trail, groping for security with my fingernails in the sandy cliff.

The inside of the trail — the exact opposite of what an experienced hiker should do! I look over the cliff instead of straight ahead. I fix my eyes on obstacles in the path, rather than on ways to get around them. Everything wrong. I am doing everything wrong.

Sweat sloshes off my brow. Does age make me less confident and more phobic? Or is it parenthood? For ahead of me march cautiously, but confidently, our 14-year-old daughter, Heather, and her same-aged friend, Nicole. Before them marches our agile 17-year-old Outward Bound trained son, Scott — too confidently, I think. And before him marches my husband with the same steady paced hiking gait I've known for 24 years.

I've never been acrophobic before.

But today I'm freaking out. The totality of *their* confidence to the contrary, *I* cannot believe all will make Kalalau Beach without mishap. Someone will slip and fall. Someone will plunge to the rocks and waves below. I am sure. It is just a matter of time.

Which one will go? Cocksure Scott, misjudging the pitch? Cautious Heather, looking back to check on her friend? Slender, sure-footed Nicole, who is not even ours to lose? Three beautiful children in the prime of youth, gifts from God to their parents and grandparents.

Damn! Why did we bring these kids to this place? How can I live with myself after the inevitable tragedy?

The girls are now behind me. I try to urge caution without revealing my hysteria. "Be careful, especially going down. If you feel tired, stop." My voice comes out in a hoarse, yet calm whisper, but my gut is knotted in a hard, still scream.

Suddenly Scott does a semi-leap around a bend and the gully to the ocean is caught for a moment in a "freeze frame" between his legs.

I lose it. "For s—t sake. Scott! This isn't the Hogback! Slow down!"

Afterward, lying under the stars, the kids asleep in tents, the "inevitable" tragedy having been avoided, my emotions are still not relieved.

My mind knows the trail was not as treacherous as it appeared to me in my highly agitated state. With caution, it was totally negotiable. I've been on worse along ridges in the Colorado Rockies.

My brain measures the trek as a great accomplishment. The kids gained faith in their skill, endurance and confidence along with more appreciation of nature's wonders and dangers. All the lessons of the outdoors we want them to gain.

But, emotionally, I gained nothing but a heightened acrophobia, which, in my youth, I was almost entirely without. And I took one step backward toward more protective mothering, at a stage at which l should be loosening the maternal reins.

The destination was a prize; Kalalau Beach a white half-moon jewel. During our cooked-out dinner, a rainbow arched from the sea and ended only 50 yards from our campsite.

But I wouldn't do that trek again, even if a "pot of gold" glittered at the end of the rainbow. At least not with such precious cargo as three teenage kids.

Yet, neither would I prevent them from doing it.

In the future, may our children (and their friends) expand their wilderness skills at camp, at Outward Bound or on excursions with their father.

Where I am only indirectly responsible.

Where I don't have to watch.

MARRIAGE:
Two Is Exponentially More Than One

How Do I Love Thee? Let Me Count the Ways

Denver Post
MARCH 2, 1981

FOR THE THREE DAYS MY FORMER COLLEGE dorm-mate stayed with us, we talked about her marriage — its highs, its lows, its ultimate failure. We talked about communication and lack of it; intimacy and its difficulty. We blamed his "macho," her assertiveness and the magical expectations of coming to age in the '50s.

It was not till the third day that she mentioned it; and she did so almost offhandedly. Emotionally spent with analysis of the relationship, exhausted by uncovering each regret, she sighed with resignation.

"I guess," she said, "I was never really in love with him."

Love. Romantic love. Marital love. Exalted in great classics such as "Romeo and Juliet," trivialized by the plethora of romance magazines; yet, in the week before Valentine's Day as I checked through my files on Feminism, Family, Psychology and Sex Roles, I found little on love.

There were lots of articles regarding the marital relationships of working wives, "helpful" husbands, female breadwinners and male homemakers.

But love? Nothing. Perhaps, heaven forbid, I have "selected out" the subject. Perhaps I need a new filing system. Or possibly I find little, because little is written.

Only Phyllis Volkens' wonderfully personal "I Am Blessed and Truly Loved" (Denver Post, Aug. 22, 1980) springs out as pertinent: "Love. I didn't know mortals could love like this, so completely unconditional, no games or strings. (My husband) sees all my faults, but he loves me as though I had none."

Love is difficult to talk about, even between couples who share it. It takes Tevye and Golde 25 years of marriage in "Fiddler on the Roof." "So you love me?" Tevye persists. "After 25 years, I suppose I do," is her final admission. For them, as for many of us, it's easier to talk about the milk horse, the daughters, the Sabbath and the laundry.

Today, everything from perversion to death is grist for the conversational mill; yet, the word love still can bring a blush, especially to those of us approaching or leaving middle age. If in love with our spouses, we fear appearing too sentimental. If not in love with our spouses, we fear depression that could come with such admission, or a vague sense of shame at others finding out.

"Love is not enough," wrote child psychologist Bruno Bettelheim. He was writing of parents and children. But his phrase applies to marriage, too. Love in itself may not be enough to overcome widely divergent cultural backgrounds, grossly unequal workloads, the stultification of one's partner's personal growth or devastating economic deprivation.

But is it possible we read about, write about, weigh and become obsessed with the potentially divisive downsides of a relationship because we are afraid to put on the scale that crucial ingredient of whether or not we are really in love?

Perhaps we don't talk about it because only the poets don't tremble when they try to put such delicately savored feelings to words:

That certain vibration that tells us that her footstep is approaching through a noisy crowd.

That happy exhilaration that catches us unaware and rails against our logic as his wheels crunch up the driveway in the snow — even though we thought we were furious with him and may still be.

That lightness and dizziness which suddenly, spontaneously reanoints a couple with delight, after days or even weeks of bumping about and mucking through the maze of household trivia.

Love may not be able to overcome our "big" marital problems. But without its force — which suddenly can render us sexy, sensitive or quixotically silly — will we even be motivated to work out the little ones? Love very well may not be enough. But is marriage "enough" without it?

"Homemaker" Still Tops My Resumé After 20 Years of Marriage

Denver Post
May 14, 1983

UNDER THE CATEGORY OF "PROFESSION," MY resumé lists: homemaker, columnist, television host, psychiatric social worker, politician — in that order.

"Why 'homemaker' first?" asked a constructively critical friend who was urging me to sell my professional qualities more strongly. "How can you say that when you are writing or on TV more than half the time?"

"I don't know," I said, and at that time I didn't.

Homemaker first. I continue to list it first in spite of the fact that I've spent much of my married life proving that I'm not defined by it. I continue to list it first even though I detest some of its more tedious aspects.

I continue to list homemaker, although maybe in my present position I may look phony, pretentious, as if I'm trying to say, "Look, you non-politicized, non-mansion-dwelling, middle-American homemakers of the world, I'm still one of you."

But the real reason I continue to list it grows clearer with time. I think it is because to me it is my primary identity, a grounding. It incorporates parenthood, love and marriage — especially marriage. For in that relationship my spirit is rooted.

I may write about big political issues: ERA, nuclear disarmament, abortion; but it is from my homemaking self, my married self, that the emotional seeds of the articles spring. Maybe "homemaker" suffices because it would be awkward to list "married woman."

My husband and I are very different people. We move at separate paces and we spend energies on divergent things. We work on common goals but are motivated by contrasting objectives. We understand and we misunderstand; we support each other and neglect each other; we love and we argue. Yet, my marriage is where I live first in my womanhood and personhood.

That is why, when his voice cuts through to me in a crowded room, I suddenly wish I were closer and could hear him better, although I've probably heard what he is saying before.

That is why I can distinguish the sound, even the vibration, of his footstep as he approaches from afar.

For me, it was not love at first sight, but love at second sight. On our second date, we watched "Richard the III" on television, talked politics in the park, had a beer on Colfax Avenue, and topped it off with philosophy and cappuccino at the old Green Spider Coffee House.

He was for love, but against the institution of marriage, he said.

I would marry him, I decided.

I did.

And since then, whatever else I've accomplished and whatever sacrifices I've made, that marriage has been my life. As Anne Morrow Lindbergh writes:

"I am married — more than married — dedicated to marriage, and I care about the man I am married to; I care intensely about his life, our life together, his beliefs, our beliefs, his actions, our actions — everything must be worked at without ceasing, all the time. Because he is in it. In the midst of the fire and always will be. And I am so made that I cannot let him 'go his way' and I go mine. No, our marriage is something else."

In this month of our 20th wedding anniversary, so is ours. And I'm glad.

Power
When a Man and Woman Become One

Denver Post
OCTOBER 20, 1985

IT WAS THE SUMMER OF 1963. DICK AND I HAD just descended from a month's climbing expedition in the Peruvian Andes. The second part of our honeymoon was about to start: a three-month bus, train, sightseeing trip through South America.

The first morning in Lima was a honeymooner's dream.

By nightfall, we were arguing about money. At least I *thought* we were arguing about money. In retrospect, I think we were arguing about something else.

The argument started when I wanted to buy a can of hair spray for 75 cents. He thought that was extravagant. I didn't.

He also thought using hair spray didn't fit my hiking, backpacking, outdoor "image." I agreed, but insisted there would be the occasional times I would dress up, wouldn't there?

He was silent.

I was silent.

We did not buy the hair spray.

The next day the argument was reignited, when "just for fun," we went into a store which specialized in articles made of llama fur, and tried on coats and jackets. Just for fun. I tried on a long, luxurious, multi-colored coat.

"Let's get it!" said Dick.

"Are you crazy?" I asked incredulously. "Seventy-five dollars for a coat, when 75 cents for hair spray was too much?!"

He was silent and looked hurt.

I was silent and felt guilty.

We did not buy the coat.

An episode I read about recently reminded me of these exchanges stored in memory over the years. It was written by Mary Kay Blakely for the "Hers" column of the New York Times, and it concerned shopping for ice cream with her husband shortly after they had celebrated their six-month wedding anniversary.

"We stopped at Hemingway's Delicatessen to find a treat to bring home. After some deliberation, I selected a high-quality brand of butter pecan ice cream and handed it to the man who was carrying our money in his wallet.

"He looked at the price, something that had not occurred to me. He handed it back, explaining that $1.95 was exorbitant for any ice cream …

"We stood there for some time, passing the pint back and forth …. His patience was melting with the ice cream when he delivered his final opinion: there was no way he was going to pay $1.95 for a pint of ice cream.

"We rode home in stoney silence. Only six months before I had been the kind of self-actualized woman who could walk into just about any delicatessen and order whatever I wanted. Dimly, I realized that this sudden loss in opportunity had something to do with the vows I had taken …

"The next day, on the way home from work, I stopped at Hemingway's and bought six pints of butter pecan ice cream."

Reading this article, I laughed so hard about Blakely's act of self-assertion and retribution that I almost cried. I imagined her husband coming home, looking in the freezer, first staring, then swearing. I thought back 22 years ago, wishing I had such chutzpah. Wishing I had bought six cans of hair spray and hid them in Dick's duffel bag.

These episodes pack so much punch not because they concern money. Big expenditures like a house or car concern money. But little expenses concern that something else: POWER.

My husband was not tight. The hair spray offended him; it trivialized me in his eyes. Yet he was extravagant in the things he wanted to buy me, in the things he wanted me to want. He just wanted to call the shots.

I was not a spendthrift. But my idea of fun and freedom

> *"When a man and woman become one, the one is mainly him. When a man's and a woman's resources become one, the power to spend it is mainly his."*

was indulging my own trivia. I didn't need him to prove his love with a $75 coat. I didn't even like the coat. I didn't want him calling the shots.

In these early-marriage power struggles, I'm not sure the wife's income, if she has one, makes any difference. Mary Kay Blakely and I both had income. But both of us lacked power, or at least we saw ourselves as lacking it.

I cite only these two stories, but I've heard almost identical episodes replayed from most of my married women friends.

And I wonder if in the "liberated" new marriages of the 1980s, these societally ingrained, power delineations still hold? In short:

When a man and a woman become one, the one is mainly him.

When a man's and a woman's resources become one, the power to spend it is mainly his.

And the lower the expense in question, the higher the perceived power stakes.

I Love You
Say It for the World to Hear

Denver Post
MARCH 30, 1986

MAYBE IT'S JUST THE SHEER NUMBER OF PEOPLE we know, but it seems that people our age — late 40s/early 50s — have been dropping like flies lately.

These are not the "normal" expected deaths of elderly people, but the "abnormal" shocking deaths of the relatively young. (Or do we all go through life thinking of "our age," and everyone who dies at "our age," as relatively young"?)

This weekend I read a heartbreakingly beautiful, as yet unpublished, account by a friend of her husband's death of acute leukemia at age 47.

With active, aggressive chemotherapy, this man, who had never abused his body in any way, had an 80 percent chance of remission. But the other 20 percent claimed him. In addition to an adoring wife, he left four children, not one yet in college.

Then there was my friend, a Planned Parenthood advocate and my son's former school counselor, who contracted breast cancer in 1983. Last spring, the cancer returned and metastasized through her vital organs. Five days after Christmas she died at age 50, at the height of an exceptional career and a developing love relationship.

Then there's my high-school friend in Hawaii whose husband of 25 years was killed in an automobile accident, leaving her with one grown child and three teenagers.

"I look around me," she writes, "and I see all the midlife crises, divorces, unhappy marriages, and wonder why us? Why D.? Our life was near perfect. I was not restless. I loved being a wife."

And, speaking of "midlife crises," relationships seem to die even faster at "our age" than people do. Last week my husband and I had dinner with a very close friend. We talked of another mutual friend from out-of-state whose husband, "the ideal husband and father," suddenly, at age 48, walked out on his family.

"I couldn't believe it of him!" exclaimed my friend. "When they visited us here in Colorado, their family seemed perfect — especially compared to ours, where there always seemed to be some underlying tension."

My friend's voice grew soft. "But we seem to be having less tension now. B. is always telling me how much I mean to him — can you believe that?" she added with a laugh.

My husband's feet shuffled slightly under the dinner table. And, to be truthful, so did mine. I was thinking how long it had been since I'd said such words of caring. And maybe he was thinking the same.

To deflect the intensity of the moment, I made the comment that maybe the best marriages start out a little flaky and shaky. And since we two couples had known each other from the beginning, this comment brought on a recounting — amidst gales of laughter — of all the demands, the sarcasm, the put-downs, the growls, that we each had suffered and dished out over the years.

For example, there was the political function where Dick was introduced as our "brilliant state representative," whereupon I blurted out in front of God and 50 Democrats, "He's not brilliant, he just works hard."

Then there was the time after our daughter was born when Dick told me in front of God, my mother, and half the maternity ward staff that he was "busy with an important client" and would have to send Heather and me home from the hospital the next day in a cab.

And the time my friend's husband had promised — for more than three weeks — to play tennis with her, but when the appointed hour came, he was "too busy" and sent his brother to play instead.

Later, I reflected upon how Dick and I, both firstborn overachievers, once found it so hard to give succor. So hard to forgive minor transgressions. So quick to grumble and growl. We were so terrified of failure ourselves, it was as if each mistake the other made was a blow to our own self-esteem.

> "We were so terrified of failure ourselves, it was as if each mistake the other made was a blow to our own self-esteem."

But I ramble. The point of this column is that relationships can end. People can die. Suddenly, without warning. Spouses can leave a formerly "perfect" marriage — even more precipitously.

And to people lucky enough to be in, as the cliché has it, a "good relationship" — one that has mellowed and solidified with age — I give one piece of advice: Appreciate it and say so! Tell your spouse. Tell your friends. Tell the world.

And before I get back into a situation where my feet are shuffling under the table and my eyes are averting his because I haven't recently said any words of endearment to my husband of almost 23 years; and partly because today is Easter Sunday — symbol of spring, rebirth, regeneration and recommitment — but mostly just because neither of us will live forever, I say, "I love you!" for him and the world to hear.

And if he doesn't read my column this week, as he sometimes doesn't (growl!), tell him to read it. OK?

After 37 Years, the Honeymoon Continues

Colorado Woman News
FEBRUARY 2001

THE YEARS, SOMEHOW, HAD DISAPPEARED. All 37 of them.

Last June, as Dick and I lurched, swayed and banged over the rutted dirt roads of Western Tibet in our Toyota Land Cruiser, I was thrown back so dramatically to our 1963 honeymoon in Peru — to those third class busses we rode high in the Andes. When I shut my eyes, I could have been there.

Had none of our other life really happened? The kids, the politics, the joys, the sorrows, the wins, the losses?

On this Tibetan "repeat honeymoon," I even found myself "talking" to my parents, now deceased, like I would from Peru, "telling" them of the marvels of the trip.

"Get a grip," I would chide myself, when a particularly spine-shuddering bump in the road would pop my eyes wide open.

But, wait a minute, you might say. "Talking" to your parents on your honeymoon? Isn't that strange? Maybe. But, then, that whole 1963 trip was strange by conventional standards.

Both being "adventure nuts," we chose for our wedding voyage the hard rather than the easy — to climb 18,000-foot mountain peaks rather than to recline on beaches. To travel in hiking boots for four months with packs on our backs and one "dress" outfit apiece in our shoulder bags.

Thus we embarked, eagerly and naively, upon a journey which would turn out to expose our differences and our faults early.

And did it ever!

Money was the first point of contention. Not that either one of us were "big spenders." We had planned to live on five dollars a day. (You could do it in South America in 1963!)

But he wanted to try to get by on less so we could stay in Latin America longer. I wanted to "blow" the whole five, eat more, see more and do more in the time we had. He usually won.

On our "repeat" honeymoon 37 years later, the money "battle" played itself out in film use. Nothing was said. Nothing had to be. Differences revealed themselves in actions and non-verbal responses.

I, the "user," tried to take a photo of almost every child in Tibet while he scowled. He, the "conserver," would not take what I thought was a perfect scenery shot from his side of the vehicle, while I sighed, "Al Gore-like," from my side.

Yet, over the decades we have learned. Money issues, which are really power issues, have shifted. No one won. No one lost. This time we each did as we pleased, and the other got used to it, helped by the meditational aura of Tibet.

In fact, the meditational aura took over the entire trip.

Lucky for us!

Because the planned goal of our Tibetan journey — a four-day, 36-mile trek on the "Kora" around the 22,000 foot Holy Mt. Kailash — was thwarted

Dick and Dottie Lamm on the "Kora," the trail that circles Holy Mt. Kailish in Tibet. / Dottie Lamm

by an unexpected storm and four feet of snow. In short, though we might have been able to proceed, the yaks carrying our supplies could not.

There we were at 16,000 feet, locked in our most dreaded scenario — two days and two nights "cocooned" in a two-person snow-blown tent, with nothing to do but read, talk, sleep and wait for the weather to clear.

It didn't. And by the time we gave up and turned back into the still whipping wind, I no longer cared.

Because it was in that tent, hung with "drying" clothes, smelling of stale sweat, damp hiking boots, BenGay and beef jerky, that we had our best talks of the trip: Where we'd been in our 37 years together, where we were still going — all the time dissolving in uncontrollable laughter over the holes burned in our wind pants when we had tried to warm our rear ends by the hearth of a yak skin "tea house."

True romance in a Tibetan wilderness "laundry tent"? Sounds unlikely, but yes.

For this Type A couple has mellowed with time. (Is youth overrated?) Ego has been softened by tenderness. We've — well almost — accepted each other faults, and modified some of our own.

But we could aim higher. Remember the devoted gay male couple in the film "La Cage aux Folles"?

In the heat of an argument, one partner becomes very matter of fact, and says, "Well, you know I love you despite your faults."

"Yes," wails the other, "but I want you to love me *because* of my faults!"

Now, that may take another 37 years.

After 50 Years of Marriage . . .

Denver Post
MAY 12, 2013

FIFTY YEARS AGO YESTERDAY, I MARRIED UP.

He was 7 inches taller, two years older, three years more educated. I even thought he might be five IQ points smarter, but then realized that, trained as a lawyer, he probably just *talked* smarter.

My choice, conscious or unconscious, was typical of the era and was smiled upon by all. That's what a woman was supposed to do in 1963, and exactly why so many college "girls" dated upperclassmen and snagged one before their own graduations — *if* they graduated.

And if they didn't? The teaching credential or the bachelor's degree could wait. The "MRS" degree was what mattered.

But that's not what matters now, not to women at least, and not by a long shot! Females — who now make up more than 57 percent of college graduates, who are a full 60 percent of graduate school attendees, who have taken most of the leadership positions in their high schools and graduated with higher grades — do not have to marry "up" if they marry at all. They are becoming fully equipped to support themselves.

Only 51 percent of American adults are married today; in 1960, 72 percent were married. And a variety of studies show that it is young males who are more eager to marry than their female counterparts. Furthermore, the statistics may suggest that it will be men who need to "marry up."

Frankly, this very terminology has become nauseating to me. Marry up? Marry down? So what? Such concepts have outlived their usefulness, and should be put in a museum display case for those who want to study marriages of the 1950s and 1960s.

Recently, my husband, Dick, asked the following question to the freshman females in a leadership seminar we were jointly conducting at Colorado College: "Suppose you meet the love of your life, who is *not* a college graduate. And you bring him home to your parents to announce your marriage plans. What will their reaction be?"

There was a stunned silence. Perhaps the quick change of subject threw them. Perhaps, as 18- and 19-year-olds, the marriage question and whether their parents would "approve" were concepts not yet on their radar screens.

Finally, a young woman piped up: "Well, I don't know what my parents would think, but if he was a good housekeeper, it'd be OK with me!" As both males and females laughed, shifted in their seats and relaxed, I realized that her comment was predictive of what's coming and, in some cases, what is already here.

In 30 percent of dual-income couples with children, the wife makes more than her husband. With college-educated couples, it is a full 42 percent. In recent decades, husbands have doubled their share of housework and tripled their share of childcare. Full-time, stay-at-home dads have jumped from 1.6 percent in 2002 to 3.4 percent in 2012. Is that a "downward" move for men? Not anymore, unless the recent recession has forced them into this position against their will.

Although only half of American adults are presently married, a full 61 percent of those never married would like to be.

Look at the recent rush of Colorado gay and lesbian couples toward civil unions and, hopefully, soon to the marriage altars. With the increase of population who can now marry, the decrease in the divorce rate, and perhaps the uniquely strong desire of Americans to wed, this basic (but debated) institution just might survive another century.

Again, I am struck by the fact that my marriage has lasted a full half-century! Forget who married up and who married down. The journey has been mostly "uppers" rather than "downers."

And to all those couples, straight or gay, who plan to "tie the knot": Hooray!

FRIENDS:

Soul Mates Forever

Friends over the Years:
Vital to Survival

Best Friends
No Rituals Necessary

Denver Post
DECEMBER 8, 1985

RIGHT AFTER MY BEST FRIEND, DONNA, GOT married at the age of 20, my grandmother asked me if I was jealous that Donna had "gotten her beau."

"No!" I snapped, and slammed the door to my room. How could I tell my "marriage-is-everything," old-fashioned grandmother that I wasn't jealous of Donna, I was jealous of "her beau."

The nuptial doors had closed me out of the best friendship of my adolescent years. Now *he* would always come before *me*. The jerk! The impostor!

This wedding was 27 years ago. But when I read Lillian Rubin's new book, "Just Friends," my initial sense of abandonment came back to me full force. When you are "just friends," says Rubin, you are often shoved aside in favor of marriage, extended family and kids.

"For most of us, kinship falls into the realm of the sacred, friendship into the arena of the secular …. There are no social rituals, no public ceremonies to honor or celebrate friendships of any kind."

I agree. But I disagree that this lack of ceremonial validation to friendship is a negative.

To me, the very strength of friendship lies in its flexibility and lack of structural or ceremonial demands. Despite my fears, I wasn't closed out of my friendship with Donna. It survived her marriage, my career, her career, my marriage, and my kids.

Although geography separated us by more than a thousand miles, we remained "bonded." More important, I was *there* for her at a stressful time in her marriage. And she was *there* for me when my father died.

"Friends *choose* to do what kin are obliged to do," writes Rubin. And therein lies the joy. A formalized, ritualized recognition would add an oppressive layer to a relationship entered into by mutual choice.

Rubin begins her book with an episode from her own life. Her best friend's son is getting married, and her friend's sister, who flies in from a distant state, is given a prominent role in the wedding. Rubin, who feels she has been more of an "aunt" to this boy than his real aunt, is given no role in the ceremony. In short, she feels left out:

"My attention is caught by the stark clarity of line between family and friend. For the first time, I am acutely aware of how undifferentiated I am from any of the other hundred or so friends and acquaintances in attendance."

I try as hard as I can to put myself in Rubin's place. I think of my own best friend in Colorado. Even though I am her older daughter's godmother, if this daughter got married, I don't think I would feel "left out" if a visiting relative took precedence at the wedding.

I know I am supremely important to my friend, and she to me. I can't imagine needing some public recognition of that bond. The two of us recognize it. And that is enough.

All of this may sound like I take friendships casually. I don't. The only time in my life I let my female friendships lapse, I ended up in psychotherapy.

In my early child-bearing years, I thought I had outgrown the need for close friends. After all, I had my husband. I had my advanced degree. I had my babies. I had my career. Why would I need any friends but the ones Dick and I shared as a couple? Why, indeed?!

> *"The only time in my life I let my female friendships lapse, I ended up in psychotherapy."*

Friends are essential to my emotional well-being: Friends listen to things my spouse would find boring. Friends accept outrageous things about me my mother might reject. Friends let me act out "subpersonalities" that my family doesn't even know exist. Friends are there for me in trauma, and I am there for them.

True, "blood is thicker than water." But water is essential to growth. It is also refreshing. Last week my best friend flew in from the Western Slope and I picked her up at the airport. The minute she was in the car, she made a comment which elucidated something I had been thinking about for a week. This kind of "coincidence" is such a normal experience for us that we barely acknowledge it.

After my friend left Denver for a visit with her daughter on the East Coast, she promised to call from the airport the following week on her way back through Denver.

She may call and she may not. And that's OK. I compare my tolerance about her phone call to how I would feel if one of my family promised to call and then didn't:

If my husband didn't call, I'd be hurt.

If my kids didn't call, I'd be mad.

If my mother didn't call, I'd be worried.

But with my friend — if she forgets, is too rushed, too busy, too tired, that's OK. When the spirit calls her to call me, I'll be here, and vice versa.

We're not "*just* friends."

We are *best* friends.

And who needs to add "ceremony" to that?

The Boundless Love of Jessica Luna

Denver Post
MARCH 1982

JESSICA LUNA DIED LAST MONTH. SHE WAS ONLY 45. Jessica Luna, woman, Chicana, artist, activist, feminist, mother of six.

Jessica Luna — woman of the strong quote, artist with the eye for the ironic, mother with both bitterness about the motherhood role and a boundless love for her children.

Married at 15, bearing her first child at 16; Jessica, the artist, was born when she turned to painting as an emotional outlet. Her husband had just entered politics, and she found herself protesting her obligation to attend boring cocktail parties "where you had to wear beige and be like nice Anglo ladies."

Later, Jessica's art turned to doll making.

The hand that wielded the paint brush thrust the needle with the same flair. Over 40 multi-colored fabric dolls, some bedecked with buttons and jewels, sprang to life over the years — all representing women: Proud, phony, pathetic, strong, or despicable as she saw them.

"These dolls are you and me," she said at a Channel 2, 1981, taping of her doll show presentation. "These dolls have been in my home — some are my friends."

The powerful narrative which accompanied her show will guarantee that Jessica shall live on in our consciousness — pricking our consciences, outraging us at certain times, making us laugh and cry with self-recognition at other times:

On men: "I don't hate men; I think men are great as long as they are in the bedroom where they belong."

On women: "Women — we give each other only the bad parts of ourselves. When we are elevated up — when our lives get better — we share it all with a man."

"Most women want to be happy. How boring — I want to be joyous! Women hate other women with joy!"

"I've never met a woman with a strong ego."

On power: "I like power — I like to have it, I like to read about it. I like to deal with men in power."

On aging: "When the wrinkles begin to show, your friends say, 'Ooooh, no, you don't have them — though they have them, too. You have to decide early what kind of an older woman you want to be. I want to be the kind of older woman you can hear coming a mile away — adorned with bells, rings and feathers. Getting old can be pure silk if you let it."

On craziness: "Going crazy is great cleansing for the soul — it is too bad it is socially unacceptable."

On civil rights and feminism: "We've only gone halfway. Now all the Chicanos work at Health and Human Services, and all the women are getting H.H.S. benefits. That's progress?"

On illness: "Being sick. It's so devastatingly boring."

On death: "If I go to heaven I'll have an affair with God. He's the only one who won't say, 'Oh, my God!' when I tell him what I've been doing all day!"

"If I go to Hell, I'll have an affair with the Devil. He's the only one who'll say, 'Jessica, you haven't been angry enough today!'"

But Jessica of the irreverent spirit, the incisive putdown, the flashing eyes, could also be soft and vulnerable:

"Why are you doing this?" she asked me, tears glistening in her eyes and lip trembling, when I helped with some public service spots for her doll show. "Is it because you feel sorry for me?"

"Friends 'one-shot' me, now that they know I'm terminally ill with cancer. They come visit: drink my tea: suck from my strength: and work out their own guilts.

Then I never see them again."

Beneath the strong, challenging, demanding exterior, there always lurked the little girl needing to be loved. Throughout our friendship, Jessica

> *"If I go to Hell, I'll have an affair with the Devil. He's the only one who'll say, "Jessica, you haven't been angry enough today!"*

criticized my husband's administration, challenged my own elitism, but one of the last times I saw her she gave me a ceramic pin.

Engraved in her personal handwriting on the back was the message — "I love you. I need you now."

Jessica Luna, dead at 45. Her friends will help her quotes, her life, her dolls live on. But we cry for our own loss and the grief of her large and loving family.

Beverly Martinez Grall, who named her new daughter after Jessica, said last summer that when Jessica died she could just see her, "in heaven on a big stage in the sky."

But in the words of Edna St. Vincent Millay. "We are not resigned." What we all wish is that we could see Jessica still on the perennial stage of earth. And as the years pass, we will not lose the yearning to hear that older woman she chose to be, "coming from a mile away, adorned with bells, rings and feathers."

Male Friends
Certain Things Men Understand

Denver Post
JANUARY 22, 1984

I READ AN ARTICLE THE OTHER DAY ABOUT MEN as friends. Not as friends to each other, but as friends to women. It began with an esoteric quote, with which I would like to start this column. But I can't find the quote. On deadline, I'll have to start the column anyway.

I think back to the men in my life who have been and continue to be friends. I never dropped them for the women's movement, but I may have undervalued them, thinking that there are some things "men just don't understand." That may be true, but there are also many things they do understand.

For instance, they understand how to keep a friendship alive through small symbols:

Last fall, I had the somewhat intimidating experience of going back to my hometown for an autograph party celebrating my new book, "Second Banana." My best and oldest male friend from grammar school was there, listening quietly as I somewhat nervously gave my "spiel" on the book to an audience filled with former classmates, favorite teachers and my parents' friends. Afterwards, he presented me with a T-shirt from our mutual high school. His gift, symbolic of our shared growing-up, was more supportive than any words he could have spoken.

Contrary to their "Playboy" image, most men understand that a romantic dalliance is not worth the price of a real friendship. Men I have known remained closer friends if there was never a romantic involvement in the first place. Former "boyfriends" I have never seen again; yet, those boyfriends' best friends, who also became my friends, I'm still in contact with, exchanging Christmas cards and occasional visits.

Men know that friendship can become as deep through shared activities as through shared sentiments:

In Colorado, I had one mountain climbing friend who led me up Maroon Bells in a snowstorm. This same person led me down in blind panic. Daylight was fast receding. I had lost my clear glasses, so had no choice but to wear my prescription dark glasses as I scrambled down rocks I could barely see. This was 23 years ago. Now living abroad, he visited us this Thanksgiving.

Men can sometimes, in some cases, understand women better than women can:

One friend, a Denver-area folk singer, was the only person besides my mother who could understand my relief and the sense of wholeness I gained when I gave up my paid career to stay home after my second child was born.

Some women friends rejoiced that I had finally joined them at home and become a "real mother." Others disdained my choice as indicating that I

> *"Contrary to their 'Playboy' image, most men understand that a romantic dalliance is not worth the price of a real friendship."*

had fallen into the sex-stereotyped role pattern of forsaking career for family. Only this special male friend knew that life moved in cycles, and that my being-at-home part of the cycle was OK.

Friendship also can involve tough, constructive criticism:

In my position, it is so easy to let people "first lady" me. How much more pleasant it is to tell the governor's wife about the column you liked, rather than criticizing the one that turned your stomach or contained the germ of a good idea developed so poorly that even its advocates wouldn't recognize it.

A recently acquired male friend and writing critic will never fall into that category: "You act like you have no confidence in your writing," he said to me recently. Elaborating, he chastised my tendency to let talk show hosts divert the conversation from my career to "Whether, When, and What-for the governor would next run."

He criticized my columns and speeches for being too full of others' quotes, adding that I appeared afraid to be my own authority. He added that I might think I was getting out of my "first lady role" when I wrote, but I actually just continued this role by playing "hostess" to everyone else's thoughts.

He told me I was a writer, a *real* writer, and that art is the way we reach across the chasm that separates us from other people's experience. He challenged me to stop quoting others so much. He dared me to be more original.

Thank you, friend.

And I guess I didn't need that esoteric quote to begin this column anyway.

Some Changes Hit Me Harder

Denver Post
OCTOBER 4, 1983

I DON'T LIKE CHANGES VERY MUCH, AND THE FALL season has brought too many. It's enough that our kids are going to new schools, I'm writing two columns instead of one, we lost one dog and gained a new puppy, my son is almost driving and my daughter didn't need me for back-to-school clothes shopping.

None of these changes is earthshaking; some in fact were sought. But the detaching and attaching, the mourning of past routines and the challenge of getting used to new ones has left me as dried up and listless as the faded, flapping beach towels hanging from the sun porch chair.

So it really wasn't fair when my former stewardess roommate and most cherished longtime Colorado friend called me on a five-minute stopover at Stapleton to tell me of another change. Her husband has taken a new job and they are moving from Aspen to Reno in the spring.

Now stop agonizing, I say to myself as she hangs up. It isn't like she lives next door. How many times have you seen her since you roomed together more than 20 years ago? Once a season at the most. Five or six phone calls each year, squeezed in between visits. In the jet age and the phone-line decade, is Squaw Valley really so much farther than Aspen?

This just isn't right

Yes, it is. It isn't just that calls to Reno are more expensive and that we as Coloradans will hardly ski at Lake Tahoe when we can ski at Aspen or Vail. It's that she just doesn't belong anywhere else. She's a Colorado convert like me — damn it! She has no business moving away!

My friend and I first met in 1959 at the United Airlines Training School in Cheyenne. Both skiers, we prayed for the Denver base to open for new flight attendants. A fling at the ski slopes for a year, and then perhaps back to boyfriends at home on the West Coast, or on to more adventure in Chicago or New York.

Fortunate enough to have our dream of a Denver assignment realized, we fell in love, not only with the men who would become our husbands — that came later — but with Colorado; with the city as well as the mountain crests, with the summer as well as the snow, with the people as well as the places.

Our year's fling in Colorado became 3½ years. We skied together, flew together, traveled to Europe together and stayed with each other's parents in Reno and Palo Alto. We were not perfectly suited. I was a recalcitrant housekeeper; she was a tad tight with the purse strings on our trips. But we were united by the same spirit of adventure, the same burning desire to make every minute count.

> *"She just doesn't belong anywhere else. She's a Colorado convert like me— damn it! She has no business moving away!"*

Sharing the big events

I was in her wedding, and she was one of the four non-family members who attended mine. We went through post-partum depression and "housewife blues" at the same time, though we were too proud to admit these stages of semi-functioning till years later. With that sharing, our friendship deepened to a new level. We no longer keep our failures from each other in competitive defensiveness. We share everything about ourselves and our kids.

And at least once a year we *become* the kids. At the end of each ski season, we leave family behind, taking a day to drink wine and ski in the sun, as giddy and foolish as we were in 1960.

I must pull myself together and stop all this agonizing and eulogizing. She is not dying; she is only moving. Our friendship won't be over, just changed.

The move will be good for her husband, and perhaps even for her. As Geraldine Davis, author of "The Moving Experience," a handbook on moving, says as she outlines the "positives" of relocating: "Moving is fun, moving is a challenge, moving is therapeutic, moving is dreaming, moving is rewarding."

I hope so, my Colorado friend.

And I still don't want you to go.

Facing the Reality of Aging

Denver Post
OCTOBER 2, 2015

MY HIGH SCHOOL "GANG OF GIRLS" WAS ONLY seven strong when we journeyed to Paris in 1987 to celebrate our 50th birthdays.

Then, after retirement, we grew to 16. Follow-up trips took us to Mexico, Maui, Aspen, and many places close to our original homes in Palo Alto, Calif.

Last month, gathering at a cabin near Lake Tahoe following our 60th high school reunion, we were down to 12, four having died in the past five years.

At the age of 78, these deaths should not be unexpected. "Necessary Losses," writer Judith Worst would say. True, but each loss has caused us sharp pain.

This attrition has not yet hit my two other "gangs of elders." My 44-year-old women's "consciousness-raising" group has not lost members for years; all seven of us remain strong and stalwart.

> *"The specter of death hovers over all of these groups …. Is it this specter that has caused the softening of so many personal 'edges,' accompanied by an even sharper sense of humor?"*

And a recent rendezvous of four couples — aging politicians and activists from the 1970s — revealed us as cantankerous as ever.

Yet an underlying reflectiveness and sense of searching surfaced as this group posed crucial questions: What challenges remain? Which do we have the time and energy for? What do we drop? What can we now just accept?

"I'm accepting the fact that I don't understand the *big* things," says one former activist with a terminal illness. "Time has narrowed in the last year. I find myself flooded and blessed by the instant."

Long pause.

"We are all terminal," reflects another in the group. "But without a 'prescribed diagnosis,' we can deny it."

Yes, the specter of death hovers over all of these groups, sometimes lightly, sometimes ponderously. Is it this specter that has caused the softening of so many personal "edges," accompanied by an even sharper sense of humor?

"I'd be happy to die of a heart attack right now," exclaims a dedicated social activist and organizer who is super involved to this day. "Then I wouldn't have to plan the funeral!"

And the fears:

"I just don't want to outlive any of my kids or grandkids," another adds in a voice uncharacteristically wistful. Silence again follows as some recall the tragic losses of progeny experienced by others we know.

About 10 years ago, I stood in front of my bathroom mirror and, startled by my aging reflection, shouted, "I don't want to die!" Where did this outburst come from? I had no terminal illness. I just suddenly realized that some time I would die and was preparing to fight back.

One member of our septuagenarian political group mused, "I can no longer be a cause of change, but I can still be a voice for change."

So can I … but on another day.

This day, I just bask in the knowledge that soon, the other six members of my consciousness-raising group, once young feminists raging at unfairness and fighting for our place in the world, will gather on my patio.

Yes, we will air our latest complaints, share the joys of our grandchildren, bemoan the politics of the world. But mostly we will just enjoy and support each other. For who knows how much time we will have left?

WOMEN'S GROUPS AT HOME AND AFAR:
Reaffirming, Reuniting

Women's Group
What These Years Have Been About

Denver Post
AUGUST 10, 1986

THE JULY 6 NEW YORK TIMES MAGAZINE featured a 12-year reunion of a women's consciousness-raising group that had met regularly in the early '70s.

Because I, too, belong to such a group, which began in 1971 and still meets once a month, I pulled out several basic questions that the article raised and took them to my group's July meeting. The following are two of those questions and the group's responses:

Did the women's movement inspire you to do more in your career, or did it just make it tougher on you if you didn't reach your goals, or if you elected to be a full-time homemaker?

Three of the women were 100 percent positive:

"It made everything easier!"

"I felt I'd found comrades in arms."

"It gave me positive linkages. It acknowledged that other women weren't all in lock step — that they were bored with the lock step, too."

One was ambivalent:

"It clarified my parenting of my two daughters, but it made me (a full-time homemaker) feel guilty I was falling short. I kept thinking, I keep preaching 'career' — should I be putting my money where my mouth is?"

And another was negative:

"It made me dissatisfied. It made me think my 'little' career was not enough. I haven't been happy since. It (the women's movement) came just at the time I was having my babies. I couldn't have turned them over to anyone except my husband, and he wasn't supportive of my pursuing a 'big' career."

Do you ever subdue or subvert your feminist instincts in order to keep the peace with your spouse or significant other?

On this one, a short silence ensued, but once broken, the women jumped to respond, almost all at once. The responses ranged all over the "assertiveness" map:

"I don't know, but I bet I've subdued it somewhat."

"I always do. With my husband, I guess I just do as I'm told. But with other men, I don't. I guess I don't care what they think — they have no power over me — it usually helps me to get along when I speak out ..."

"Yes! Me too. It's OK to act like a feminist out in the world. But at home it makes me act 'bitchy.' I feel the power difference, and with the things

75

that mean the most to me — when I try (to assert myself) — I just get this, 'what is this s—t anyway?' Let's face it, men are (expletive deleted)!"

"I feel comfortable as a feminist with my spouse, but when I first claimed it with G. and my sons, it made me realize how fragile they were. It was like they were saying, 'We understand, but we wish you would stay where you were.'"

"When something is really important to me, I have to write K. a memo. I get too emotional when I talk and he shuts me out. It works, but it's crazy I have to do it. I can't image *him* writing *me* a memo! When he feels strongly about something, he just lets it all hang out."

"My husband likes my dependence. And part of me likes it, too. So I have to fight to keep my feminism and independence alive."

"I *never* back down from my feminism! Maybe that's why I don't *have* a significant other …"

A couple of comparisons with the New York group. We've been together 15 years and they've been apart for 12. But we, like them, seem to have reached two tentative conclusions about the women's movement:

It's been a powerful, positive force for women in society.

But it is not easy to put in practice on the personal level.

And as I read over this column, I can't help but feel some sadness. Sadness that some of us — myself included — have not progressed that far from where we were in 1971.

My head knows that we really have moved.

Yet, my heart and gut still wish for more.

I want to yell — WHAT HAVE THESE LAST 15 YEARS BEEN ABOUT IF WE HAVEN'T COME TO TERMS WITH ALL THIS!!

But I smile as I yell. Because I know what it is about. It's about the non-linear growth and development of women. It is about life cycles — big cycles with smaller ones intertwined. About an evening that uncovered only one slice in the bread of our lives, whereas another evening might have revealed a different slice.

It's about claiming power and backing away from it. About bonding and breaking away. About loving and letting go. About getting stronger and showing it — sometimes.

It's also about friendship. And that part makes me happy. Happy to have a whole group of friends that don't "one-up" each other. Thankful to have a group where none of us has to act as if we've made great, big, unambivalent strides if we haven't. A group in which no one has to pretend.

35 Years of Solace, Sentiment, Solidarity

Rocky Mountain News
SEPTEMBER 10, 2006

THIRTY-FIVE YEARS.

I was 34 in 1971 when I joined the Women's Encounter Workshop that would become my lifelong support group. I am 69 now.

We numbered 20 then. We number six now.

We were searching then — desperately trying to find peace and balance between the prattle of small children and some semblance of an intellectual life; between the new mandates of feminism and the old mandates of husbands or partners who talked "liberated" but didn't quite act it.

And, 35 years later, we are searching now. What is the meaning of growing old gracefully? Who are our role models? How did we get here anyway?

At our most recent monthly meeting, one woman told of suffering an undiagnosed illness for two months. A widow living alone, she became depressed, was sure she was dying and started agonizing over who would take care of her animals. Finally, her new doctor, the *fourth* in a series, actually listened to her and prescribed the right medication.

Another told of her 90-year-old "fiercely independent" mother who has decided she needs to sell her house and go into assisted living. "This is probably my last year," she told her daughter. "And you know," added the daughter, "she is probably right."

This story was followed by a silence poignant with memories. All of us have lost parents, three of us have lost husbands, three of us have lost a child or a grandchild. One woman's mother who died 11 years ago was also a member of our group.

Not that there haven't been joys too — children grown through tormented teens to productive adulthoods, our own professional successes and "perfect" grandchildren. But neither the sorrows nor the joys are what this article is about — they are only the subtext.

This is about our cohesiveness, our uncompromised loyalty, our very selfishness, and the importance of the group in our lives.

Many members dropped out over the years for various personal, philosophical or professional reasons.

What remains is a small group of embarrassingly nondiverse white middle-class women, all in the teaching, health or helping professions. Women whose marriages have survived — at least until death did them part. Magnanimous and inclusive in the world, but protective and even ruthless about the sanctity of our group.

"This is about our cohesiveness, our uncompromised loyalty, our very selfishness…"

For example, a professional we once hired to help us with our "process" told us that our group was dying because of the "dysfunctional relationship" between the mother-daughter duo in the group. She demanded that for appropriate functioning we must "kick the mother out." We broke the paid contract and kicked the professional out instead.

Then there were the three former members who dropped out years ago and recently asked to come back. Although we mourned when they left, our answer was no. Just too much personal history had gone by without them.

Decades ago while talking about our children, one woman in attendance with her infant at her breast laughingly predicted that someday we'd be sitting in rocking chairs on someone's porch discussing our old age. In unison we moaned at the thought. Then about 10 years ago, it actually happened, right there on a porch in Capitol Hill, two of us in rocking chairs to boot!

Recently, our sadness about one woman's mother suddenly turned practical. What are the pros and cons of various retirement homes and assisted-living centers? Whose parents have had the best experience? Then came another of our common bursts of laughter laced with irony.

"We're no longer talking about our parents," exclaimed one woman. "We are talking about us!" Will there be that "dream" assisted-living place close to the city, close to nature, designed with one-pod cottages, replete with wildflowers in between? That we can afford? That will take us?

All of us — *together*, of course!

The "Cancan Girls" Go to Paris
A French Rendezvous to Celebrate Turning 50 Together

Denver Post
JULY 5, 1987

FOR OLD TIMES' SAKE — A RENDEZVOUS IN PARIS with the old gang! What a wonderful way to celebrate turning 50.

When Joanna Morrison Liston called me from Palo Alto, Calif., last November, I thought someone had died.

Joanna and I had been friends since the fifth grade, but she never called long-distance just to chat. Bad news about someone in the old gang, I thought, as I walked slowly, apprehensively to take the call.

Her instant laughter relieved me. Jo did have some news about the old gang. Good news.

"We are going to have a birthday party!"

We all turn 50 this spring, she reminded me. "We are going to take a trip together. No husbands. No kids. Just us — Linda knows a travel agent with great excursion fares to Paris. What are some of the times you can go?"

Paris trip members in the 1954 cancan skit were Joanna Morrison Liston (fourth from left); Dottie Vennard Lamm (fifth from left); Linda Gordon Sawyer (fifth from right); Ginny Drake Reiss (third from right); Mary Hill Ashworth (second from right). / Dottie Lamm

I hung up and sat still. A trip with the old gang in the spring of 1987, 41 years after I had met them. Fantastic!

I would be there.

The "gang," after all, is my oldest women's group, predating feminist consciousness-raising by two decades.

Suddenly I recalled the glossy black-and-white print in my high-school scrapbook. Ten of us had danced the cancan for the Girls Jinx, the Palo Alto High School all-female variety show, in the spring of 1954.

Well, at last! I laughed. The "cancan girls" go to Paris!

There were about 15 in the old gang. Of these, seven made a firm commitment to the trip.

And seven showed up at the Hotel Ambassador Concorde in Paris on Friday, April 3, 1987.

Who were they? Only some of the greatest women in the world. Friends whose bonds were formed in the quiet, patriotic era immediately following World War II. Girls who came of age in the conventional '50s. Women who learned to achieve professional success without sacrificing home-centered values.

There was Mary Hill Ashworth who, in our Palo Alto days, was a "picture perfect" petite blonde who could play in the mud all day without getting dirty. A talented pianist and ballet dancer — and still picture perfect and petite — Mary became my very best friend and, at 20, became the first person I ever knew to have a "nose" job.

A respiratory therapist who has taught ballet and still dances five days a week, Mary has been married for 28 years to her high-school sweetheart, Jim Ashworth. Mary and Jim, who were separated for a year in 1981, now conduct Marriage Encounter courses for couples with troubled marriages. They have three grown children and two grandsons and live in Orinda, Calif., where Jim is a businessman.

Then there was Virginia Drake Reiss — peppy and pigtailed "Ginny," a natural-born initiator who brought energy and humor to everything she did. Through our grammar-school years, Ginny and I competed heavily for position of "gang" leader. (We're still not sure who won, nor do we care.) Married 14 years to her second husband, psychiatrist Art Reiss, Ginny is an educational psychologist, a photography enthusiast and an avid feminist with three grown children and four grown stepchildren. She lives in Greenbrae, Calif.

Jill McCutchan Robbins arrived at "our" grammar school (Walter Hays) when she was a 10-year-old fifth-grader, and we quickly embraced her friendship. Red-haired, freckle-faced and exceptionally pretty, Jill rubbed lemon juice on her freckles, hated her red hair and longed for skin that would tan. When we were growing up, she went on so many outings with my family that my father had a standard joke: He said if he ever left the car running in the driveway, it would "automatically drive itself over and pick up Jill."

Today, Jill and her husband, businessman Grant Robbins, live in Corona del Mar, Calif., where Jill is an elementary-school teacher and all-around outdoor enthusiast whose dream is to climb all the 14,000-foot peaks in Colorado. Jill and Grant have two grown daughters and an 18-year-old son.

Joanna Morrison Liston also entered Walter Hays School as a fifth-grader — a very blond, very shy 10-year-old. But Joanna evolved into a giggly, flirty adolescent who attracted more boyfriends than she could handle.

After college, she married her high-school sweetheart, Laurie Liston of Palo Alto, a banker. An antique and gardening enthusiast, Joanna is an elementary-school teacher and has taught blind adults for 11 years. The Listons, both deacons in their church, have three almost-grown children. Joanna, who more than any of us kept track of the gang, instigated and organized the Paris trip.

Linda Gordon Sawyer joined our gang as a ninth-grader at Jordan Junior High School when she moved to Palo Alto in 1951. A tan, lean brunette, Linda was as soft-spoken as she was multi-talented. Pianist. Artist. Tennis player. Linda, now a successful painter and print maker, was the one person I knew the least in our group and admired the most. The first of our group to marry, Linda celebrates her 30th wedding anniversary to dairy farmer Tom Sawyer this year. The Sawyers, who have four grown boys and one grandson, live in Waterford, Calif.

Annie Lease Irons. Scatter-brained, giggly, and gregarious with an infectious smile, Annie was elected "most popular girl" in the class of '55, three years after joining up with our Palo Alto "gang." Annie is artistic, musical, emotional — and after college she moved to Hawaii and fell in love with a naval officer, David Irons, who later became an attorney. They were married 23 years. Widowed in 1984, Annie sang the "Lord's Prayer" at David's memorial service. She has three grown boys and a 14-year-old daughter. A former paddler for Hui Nalu canoe club in Honolulu, Annie is a longtime

teacher of art and English. As well, she paints and exhibits — "striving for an artistic breakthrough."

I completed the gang. Dottie Vennard Lamm. Bossy to a fault, I often alienated the members of the gang I tried so hard to lead. In junior high I wised up and became known for my ability to listen to personal problems with open ears and closed mouth.

Since then I've become a flight attendant, a skier, a social worker, a political spouse, a feminist and a writer.

As a writer, I would chronicle this trip.

And I was eager to get started as my plane landed in Paris on the morning of April 3.

My flight arrived 12 hours before the others were due to land, so I spent the day in Montmartre, strolling along the crooked streets and taking pictures. Usually, I like touring alone, but on

In Paris, Dottie Lamm shares a seat on the Metro with Annie Irons. / Dottie Lamm

this day I was hyper with the promise of seeing the old group.

And, Lord, when they finally arrived at 10 p.m. — three hours late — the sheer *fun* of our friendship instantly caught us all up and immediately we were "us" again. Hugging. Crying. Laughing at things we knew were funny without having to explain why. Warmed by the sight of one another. Comfortable in our acceptance of who we are.

So — why not? — off we went to the nearest café on the Boulevard des Italiens. We had wine. We had dinner. Immediately, we picked up where we had left each other last. For some, our last meeting was at our 30-year high-school reunion. For others, like Jill, the separation has been as long as 10 years. No matter the time lapse, the bonding was instant.

Is this a dream? I ask myself after two days of sightseeing. The tenderness floats up from my gut, touches my heart and catches in my throat as I ride the elevator up to my room.

Is it possible that we are all still such friends? That we move easily among one another, our talk like a rhythm or a dance? That there is no forced conversation?

In the recent book "Women's Ways of Knowing," the authors refer to the "play patterns" of fifth-grade girls: "intimate rather than impersonal, relatively informal and unstructured …. Women have been practicing this kind of conversation since childhood."

And here we were, practicing still.

I was scared before I came. Eight days with six women I'd seen only superficially over the past 33 years! Would I, in my efforts to get photographs and a story, revert to my grammar school "bossy" self? Would we get along?

I just didn't know if it would work. One friend of mine, born of the women's movement, told me it wouldn't. "Especially with you as a journalist," she said. "If you try to write it, you will be viewed as an outsider."

But I wasn't. Yes, I asked questions — but they were sincere questions and I got sincere answers. Poignant, confidential answers — the kind that would not have been shared if we'd come together 20, or even 10, years ago.

For me, there was close to a decade in which I had lost contact with my friends. They had thought that I, as a still-single flight attendant, was living the life of an "Adventuress Extraordinaire." I wasn't.

I had thought that they, who had started their families earlier, shared something special, something that excluded me. They hadn't. In fact, they shared very little.

Joanna, who has since adopted children, had not shared her grief over infertility. Ginny, who had three babies by the time she was 25, had not shared the trouble in her marriage.

"How could I admit," she asked, "that the 'Fifties marriage dream' fell short of the promise? Especially when everyone else was living the 'dream.' Weren't they?"

But here we were in Paris sharing almost everything. On the Metro. In the bistros. On the tour bus to Versailles. At the Chateau de Chantilly, the cathedral at Chartres.

And Giverny! Giverny, home of the famed country house of impressionist Claude Monet, stands out as the heart and soul of the trip. Perhaps because it was the third day, and we had become totally relaxed. Perhaps because "overdosing" on Monet's huge painted waterlilies engendered an abnormal "high." Or, more likely, it was just that clowning around and devouring *glace* in the bright Giverny sunlight brought back our childhood full force.

Through the whole trip, I marveled that everyone who had committed to the rendezvous had actually made it. Even Linda, whose father had died just six weeks previously. Even those of us with teenagers still at home. We are, after all, the "sandwich generation."

Nobody had changed that much. Although none of us "self-destructed" into her least attractive childhood trait, our mature selves still reflected those same children who had stepped up to bat on the grammar-school baseball diamond. Or the same adolescents who "bunny-hopped" around the dance floor at the junior prom.

"Maturity," however, had made us intensely aware that what is sure today may be gone tomorrow. We are women who understand life's vagaries: accidental death. Illness. Job loss. So the very spirit that brought us to Paris permeated our time together.

> *"'Maturity' had made us intensely aware that what is sure today may be gone tomorrow."*

We know how fast life can go. Reach for it while we can. Grab life by its neck and live it. Renew old friendships before it's too late. Take Paris by storm before aging "cancan" dancer legs become too slow to maneuver the Metro. Life must be lustily consumed, not just spent. Don't hoard what you are given. It's criminal not to use it.

We relived the hilarious (though tame, by today's standards) adventures of our youth — climbing over fences into private swimming pools, sneaking out of slumber parties to meet boyfriends, organizing forbidden "street dances," smoking or drinking beer in dark, wooded back alleys.

We relived childhood hurts too:

"You wouldn't let me in the 'Junior Police Club,' because I failed the 'shinny-up-the-pole-test!'" I reminded Ginny.

"So! You got even. You wouldn't let me in the 'Ten Tiny Tailors.' I didn't get to make a poodle skirt like the rest of you."

At one point, Mary confided: "When you started going with my ex-boyfriend in the ninth grade, you didn't know it, but I cried for weeks."

"I knew ...," I answered.

But most of all we recalled the positive things that had lasted a lifetime. Friendship things. Value things. At times we felt like no time had passed.

But of course, time had passed.

Our faces showed it. So did our bodies. We joked about how good we looked, and prided ourselves on the fact that at least none had "gone to pot." But we didn't look 9, or 19, or even 39 anymore. And we knew it. That's why we were willing to throw fashion to the winds and wear Adidas and Nikes everywhere, and with everything.

We were "little old ladies in tennis shoes" — and we were having a ball. Let others laugh! So what.

The novelist Madeleine L'Engle wrote: "It's amazing what passing the half-century mark does to free one to be an eccentric."

Is that why Annie could vault over the turnstile when she forgot her Metro ticket? Is that why Mary, once the most "proper" of the group, could spin round and round and *round* the pole on the Metro car — her blue down coat making a tent of wind — while startled, but indulgent, Parisians stared?

Is that why Joanna and I could ride the merry-go-round with abandon, smiling and yelling like cowgirls while the others took pictures?

Is that why Jill, once the shyest, could bargain at the market with gusto? Or why Linda, the artist, could pose, unabashedly "mimicking" the sculptures on the terrace of the Centre Georges Pompidou? Or why Ginny could yell across the courtyard to wake us up in the mornings and then snap pictures of us as we peered out the windows, eyelids at half-mast?

Or why the whole gang of us could sing at the top of our voices, accompanying the pianist at a restaurant in Montmartre …?

Wait a minute. All this is beginning to sound gooey. Of course it wasn't laughter every minute, the whole group in "sync," tripping through Paris on the tips of our tennies.

Of course we argued.

We argued about the big things. Whether or not women had always received the short end of the stick. Whether Mary Beth Whitehead should've been allowed to be a surrogate, and about Whitehead's rights to Baby M. Whether single people should be allowed to adopt children.

Whether gays and lesbians should be prohibited from being foster parents.

And we argued about little things: Where to go and when to go and where to meet and whether we should wait if someone was late. We argued about whether to Metro or taxi or walk. Whether service was included, who to tip, whom not to tip, how much to tip.

We criticized each other's clothes, just as we did when we were girls.

"Take off the earrings. The earrings don't go," Annie said to Ginny one evening.

"Go to hell," Ginny replied, laughing. "I think they're fine."

But the criticism had little anger. It didn't matter what we argued about. It usually didn't matter who won.

Because the content of our trip was in our caring. Our solicitousness of Jill, who got sick. Of Annie, whose wallet was stolen at the Musee d'Orsay. Of Mary, whose husband's plans to join her in Paris might have to be canceled because of his father's impending surgery. The group even indulged my need to have an ice-cream "fix" every afternoon as if I were still 30 and pregnant.

Therefore, the trip in which we scarcely ever got to bed before 2:30 a.m. became a period of renewal more than exhaustion. At times we careened around Paris on half-empty fuel tanks, but we all left for home on "full."

Our sorrows were a recurring theme amid our joy. Most of us have lost parents and/or in-laws, some to long debilitating diseases. Others of us will face this soon. (Ginny's father died unexpectedly three days after she returned home.) Annie had lost her husband in a car accident, and all of us had lost friends, including group member Donna Arnold Haywood, who died of a tubal pregnancy at the age of 35.

We chastised ourselves for not reaching out to each other earlier when our children were little. Those supercompetitive, lonely days.

OK, so that past is past! All the more reason to celebrate the sharing that is possible now, when "success" and "happiness" are defined differently.

Because, who cares if somebody's husband didn't get the promotion he deserved?

Or somebody's career was cut short by family obligation?

Or somebody's, *everybody's* kids aren't perfect?

What matters is that we are still friends. Close friends. And that we all have networks of other friends too. That we grew into mature and giving women, sincere enough not to be defensive about who we are. And free enough, for at least one week, to make our oldest female friendships not just a priority but *the* priority in our lives.

> *"Our sorrows were a recurring theme amid our joy."*

Some of us had become, and remain, deeply involved in the Women's Movement. Others merely tolerated it. But each of us has absorbed many of its tenets and made them work on a societal and/or personal level.

We wouldn't have decided to come to Paris without our husbands, I'm convinced, if we hadn't been influenced by the Women's Movement in the '70s.

But if we had not been "growing up" friends in stable, traditional Palo Alto of the '40s and '50s, would we have formed such lasting bonds? And would it have occurred to us to take this trip together at all?

In the middle of our rendezvous Joanna and Ginny told Mary and me to be sure we pulled our shades tight at night, as they had been able to see us undressing from their window across the courtyard.

"Never mind all that!" said Mary eagerly. "How did we look?"

"You looked 50," replied Joanna with a grin.

C'est la vie.

Years Fall Away at Reunion
15 Friends from the Class of '55
Catch Up in Mexico

Denver Post
April 3, 2002

Barbara emerged from Customs, her radiant smile and jaunty, eager step belying her age and recent widowhood. As she approached the gate, I saw not a 64-year-old woman on vacation, but that spry, slender 13-year-old girl with the bouncy hair, over whom the most handsome boys in our 1949 ballroom dancing class constantly fought.

Ginny raced from the condo, yelling in a high-pitched voice, "Wait for MEEEEEE!" Suddenly the persona of the sophisticated psychotherapist taking a respite from her intense practice dissolved. In its place I recognized that 9-year-old pigtailed ball of energy who, starting last, and never failing to keep the "gang" waiting, always *finished* first.

Jill stopped on the beach, tenderly picked up a tiny crab shell, then with rapt focus slowly coaxed its inhabitant out of hiding. At that moment her adult, accomplished-fly-fisherwoman mystique faded away. In its place arose my red-headed freckle-faced childhood friend, whose nurturing of small creatures, especially her dog "Ruffles," would shut out all "people" concerns.

That's how I saw them. And that's who we became when, early this year, 15 of the "girls" from Palo Alto High School graduating class of 1955 gathered for a week in Sayulita, Mexico, to celebrate our joint 65th birthdays.

I'm sure others in that sleepy coastal town north of Puerto Vallarta thought we were just a bunch of grandma-aged *gringas* ready to bargain and ready to buy. But they were wrong.

Wasn't it obvious that we, all 15 of us, were the uniquely individual and competitive girls of the gang, reliving our youth and reclaiming the friendships forged in the 1940s?

Five of us have known each other since the fourth grade. We called ourselves the "Five Musketeers" and, defying the feminine "little girl" roles assigned to us at the time, we picked teams, built forts in the mud and lobbed dirt clods at each other with an intensity that equaled the fierceness of the boys in our post-World-War-II era.

At least two of our group met way back in the first grade, forming friendships that have lasted 60 years.

Motivated in September 2000 by the gracious invitation of Anne, classmate and half-time resident of Sayulita, we began planning. Then, stimulated by the events of September 2001, for some the wish to reconnect moved from desirable to imperative. Not one canceled out of fear of flying or fear of terrorism.

Maybe it's *the* age, maybe it's *our* age ... because all of us seemed to have shed any negative childhood traits, and only our best youthful personalities emerged.

Not once did I hear a sharp comment.

Not once did an unseemly competitive, defensive "edge" cut its way into the mellow atmosphere.

Though we were clearly "fourth-graders" once again, we managed to leave the dirt clods in the forts. And when Martha broke her kneecap on the last day, our solicitousness and caring knew no bounds.

Like the gently winding walkways connecting our three condos to one another and the beach, our strand of seamless conversation rose and fell through uproarious laughter, poignant memories and, occasionally, tears — all enhanced by Frank Sinatra and Elvis Presley crooning '50s and '60s songs from a boombox at our kitchen window.

The week's time allowed me to catch up intimately with each friend.

The "Five Musketeers" — clockwise from upper left: Marcia Beals, Dottie Lamm, Jill Robbins, Ginny Reiss-Brenner, Mary Ashworth. / Dottie Lamm

And as we walked and talked, romped in the surf and talked, drank margaritas and talked, and played — especially the last night, when we created a fiesta and banged at a birthday piñata with all the strength and abandon of our youth — and talked, most superficialities peeled away.

Statistically, we are quite "predictable" middle-class, educated women who came of age in the 1950s and are about to receive our Social Security checks.

Out of 15 women:

There have been 19 marriages and four divorces.

Three women have been widowed — two quite young — and only one has remarried.

Twelve are married at the present time and our marriage satisfaction comments ranged from:

"Divorce? No Way! Life's too short; besides, no one's perfect" to "We've been madly in love since we met and are even more so today."

Eight of us have been married only once and to the same man we married in our early or mid-20s.

We have had an average of 2.5 children each.

Two women have lost children — one to an early crib death, another to an illness suffered as a college student.

We have too many grandchildren to count!

Almost all of us have had careers, and most are now retired or work parttime.

But we don't *feel* predictable! We feel unique, special and fortunate in the knowledge that we have kept such close ties over the years and that we have not feared getting together periodically to leave the present behind and to become kids once again.

As most of our parents, and some of our siblings, have died, we have become, in a real sense, each other's "family of origin" — sharing memories, episodes, incidents, and special humor that we and we alone can understand.

All 15 of us — relatively healthy, "well-preserved" and strong as we are — nevertheless have suffered the sudden and recent loss of friends our own age.

We know that time will no more stand still for us than the waves of the ocean upon which we gaze.

It is not that we don't have other friends or groups — we do — the latter ranging in names from "The Cup Cake Club" to "Hot Flash Investments."

But in none of these can we revert to our own best and freshest childhood selves and have the others instantly recognize that original, creative young girl who still peeks out from under out those dutifully acquired layers of life.

When I suggest we celebrate age 70 in Aspen in 2007, Brenda looks startled.

"Seventy?!" she exclaims, "Why not 69?"

"No! 68!" ventures another.

"What about 67?"

We laugh with relief. Why not? So age 67 in 2004 it is. We all know we are older than we look and *much* older than we've acted this delightful, delicious week. So why wait?

Many books and articles have been written about "reclaiming your inner child." Most suggest intense introspection, artistic endeavors or throwing all conventions to the winds.

I have a better idea. Spend a week with a friend who shared your childhood — 14 if you can.

"To be young, really young, takes a very long time." — *Pablo Picasso*

> *"As most of our parents, and some of our siblings, have died, we have become, in a real sense, each other's 'family of origin.'"*

Feminism:

Absorbing Its Power, Facing Its Challenges

HISTORY OF BLATANT MISOGYNY:
The Patriarchy Ain't New

Tracing Anger
Its Roots Are in History

Denver Post
NOVEMBER 6, 1983

IN LAST SUNDAY'S COLUMN, A WOMAN READER said, "It's fine to say we should move from 'confrontational' feminism to 'transformational' feminism, but many of us are still *angry*. What do we women do with the anger?"

What *do* we do with the anger? The vague rumbling annoyance, the red hot rage, the fury that "explodes" unexpectedly and sometimes "irrationally." From where does such female anger come?

It well may come from our history — not women's history, not American history, not even Western history, but the history of the ages from the time the pen was first put to parchment.

In the November/December issue of Humanist magazine, sociologist Meg Bowman shares what the "best" of men have thought of women over the centuries:

"One hundred women are not worth a single testicle."

— Confucius (551-479 B.C.)

"A proper wife should be as obedient as a slave .... The female is a female by virtue of a certain lack of qualities — a natural defectiveness."

— Aristotle (384-322 B.C.)

"Do you know that each of your women is an Eve? The sentence of God — on this sex of yours — lives in this age; the guilt must necessarily live, too. You are the gate of Hell, you are the temptress of the forbidden tree; you are the first deserter of the divine law."

— Tertullian (22 A.D.)

"In childhood a woman must be subject to her father; in youth to her husband; when her husband is dead, to her sons. A woman must never be free of subjugation."

— The Hindu Code of Manu (c. 100)

"Among all savage beasts, none is found so harmful as woman."

— St. John Chrysostom (345-407)

"Any woman who acts in such a way that she cannot give birth to as many children as she is capable of, makes herself guilty of the many murders ... "

— St. Augustine (345-430)

"Are Women Human?" (In the year 584, in Lyons, France, 43 Catholic bishops and twenty men representing other bishops, after a lengthy debate, took a vote. The results were: 32 yes; 31 no. Women were declared human by one vote.)

— Council of Macon, France

"Men are superior to women."

— The Koran (c. 650)

"Women should remain at home, sit still, keep house, and bear and bring up children …. If a woman grows weary and, at last, dies from childbearing, it matters not. Let her die from bearing, she is there to do it."

— Martin Luther (1483-1546)

"Woman in her greatest perfection was made to serve and obey man, not rule and command him."

— John Knox (1505-1572)

"The souls of women are so small that some believe they've none at all."

— Samuel Butler (1612-1680)

"What misfortune to be a woman! And yet, the worst misfortune is not to understand what a misfortune it is."

— Kierkegaard (1813-1855)

"It seems to me that nearly every woman I know wants a man who knows how to love with authority. Women are simple souls who like simple things and one of the simplest is one of the simplest to give …. Our family Airedale will come clear across the yard for one pat on the head. The average wife is like that. She will come across town, across the house, across the room, across to your point of view, and across almost anything to give you her love if you offer her yours with some honest approval."

— Episcopal Bishop James Pike (1968)

"Blessed art thou, Oh our God and King of the Universe, that thou didst not create me a woman."

— daily prayer of the Orthodox Jewish male

Certainly, all women today are not angry all the time. The majority of men we know harbor such thoughts in neither heart nor head. But most of us are angry some of the time. And when our anger appears "irrational," when we are written off as victims of "raging hormonal imbalance," we probably aren't angry at much. Just the history of the world.

Mankind
Language a Symptom of Social Inequities

He and Him
Man and Mankind.
His thoughts.
His philosophies.
His Women.

The Denver Post / Maureen Scance

Denver Post
MARCH 4, 1990

THE WORDS, THE PHRASES, JUMP OUT AT ME from everywhere:

Mankind.

Manpower.

The history of Man.

Since Man set foot on this earth.

Chairman.

Whether it's a publication of essays written by high-school students, an article from The New York Times, an editorial in The Denver Post, a speech by an otherwise enlightened public servant, or a Colorado charity called "The Friends of Man," these references to the whole of humanity by a noun that covers less than half of it strike like small arrows into my consciousness.

I wiggle, pluck them out, try to ignore their hurt. But they deflect my focus, dilute my concentration from the article, the passage, the speech at hand.

Why not humankind? I want to scream. Why not the history of Humanity? Why not Humanpower? Workerpower? Chairperson?

But the scream dies and turns inside. It saddens rather than angers. To argue about semantics is foolish, I tell myself. What does it matter what women are named or that they are *not* named? What does it matter that efforts toward inclusive language have regressed in the last decade?

Language? What is language?

A trivial matter when compared with the "real" problems of women. Should I not, instead, be moved to tears over a low-income woman's botched self-abortion because her right to reproductive freedom has been taken away? Or over a woman who can't quite break the poverty cycle because to leave welfare for paid work gives her such poor wages she cannot cover medical expenses? Or over the battered woman — rich or poor — who feels if she would just "do a little better" she wouldn't "deserve" it?

Yes. But somehow this language issue feels basic and connected, even rooted, to all of the above.

If women are ignored in our language, not seen as people, isn't a logical next step to not see us at all except as vessels for the fetuses we carry?

If women do not exist as persons in their own right, what does it matter if we suffer more poverty than men?

If women are classified within the term "mankind" and not as 51 percent of humankind, if females are viewed — as Sigmund Freud viewed us — as lesser, anatomically defective males, who cares if we are battered or even murdered by our significant others?

Studies of war psychology show that projecting "nonperson" status onto the enemy allows societies to kill or maim with a clear conscience. If the enemy can become nonhuman, out of sociological or political convenience in war, is it so surprising that our language can render women less than human in "peace"?

> *"These references to the whole of humanity by a noun that covers less than half of it strike like small arrows into my consciousness."*

Haggling over words is out of fashion now. Kind of like the word "feminist." We don't want to get hung up on words. I wrote a whole column defending that position in January.

Readers agreed.

After all it spoils the style, the rhyme, the rhythm, the grammar, especially of old texts, to revise them for modern linguistic/political purposes.

But forget rewriting old texts. That's a topic for another day. Couldn't we just clean up our verbal act in the present?

Is it so hard to teach and use nonsexist phraseology in our schools, in our media, in our places of worship, in our public dialogue?

An opponent in my husband's 1974 gubernatorial campaign spoke of "men and women," "businessmen and businesswomen" so easily and naturally, it became a standard for all the candidates to emulate. What had been unnatural became natural, and fast.

But since those days, what became natural seems, again, to have become unnatural.

Riane Eisler, a prominent lawyer and author about my age, recently said in a speech:

"Remember how we sat in classes and they kept telling us about *he* and *him*. *Man* and *mankind*. *His* thoughts, *his* philosophies. And *his* women. Wow!"

Suddenly Eisler had realized that her feeling of being "one down" in those classrooms wasn't some personal neurosis, but a societally generated psychosis.

If it seems ridiculous to dwell on such linguistic subtleties, let's turn the tables for a minute.

Let's tell our men and our boys that it's "OK" that all humanity be called "Woman." That the study of the human species be called the study of Womankind. That, of course, those are just words. That, of course, they are included in such language.

What's the matter with them, anyway, are they paranoid or what? Please boys (sigh and roll your eyes) don't bother us with such trivia in the face of the world's *really* pressing problems.

Ridiculous?

Of course.

But what is more ridiculous, sad, discriminatory, and demeaning is not the fact that we women who are "fiftysomething" used to sit in classes and lectures in which we were as often as not ignored as full human beings — those, after all, were the "olden days" — but that our daughters who are "fifteensomething," in 1990 America, still are.

Discounted
Women Must Demand Respect
for Their Gender

Denver Post
C. MID-1980S

SHORTLY AFTER I TURNED IN MY OCTOBER
column on the "Daughter Track," I came
across an article in the New York Times headlined,
"Daughter of ..., Wife of ..., Mother of ...."

I didn't even read the article, which was actually
the review of a book, because just seeing the title
pushed old buttons and sent me spinning.

"What about '*Grandmother* of ...'?" I yelled
to myself. Isn't that the next logical step? The
last sequence of women's lives where we are "of
somebody." And, of course being "of somebody"
usually denotes taking care of that somebody.

The "Grandmother Track," although it may
engender the most "reverence," also could become
the most discounting. Because the *only* way we
like to see old women is as grandmothers, if we
like to see them at all.

"When women are 'over the hill,' that means
they're out of sight, and the hill is power," proclaimed feminist author Baba Copper before her
death last year.

Although 51 percent of the U.S. population —
indeed, a full 75 percent of the elderly — is female,
we women have historically been discounted, and
if not discounted, overlooked in our uniqueness.

I was a psychology major back in the 1950s.
Yet it wasn't until reading Carol Gilligan in the
1980s that I realized all of those developmental
parameters I studied — parameters that denote
the "normal" progression of the human psyche —
were derived by male researchers examining male
subjects. The researchers then simply "extrapolated"
their findings on men to women!

And it wasn't until this year — when Rep. Pat
Schroeder revealed the shocking fact that most
federally financed medical studies have, again,
been done solely on men, even though the diseases
researched (cancer, heart disease, stroke) also afflict
women — that I realized things haven't changed
that much since the '50s.

But perhaps I digress from my original point,
which is not that women are always discounted,
but that they are far more likely to be discounted if
they are not performing their expected, caretaking
roles.

"I'm *not* your mother!" proclaims 76-year-old
writer/feminist/activist Barbara McDonald from
the pages of the premier issue of new Ms. magazine.

That's right. She's not. Nor my grandmother,
nor her sister's keeper, nor nurturer of anyone, if
she does not wish to be. Yet, I choke a little on
the stridence of her tone.

McDonald insists that older women who consider it their destiny to become "mothers" and
"grandmothers" of society merely perpetuate
the female caretaking stereotype; that it is older
women fighting for *themselves* that will engender
respect for women and will, at last, change the
ethic that men "produce and create" while women
"take care of and clean up."

Well and good up to a point.

But perhaps a part of me resists McDonald's message because my own "message" recently has called upon the elderly to make sacrifices for the young. And I do so not because the elderly are *mostly* female beings, but because the elderly are *all* human beings.

Or maybe I react because her cry of "personhood first," obviously valid, nevertheless, reminds me of the early days of the 1970s feminist movement. At that time women in the paid work world seemed to designate themselves as the only "true feminists" while women in the home — the full-time nurturers, whatever their beliefs — were discounted.

And if we women continually discount a large segment of our own population — the segment which puts nurturing first — how can we expect the Patriarchy to stop discounting us all?

McDonald fears that the armies of old women we are becoming will be vanquished from the power scene despite our numbers, and valued *only* for our ability and willingness to sacrifice for the next generation.

And she has good reason to fear.

The flip side, of course, is that this very role may be a determining factor in *why* we are three-fourths of the elderly. We nurture more, are nurtured more, and we live longer — eight years longer. (Either that or we are simply biologically superior.)

But, must this dichotomy between nurturing and independence remain forever either/or? Men are not expected to give up

their power, their rights in the world when they nurture the next generation.

Renowned psychoanalyst Eric Erikson's 1968 book, "Stages of Man," includes the seventh stage of "Generativity." This is the stage where an older man is both inclined and expected to pass on his knowledge, his wisdom to a new generation. This mentoring process is not a diminution of his power, but an extension of it.

We women, who, following our mothers, orient ourselves to others most of our lives, could also learn to see this "caring for" process as an expansion, not a contraction of our power.

And, of course, to be able to do that fully — to form a society where male generativity would start earlier and female nurturing could become more creative and less energy depleting — we *will* have to bring about the structural and workplace changes McDonald, Copper and other feminists have been pushing for 20 years.

As an old woman, as an old person, I expect to mentor my own grandchildren and those of others in my own special way. Yet, I refuse to be defined by that role.

I also expect to fight for my place in the sun, write more radically, speak from the soul, scream when I feel like it, climb the 30 plus Colorado 14,000 foot mountains I did not "bag" in my youth, and perhaps take up sky diving.

So, yes, future generations, I *am* your mother! And I will pass on to you, not my passivity, not my "invisibility" but my own unique power.

> *"If we women continually discount a large segment of our own population ... how can we expect the Patriarchy to stop discounting us all?"*

We've Come a Long Way, Baby

Denver Post
DECEMBER 9, 2012

"THE 2012 ELECTION WILL GO DOWN IN HISTORY as a groundbreaking, glass-ceiling-smashing milestone for women," political reporter Laura Bassett wrote in The Huffington Post.

With a record 20 women elected to the U.S. Senate, an all-time high of 81 females joining the U.S. House, and a whopping 20-point female gender gap re-electing President Obama, history was clearly made.

Retired U.S. Rep. Jane Harman, D-Calif., added her voice to the euphoria. In a National Public Radio interview, Harman recalls sitting with Denver's former congresswoman, Pat Schroeder, at an Armed Services Committee session where the men were all screaming at each other.

"Pat then nudges me and whispers, 'Let's give them all estrogen shots!'"

Suddenly, I was propelled back to that banner year when Schroeder was first elected: 1972. What were we women doing then and how have we progressed since?

A Time magazine I found from March 20, 1972, provides some clues to the first half of this question. Headlined "Special Issue: The American Woman," the cover (showing the inner workings of a young woman's head filled with a collage of mostly domestic concerns) reveals that despite the beginning of women's lib, we were still pretty traditional.

A few nuggets from Time's inside scoop:

- In 1972, the U.S. boasted only one female senator and — before Schroeder's election that fall — only 11 congresswomen.

- There were no female Supreme Court justices. (There are now three.)

- There were only 200 female judges out of 10,000 in the U.S. judicial system. That's a mere 2 percent, compared with between 19 percent and 26 percent today.

- In 1972, twice as many men as women were in the paid workforce. And the women who did work made just 59 percent of what men made. Today, we are almost 50 percent of the work force and we earn 82.2 percent of the men's earnings.

- Although 50 percent of both males and females graduated from high school in 1972, only 41 percent of the female graduates entered college, as opposed to 59 percent of the male grads. Now, more women enter college than men. We earn 57 percent of the bachelor's degrees and 59 percent of the master's degrees, making education by far our biggest 40-year gain.

The report — replete with photos of *individual* feminist icons — not only touches on what the average woman was doing but also what she was thinking:

- A majority of women felt that the nation simply was "not yet ready" for a female president.

- Although women had obtained the vote 52 years before, very few of them voted differently from their husbands. Compare that to this year, when politics divided not only men from women, but also spouse from spouse, sometimes bitterly.
- Women comprised less than 10 percent of doctors. Yet even if there had been more, they may have lacked patients. Seventy-five percent of women (and a full 84 percent of men!) preferred a male physician.

The "pill" had set women mostly free from reproductive slavery for a decade, but attitudes toward abortion were mixed. Although 16 states (Colorado being the first) had slowly liberalized their abortion laws, the Roe vs. Wade Supreme Court decision giving women total freedom to choose abortion in the first trimester was still a year in the future.

In the 2012 election, despite the vitriol from the anti-choice, anti-Planned Parenthood conservatives, Democratic women and independent women remained almost 70 percent pro-choice, and voted that way.

So where are we today compared to 1972? Euphoric, yes — but, let's be wary.

We have made some gains in the professions, huge gains in education. Yet reproductive choice is still under attack.

And in politics, 20 percent of Congress is not enough! Schroeder weighs in by e-mail with her usual sense of irony and humor:

"Yes; It would take a 45-50 percent 'critical mass' of females to change the culture and eliminate the need for those estrogen shots."

"[In the early 1970s,] a majority of women felt that the nation simply was 'not yet ready' for a female president."

Female vs. Male:
Partnership, Planning, and Paradox

Women and Careers
A "Second Banana" Answers the Call of Independence

Denver Post
SEPTEMBER 24, 2006

MICHAEL NOER'S RECENT FORBES ARTICLE titled "Don't Marry Career Women" — which advises men in the marriage market that wives with careers will neglect their children, avoid the house work, make husbands' lives miserable, seek divorces and, worst of all, indulge in extra-marital affairs — catapulted me back 25 years.

It was 1981, and as first lady of Colorado, I had just written a column in The Denver Post titled "Second Banana." I described the challenges and frustrations of being a social worker/aspiring writer, and yet, no matter what my career needs or accomplishments, always being viewed as "second" to the "Big Man" I was married to.

Responses piled up on my desk with each day's mail, close to 100 from women declaring that my dilemma was hardly just a political one.

Women from all walks of life, married to CEOs, small business owners, entertainers, school principals, ministers, rabbis and other professional men, shared their frustrations about the fact that their lives always had to dovetail into their husbands' lives, when just occasionally, they would like to put their lives first.

The wives who wrote ranged from career-track executive working mothers to aspiring playwrights, teachers and artists who worked at home.

The Denver Post / Cindy Enright

The very few husbands who wrote to me were "stay-at-home-dads" — still uncommon in 1980 — or "Big Men" themselves. Some were sympathetic, others complained that it was the higher salary that created the "Big Person" syndrome, not gender. In short, get over it, ladies!

Recently I had the chance to speak of this subject again with two married women who, like me, came of age in the tumultuous '60s or the feminist '70s.

One of them, a freelance writer with three grown children married to a politician/ambassador, mused, "Yes, I realized I was marrying not just him, but his *life*! That's why it took me 11 years to make up my mind to marry him at all."

Another — a self described "political radical" who along with her husband and kids once lived in a commune — laughed when I asked her how her marriage had held together through her career and her activism.

"Whenever we got close to divorce," she said, "negotiations broke down over who *wouldn't* get the kids."

But perhaps in 2006 how we "older" career women did or didn't come to terms with the "second banana syndrome" is outdated and irrelevant. Let's take a look at the younger generation, the real women, and the real men, not those falsely warned in Forbes. What are they thinking and living?

First, and of primary importance, many men are rebelling against the "big-man, me-first, career is all" stereotype, especially now when the expected "Type A" performance for an aspiring executive is not 50 hours a week, but 80.

Married (to each other), authors Matt Miller and Jody Miller, who both could be described, among others things, as corporate consultants, wrote an article in the Nov. 28, 2005, issue of Fortune titled, "Get a Life!"

This piece seriously questioned whether the 20th century, Big Person, 80-hours-a-week model is actually good for people, their families, their businesses or even the national economy.

After describing the frustrations of one male executive at a top accounting firm whose "quality time" with his 4- and 6-year-old children consisted of early evenings when his wife "would bring the kids to his office in their pajamas for some romping around time," the Millers make the following points:

- Shared job arrangements, which used to be seen as the prerogative only of support staff or type B achievers, are now being tried and are working for top-level executives as well. The Millers cite Los Angeles Times editor Dean Baquet and his idea to divide the job of managing editor into not two, but three positions.
- "I like the idea of them having lives," says Baquet of his senior team.
- "Men are willing to talk about these things (job overload) in ways that were inconceivable less than 10 years ago," echoes Howard Schultz, chairman of Starbucks. (Yes! Remember when paternity leave was first granted by some progressive companies, yet 90 percent of fathers refused to take it out of fear of

appearing at best B players and at worst sloths or laggards?)

- And the younger a man is, the more willing he is to succeed professionally and "get a life" as well as a wife with a career. My son-in-law could not imagine taking a job that would limit his care of his 27-month-old son Jasper to "pajama romps" in his office. And would my daughter leave her own executive job to schlep Jasper to daddy at dinnertime? Hardly! These two, with the help of a nanny, share childcare, child "grunge" and child delights more than I can even imagine my husband and me doing in the supposedly liberated '60s and '70s.

But we need to be talking about women's careers in terms of more than lifestyles, family time or psychology — whether or not a wife is a top, second or equal banana in her own mind or the mind of others. Or whether a man, God forbid, should marry a career woman.

Syndicated columnist Ellen Goodman recently wrote of dedicated homemaker and "anti-feminist" Terry Hekker, a woman about my age with whom, years ago, I used to spar in friendly visits over tea at the Governor's Mansion.

Hekker, who in the 1980s wrote eloquently about the joys of full-time motherhood in The New York Times, was just handed divorce papers on her 40th wedding anniversary. Now, feeling like "an outdated kitchen appliance," Hekker urges young mothers to plan for a career whether they plan to use it or not.

For no matter how much more enlightened the work place has become, or how equal male/female roles evolve, a good career for a wife could mean not just an elevated ego, but economic survival. (Yes, "career men" seek divorces too, yet no one ever advised a woman not to marry one.)

Truly secure husbands will applaud, not grumble over, a wife's career and what it can bring to the family, and to him. Forty-two percent of college-educated women now out-earn their husbands. Many of those husbands welcome that. And they just might encourage their wives' careers for another reason.

The reason is this: A recent University of Wisconsin-Madison study of 500 married couples, cited by Women's eNews writers Caryl Rivers and Rosalind Barnett, reports that for both men and women, "The highest sexual satisfaction was among couples who both worked and experienced high rewards from their jobs."

In other words, a good job is good for your sex life.

No affairs needed, it seems.

On Planning
Women Need to Make Long-Range Plans

Denver Post
JANUARY 1, 1984

COLUMNIST MELVIN MADDOX WRITES, "(THE month of) January was named after Janus, the Roman deity who possessed a second face so that he could look in two directions at once …. Was he looking back at December and ahead to February?"

Most likely, the god Janus *was* looking both backward and forward, as, on this New Year's Day, we mortals also are prone to do. Yet, just how *far* past February we look may be a measure of how much planning power we have, or perceive we have, over our own lives.

Gloria Steinem, in a 1980 essay, "The Time Factor," writes:

"Planning ahead is a measure of class. The rich and even the middle class plan for future generations, but the poor can plan ahead only a few weeks or days."

Steinem elaborates on the fact that women — no matter what class or caste they are in — also tend *not* to plan ahead too far. Even ambitious women feel they must remain flexible. Available. Malleable. "Living their lives in day-to-day response of any possible needs of their husbands and children." Even potential husband and children. Even if they don't have them yet. Even if they're not sure they want them at all.

Steinem's essay took me back 22 years:

"What do you expect to be doing five years from now?" asked a 26-year-old attorney on our third date. The question stunned me. I had no idea.

"It will probably depend on whom I marry and what situation he's in," I answered tentatively. My date was visibly disappointed. He had goals. Why didn't I?

It's not that I had *never* had long-range goals. I had planned college and I had gone. I had planned to save work money for a trip to Europe between my sophomore and junior years, and I went. I had aimed for certain honor society memberships by the time I was a senior, most of which I achieved. And I had planned a temporary career as an airline hostess, and that's what I was doing.

But, at that point my life plans became hazy. As I reached legal adulthood, my assertiveness diminished. Competently and purposefully flying around the skies, I lacked direction and deliberateness on the ground. I was a college-educated dilettante, waiting to see "what would happen."

"What happened" was that I married that attorney who valued so highly the organized planning of goals. The "husband" part of my life was now realized; slowly, tentatively, I began planning again, too.

I planned for us to stay in Venezuela after our mountain climbing honeymoon. He planned we would come home. We came home.

> *"Competently and purposefully flying around the skies, I lacked direction and deliberateness on the ground."*

I planned a career in social work. He planned a career in law and politics. We both planned children. When the second one arrived, the social work career was the one shelved. Naturally. No questions asked.

I don't relate this interrupted planning with bitterness. I have been repaid tenfold for the career interruptions and the "detours" I have taken. My story has a "fairytale ending." I did what wives are supposed to do. I was flexible. I shelved my plans and was duly rewarded: a mansion, a cook, a platform from which to speak, and a room of my own from which to write.

But other women who dovetail or give up their long-range plans are not so fortunate by the time they reach middle age. Planning, or not planning, is more than a dilemma. Either can become a trap.

Many women protect themselves by only planning in little short blips. They assume grander plans will be interrupted. But since their plans stay "Lesser," they have no equity in a marriage. Then even their minor plans are easily curtailed.

Eventually they are living, or perceive themselves as living, a purely reactive life. And the "positive" trait of flexibility can turn vicious. A friend of mine, at the low point of her "powerlessness," by her own admission became "super-controlling" over the "little" things:

The baby would sleep at exactly *this* period. They would eat at exactly *this* time. They would have guests on *this* particular date. They would do Christmas *this way* this year.

Gloria Steinem points out how the women's movement itself can fall prey to lack of long-range planning.

"As a movement, women have become painfully conscious of too much reaction and living from one emergency to the next, with too little initiative and planning action of our own; hence many of our losses to much smaller but more entrenched and consistent (and continually *planning*) Right Wing."

Come to think of it, I'll bet the god Janus was looking *way* past February! But would "he" have dared to plan so far ahead if "his" name had been "Jane"?

What Does It Really Mean to "Keep Your Own Counsel"?

Colorado Woman News
MAY 2001

"A GOOD WOMAN," THE ELDERS OF MY CHILD-hood would say, nodding approvingly in the direction of a certain wife, mother or community matron. "She keeps her own counsel."

In other words, she keeps her mouth shut.

But, at the time, I really didn't get the message this "compliment" was meant to convey.

Then, years later, in the early Seventies, when I was trying to decide if the Women's Movement was for me, I heard the phrase again. This time its implications burst into my brain with a loud feminist CLICK!

- If "keeping one's own counsel" is the virtue which best defines a "good woman," why is it never used to define a "good man"?

- Isn't "keeping one's own counsel" just another way to define away a woman's personhood?! She speaks, therefore she is. For shame! Don't let her speak.

- And couldn't it be just a "polite" way of saying that women, like children, are best seen and not heard, and for God's sake, don't bother me with s**t?!

I joined the Movement.

Much has changed since the early Seventies, thanks to The Deity in Her Heaven. And thanks to the many women who, sometimes at great risk, have given the following "counsel" freely to others — and to the world:

You deserve equal pay!

If men needed abortions they'd be legal and available!

Challenge sexual harassment!

Do not trash the environment!

Domestic violence is WRONG — You did NOT ask for it!

Prevent Nuclear War!

Protect our kids from gun violence!

Yet, with due respect to such crucial activism, political "counsels" can be the easiest to give.

The tougher challenge is giving the personal "counsel" — the one that may threaten a relationship, a job, a promotion, the love and respect of one's intellectual or emotional community.

The closer to "home" the thought of speaking up comes, the tighter the knot in one's throat. Yet also the greater the danger in NOT speaking up. To paraphrase Maya Angelou's splendid metaphor, "Sometimes, when a caged bird doesn't sing, it dies."

I was in therapy between the birth of my first and second child. "Situational stress and mild post partum depression" was my diagnosis.

But looking back on it I realize that I was there partly because, as a "good wife who kept her own counsel," I ASSUMED I couldn't possible tell my husband about the things that were distressing me.

Years later I found that my best friend was in therapy at exactly the same time for almost exactly the same reasons. But we both ASSUMED we could never give counsel or, heaven forbid, confide in each other. To talk about our problems or our needs would have been to admit we were not "good enough" wives and mothers and that our lives were not "perfect."

In short, keeping our own counsel, keeping up pretenses, buying into the Patriarchy's (or even the Sisterhood's) concept of female goodness can paralyze us.

A no less seemingly fearless personage as Oprah Winfrey writes movingly in the April edition of her magazine, *O*:

"Over time I realized that I had often seemed so brave on the outside but had lived much of my inner life in bondage. I was afraid that others wouldn't like me …. I was terrified that if I said no to people they would reject me.

"Everything I did, thought, felt, said, or even ate, was connected with the fear I carried around with me — and I allowed it to block me from ever knowing who I really was."

Not that there isn't reason to be frightened.

Over the years, I have seen marriages flounder over women asserting themselves and becoming "who they really are." But I have also seen them flounder when women have given up every bit of who they are for the specific sake of "saving the marriage."

A good friend of mine who risked losing her parents when she came out as who she really was — a lesbian — did, indeed, lose them. The loss saddens her to this day, but there is no way she could have continued to "keep her own counsel."

Often, however, we win when we speak up.

A University of Denver Women's College student of mine was terrified of losing her job when she told her boss that a client worth megabucks to their company had sexually harassed her.

She held her breath for his response while he grew silent and gazed out the window. Finally he turned to her and said, "Well, I don't think we need that client any more." Slowly she let out her breath.

"I don't think I've ever felt so supported," she reported later.

We are in a very conservative time. (You've noticed?) Not only politically, but economically as well. The massive middle class feels less secure than it did only a year ago. Americans' net worth fell a collective 2% last year — the first such setback since 1945. And women feel particularly vulnerable. Therefore it's not easy to let our "counsel" fly.

But our voices must become stronger even when we're scared.

So write to the President and to your Congressperson about the country's and world's injustices, and give them your counsel where they need it. That's the easy part.

Then speak up to your friend, your lover, your husband, your co workers and your boss about your own needs and any "local" injustices you feel need correcting!

For in order to change the paradigm for women's potential power, we must risk giving our "counsel" not only where we march and vote, but where we live and work.

Quote: *"… the true meaning of courage is to be afraid, and then, with your knees knocking and your heart racing, to step out anyway …."*

— Oprah Winfrey, *O* magazine, April 2001.

Feminist, First Lady: No Conflict

Denver Post
NOVEMBER 7, 1993

I HAVEN'T HEARD ANY HILLARY JOKES LATELY. That's not surprising. Who would dare? When excellence is the issue, "role" becomes a non-issue.

I watched the first lady's performance at the congressional health care hearings in September and October, and then again last week as she took on the insurance industry, with more amusement than amazement.

Hillary Rodham Clinton's command of her subject did not surprise me in the slightest. I saw that command back when we were in the Governors' Spouses association together.

What amused me was how the Democratic senators, seeing a political rocket rising, clamored for her presence. Some literally slobbering over her presentation.

"You were maaaarvellous," crooned House Ways and Means Committee Chairman Dan Rostenkowski after she testified.

Some of these guys still don't get it.

Don't they know that to *over*-praise is not to compliment but to condescend? To *over*-praise doesn't say, "Wow, you did it!" but, "Wow, as a woman, a first lady, a wife, we didn't think you could."

Political pandering aside, the dearth of Hillary/Billary jokes is a refreshing respite.

Recently, however, I have heard some strange criticism of Hillary, and even of those who introduce her, from an unusual place. A feminist friend of mine at a breakfast roundtable complained about the fact that Hillary is always introduced not only as chairwoman of the Health Care Task Force, but also as the first lady or the president's wife.

"But she *is* the first lady and the president's wife!" I responded.

"Yes, but she's *qualified* to head this task force from her own experience," insisted my friend.

"Yes, but she *wouldn't* be doing it just from her own experience …."

With which the breakfast table erupted into an impassioned discussion.

Have feminists, myself included, gone so overboard in "becoming persons in our own right" that we forget that the person to whom we are married is at least part of our identities?

The fact is that Hillary Rodham Clinton — Wellesley graduate, former chairwoman of the Children's Defense Fund, and one of the top 100 lawyers in America — would not be chairing the President's Health Care Task Force if she were Jane Smith Esq., practicing law in Little Rock. She would not be chairing it even if she, as Jane Smith Esq., had been appointed to the cabinet.

> *"Have feminists, myself included, gone so overboard in 'becoming persons in our own right' that we forget that the person to whom we are married is at least part of our identities?"*

If President Clinton had simply wanted a smart, able, female cabinet member to head up health-care reform, he'd have picked HHS Director Donna Shalala.

At another recent feminist luncheon (I eat a lot of feminist food!), I heard Marion White, wife of former Supreme Court Justice Byron White, introduced with no mention that she was married to the native Coloradan who had served on the nation's highest court for almost 30 years.

Strange, I thought. And sad. Because as I looked around the room I realized that over half the women, and virtually *all* the younger women, had no idea that this accomplished, venerable woman sitting in their midst was also married to an accomplished, venerable man of whom they must have heard. Wouldn't they at least like to have *known* that?

When Hillary Clinton first went before Congress to testify on health-care reform, she said that she came as "a mother, a wife, a daughter, a sister, a woman."

Wise move, I thought, to emphasize her family side. Especially in an area like health care, where female relations assume the major responsibility.

If Hillary Rodham Clinton can use "feminine, associative" words to at least partially describe a very "feminist, independent" self, what are the rest of us afraid of?

Fear of Success Isn't the Issue

Denver Post
July 3, 1984

Last month at a dinner party, I sat next to the managing editor of a major East Coast newspaper, and we got to talking of the progression of women up the journalistic ladder.

According to this gentleman, who has "mentored" many women journalists, there is a point at which some women "level out." And it isn't because they don't have the ability to go further. (This gentleman said — and I don't think he was putting me on — that women, in certain ways, are smarter the men.) But at a particular point in career advancement, some *choose* not to go further.

We both agreed that the cliche "women fear success" is hogwash. But if they don't fear success, what do they fear?

He said that some women fear taking the jump to a managerial position, because they are more sensitive than men to the fact that some of their associates (especially their female associates) no longer will like them.

I said that it isn't gaining success that some women fear, it's losing a degree of intimacy with family and friends.

Women may yell bloody murder, hassle their husbands, and cry to their support groups about the diapering, the driving and the tear-drying. Yet, when push comes to shove, they really don't want to give up the goodies of child raising:

Hearing the stories from school when they are fresh — not retold the next morning over a hurried breakfast. Occasionally, being home to receive a hand-picked bunch of dandelions. Tucking in their kids without the tug of a high-powered job — always nagging, nagging, nagging them back to office or phone.

Sticking with favorites

He said that some women don't like the job trade-offs, either; they would rather stay in writing if that's what they love than rise to editor or manager and supervise others who still get to do the work they enjoyed.

I said some women might be more idealistic then men — in that satisfaction is more important than prestige or money.

He said that some men might like to "level out" too, but that the "Top Success at All Costs!" message is so ingrained in men that they feel they are copping out if they don't keep pushing and climbing.

I said that some women feel like they're copping out if they delegate too many of life's intimacies to impersonal others.

We both agreed that that's exactly why some women might be smarter. To them, job success is just one part of the success gestalt. And some men might be wise to learn from their values.

We also agreed that the problem with all of this is not that the desire to level out is true for some women, but that bosses, editors, CEOs and executive directors form their stereotypes accordingly. That in the minds of some men:

Some women not wanting the trade-offs of top success becomes *all* women won't make the trade-offs. *All* women not wanting the top jobs becomes, why train *any* women for the top if they won't go for it? And if you aren't going to train them, why hire them? And it's probably best not to hire them anyway, because, of course, they'll quit when they have babies!

Some do, some don't

So what's the answer? The answer is, we don't assume anything. Some women might want to "level off." So may some men. Some men may want to "go for it." So may some women.

Now I've spent a lot of time in this column advocating the balanced life, the taking of "time to smell the flowers," and half of me believes it.

But, then I came home from this dinner conversation and read the June 11th Denver Post article on the five top achieving career women honored by the WomanSchool Network as "pathfinders" and my "other half" was activated. The determination and sacrifice of these women renews my hope that even more women out there will be willing to scramble up that path.

If they aren't, we all may be "leveled out," not by our own choice — but by that pervasive historical interpretation which says not, "some women *won't* go for top," but that "no woman *can*."

Censorship a Sexist Issue

Denver Post
NOVEMBER 12, 1985

"**D**OES YOUR HUSBAND EVER CENSOR WHAT you write?"
This time the question was asked by the wife of a newspaper editor who attended a speech I gave. But it has been asked before. And I'm sure it will be asked again.

Perhaps the question stems from the days when a political wife was supposed to sit with legs uncrossed, hands folded and mouth drawn in a smile tight enough to prevent anything controversial from escaping her lips.

But I digress.

The answer is no. My husband does not censor me. Generally he does not see any controversial column that escapes my word processor before it hits The Denver Post.

Yet, for some reason, the question is beginning to bug me.

Perhaps the reason is this: I can't imagine anyone ever asking my husband the same question. I asked him if anyone had. He said, "no," which is what I expected.

Sometimes I get tired of how my feminist anger rises to the surface over sexist discrepancies like this. I'd like to get rid of the prickles I feel in the back of my neck. I'd like to

> *"Cold water is likely to be thrown on the expressiveness of women no matter where they work or what they do."*

exorcise the tightness that grips my throat when I begin to sense some subtle kind of assumed power delineation which puts women in second place. And the assumption that wives will be censored by husbands, but that husbands will never be censored by wives, is one of those subtle delineations.

Unsubtle sexist discrimination is easier to get angry about: Blatant discrimination in pay. Obvious discrimination in promotion practices. These are things over which one can mobilize one's anger, things one can fight.

But when one becomes angry over the *subtle* feminist issues, there's no place for the anger to go. One can't direct it at the woman, a product of societal expectations or her own experience, who asks the question. It isn't her fault. One shouldn't direct it at the husband who has never censored. It isn't his fault.

But which sex censors which in the fields of politics or newspaper writing is only the tip of the iceberg. For cold water is likely to be thrown on the expressiveness of women no matter where they work or what they do.

Recent research on the conversation patterns of males and females has shown that men are twice as likely to interrupt women, or change the subject at hand when a woman is speaking, than vice versa. It's as though adult boys are expected to outgrow their need for the censorial "mother," but adult girls will always need the censorial "father."

And what is considered bold for a man to express is often considered brazen for a woman.

Take the woman who asked me the question. It turns out she was a political cartoonist. After my talk, she showed me the most incisive cartoon I've ever seen depicting President Reagan's ongoing love affair with the MX missile. It was extremely clever, marvelously drawn, and in questionable taste, though no less tasteful than others I've seen on the same subject, penned by male cartoonists.

The cartoon never saw print. Her husband, the editorial page editor, censored it. He not only banned it from "his" paper, but forbade her to submit it elsewhere.

"Well, I can see why he censored that. I don't blame him!" exclaimed another woman after the cartoonist left. And maybe the cartoon should have been censored.

But that isn't the point. The point is, if the roles had been reversed, if *she* had been the editor and *he* the cartoonist, I can't imagine *her* censoring *him*.

Can you?

The Bathroom Wars
Money and Power in the American Home

Denver Post
DECEMBER 4, 1988

I'M NOT MAKING MUCH MONEY THIS YEAR. YET I've got a wish list that includes a rather costly project at our house.

I want to convert a long, narrow storage room in our basement into a bathroom, requiring a tidy sum that now exceeds by almost $2,000 the estimate we got when we bought the house two years ago.

There are other financial factors — namely, the fact that we'd probably not recover the cost of this little project should we sell the house any time soon. The housing market is soft right now.

But as my husband and I wrestle with the decision — to remodel or not to remodel — the "money" issues feel more and more like "power" issues.

You've probably guessed it already: I want to get the bathroom done. My husband only wants to get it done, sort of.

And since he brings in most of our income now, his opinion on the matter feels as if it carries more weight. (But more on that in just a minute.)

Meanwhile, I am ready to get moving. I'm home this year and have time to oversee the project. Next year, when our daughter, Heather, is out and off to college, I plan to be out and off, too.

Our 20-year-old son Scott's room is in the basement. When he's home from college — from Thanksgiving to New Year's in the winter and various times during the summer — he clutters and spreads all over *both* the tiny guest bathroom and our larger master bath with his shaving gear, post-shower "waterfalls," and sopping towels. A bathroom on his floor would stop that.

Scott also brings friends home, and when we, or Heather, have house guests at the same time — well, you get the picture.

My husband agrees with most of this, kind of. Except that we have other redecorating costs. (New drapes are being installed as I write.) It's better, he thinks, to buy art and things we can "take with us." (Where are we going?) Also, "I kinda like Scott in our bathroom," he says. "Gives me a chance to relate to him over the sink. Besides, how often is he home anyway?" (More than we realize.)

My psychological and family sense says, let's do it! Ever the peace keeper and the "smoother-over" of potential conflict, I naively may be assuming that more space and more privacy automatically promote family harmony.

But the fact is, I *don't* "kinda like" relating to our son over the bathroom sink.

Last week I almost gave up. After finding, for safety and efficiency reasons, we must replace our two furnaces for a full *third* the cost of the proposed bathroom, I said to Dick, "After this, I'm not sure we can afford the bathroom."

He did a double take, looked at me strangely, and said nothing.

The Denver Post / Maureen Scance

But we can afford it. He knows it. And I know it.

What I was doing, of course, was taking the initiative on what I thought *he* would say. All of a sudden, I wasn't sure if I cared diddly-squat about the bathroom per se. But I did not want my "request" denied. I would rather surrender, take control myself, than be "beaten."

Request? Beaten?

Clearly, this is even more of a power issue to me than I thought! Why?

Because I *feel* powerless. My present meager income contribution to the family seems to have reduced my familial status. I'm convinced if I were earning a third of our income, as I have from time to time, there would be no "soul searching" and "processing" over the bathroom. We would simply do it.

"In the back of my brain the old feminist 'click' explodes, and I realize how thoroughly I've bought 'the system.'"

On the other hand, why bother with the bathroom project? A generation ago whole families got by with just *one* bathroom, and some still do. Besides, it's exhausting to struggle from a sense of powerlessness, real or imagined. One has to fortify oneself with self-esteem hype, fake energy, and a sense of urgency that rings shrill.

After all, I don't work outside the home to the frenetic degree my husband does. Neither do I work inside the home to the exhausting extent that I used to when our kids were younger. And this year — our last child's last year of high school — I have *chosen* this laid-back, unpaid course, and if that choice gives me less power, so be it.

STOP! What kind of thinking is *that*?! In the back of my brain the old feminist "click" explodes, and I realize how thoroughly I've bought "the system." Such "system buying" rails against everything for which I, and this column, have stood for the past 10 years.

Why should my value, or that of any spouse, be measured *either* by money earned or hours "served"? Marriage is an equal partnership of equal individuals rich in their own, sometimes unmeasurable, characteristics and contributions. This equality is recognized by the law, but often not by the female psyche.

Our house is jointly owned, and this bathroom project is not some personal, selfish indulgence of mine, but something that will contribute to both home value and quality of family life. I *know* that. That knowledge is part of my familial contribution, and if, by age 51, I haven't learned to honor my own knowledge, how can I expect my family or anyone else to honor it?

Suddenly my power no longer feels lost.

Let's get the bathroom done!

Women Competing: Brilliance, Beauty, Ambivalence
Successes Can Be Intimidating

Denver Post
February 2, 1981

Twenty-five to 30 governors' wives sit in an informal circle. Quiet after the carefree spontaneity of the preceding luncheon; the only sound heard is the flipping of pages of their activity reports.

A very personable and highly respected woman from a Southern state breaks the ice:

"Intimidated! That's what I am — intimidated — at what you-all are doing!" she exclaimed. The rest of us laugh, identifying instantly with her reaction.

Another woman speaks up.

"Me, too — intimidated — but look at us — all threatened by each other's accomplishments and taking our own for granted."

The second woman's comment reminds me of the recent statement of an editor. "Women view their virtues as qualities belonging to everyone, and their 'vices,' or their 'lacks,' as sins which are theirs alone." Hmmmm.

Later I compare the governors' wives' discussion with that of another group. My husband and I are taking part in a "President's Association Seminar" in Carmel, Calif. Around the table are about 25 male presidents of businesses — large and small.

The moderator asks them, "If you were all vice presidents, how many of you would just know you could do the job better than the president over you?" There is unanimous acclaim. Each one feels he can do the job better than his superior. Or at least he says he can!

Maybe I'm really comparing two unalikes. The group of male presidents who have "made it" is at the seminar for that reason; whereas the group of females, whatever their achievements, is at the governors' conference because of whom they happen to be married to. And maybe I'm comparing genuine female sharing with male ego strutting. Who knows?

Nevertheless, it does appear that we women orient ourselves to our weaknesses rather than to our strengths, and our tendency to chide ourselves for what we lack rather than to congratulate ourselves on what we have, seems to start early. Few of us ever have broken arms patting ourselves on the back!

Women even become intimidated by other women's successes on items we have placed at a low personal priority.

"Her perfect house — with no help — and 'homemade everything' pulls on 'old strings,' even though I rejected those priorities long ago. She's intimidating! She's such a good housekeeper …," says my administrative assistant.

And shouldn't I accept more positions on boards and commissions?

I wonder, as I read one governor's wife's resume filled with important board appointments. She does so much for the community — she is such a good person ….

"So why don't we play to our strengths as men do—or as men at least pretend to?"

A woman may compare herself with a colleague: "Since she is a good person and has done all that — and I haven't done 'all that' — how can I be a good person?"

How self-defeating! Since we alone know the darkness of our own soul, and others don't wear their "darknesses" on their sleeves, we naturally place last in our comparison trap.

In "Pulling Your Own Strings," Dr. Wayne Dwyer points out: "The first step is to realize there is only one you." So why don't we play to our strengths as men do — or as men at least pretend to?

I will, I resolve. Yes, I will.

Sidetracked by an article on the new president of Wellesley College, Nan Keohane, my eyes skim avidly, fascinated.

At age 40, Ms. Keohane has four children who help her and her husband with all the housework … is described by colleagues as "brilliant and easy to work with," is "a first-rate scholar" who has just published a book called "Philosophy and the State of France: The Renaissance to the Enlightenment," … runs 4 miles a day … is "thoughtful, sensitive and graceful in interpersonal relations," and according to Stanford University's new president, Donald Kennedy, "… she probably can walk on water, too."

Something in my throat clutches momentarily, I'd like to meet her, I think … except that she sounds so … well … intimidating ….

Competition
Women Can Do It Too

Denver Post
JANUARY 20, 1985

WHEN I WAS A GUEST ON TRISHA FLYNN'S KNUS talk show (as she substituted for Woody Paige) the question came up about whether we two women "co-columnists" at The Denver Post "collaborate."

Shortly after the show, a woman wrote me a letter with a second question: "What I'm really interested in is not whether you collaborate, but do you compete?"

The answer to the first question is simple. Yes, we collaborate occasionally, but not usually. We're very much on the same "wave length," and sometimes we refer information to each other. But if our columns on similar subjects appear together, it is almost always a matter of chance.

The answer to the second question, "Do we compete?" is more complicated. Things are always "complicated" when one is tempted to smooth over, to sugar-coat, in short, to lie.

I'd like to answer the question with a resounding "NO!"

I'd like to tell you, in the voice of my 1950s upbringing, that competition makes me feel too assertive, too aggressive, too uncharitable and too unfeminine. If I were a competitive person, I would not be a really *nice* person; I might even be, heaven forbid, "masculine."

And I'd like to tell you, in the voice of my 1970s Women's Movement passion, that women *do* not compete and women *should* not compete, because they must stick together. Sisterhood, not competition, is the name of the game.

Competing sounds like "trashing" and that's a no-no. And if we women do compete, then we shouldn't ever let anybody else know about it, especially men. So, the second name of the game is silence.

And this game of silence takes strange forms. On March 25, 1984, Contemporary reprinted a Washingtonian Magazine article by Judy Bachrach titled, "Female Rivalries; Behind the Mask of Sisterhood."

Bachrach wrote of an intriguing phenomenon: Those women she interviewed for the article who admitted to competition with other women insisted on anonymity. The ones who allowed their names to be used disavowed any competitiveness and instead said things like this:

"I don't think women want to compete against each other. Only pussycats whose goals are lesser are interested in competing with other women." — Liz Carpenter, feminist, former press secretary to Lady Bird Johnson.

"I was married young and never had a career, so I've never been competitive with other women, and I don't think women are particularly rivalrous with one another." — Socialite Buffy Cafritz.

Come off it! With all due respect to these women and their accomplishments, I don't believe a word of what they say, and I wonder if they do.

You see, I don't think it's overt competition between women that destroys the sisterhood. It's underground competition; unacknowledged, simmering competition that's destructive. And much of this non-acknowledgment of our combative instincts is due to our conditioning.

Later in the article, Mary Crisp, former co-chair of the National Republican Party, was quoted in her customarily blunt style:

"Men are accustomed to rivalry with each other. They've known this from the time they were kids. They could even resort to violence and punch a friend in the nose and still be friends. But rivalry with women … well, it's considered distasteful. We aren't open about it, so it becomes surreptitious, and takes different forms."

And others have said it even more definitively. Regarding the maintenance of that competition/friendship/tension in one relationship: Boys can do it. Girls can't. Period.

But back to myself and Trisha.

I'd also like to tell you, in the voice of the 1980s Leo Buscaglia-type self-esteem ethic, that I don't compete with Trisha because I am a unique individual and my only competition is with myself. That copying another is self-defeating. And this last part is true. I don't "copy" Trisha.

But do I compete with her? Of course! I compete with her and I collaborate with her.

I compete with her, and I'm glad she's there. Through the stimulation of her being there, I'm a better writer than I would be if she weren't there. In fact, I'd feel a real loss if she weren't there. I would immediately look around for another columnist who *was* there — one with whom I could compete! Otherwise, I might get lazy.

So yes! I compete with Trisha.

And yes! She is my friend.

And who says that "boys" are the only ones who can "do it"?

Our "conditioning" to the contrary, we "girls" can "do it" too!

> *"If I were a competitive person, I would not be a really* nice *person; I might even be, heaven forbid, 'masculine.'"*

Alliance
Seeking a Meeting of Women's Minds

Denver Post
APRIL 22, 1984

TWO WEEKS AGO I HAD TEA WITH A FASCINATING woman whose political views couldn't be further from my own:

She is anti-ERA. I am pro-ERA. She is "pro-life." I am "pro-choice." She is for a constitutional amendment permitting organized prayer in the public schools. I'm against such an amendment. She is against the sex education presently being taught in the schools, especially when it is taught in mixed sex audiences. I'm for it in any audience.

She believes women who can afford to stay home with their children full time should do so. I believe a mentally "suffocated" mother is a poor mother, and that even a "well-off" woman is entitled to work outside the home if she wishes.

The woman whose views contrast so sharply with mine is Jimmie Nell Ecker, the Colorado representative of Concerned Women for America, a conservative Christian-based organization founded five years ago in California by Beverly LaHaye.

Jimmie Nell Ecker and I could have spent our hour and a half together disagreeing politely. We could have spent it arguing vociferously. We even could have spent it tearing down each other's idols and mocking each other's beliefs. But we didn't. Why?

Well, first of all, contrary to each of our probable stereotypes of the other, we both have a sense of humor. If I had anticipated a grim and dour church woman, I would have been shocked. If she had anticipated a humorless radical feminist, she would have been dead wrong. Much of our time was spent in laughter over the antics of teen-age children.

But our shared humor was not the destination of our discussion. Instead, it was the path by which we reached agreement on more important issues. For in spite of our opposite positions on the political spectrum, we found ourselves in consensus on certain vital concerns. For example, we both believe:

- That the radical right, as exemplified by *some* spokeswomen, is not reaching the traditional woman who would choose to stay home but who must be employed for financial reasons. The message, "You must stay home or you are not part of God's plan," is an undermining one to a woman who must support, or help support, her family.

- That *some* radical feminists have been guilty of putting down homemakers and undermining the values of the family. (Although Ecker views these putdowns as a deliberate attempt to destroy the family and its relationships, and I view them as an over-zealous attempt to correct past inequities in the work place, we both agree that the denigration of the full-time homemaker role has occurred.)

- That there are biological differences as well as socially-conditioned ones between men and women that may affect behavior.
- That *all* women need to get involved in the world and work for what they believe in; that the feminist movement has been instrumental in inspiring even non-feminist women to do just that.
- That, whatever the reason, millions of American children are neglected. That the children should be the first priority of both parents, emotionally as well as financially. That when both parents must work, or when a single parent raises a family, creative new ways to nurture these children must be found.

Today is Easter Sunday. Whatever a person's theological belief, Easter is a symbol of rebirth, enlightenment and new beginnings. A time for healing differences. A time for pulling together.

Now, I'm not suggesting a formal alliance.

Not for a minute am I naive enough to think that because of a few tenuous agreements between two women philosophizing over tea, "Concerned Women for America" and NOW (National Organization for Women) could pool resources and structure a joint platform. The pressure of maintaining the alliance would surely pull the planks of the platform apart, not together.

But an informal, emotional alliance might be possible. An alliance in which, at the very least, one faction does not automatically pose the other as the enemy. An alliance that could support certain kinds of privately-sponsored child care. An alliance that would fight pornography from both the standpoint of morality and the non-denigration of women. An alliance that could re-elevate the woman who chooses to stay home and care for her children (and who, increasingly, provides after school care for everyone else's children, too!).

Why not such an informal, emotional alliance?

For at the bottom line, we are *all* Concerned Women for America. And the agenda items we can agree on need to be tackled NOW.

Gifted Females
Support Important

Denver Post
JANUARY 13, 1985

FOUR YEARS AGO, THE DAUGHTER OF SOME VERY good California friends was accepted at Princeton, Amherst and, as I recall, a couple of other highly academic and prestigious institutions.

Her high school friends were amazed at these acceptances and so were their parents.

"We knew Hannah was achieving very high academic marks," said her own parents, "but apparently no one else did."

Whether she did it consciously or unconsciously, Hannah, an accomplished basketball player, concealed her intellectual giftedness from her peer group, which consisted mainly of athletic companions with varying degrees of academic prowess.

Isolated from her friends in the accelerated classes of a huge inner-city public high school, Hannah was able to keep her academic life and social/athletic life almost totally separate.

Hannah came to my thoughts recently as I read a paper by Linda K. Silverman, Ph.D. psychologist, titled, "What Happens to the Gifted Girl?"

Hannah's story to the contrary, one of the things that happens to many gifted girls is that their grades (which are usually superior to those of gifted boys in elementary school) drop off markedly in the junior high school years.

Why? Mainly because most gifted girls cannot find a way to hide their talents and still keep achieving. Even in the "liberated" 1980s, too many "smarts" in an adolescent female is not considered "cool" by her peers. And if a girl has to pick between "smarts" and acceptance by her friends, she'll pick the acceptance.

One girl quoted in the Silverman paper said that the biggest accomplishment of her life was graduating third in her high school class without letting anyone know of her academic standing!

Adolescence is a time of peer conformity in both sexes, but because the male senses more societal rewards in deviating from the norm toward excellence and difference, he is more likely to take risks in that direction.

> *"Even in the 'liberated' 1980s, too many 'smarts' in an adolescent female is not considered 'cool' by her peers. And if a girl has to pick between 'smarts' and acceptance by her friends, she'll pick the acceptance."*

With all the progress women and girls have made of late, I still see indications of this adolescent female reticence to excel, especially if the girl's giftedness lies in a non-traditional field. The 15-year-old daughter of other friends recently tested in the gifted category in math.

"Yes, math is easy," she said flippantly to her parents, "but I do not like it, and I don't plan to do anything with it!"

According to Silverman, and other authorities she cites, gifted girls who "hang in there" will find an adequate peer group as a college student and as an adult, but it's almost as if they have to go "underground" in their teen years. And some of them never reemerge.

The "gifted girl," writes Silverman, "has more reason to hide her abilities than to demonstrate them, and hide them she does, until she no longer believes they exist."

So what are some of the ways to support female giftedness in these precarious years?

In a follow-up phone conversation, Silverman urged that parents and teachers of potentially gifted girls have them tested, identified, and placed in special classes or special project groups with other gifted youngsters. "Being different" is not so scary if there are others with whom to be "different."

Silverman stresses the critical role of fathers, citing an article, "Women in Male Dominated Professions," by J.A. Lemkau. She writes: "early experiences with a supportive father may 'inoculate' these women against later pressures to be sex 'appropriate,' and may predispose them to seek the companionship of males unthreatened by their unusual interests."

It is no accident that fathers without sons tend to encourage daughters — especially a first born or an only daughter — to develop along challenging, expansive, non-sex stereotyped lines. Such a father will both enjoy his daughter's "femininity" and teach her to play baseball and do math puzzles too!

But a daughter with brothers also needs that kind of father guidance; otherwise the female sibling, gifted or "average," may become programmed to make the diminutive and passive role of "little sister" a lifelong pattern.

Mothers, of course, are important, too. Silverman does not give quite as explicit advice to mothers, but I have some pointers of my own:

- Acknowledge your own accomplishments. Females of all ages will invariably attribute their own personal success to "luck." Don't.

- Maintain an authoritative position in the family. If Dad is always perceived as the "Boss," your daughter will project that "boss" authority onto her male teachers, colleagues, boyfriends and husband.

- Show, by your own example, that nurturing friendships and personal accomplishments are *not* mutually exclusive. If you don't act as if they are, chances are, neither will she.

Different? So What!

Denver Post
SEPTEMBER 3, 1985

A MAN I KNOW AND RESPECT HANDED ME A short article from the June 18 Brain/Mind Bulletin.

The article featured Sophie Germaine, who attended math classes dressed as a male in 18th-century France where women were prevented by law from studying math.

By the time Germaine's true identity was discovered, she had become such an outstanding student she was allowed to continue.

Eventually Germaine won a French Academy of Science contest. Later her research led to the invention of elasticity theory.

"I thought this story might make good column material," the man said, "even though I guess, on average, men do test higher than women in math, don't they?"

"Yes, they do," I answered.

"Here we go again," I said to myself, at the same time reminding him that we still don't know how much of that male math superiority is biological and how much is culturally determined.

He left. I pondered our conversation and suddenly a radical thought entered my mind: "So what?!"

So what if we could isolate out all cultural influences, and still found men were slightly superior to women in math and science?

The fact that is important is not the comparison of group medians in a specific talent or trait, but the fact that *any given individual*, male or female, can range anywhere from the highest to the lowest spot on that trait's continuum.

So what if the "average" man has a greater degree of upper body strength than the "average" woman? That doesn't mean we should "protect" any individual woman by not allowing her to take a high paying job which involves lifting.

So what if males measure consistently higher on tests of aggression than do women? That doesn't mean that a woman should be eliminated from military combat.

We do not sentence all men between the ages of 18 to 22 to prison, even though they have the highest criminal record of any sex/age group. Why should we sentence all women to an ideological prison walled by statistical averages?

On Aug. 29, Heather Larson became the first female firefighter hired by the Denver Fire Department. In support of this hiring, a newspaper editorial pinpointed the generality/specificity issue:

"Why should we sentence all women to an ideological prison walled by statistical averages?"

"Naturally, a firefighter needs to have greater strength than, say, a clerk in a doughnut shop. And more men than women no doubt possess the required strength. But surely some women have the necessary physical attributes to operate as first-rate firefighters."

Gender and other biological generalities are dangerous. They have spawned societal sexism and racism. Apartheid and the Holocaust.

Many, even in 1985 America, embrace such generalities in order to keep hierarchies intact, in order automatically to eliminate whole groups of people from competition.

It is not surprising, then, that other Americans are so frightened by these attempts to stereotype and discriminate they become blind to data that might show innate differences between males and females. Or between blacks and whites. Or whatever.

But intellectual blindness does not enhance enlightenment.

So what if some differences in the "average" exist between two groups? If the data is there, it should be looked at and countered only by other conflicting data.

The important thing is to be able to accept possible differences in range without ever presuming where a certain individual will fall in that range, or even presuming that he/she doesn't have the possibility of expanding that range.

As Sophie Germaine did.

Catch-22
Female Beauty and Success

Denver Post
JULY 13, 1986

BACK IN 1972 WHEN COLORADO VOTERS approved the state's Equal Rights Amendment, a locally prominent feminist was interviewed on television about the victory. She did a great job. But her major worry after the interview was not if she *did* great, but if she *looked* great. "They shot me in my bad side," she moaned, as she descended from the studio set.

I was reminded of her complaint three weeks ago at the National Organization of Women Conference when I met another prominent feminist. The second thing she said to me, as she ran frantic fingers through her hair, was, "It's so flat — I just didn't have time to do it this morning."

The first woman worried about her appearance in a decade when some feminists made a political statement by "not caring" how they looked.

The second woman fussed about her hair in a radically different decade: Unshaved legs, unstyled hair, sloganed T-shirts have long been discarded for "dress for success" neatness and respectability.

But no matter the decade, and despite the feminist emphasis on achievement over appearance, both women cared more about personal good looks than either might have liked to admit. And the pressure, at this time, to be gorgeous seems to be growing.

"You don't have to be a movie star, (you can be) people just like us, who want to feel good about themselves," croons one local advertisement for plastic surgery.

Another local ad even suggests that if you don't have those lumpy thighs surgically smoothed out, the "real you" won't be able to "shine through" such an unattractive body.

A longer running national ad for a cosmetic shows an older woman fussing over the brown spots on her hands. "I'm so *ashamed*," she laments. Ashamed? Ashamed of what? Her heredity? Her age? Her lack of "perfection"?

"You all aren't any good just the way you are — *Are* you?" challenged Phil Donahue as he opened a TV show on the cosmetics industry a few months ago. The mostly female audience tittered nervously.

For the fact is that most women are *not* happy with themselves the way they are — especially their bodies. A 1985 New York Times report cited numerous studies which revealed that both women and men have unrealistic expectations about how others view their bodies — but with this difference: Men think their bodies look better than others think they do. Women think their bodies look worse!

But women should think twice before seeking the surgeon's scalpel. Because perfect trimness and model good looks, whether naturally endowed or otherwise achieved, may actually *hinder* a woman seeking professional success.

Madeline Heilman, a New York University psychologist, found that although beauty served a female very well in childhood and adolescence, it only served her well after that if she chose a traditionally female occupation.

When groups of people studied resumes with attached pictures of politicians and corporate executives, who did they rate the "most competent"? The "attractive" men and the "unattractive" women!

Yet, in spite of the "beauty and brains can't mix" stereotype, Heilman did not suggest that women hide their looks, or wear "masculine" clothes. For women who try to look like men are not trusted. Catch-22.

Does any woman have a chance then, aside from a plain Jane in a ruffled collar? And why should looks matter so much anyway?

I don't know, but they do. Or, at least, women are convinced they do. And how much time, energy and money will women continue to put into the looks area, while plastic surgeons and cosmetic manufacturers laugh all the way to the bank?

I can't answer for my generation.

And I'm not sure the youngest supposedly "liberated" generation can answer either.

Witness the following conversation between New York Times writer Lois Gould and two pre-adolescent girls, Sandy and Nicole.

Gould: What if you had a choice, I mean in real life? You could be smart and strong — or you could be beautiful. Which would you choose?

Sandy: Why couldn't we be all three?

> *"Men think their bodies look better than others think they do. Women think their bodies look worse!"*

Gould: Well, first *off*, because hardly anybody gets to be all three. And hardly anybody gets to have a choice. So I'm giving you a choice. Beautiful but dumb and weak. Or smart and strong, but ugly.

Sandy: (frowning) Hmmmm.

Nicole: (cocking her head so that her long mane of naturally frosted curls tumbles gently around her shoulders) *How* ugly?

ON MEN:
Disregarding 49% of the Population?

Women "on a Roll" Exceeding Limits?

Denver Post
JANUARY 10, 1984

POSTED ON MY FILE CABINET TO THE RIGHT OF my desk is a "female superiority" sign. It reads: "A woman has to do twice as much as a man to be considered half as good. Fortunately, it isn't difficult."

When I received that sign from a friend over two years ago, I was amused. I liked it. It made me feel good. You know, the kind of "good" that comes from feeling "one notch up." Smug. A little better than the next person. Particularly if the next person happens to be a male.

For a while I chuckled over that sign each morning as I sat down at my desk. But, eventually the sign and its message kind of disappeared into the woodwork — or the metalwork — the way all new decorations start to fit in, slowly take their place, then become almost unnoticed.

> *"Subtly to deride men just because they are men smacks of a sexism we women would not tolerate if directed toward ourselves."*

But, now I find I'm noticing it again. And I'm not chuckling. Maybe I've lost my sense of humor, but it doesn't seem funny anymore. And I think I know why.

I'm getting tired of the subtle "put downs" of men with which we women indulge ourselves. Too many of us have moved from protecting individual male egos at any cost to putting those egos all in one generic basket and trampling them with innuendo.

It isn't that we shouldn't "take on" individual men when they offend us. I vengefully attack columnist Patrick Buchanan's Neanderthal views of women everytime I get the chance. I attack his biases and diatribes, not because he's male, but because he's sexist male, and obviously proud of it.

But subtly to deride men just because they are men smacks of a sexism we women would not tolerate if directed toward ourselves. Recently, I attended the first large public event of the Denver Women's Partnership's "A Year for All Women."

The 1,000 women in attendance were on what could be described as a "roll." When the keynote speaker, MacNeil-Lehrer television host Judy Woodruff, interjected into her speech the comment, "Women who seek only to be equal with men lack ambition," the crowd applauded and laughed, "knowingly" and comfortably.

Yet, I couldn't join them. To me, Woodruff's comment — although delivered in a soft "lady-like" manner — wasn't "knowledgeable" or funny. Sitting at a table of Mountain Bell executives, most of them male, and their spouses, I couldn't help wondering what these executives and the other corporate sponsors of the event were *really* thinking as they smiled warmly and joined the applause.

The women's movement has come of age. We have learned not to allow men to "trash" us simply because we are female. We women also have learned not to trash each other. But, does this give us the right to trash men, even ever so gently, just because they are male?

Another women's event last year where hundreds of women were clearly on a "roll" was the "Take Back the Night" march of late September. Here, also, a small but supportive group of men attended, men who were as dedicated to the eradication of rape and violence as the women they accompanied.

It angered me that in order to attain an all-female front, the leaders of the march relegated Colorado men to the back of the procession, like Alabama blacks were once relegated to the back of the bus.

As one person, there isn't much I can do to prevent women "on a roll" from being insensitive. But, yes, there is one thing. Reform always starts at home. The "female superiority" is going where it should have been relegated in the first place. *Trashed*. To file 13.

Is "Entitlement" a Man's Right?

Denver Post
AUGUST 16, 1983

THE WOMAN STOOD AT THE WINDOW AND watcher her teen-age son and his friend play touch football in the park across the street. The Saturday afternoon ritual was not a formal team effort. It was not a do/die, win/lose situation. Yet, their play evoked a do/die, win/lose feeling. Sweaty bodies clashed in earnest. Expletives abounded. Laughter was not in evidence.

Suddenly the mother wondered, "Would teenage girls play the same way?" No, she decided, they would not. They would play with determination, they would play with vigor, they might even play with abandon. But they would play differently.

The game ended. One of the boys flung himself through the kitchen door for a drink of water. His energetic presence filled the kitchen. He gulped one, two, three glasses of water, then flashed a big grin, wiping the sweat from his forehead with the back of his hand. "Thanks," he said, amicably.

The woman smiled back. "You guys play as if what you're doing is really important!" The boy stared at her.

"Of course it's important or we wouldn't be doing it."

Masculine viewpoint

"It's that male sense of entitlement," the woman said to me after describing the episode and shaking her head in wonder. "From a very young age boys develop that sense that whatever they are doing is earth-shakingly important because they are doing it."

Sense of entitlement. The phrase found a home in my brain, touched a chord in my subconscious. It was the phrase I had been searching for to differentiate my husband's self-confidence from my self-scrutiny, a phrase that may explain why when I do something part of me is always wondering if, in fact, I shouldn't be doing something else. In contrast, my husband is certain that whatever he is doing at an appointed time is what he ought to be doing at that time. Period. No doubt.

If he is writing, he is fully absorbed. If he is napping, he needs a nap. If he is jogging, his knowledge that the activity is right at this particular time exudes with every stride.

He may not be "right" in the absolute sense. His writing may be off base. He may not be doing what others wish him to do or need him to do. It's not that he may not stumble as he jogs, or quit a mile early; but if he quits, he will feel right about quitting. No self-doubting inner-dialogue: "I should do one more mile." Guilt.

Another woman I know has said: "Men seem to take up space more than women. Even small men." Her pronouncement also hits home. My son had that proclivity for filling space long before he became 6 feet tall.

A personal experiment

This spring Carol Lynn Mithers wrote a series of articles for the Independent News Alliance.

Carol wanted to find out what it would be like to be a man. Her experiment began by the donning of a total male disguise, complete with beard and breast wrap. For a part of each day or night for three months, Carol became David. As David, Carol found that not only did people respond to her differently but also she began to act differently in certain subtle ways.

"As David, all hesitation was removed from my voice and all traces of the 'tag question' ('this is a great movie ... don't you think?') as well as that particularly female inflection that hedges its bets by placing statements in question form. ('I'm going to the gym now?')

"As David, instead of politely requesting service in bars and restaurants, I politely demanded it ....

"As David, I didn't smile much at all, and I was becoming uncomfortably aware that when I was a woman, a little 'hi, excuse-me-for-taking-up-room' deferential smile seemed always on my face."

As David, Carol also began to walk differently. Before her experiment her boyfriend had explained to her the "politics of a masculine walk":

"'When you walk, take your time. Women always hurry. They move as if they are going somewhere specific, as if they need a reason to be where they are. As a man you can just inhabit the space. The public space is yours to take.'"

So Much for "Cinch" Column

Denver Post
MAY 1, 1984

I STARTED THIS COLUMN ON A RECENT SKI weekend. My notes were in order on the desk in my hosts' guest room. Pencils and mind sharpened. Thoughts ready to move.

The column would deal with certain kinds of stress particular to women. Focus would germinate from studies I had been reading on how women are more likely than men to be vulnerable to "vicarious stress" — stress caused by traumatic life events experienced by a family member, neighbor or close friend.

The theory had a comfortable "deja vu" feeling about it. For not only have I read about this phenomenon, I have observed it.

I have known wives who were more bereft by the physical and mental demise of a husband's parent than their husbands were. I have seen mothers "work through" with their children the death of a pet, pack the children off to school, only to call in sick themselves — too emotionally shattered to go to work. I have talked to women who have given up their entire day to listen to the despair of a friend's divorce, women who then stayed up all night completing the nitty-gritty tasks of their own lives left undone.

All but on paper

So this column, a delightful uniting of the academic and the experiential, would be a cinch. Before I began it, it was almost written in my head. Finished. Until the next day, when I was involved in an exchange that just didn't jibe with the theory.

"I don't think there's anything that tears me up like a problem one of my kids is having," said my host as we rode up on the ski lift. "Work problems, anything else, I can leave it behind — but not my kids." For the nine-minute ride, this father agonized over his 16-year-old daughter, who had just completed her spring vacation and returned to a fine arts boarding school in the East.

His daughter's problems were not serious by societal standards — no drugs, alcohol, academic failure, gross adolescent rebellion. Hers were problems of an overachiever, not an underachiever; an adolescent whose maturity level had not caught up with her talent or sensitivity level; a child whose most pressing practical trauma was that she had messed up in planning her spring schedule and missed a flight connection on the way back to school. Yet, this father was not merely vicariously stressed, he was the *epitome* of vicarious stress.

Reinforcement

Listening to him brought to mind a letter from another man whose experience did not jibe with one of my theories. This man, a seemingly self-assured journalist, challenged an August column in which I implied that men inherently come by a swaggering personal self-confidence, whereas women seem to lack it. He wrote:

"I thought your August 16th column on 'Entitlement as a Man's Right' was — well … baloney! Sorry. I heard you implying 'all men are self-confident, suffer no guilt, take up psychological space comfortably, etc.' Do your observations of people *really* confirm that analysis from the articles you quoted?

"My experience is quite different. I know how often I vacillate about big and little decisions — before and after I make them. I know how scared I am sometimes when I walk into a room or situation and don't know the turf. I know that sometimes I am confident and sometimes I am hesitant. I doubt very much if I am the only man that runs scared, sometimes lacks assertiveness, etc.

"Think I'm wrong? Next time you walk down any business or campus street — except 17th Street, which may still be prime male dominance territory — really look at the people you pass. Some will walk confidently, taking up all the psychological space you will give them. Others are more tentative. It depends on (their) personal style in the situation, not (their) sex ….

Thank you, gentlemen, for not allowing my analyses to become too pat. *My characterizations too stereotypical.* Thank you, in short, for keeping me honest.

Just Like a Man
Are We Headed for an Era of Sexist Xenophobia?

Denver Post
August 4, 1991

I observed two young fathers with their preschool children recently.

The first father, at a Vail resort swimming pool, repeatedly admonished his three kids, "No crying, now — anyone who cries won't get to go on the chair lift." His voice was nasal and whiny, almost feminine. His manner grated, if not on his kids' nerves, certainly on mine.

The second father, halfway up Grays Peak, pushed, encouraged, prodded, and alternately hoisted his three youngsters (none older than 5) up the mountain. His voice was gentle, strong; his patience endless.

But he carried only a small pack with lightweight jackets and minimal food! Grossly unprepared, I thought, my silent criticism zeroing in on his neglect like a hawk diving on its prey. It could rain, hail or snow here. Not thinking ahead. Just like a man.

Only later did my judgmental attitude about these fathers strike my suddenly raised consciousness like a bolt of summer lightning.

After all, the pool dad was at least "doing it" — in the water and totally engaged with his kids. So what if he sounded no better, no worse, than the millions of worn-out moms who chide and

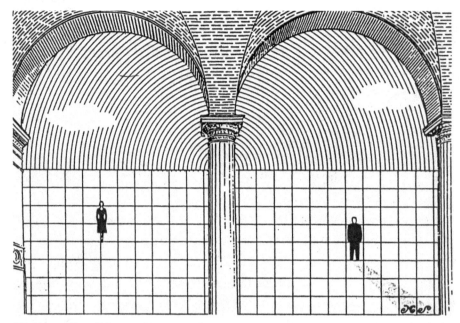

The Denver Post / Maureen Scance

But suppose his "fair lady" *had* become more like a man? Would he still have fallen in love with her? Would he still, in the title words of another of the show's songs, have become so "Accustomed to Her Face" he was forever smitten?

In order to succeed in the paid work world, some women have become like men: the older ones, the "queen bees," the ones who climbed up the hierarchy before it started to mellow and flatten, the ones who say, "I made it without help, without child care, why can't you?"

gently threaten their kids through yet another hot summer day.

And the mountain dad? Although Grays Peak is not Disneyland, on a weekend it's more like a group pilgrimage than an isolated wilderness experience. If this young family had become threatened by the elements, at least 100 other "pilgrims" would have handed over their own down vests and trail mix.

Yet, I had been damning both these fathers; one for fathering "like a mother" and the other for fathering "just like a man."

Women, of course, have dealt with this "damned if you do, damned if you don't" attitude all their lives.

"Why can't a woman be more like a man?" crooned and complained the legendary Henry Higgins in the 1956 smash musical hit "My Fair Lady."

Yet fewer than 45 percent of the women at the top of corporate America have children, while 95 percent of the men do. It's a cruel paradox that in becoming like men, they became not like men at all. These top women, with no "wives" at home, didn't just have to give up kid care, they had to give up kids!

It is now 1990s America. Yet, women can still be damned if they "do it" like men and damned if they don't. If they try to emulate the traditional success-producing characteristics of men, they immediately run into the double standard.

Men are assertive; women are pushy.

Men are commanding; women are bossy.

Men are verbally forceful; women are shrill.

And if they try to remain as "female" as possible, or even make their decisions with no regard to expected sex roles, they run into a double bind.

A recent report on the choices women doctors make lamented the fact that women almost *have* to choose a stint at emergency room work. The emergency room is a dangerous place: who knows what drugged-up crazy will stagger in the door? Therefore, if a women avoids it, "weakness" is assumed, whereas if a man avoids it for a more prestigious placement, "normal ambition" is assumed.

Take the case of Stanford University medical school. Recently, a 50-year-old neurosurgery professor, Dr. Frances Conley, quit in protest, citing "a quarter of a century of sexism and sexual harassment." According to a July New York Times article, women physicians at the school who dissent at faculty meetings are often labeled "premenstrual."

Is this labeling a way for men to be sure women will remain stereotypical females and then to damn them for it?

Or is it a way for men to deny their unique emotionality that can detonate capriciously on the world like some Third World nuclear weapon run amok?

Such "male emotionality" has been labeled "testosterone poisoning" by former Reagan speech writer Peggy Noonan. If we have to label, I'll take

"Will women finally achieving 'critical mass' in the workplace simply render us 'massively critical'?"

my chances on "premenstrual" over "testosterone" any day! At least *our* moods are cyclical, predictable and modifiable.

Yet women (as this one just was) can be every bit as smug and pejorative. I heard recently of a premed program at a Colorado university that is more than 50 percent female. The women there have little use for the men, castigating them for not working hard and not being as prepared as the women.

Is our 1990s world turning into a macrocosm of majoritarian sexist xenophobia?

Are we, in effect, saying: "If my sex is in the majority, any one of the opposite sex who does it differently from me is lesser. And any one of the opposite sex who does it the same as me is a fool."

Will women finally achieving "critical mass" in the workplace simply render us "massively critical"?

I hope not. Because men will need our understanding, not our judging, just as we need their acceptance, not their labeling.

If we can't stop damning each other for being different, and in the same breath damning each other for being the same, we'd better *all* stop trying to run the world and call in the robots.

Unisex ones, please!

My Space
Why Are Women "Territorial"?

Denver Post
JANUARY 15, 1984

ONE SPRING DURING THE LONG YEARS OF World War II, two young girlfriends and I decided to plant our own flowers.

Excitedly, we carved out our planting space on the edges of our neighborhood "Victory Garden."

In late March, as the wide ground cover of gray New York snow slowly inched away, we began to cultivate the small patches of dark earth we now saw as our very own.

But our carefully planted flowers never were to bloom. For one April day as we approached our project, our giggles were cut short. We stared at what had been our garden.

Footprints revealed that vandals had destroyed most of our creation by stomping. And any remaining seedlings had been flooded out with a garden hose.

I remember sharply my immense sense of vulnerability, violation and loss. "Our" *space* had been invaded. Our dreams destroyed.

But wait a minute.

As I read over these introductory paragraphs, I am aware that this is not the column I had intended to write. This was going to be a light-hearted column about personal space, and what it means to different members of a family.

The column would be a parody, replete with illustrations of why, in a house with nine bathrooms, three members of our family fight over one; why my son and I, who have the choice of exactly 18 couches in approximately 25 rooms, square off and try to beat each other to the chaise in the center of the family room.

I wanted to make light of the issue of personal space, to mock the "territorial imperative." Yet, I'm finding it hard to do. As a child, through the vandalization of my garden space, I felt not only the loss of potential summer flowers, but terror at my absolute powerlessness.

As an adult with my share of power, I now think I can make light of this space/power theme. But, as I try to write about it, "space" again becomes an emotionally loaded word. Why?

Maybe it was the garden destruction at age 7. Maybe it was growing up female to almost 47. Maybe it was not having a room of my own from 1955, when I left the home of my parents, to 1975, when I moved to the Governor's Mansion.

Whatever it was, I am realizing, right now, for the first time, and with some sense of shock, that I am, by far, the most "territorial" member of our family.

Something in my throat growls like a thwarted bear when I find another family member stalking my room, rummaging at my desk, searching for something in my shelves. Even if they have a totally legitimate reason for being there. Even if I might have sent them there!

It's not that I'm super neat. I'm not. It's just that my own pile of clothes has its own casual order — my order, not their order. My books sit at my own crazy angles, gathering dust in my own special patterns. Even my bathtub "ring" is my ring, at *my* water level, not theirs. And that's the way I like it.

My husband seems to lack this territorial defensiveness. Maybe he wasn't traumatized at age 7. Maybe growing up male gave him that sense of "entitlement" to both space and power which renders guardedness unnecessary. He does have one "territorial" sign on his bathroom door. It reads: "A dirty old man is a man with one bathroom and two teen-age kids." But, the kids take this as a joke, and so does he.

When we lived in an average-size house on South Logan Street, Dick had a large and roomy study. My "study" was a desk in the small sitting area of our bedroom. I did not make long phone calls from his study when he was working, yet he often did so from mine when I was trying to concentrate.

I resented his phoning from my space, but I couldn't tell

> *"Perhaps the human female holds her own personal space sacred, not only to nurture her young, but because it is the singular birthplace of her ideas, her dreams and her power."*

him, partly because I knew he *wouldn't* resent it if I did the same. He *would* be able to concentrate while I was talking on the phone, and this made me feel both guilty and angry! Anthropologists and zoologists say that female animals define and protect their territory because of the nesting instinct. The nest is where they give birth to the young. Perhaps I am more closely related to that thwarted bear than I like to admit.

And perhaps the human female holds her own personal space sacred, not only to nurture her young, but because it is the singular birthplace of her ideas, her dreams and her power.

According to Robert Ardrey, author of "The Territorial Imperative," "The female has a territory of her own which she defends against all comers, including males." Ardrey has other quotable comments on the subject, which I'd like to use. But, even in a column, one suddenly can be out of space.

Feminism and Family Policy:
Who Stays Home with the Kids?

Newborns
Maternity Policies Should Be Flexible

Denver Post
September 29, 1985

In January of 1968 our first baby, Scott, was 4½ weeks old and had been breast-fed since he was born. Time was closing in and I knew it.

In order to return to my part-time social work position, six weeks post-partum, as I had promised, I would have to train him to take the substitute bottle the baby sitter would give him while I was gone. And I would have to do it NOW!

The first attempt was a disaster. His soft baby lips pursed into a straight line. No way was he going to take that bottle! After 15 minutes I gave up, returned him to the breast, and burst into tears.

The next afternoon I got smarter. Feeling like the personification of the Wicked Witch of the West, I let him scream with hunger for a half hour.

It worked. He then took the bottle with relish, ingesting it with what seemed like less than a dozen large gulps. But, again, I burst into tears — first with relief, then with fear. Would my baby now grow to like the bottle better than me?

All these feelings came flooding back to me recently when I read an article titled "The Maternity Backlash: Women vs. Women" in the March edition of Working Woman Magazine.

The article told the story of a young vice president of an insurance company who gave birth to her first child after negotiating a three-month maternity leave. Then, at the last minute, this VP decided not to go back to work at all, as her baby had become "Top Priority."

I identified with this new mother.

Yet, I also identified with her female boss who was stunned. "I had especially wanted to reassure this woman that her job was safe (that her temporary replacement was only temporary), yet she turned around and left me high and dry," said the boss.

And I can also identify with the next woman in that agency who will get pregnant.

Will it now simply be assumed that she, too, will not come back to work? Because of the example set by the VP, who was the "first woman" agent in the company to get pregnant, will the "second woman" be fired? Or will she merely be sidetracked to less important accounts?

Leaving an infant, especially a first one, is excruciatingly difficult even when good substitute care is available. A new mother must prepare herself to feel the compelling emotional and physical "pull" of her infant most, if not all, moments she is away. She also has to be prepared to face the potential animosity of co-workers, who may resent her "new mother" status once she returns to work.

A local professional woman who took a six-month maternity leave recently related to me the enervating hostility that greeted her when she returned to work. The woman analyzed the hostility this way:

"First, there are the people who pick up the workload when you are gone, usually for no extra pay. Then there are those women who don't have babies and wish they did. Then there are those women who have kids but could not arrange or afford to take six months off when their children were born. Then there are the women who, if you are very successful at your work and also have a baby, think you are some kind of superwoman, though you sure don't feel like one!"

So what's the answer? The answer, perhaps, is a changed company perception of its own long-term self-interest. For example:

- The company acceptance of temporary leave and/or temporary part-time work in exchange for the idea that most professional women who get pregnant will eventually come back full time with renewed vigor and determination.

- The provision of enough other kinds of benefits on a "cafeteria style" plan, so that those who do not take parental leave can choose to take some other work "perk."

- Understanding that the people skills learned in becoming a parent often will make one a better employee on the job.

- And bottom line, the acknowledgement that a generous maternity/paternity leave policy and flexible work hours are ways to attract talented young workers and to bind them to the company.

But we are still in the short term, and for the short term I have two messages of advice:

To managers: Be as flexible and generous as you can. Be creative in convincing the top echelon of the importance of looking at parental leave in fresh ways.

To pregnant professionals: If you choose to quit, quit — but give plenty of notice. If you plan to return, negotiate the best leave conditions you can, but start that "substitute bottle" early. And don't go back on your word. Barring an extreme medical emergency, when it's time to show up, SHOW UP!

Other new mothers are counting on you.

> *"Leaving an infant, especially a first one, is excruciatingly difficult even when good substitute care is available."*

Family Leave
Let's Try Something Radical

Denver Post
July 1, 1990

THE PRONOUNCEMENTS FROM ON HIGH BOGGLE the mind.

First, the American Academy of Pediatrics proclaimed that full-time working mothers "imperil" their kids — especially their infants.

Second, last week the Bush administration announced the president's intention to veto the Family Leave bill, which would mandate that businesses allow the parent of a new infant to stay home with her or his baby for up to 12 weeks.

A corporation's leave policy should be "voluntary," the president says. Companies should only grant it if they choose to grant it, even though the mandated leave in this legislation would be unpaid and would affect only those companies with more than 50 employees.

The Catch-22 here is so blatant that even an "imperiled child" might grasp it.

As one employed mom exclaimed, "The pediatricians value mothers at home. The

president says he values mothers at home. George Bush's wife *stayed* home for 30 years. But he won't even guarantee that I can *go* home for 12 weeks!"

Fifty-one percent of American mothers with children under 1 are now in the paid workforce. Most of them march off to work each day not out of choice but out of financial necessity.

And that statistic may not change. What needs to change is our policy toward those young parents.

Furthermore, if we want a *real* discussion of the welfare of our nation's infants, both the president and the pediatricians should take into account two other things:

First, the vast difference in financial circumstances of both employed and unemployed moms.

Second, the huge individual discrepancies in the parenting skills of mothers in both groups.

One working mother may be a highly paid married professional with the services of a full-time nanny or a nurturing child-care home.

The Denver Post / Maureen Scance

Another mom may be a single fast-food chain employee, just one dollar away from welfare, with caretakers moving in and out of her infant's life as fast as her customers move up and away from her window.

One stay-at-home mom may be an earth mother who will take time to hold, soothe and stimulate her baby.

Another may be one of the mothers columnist George Will calls "the mothers who don't know how." These mothers — often teenage, usually single, most likely on welfare — don't know how to cuddle an infant while it sucks or to jabber playfully at a 6-month-old.

In short, parents' needs, skills and circumstances vary enormously.

Kids' needs, however, do not.

For beneath the scare headline predicting "impaired kids," beyond the oversimplification of the issues, the pediatricians are reiterating a truth that we have known in our gut for a long time: **infants need to bond**.

To ensure an emotionally healthy childhood and adulthood, every baby needs a close *ongoing* physical and emotional relationship with a loving, caring adult.

That loving, caring adult does not *have* to be the biological mother. It can be an adoptive mother, a father, a grandmother, a nanny. Any person who will cuddle, rock and care. And it can be more than one person.

But it *cannot* be a huge number of rotating caretakers who, at best, may treat the child with the offhand, casual affection usually reserved for pets and house plants.

OK. So the loving, caring adult *can* be anyone. But isn't the mother or father the *logical* one?

And is it so outrageous to think that corporations owe parents this time off for bonding with their kids?

> *"Parents' needs, skills and circumstances vary enormously. Kids' needs, however, do not."*

Other countries mandate parental leave. And their businesses are thriving. France and West Germany have productivity rate increases as high or higher than ours, and they have mandated not mere *unpaid* leave but partially or fully *paid* parental leave for years.

So let's say the president has changed his mind. Or that the Congress overrides his veto. Either action would guarantee that over 60 percent of employed American parents could fully bond with their own kids for the first precious weeks of their lives.

But even then, huge problems would remain for our American infants.

First, the people who need this leave the most, single parents, would not be able to afford to take it because it is unpaid.

Second, it does nothing to improve the chances of the truly imperiled infants in our society: those at home not with substitute care but with mothers "who don't know how."

Therefore I offer a radical three-part solution:

- We pass a family leave bill with *paid* leave, so that all employed parents can take off those first precious 12 weeks to bond with their infants.

- We insist, as the current bill does, that companies provide unpaid leave for employees who need to minister to a sick child or an aging parent.
- We allow employees who do not have the demands of either children or parents to take up to four weeks of unpaid leave time to do volunteer work. That we give incentives for companies to initiate pro-grams in which employees with nurturing skills can go into homes to "mother" those mothers who need role models and to teach them parenting skills.

If George Bush is really interested in volun-teerism, he should provide the opportunity for full-time employed workers to volunteer.

If he sincerely wants to promote a "kinder, gentler nation," he might begin with its kindest, gentlest citizens: Our infants and our kids.

Sick Kids
A Problem for Parents and Employers

Denver Post
May 11, 1986

M Y MATERNAL GRANDMOTHER WAS OBSESSIVE about keeping her children germ free. According to my mother, her mother drove her crazy with her admonitions: "Wear your rubbers!" "Get your coat!" "Wash your hands!" "Don't sit in that draft!"

Yet there was no one like my grandmother when, despite her fanatic doses of prevention, the germs prevailed. As a Latin teacher for the 17 years before she was married at age 39, her professional expe-rience had been in the classics. But when a child of hers became ill, one would have thought her profession had been nursing, child psychology and recreational therapy — all wrapped in one.

And my mother was much the same when I was sick as a child. And I hope I've been the same with my two children. But many parents today, now that 70 percent of mothers are in the paid work force, don't have the chance to be that in-home nurse and recreational leader.

In fact, even to get one day off to care for a sick child, a parent might have to lie. Little sympathy may come from bosses. One executive I heard speak recently wanted to be sympathetic, "But when you have a team of five assigned to a priority project and three call in with a sick kid, it's a problem," he said.

It's particularly a problem if you happen to be a male parent. Donna Chitwood, director of the Child Development Center at Metropolitan State College, told me of a male friend who pleaded with his boss for some time off, explaining that his child was sick and his wife had already stayed home from her job for two days.

"That's what you have a wife for!" his boss interrupted, closing the subject.

In answer to this sick-child problem, sick-care programs are sprouting up around the United States.

With names like Chicken Soup, Wheezles and Sneezels and Grandma's Place, many are "sick bay" areas of already established child-care centers. Some are situated in unused wings of hospitals.

Others, like that sponsored by Denver's YWCA and Pound of Care in Boulder, are not centers at all, but are programs that help parents bring paid caretakers into the home on a pay-per-hour basis.

Centers for sick children are more expensive than regular child care. So businesses that want their employees on the job may need to pick up some of the costs.

But are sick-care programs, or even sick-care baby sitters in the home, the wrong answer to the right problem?

At a recent child-care conference in Denver, Andrea King, a child-care licensing specialist from Jefferson County Department of Social Services,

"Is sickness a time in which a child, any age child, needs to regress, and whose regression is best catered to by a loving parent? Is a child's illness an event for which 'time out' should be called, rather than the relentless, never ending 'time in'?"

stated that such services, especially when subsidized by employers, might put pressure on parents to *never* stay home with their sick children, even when that child is seriously ill.

"We are still not putting the welfare of children first. We are thinking of parents as employees first and parents second," King said. "What kind of parents will these kids grow up to be if they are never even allowed to stay home when they are sick?"

But other social workers and child-care professionals emphasized the fact that sick-care centers are designed only for children on the recuperative end of an illness, and that we need to educate employers to that effect.

Registered nurse Loni Tracey, who with her partner, Judy Lovin, is opening Cradle Care, a center for both well and sick infants in Aurora later this spring, argued that leaving a sick child with a pediatric nurse can alleviate parental guilt, and that a recuperating child could even benefit from a fresh environment.

But *can* the child benefit? Is sickness a time in which a child, any age child, needs to regress, and whose regression is best catered to by a loving parent? Is a child's illness an event for which "time out" should be called, rather than the relentless, never ending "time in"?

I certainly don't want to throw cold water on *any* attempt to help sick children and their families. I think well-staffed sick-care centers are an idea whose time has come. So are health-care professionals who will come to the home. As Jan Pagliasotti, coordinator at the Boulder Child Care Support Center, said, "Parents have told us they would have lost their jobs if it weren't for the services provided by Pound of Care."

But would it not be preferable in the long term for employers to give parents generous sick leave which would include the illnesses of both employee and child?

"Yes!" say many child advocates.

Yet, according to Pagliasotti, it's the very companies who have generous sick-care leave policies that are also likely to subsidize in-home sick-care professionals or sick-care centers.

"It's the other companies we have to educate, companies who, thus far, are willing to do neither."

In the meantime, both mom and dad need to be on the job.

And grandmother is far away.

Gender Roles:

In Marriage, in Partnerships, in Life

MARRIAGE:
Push-Pulls and Parity

One Morning, I Awoke, and No Longer Felt Tired

Denver Post
JANUARY 11, 1982

ONE MORNING WHEN MY FIRST CHILD WAS 5, I woke up and found that I wasn't tired anymore. Like a blind person suddenly given sight, a dimension was added to my life. Flowers smelled sweeter, the sunshine was friendlier, even the house seemed cleaner — though it wasn't.

Had I really been tired for five years? So tired I didn't know it; so tired I thought backaches, headaches, and depression and fuzzy thinking were normal? So tired I thought my irritability was paranoia and sought therapy instead of rest?

No actual milestones marked the change that 35th year of mine and the 5th year of my son. He was yet to enter kindergarten. The "pre-school" years were hardly over. I still don't know what resurrected me, but I took steps to see that I didn't slip back into exhaustion.

I often think of this period in my life when I read articles that speak to the "biological timeclock." The "timeclock" usually refers to the fact that the reproductive years for women (20-35) are the same

years that, if they want to succeed career-wise, they should be giving their all to their jobs.

But the biological timeclock operates on men, also. Males can physically father children longer than women can conceive and give birth. But biologically the biggest drive for success, identity, and "making one's mark" occurs for men at the same time it does for women — concurrent with when they are raising young families. For both sexes, reproductive and nurturing drives can be in conflict with self-actualization drives.

"The decade between 25 and 35 is when men either succeed or fail," writes economist Lester C. Thurow. "It is a decade when lawyers become partners in the good firms, when business managers make it to the 'fast track,' when academics get tenure at good universities, and when blue collar workers find the job opportunities that will lead to training opportunities and the women they are married to — whether they leave the paid job market or not — feel urgent pressures to succeed." Those who choose to continue career goals try to become "super-women." Those who make the decision to stay home full time find their self-actualization drive turns into a singular herculean devotion to family and children. Often, out of financial necessity or pride, such homemakers will endeavor to "do it all" by themselves, hire no help, and use no support system.

For both young parents the pressure is on to "make it" — everywhere; give your all to work, your all to family, keep up your social contacts, your community obligations, show your own parents how successful you are — all to the point of exhaustion.

A workplace more sensitively in tune with family needs would help. As Betty Friedan states in a New York Times article, "These conflicts (besetting young parents) seem insolvable because of the way the family and the work place have been structured in America."

Like Friedan, I'm for on-site child care, flexitime, and three-quarter time work schedules for any parent who can get one and survive on one. I'm for parental role sharing, maternity and paternity leaves, for communal living arrangements, and neighborhood drop-in child care centers for full-time mothers who need a break.

But even if all these ideal supports were in place, would people in the 20-35 age bracket actually slow down? Would an ambitious person live within a 3/4th's time job, or would he/she just simply round it out to full time to pass the competition and to please the boss?

Is there a less stressful way through that period? A period where marriages are at risk and children sometimes are hurt by parental over-extension and even by the over-dedication and intensiveness brought to their "upbringing."

Any answers out there? Those of you who are a half-generation behind me? Are you still struggling with how to have it all? Do you have answers to continuous exhaustion? Do you even know when you are tired?

Saving the Marriage
Does Feminism Help?

Denver Post
DECEMBER 7, 1986

I WOKE UP THIS MORNING THINKING ABOUT A character in a book. The character is the grandmother in "The Good Mother," the recent best-selling novel by Sue Miller. This grandmother, a staunch New Englander, had "kept her own counsel," had never told her innermost thoughts to anyone, and had never once "stood up" to her husband of nearly 50 years.

But late in this woman's life, she was forced out of her passivity and she rebelled when a divorced granddaughter came to her husband to ask for money to fight for the custody retention of her 4-year-old daughter.

The granddaughter had approached her grandfather in privacy, when suddenly her grandmother appeared at the doorway.

"Hadn't you better help her?" she demanded of her husband.

Then turning to her granddaughter, she added, "You could ask *me*. I have money, too. My own money. You could ask *me* for money." And the case was settled.

This episode was a mere sub-drama in a much longer, dramatic plot of divorce, custody, love, passion, personal identity and sexual morality. But the vignette sticks with me.

People, especially women who "stoically keep their own counsel," who never ask anything of their mates and who don't share feelings easily, occasionally have confided in me.

One "older" women, actually only about 10 years older than I, raised in New England, expressed astonishment at the idea of my woman's

The Denver Post / Maureen Scance

support group, which began as a "tell-all" consciousness-raising group back in 1971.

"What do you talk about?" she asked a few years back.

I told her we talked about things that were bothering us, that we couldn't quite tell our husbands about (yet). Or that we talked about things that we thought were unique to ourselves, finding out with relief that we weren't "alone" after all.

She was aghast and at the same time envious.

"We never talked about emotional trauma to anyone," she said. And then proceeded to reveal, guardedly, some of the traumas of her own early childbearing years. "But we made it through," she said, suddenly cutting herself short.

"But wouldn't you have liked to have talked it all out?"

"Somehow you just did what you did and got through," she replied.

New England, like England, I thought: "Stiff upper lip. Carry on, carry on."

Yet, maybe there is something to this "Stiff upper lip." This New England stoicism. Maybe we have discarded too much of the emotional guardedness brought ashore from the Mayflower. After all, marriages lasted in those days of my grandparents and of my parents, and even those of my "older" friends. Not just in New England, but everywhere.

Suddenly I think of the New York Times article I read last summer about the Woman's Movement. The article featured a 1986 reunion of a consciousness-raising group that began in the '60s and lasted for two years.

At the reunion, only one woman said the assertiveness and openness generated by the movement had "saved" her marriage. For this woman, it had provided her the strength to approach her husband on the things that she cared about. And he had responded.

The rest of the women in the group had found that the women's movement had complicated personal male/female relationships. Thus they had become "feminist" outside the home, but "traditionalist" inside the home, employing, just as their mothers and grandmothers before them, a "keep your own counsel and save the relationship" stance.

Everyone makes adjustments in a relationship, but from what I've observed, men are more likely to make adjustments in what they *do*. Women are more likely to make adjustments in who they *are*. "Every marriage is two marriages," said one. "His marriage, her marriage, and his is the dominant one."

All of which makes me realize why I thought about that fictional grandmother this morning. It's not what I read about her last month, it's what I read about myself last night.

Sorting out some stuff for the impending "Big Move" out of the Governor's Mansion, I came across a poem I wrote when I had been married about six months. "Where can it be, this thing called me?" the poem was titled.

It wasn't a very good poem. But it forcefully represented my fear that I was losing myself in this thing called marriage, and I might never be found again. I don't remember feeling that way at that early time.

But I do remember feeling that way later.

And like the woman in New York, it was the woman's movement that gave me the strength to stand up and be counted. To approach a husband, who was far more flexible in his thinking than I was in my own strict code of what women "should" or "should not" do in a marriage.

Did the woman's movement then "save" my marriage? I don't know, but maybe. Repressed resentment can do two things. It can stay isolated while the rest of the relationship goes on. Or it can spread like poison, contaminating the very thing you were trying to save, by "keeping your own counsel" in the first place.

All of this said, there are no guarantees.

I know a woman who submerged herself to all of her husband's wishes. He was not unkind, just not conscious of who she was. She gave up her professional career plans and the desire for a child to "save" her marriage. Eventually, he left her anyway.

And I know another woman who latched onto the assertiveness ideals of the woman's movement, feeling their implementation would enhance her marriage. If she could just become "real" with her husband, things would work out, she believed. She became "real," the structure of the marriage shifted, and he also left.

So, is keeping one's counsel and a "stiff upper lip" the best way to "save" a marriage. Or is being "real" the best way?

The answer has to be, it depends.

And are some marriages even worth saving?

And should women always be the "saviors"?

Those questions are a whole other column.

> *"Everyone makes adjustments in a relationship, but ... men are more likely to make adjustments in what they* do. *Women are more likely to make adjustments in who they* are.*"*

Undercurrent Rates an Airing

Denver Post
JANUARY 22, 1985

ONE NIGHT DURING THE CHRISTMAS HOLIDAYS, an "old" married couple and a not-so-old married couple began talking about movies they had seen. "Falling in Love" was the second movie mentioned, and the couples never got past it.

One of the men thought that the movie (a story of two people, both married to others, who meet by coincidence and fall in love) was engaging but superficial: "It never could have come off without the acting strength of (Robert) De Niro and (Meryl) Streep."

One of the women found the excluded spouses incredibly naive: "How could they not know something was going on?" she asks.

One if the men exclaimed, "The logistics were impossible; the coincidences — beyond belief."

One of the women countered that the coincidences were believable, because they weren't real coincidences. "From the first time the two met on the train, they kept arranging, consciously or unconsciously, to meet again and again," she argued.

Serious subject

And so on. But the real conversation began when one of the women said, "No one ever talks about the gradations of sexual attraction a married person can have for someone besides his or her spouse. People can talk flippantly about affairs,

divorces and remarriages. Yet they can't talk about that undercurrent of sexuality which is just *there*, right under the surface, though often not acted upon."

But this foursome did talk about it. Slowly, haltingly at first. And after a subsequent hour and a half of conversation, both members of both couples agreed that even such good friends as they could not be discussing this subject, comfortably, if it weren't for the "safety" of all spouses present.

But back to the movie. As one of the women in that foursome, I found the dialogue in the script so realistic it was funny. I had expected "Falling in Love" to be a movie to make me cry. Instead, it made me laugh. But some of my laughter may have been nervous laughter.

And the nervousness may have come from the very vulnerability of all the characters, from the fact that these two strangers were falling in love against their will, not because of bad marriages but in spite of basically good ones.

A step beyond

The strangers were simply struck by a special magic that goes beyond mutual, unspoken and controllable glow of mere physical attraction. The "jilted" wife captures the essence of the story perfectly when her husband tries to explain, "We didn't — it's not an affair — it's nothing like that."

"No," she answers, "It's nothing like that — it's worse!"

The movie reminded me of two other films:

In the first one, "Shane," the title character leaves the home of the family — mother, father, and son — he was visiting, because that "magic" was happening between himself and his host's wife.

In the other one, "Dr. Zhivago," Zhivago gives into the overpowering magic of a new love, although his relationship with his attractive, pregnant wife had been satisfying until he met Lara.

There is a story, perhaps apocryphal, about a famous artist. One night he and his wife met a new friend and the friend's wife for dinner in a restaurant. When the artist's eyes and his friend's wife's eyes locked over the candlelight, click! That was it! The two simply got up and left the table together. Never to return. Never even to explain.

Different responses

I heard that story, years ago, while relaxing with a group of skiers in a resort lodge around a fireplace. But I remember the reactions it generated as if it were yesterday:

The men in the group immediately identified with the "conquering" artist. "Cool," they said. Or "terrific story," as they stretched their legs, slapped their knees, rose and swaggered toward the bar for another drink.

The women, most of them wives of the men at the bar, were quieted and somewhat intimidated by the story. Each of them could have identified with the "conquering" woman, anointed also with the magic. But, somehow, none of them did. And one woman, twirling her ice cubes in her glass and staring into the fire, spoke for the others when she mused:

"I wonder what happened to the two who were left behind?"

It Adds Up
Wife's Hours Staggering

Denver Post
February 17, 1985

Last month I had lunch with a friend who told me of the various ways she had prepared for a settlement of her "worth" before her divorce.

One way was by making a list of how she had spent her time during her marriage, a marriage in which she had "stayed at home" and raised children.

I asked her to send me the list. She did. Here goes:

"During the course of my 22-year marriage I have:

Made over 1,500 trips to the grocery store

Prepared over 25,000 meals

Run around 10,000 errands

Taken my four children to approximately 400 doctor, dentist and orthodontist appointments (100 per child)

Driven carpools to at least 1,000 events, lessons, or activities

Attended 24 field days at our elementary school

Been to at least 50 back-to-school nights."

Out of curiosity I calculated my friend's duties on an hour per week basis. Figuring conservatively, I assigned a half-hour each to errands; one hour each to grocery store trips, meal preparation, and carpool trips; two hours each to doctor's appointments, field days, back-to-school nights.

I came out with an average of 29 hours a week. This figure, of course, doesn't measure the *immeasurable* hours: doing the laundry, diapering the babies, dressing the toddlers, monitoring the television, reading to young children, doing homework with older children, nursing sick children, playing with well children.

It also doesn't include listening, lecturing, laughing, disciplining, drying tears, scouring toilets, weeding gardens, making lists, making plans, making phone calls, answering the phone, answering the mail, paying the bills, waiting for the repair person, waiting for the babysitter, waiting for the husband, etc., etc., and so forth — all of which has got to add up to double that 29 hours — more like a 58-hour week.

Add to this two more hours per week for anything I didn't think of. And you have 60 hours — a time-and-a-half work week!

More than 40 percent of married American women still are fulltime homemakers, and most of those who take jobs outside retain the major responsibility for running the home. It has always been curious to me that a wife knows more about what her husband's job is at his office — when she hardly ever goes there — than he knows about her job at home — when he actually lives there.

But at least one man knows. Sey Chassler, former editor of Redbook magazine, is a man. In an article he wrote for the Jan. 13, 1985,

> *"It has always been curious to me that a wife knows more about what her husband's job is at his office—when she hardly ever goes there—than he knows about her job at home— when he actually lives there."*

edition of Parade magazine, he writes of his own painful enlightenment about "women's work."

"About 20 years ago, my wife and I were having one of those arguments that grows into fury — the kind that leave a dreadful pain that lasts for years. Suddenly, unable to stand my complaints any longer, my wife threw something at me and said: 'From now on you do the shopping, plan the meals, take care of the house, do everything. I'm through!'

"I was standing in the kitchen looking at the shelves, the sink, the refrigerator, the cleaning utensils. At my wife.

"I was terrified. Tears trickled down my face. No matter what, I knew I could not handle the burden she had flung at me. I could not do my job and be responsible for the entire household as well. I had important things to do …

"How could *any* one do all that and stay sane? Natalie simply watched me for a while. Finally she said, 'OK. Don't worry. I'll keep on doing it.'

"If you're watching Monday night football, who's doing the laundry? The wife, of course. But if you are watching it together, where will the clean laundry come from? In most homes, we don't even ask the question. We simply assume — both women and men assume — that the laundry will get done, that the woman of the house will see to it.

"… I wonder how many of us men could handle the (woman's) job. And I wonder why we have learned to belittle women and why we persist in doing it."

Suddenly I have a new insight as to why, according to Ann Landers' much publicized survey, a surprising 68 percent of married women questioned declared that they would prefer a "hug" to the "sex act."

It's not that most women are undersexed.

It's that many are underappreciated.

For there's one word a hug demonstrates better than sex, and even better than the speaking of the word itself.

And that word is "thanks."

Woman's Place Must Be Precise to Avoid Stress

Denver Post
MARCH 13, 1984

SINCE 1981, I'VE BEEN KEEPING A FILE CALLED "Men and Women: Changing Roles." For three years, this file has been the receptacle of articles, studies and columns, many of which were tossed into the folder barely read.

When, last week, I accepted a speaking assignment titled "The Changing Roles of Men and Women," I looked forward to its preparation. Finally, I would get to that file and make some sense of its contents!

I got to the file. I gave the speech. But I'm still not making much sense of the file. Not only are changing male/female rules somewhat conflictual for the men and women involved, but the articles themselves are conflictual about the effects of such changes.

Take, for example, the recent march of wives into the paid work force, their climb up the economic ladder and the effect of this "march and climb" on a married couple's mental and physical health.

That six-letter word

Certain studies in my file portray the employed mother as tense, conflict-ridden and harassed. The compounded guilt over leaving a child, worry about day care and resentment over her disproportionate share of housework adds up to one six-letter word: STRESS.

Yet, another study in Science Digest magazine says the woman who combines career and homemaking, in fact, has a lower degree of stress-related diseases than the full-time homemaker. The reason: Her paycheck gives her a sense of financial security and a heightened self-esteem.

Some studies in my file reveal that husbands benefit psychologically when their wives share the burden of "breadwinning." Years ago, Gloria Steinem urged males to support the woman's movement: "They have nothing to lose but their coronaries," she said.

But Steinem was right only up to a point. According to a recent report, researchers Carlton Hornung and B. Claire McCullough warn that in the 17 percent of dual-income families where wives' salaries surpass those of their husbands, those male coronaries can come back — fast!

Hornung and McCullough's research, in fact, revealed that when underachieving men are married to overachieving women who earn more than they do, these men run a four- to five-fold greater risk of dying from heart disease. Among 40- to 50-year-old husbands, the risk is 11 times greater!

Going home again

Some clippings reveal a minitrend toward, rather than away from, full-time homemaking. Some employed mothers (who can afford it) are marching out of the paid work force instead of in. This choice also has its psychological downsides. No matter how worthy their reasons, when mothers quit their jobs to stay home with young children, most suffer depression and a feeling of extreme isolation.

And even if a husband verbally supports his wife's choice to leave paid employment, his actions may not. His share of household chores, disproportionate even when his wife is employed, can plummet to zero proportion when his wife decides to stay home.

Some husbands do not support, even verbally, a wife's choice to temporarily retire. A teacher I know who did just that in order to care for her infant daughter found the pressure from her husband intense. He wanted her employed so they could afford a new car!

But, back to the file on my desk. Suddenly, it does seem to make some sense.

For one thing, its contents clearly have less to do with "roles" and more with "place." If a couple is to avoid female depressions and male heart attacks, a woman's "place" is no longer in the home, but at work, perched midway up the economic ladder. Exactly *midway*, mind you! If she reaches a higher rung on the ladder than her husband, falls off or voluntarily climbs down, she becomes a prime candidate for STRESS. And so, apparently, does her spouse.

Is Single Parenthood Just Too Much?

Denver Post
APRIL 21, 1980

DOZENS OF ARTICLES ON ROLE SHARING, contract marriages, male homemakers, grateful wives, angry wives and the latest statistics on who-does-what within the household again spill over my desk. For the 67 percent of American adults who are married, these are crucial domestic issues of the 1980s.

For most women, the "should I work outside the home" question has long been resolved. For men, the "should I even pick up a diaper or dishrag" question has evolved into "I will — but under what circumstances and how often are still negotiable!"

But these questions don't grab me with their usual urgency today. Perhaps that is because of my friend, Sally.

Sally has been divorced for two years. She has a daughter 8 and a son 4, a highly challenging job with a corporation recently located in her city, a former husband who usually sends his support money, but never sees the kids.

Sally is a good mother. Her children go to two excellent schools and to three experienced after-school babysitters. Every minute away from her workday, Sally spends "quality" time with her kids. I know because just last month my daughter received a birthday invitation, clearly handmade by mother and child, to Sally's 8-year-old's birthday party.

Sally seldom dates. Tall, vivacious and attractive, she always is invited to her company's social events, but seldom does she attend them.

She was full of energy when first divorced. She was glad to be free. She could do it all, she thought. She and her nextdoor neighbor, Ann, also divorced with a child, could conquer the world with each other's help. And so they did for a while. But a year ago Ann remarried and moved away.

Yesterday I heard secondhand about Sally. She was ill with the flu, so ill that she could not take the children to school, she said. She called a friend who was to take them for her and told her not to come. She couldn't even get out of bed to help the 4-year-old get ready.

Alarmed, the friend drove over immediately to find the neat, middleclass home in disarray and Sally incoherent.

Sally had pushed herself so hard and given herself so little, she was close to a nervous breakdown. The flu had precipitated her dangerously beyond the precarious balance of mental and physical health — or else the dangerously stretched balance of mental and physical elements had precipitated the flu. Whatever, the reluctant call for help, even in the negative phrase, "Don't come!" was Sally's salvation and her recognition that nobody does everything alone.

> *"What tremendous burdens exist out there for the 12.5 percent of American families headed by a single parent who alone must earn the bread and nurture the brood."*

Sally, an admitted over-achiever, will be okay. She'll key down and turn to her friends, her church or her former support group. Perhaps all three.

Yet, what tremendous burdens exist out there for the 12.5 percent of American families headed by a single parent who alone must earn the bread and nurture the brood!

Among these families are the very poor; those much poorer than Sally; those who don't even have the opportunity or the skills to become over-achievers. Also among them are the large percentage of working women with secretarial, factory or retail jobs. These women, according to a recent New York Times report, are becoming the most stressed workers in America and the most likely group to develop heart trouble. Among them, too, is the increasingly frequent single male parent who, like Ted in the film Kramer vs. Kramer, must struggle alone with French toast and fatherhood.

I think again of the challenges of role sharing within a marriage. Whatever kind of tentative agreement, firm contract, adequate or inadequate arrangement we make to find a new space or protect an old territory, we married ones seem lucky.

For no matter how the jobs are divided — two, after all, is twice as many as one.

Woman's Role as Communicator

Denver Post
c. 1982

THE GOVERNORS' WIVES WERE REALLY TURNED on to the subject! Their lively dialogue on family communication burst forth honest, frustrated, creative, grappling, and sometimes angry.

This interchange, unburdened by the presence of press and security guards, was real. This was earnest. This was special. The recent Communications Seminar in Washington D.C. was the best program to come out of the National Governors' Conference spouses' organization in eight years.

Yet, something seemed slightly off, out of whack, not quite right. Something was being taken for granted that shouldn't have been, but what was it?

That night in the Hyatt Regency Hotel my eyes fell on Ellen Goodman's column in the Washington Post. Reading her column, I suddenly realized what "it" was.

Goodman wrote of the communications role of a close female friend.

"The people in her home communicate with each other through her. She delivers peace messages from one child to another. Softens ultimatums from father to son; explains the daughter to father. Under her constant monitoring, the communication lines are kept open; one person stays plugged into the next."

Goodman continues:

"But sometimes I wonder whether she has kept all of these people together or whether she has kept them apart. Does she make it easier for them to understand each other or does she actually stand between them, holding all the wires in her hand?"

And finally:

"I know it is a skill to be able to understand and analyze one person's motives and psyche to another. It requires time, attention, emotional dexterity to run these switchboards. Yet, it can also overload the operator and cripple the people from talking across their own private lines ...."

Communication — a woman's job. Switchboard operating — a woman's trap. There we all were at that meeting taking responsibility. Again, we had tacitly accepted the premise that it was as much our role to grapple with new communication techniques as it was for our husbands to struggle with the "New Federalism."

Like Goodman, I agree that communication is a skill, and that sometimes we women need to explain a father's discipline to a son, so that he can receive it in a softer way. Sometimes we need to keep a family reunion peaceful by reminding each member in private what another may be expecting of them. Sometimes it is absolutely necessary to explain to a father an adolescent girl's behavior, drawing on our own experience as a girl years before.

But, also like Goodman, I think sometimes maybe we need to let go. We need to let our loved ones explain themselves, or not explain themselves, to other loved ones in their own ways. We need to let family members confront each other in awkward and sometimes angry modes that can shatter the peace.

Occasionally we need to drop the connecting wires that emanate from our head, our heart, and our gut, and see what new family communication patterns will emerge without us.

Knowing when to connect the "wires" and when to drop them is one of the new dilemmas of choice we women have won for ourselves. If we no longer take it as a given that we always will assume the prescribed role of traditional "peace maker," we have to decide each situation on its own merits. And that's much harder. Sometimes we make the wrong choice. Sometimes the results are complicated.

Once, a dozen years ago, at a large family gathering, I had an inner sense that I was the only one who could smooth the antagonistic ripples lurking under the waves of forced joviality. And I was tired, and I refused. I dropped the "wires" and went to bed.

The short term effect was near disastrous, and I felt guilty for weeks. But long range, springing from that incident, new communication patterns formed; healthier family relationships slowly and tentatively emerged, all of which are more or less entrenched today.

It's scary and risky for women, early trained to be peacemakers, to pull back from the switchboard, to drop the connecting wires that might energize a potential peace. You never know what the results of an action will be until you try.

Or perhaps you never know until you stop trying. And sometimes you don't know if you made the right decision till years later.

THE MALE FACTOR:
In Conversations, Choices, and Caretaking

Yes, Men Transform Women's Talk

Denver Post
SEPTEMBER 22, 1980

MY SISTER AND I WERE "CATCHING UP." At last we had a whole morning together. As we sat on the carpet, stockinged feet curled under us and coffee mugs in hand, our talk and laughter ran free and relaxed, interspersed, but not interrupted, by children and household noises.

I don't remember what we were talking about when my husband walked in, but our conversational direction shifted. Suddenly our tone and pace were altered. The flow of words moved at a different beat, a faster cadence, a more "masculine" rhythm.

Louise Bernikow, in her new book, "Among Women," describes the dialogue between herself and a friend:

"The talk was intimate and non-linear, moving from books to people, literature to life, mixing domestic with philosophic quickly, with few bridges. There was an interplay of mothering behavior — Do you need more of this or that? Is it going well for you today? — A certain solicitude, and a hint of reassurance. We were personal."

Personal.

It isn't that conversations with men present cannot be personal. My husband often is the one who will infuse life into a sterile conversation with: "But does that kind of work really satisfy you? How's your social life in Boston? Do you really live alone in Greenwich Village?"

Men have been charged with being too conversationally aggressive. Supposedly, they interrupt more, especially when women are speaking.

Yet, when a female conversation becomes mixed, women do their share of controlling and subverting. Suddenly we are more likely to censor ourselves: I won't say that, we think; it's trivial, it's not clever enough, it's too revealing, it's too assertive.

Some women work consciously to make certain a conversation will be stimulating to any brother, husband, friend, father, or lover present. Others who would deny such efforts still find their conversation somehow transformed by the presence of men.

Anne Morrow Lindbergh, in "Gift from the Sea," describes herself and her sister:

"We work easily and instinctively together, not bumping into each other as we go back and forth about our tasks. We talk as we sweep, as we dry, as we put away, discussing a person or a poem or a memory. And since our communication seems more important to us than our chores, the chores are done without thinking."

"What can you women talk about for eight hours?" asked the husband of a member of my all-female support group. We invited him to join us, but he grinned and declined.

It is not really what we talk about, but how we talk about it, I mused quietly as he left.

Putting Self First Not Easily Done

Denver Post
NOVEMBER 20, 1984

L AST DECEMBER I WROTE A COLUMN TITLED, "Self-Esteem and Solitude Are Partners," in which I suggested a number of ways a harassed mother could find some alone-time to put her feet up, relax and to recharge her sense of self.

The silence with which the column was greeted was deafening. Not a letter. Not a phone call. Not a comment.

Its publication date, Dec. 20, may have been a factor in the lack of response. It's very likely that, five days before Christmas, no mother had even the alone-time to read the paper. Mothers' feet don't go up until after Christmas dinner goes down. Everybody knows that!

But there could have been other reasons for the zero feedback. Taking "self time" is threatening and conflictive for many people, and some would rather continue to be harassed than to deal with it.

Suit yourself

This week, I talked with an educational consultant, who, as a part of a 40-hour self-esteem course for teachers, assigned a special five-hour time block during which the teachers (most of them parents, too) were to leave class and do something *strictly* for themselves.

Only six of these 28 teachers reacted with unmixed joy to the assignment. The others found that conflicting emotions complicated the sudden permission to put oneself first. Emotions including:

Frustration and ambivalence — One teacher found she simply "couldn't do it." She had made plans to swim and to "hot tub," but when some (non-emergent) family demands came up, she responded to them instead.

Worry over "wasted" time — One woman spent the afternoon shopping and walking in the park and hated it. "I felt so aimless!" she exclaimed.

Overanticipation, followed by letdown — One woman was thrilled that she would have some time to get some personal friends together, but her friends (not able to take the same five hours off) couldn't join her. Others suffered from the "kid at Christmas" syndrome. Even when their plans "worked out," the "real" didn't live up to the fantasy, and mild depression ensued.

Fear and confusion regarding choice — "I thought of 100 things to do, and when I finally picked one, I was still thinking of the other 99!" reported one woman.

Anger — Another was just plain mad. Her idea of doing something for herself was getting what she paid for from the educational consultant, by whom she felt cheated by the assigned five hours off.

"Mothers' feet don't go up until after Christmas dinner goes down."

Fear of others' reactions — One woman, who had lost some weight, went on a shopping spree for new clothes. She loved every moment and every purchase, but remarked that her husband "wasn't too pleased," and that the anticipation of his reaction took the "edge" off her joy.

Guilt — A 28-year-old mother of three admitted she hadn't any time off for herself in the seven years since her first child had been born. But since her mother-in-law was watching her kids, she felt guilty taking time off. It was OK for her husband's mother to watch then while she was in class, but not while she was eating popcorn at a movie. Or so she thought. But she went.

Upon returning home and still feeling guilty, she confessed, only to find her mother-in-law was overjoyed that she'd finally taken some time off for herself.

But who were the six teachers who were not ambivalent about the assignment? The six — you guessed it — were the men! The men teachers took it somewhat as their due. As their *entitlement*. Which reminds me of another column I did, and another subject I could get into. But I won't. I'm out of space.

Besides, it's time for the 3 p.m. movie.

And the popcorn.

Gender Traits Can, Should Be Mingled

Denver Post
SEPTEMBER 11, 1983

MY MOTHER CALLED THE OTHER NIGHT TO tell me of a wedding she had attended. The minister had not only encouraged the young couple to cherish each other but also had counseled the young man to cherish the feminine in himself, and the young woman to value her masculine traits.

The next day I read a letter from a reader who wrote in response to my column on "male entitlement":

"Women should be able to feel they 'can just inhabit space.' Men should be able to express what they feel. Shouldn't we, couldn't we help each other see (that) women could live outside the restrictions of being female, and that men could stretch beyond the real limits of being males?"

This kind of talk, taking males and females out of their stereotypical roles and attributing to them traits of the opposite sex makes some people foot-tapping nervous. It brings out "homophobia" and fear of "godless androgyny." There are many who, even in 1983, still argue that "women don't like men who show too much tenderness; men are not attracted to assertive women."

I don't believe this, and I'm not sure I ever have. I can't help but think that Alan Alda, with his sensitive, vulnerable portrayals, has become hero to far more women than John Wayne ever did. And who cheers the loudest for the Unsinkable Molly Brown and Annie-Get-Your-Gun females of the world? Men, of course.

I remember incidents through the years when my husband has melted; his brusque, no nonsense, even antagonistic demeanor gone in an instant at the sight of a rosy-cheeked child, a new puppy, or the reading of a sensitive poem. The times when he chokes back tears and can't get through a reading dealing with loss or pain are the times I love him the most.

> *"I remember incidents through the years when my husband has melted; his brusque, no nonsense, even antagonistic demeanor gone in an instant at the sight of a rosy-cheeked child, a new puppy, or the reading of a sensitive poem. The times when he chokes back tears and can't get through a reading dealing with loss or pain are the times I love him the most."*

And how does he respond to my assertive "male" characteristics? One example may suffice. When we were first married, we bought at his insistence a used vacuum cleaner for $15 at a second-hand shop. It was one of those sausage-looking things, with a long, thick hose. It worked perfectly when demonstrated at the store. The minute we got it home, it sputtered, choked, fizzled, and stopped dead. "No cash refund" the sign had said.

Silently furious, I grabbed the old sausage by its hose, swung it into the car, drove it back to the store and talked the proprietor out of the cash refund in spite of the sign. I was home with the money in 15 minutes, wondering if I would be scowled at, wondering if Dick would be annoyed at my "taking over." I was met at the door, not with a scowl, but with an ear-to-ear grin.

Jungian therapist Laura Sue Dodson writes of the societal archetypes we all carry in our collective unconscious: "Every archetype has polar energies that could be described as masculine and feminine aspects of the archetype. An ego state that could be described as embodying wholeness is one in which the ego is not identified with one side of the archetype to the exclusion of the other." Dodson also writes of the Oriental concepts of Yin and Yang. "Yin and Yang energies, like all seeming opposites, can be likened to electrical current polarities. The Yang (masculine) pole is positive — assertive, outgoing; the Yin (feminine) is negative — receptive or passive. The two together allow the current to pass. One is the perfect complement to the other, not the opposite …."

The best, most creative people, the best, most functional organizations have always been a blend of the masculine and the feminine. It's just that it has been taboo to mention that a female's most creative qualities may be her "maleness" and vice versa.

University of Pennsylvania sociologist Frank Furstenberg calls it "pluralistic ignorance" when people believe something that almost everyone else believes — while individually, each is convinced that he/she is the only crazy person believing it.

But perhaps we are finally becoming "pluralistically smart." John Naisbitt, author of the best seller, "Megatrends," gives validity to this blending of the male and female in an 11th trend he adds to the 10 listed in his book:

"The 11th megatrend is a shift from sex roles to synergy," said Naisbitt in an interview with writer Connie Zweig. "It reflects a reconciliation between the sexes at a deep level, a greater harmony between qualities we used to consider either masculine or feminine. It could well mean the end of the battle of the sexes."

Mr. Mom in the 21st Century

Denver Post
JUNE II, 2008

MATT SCHNEIDER IS A RESIDENT NEW YORKER who grew up in Englewood. You'd think this young stay-at-home father of two and I would have nothing in common. But we do.

His wife works in an all-consuming career: global real estate private equity. And my husband once worked in an all-consuming career: Colorado politics.

As the stay-at-home parent Matt faces the same joys, jobs and frustrations of full-time kid care as I once did:

- Complete discretion over when to take the kids (his are boys ages 5 and 2) on excursions.
- Total relationship with the children's preschool. They always call dad, not mom, when a child is sick.
- Inner conflict: What do I do with any bit of free time I get? Indulge my own interests? Or scrub the floors, fold the laundry, etc.?

Of course, there is one big difference between what Matt does now and what I did in the '70s. Where I was a follower, he is a leader. Where I was living the still-conventional life of a mom, he is charting a brand new path for dads.

Although fathers now do twice the amount of child care that they did just back in 1995, fewer than 200,000 enter full-time stay-at-home parenting by choice.

I suddenly recall a Newsweek cover story from last fall: "MAN UP!" shouted the headline.

The cover photo does not show some pumped-up athlete, a finger-pointing politician or gun-toting militiaman. Instead, filling the entire page is the shirtless back of a young man of average build, holding a small boy who peers questioningly over his shoulder.

The article bemoans the fact that as women have expanded their roles in many professions once closed to them, men have "turned to old models and mores of manhood for solution."

Yes, more than 20 percent of wives in dual-income families now make more than their husbands. Yes, 80 percent of jobs lost in the recession have been traditional male jobs. So there are plenty of reasons for men to feel demeaned and sometimes useless.

However, those body-powered, super-masculine industry jobs of the past are not coming back. Neither are the sexist, male-dominated work environments portrayed by such TV favorites as "Mad Men."

Therefore, "if the traditional male is an endangered species, it's time to rethink masculinity," says Newsweek. And one of the ways to rethink masculinity is to rethink fatherhood.

Some dads not only "rethink," they jump in with both feet from the get-go.

"But how can they do it!" exclaim some skeptical — mainly male — responders. Aren't moms the "natural" nurturers? "Dads just have too much testosterone!" Perhaps, but testosterone is more malleable than we think. The actual act of early fathering can reduce it!

According to a study by biological researcher Katherine Wynne-Edwards and psychologist Anne Storey, "dads holding either their baby, or a doll wrapped in a blanket that had recently held — and still smells of — a newborn, experience a rise in ... hormones associated with breast feeding, accompanied by a drop in testosterone."

Don't panic, guys! The changes are temporary! Early daddy time benefits the kids, too.

A British survey of 1,900 children born in 2000 or 2001 has revealed that, by the time the youngsters reached 3, emotional and behavioral problems were more common if their fathers had not taken time off from work when they were born or had not used flexible work hours in their early years.

Matt Schneider is not surprised. He wrote in an e-mail to me: "When Dads are active in our children's lives from the beginning, we develop a skill set and confidence that allows us to parent as a partner, rather than as an assistant. What a gift for our children — two engaged, nurturing, and competent parents."

All Boys

Rocky Mountain News
c. 1999

THE ONE COMMONALITY OF THE NINE perpetrators of the seven school shootings in the last four years was gender.

Nationwide, 95% of violent crimes are committed by men or boys, yet as we agonize over the Columbine tragedy and search for reasons, we don't talk much about the fact that youth violence is, in fact, *male* violence.

Are there genetic factors that make boys more violence prone? Of course. Scientists, traditionalists, feminists alike would be hard pressed to deny it.

The robust cry, "It's a boy!" when a male baby is born could be the heralding of a potential killer. This does not, however, mean that biology is destiny. Just because 95% of violent crimes are committed by males does not mean all males are violent. The vast majority are not.

So what are the ameliorating factors?

Different cultures have found different ways to direct male aggression into "constructive" outlets.

Traditional Western societies have tried to channel aggression into war and into organized sports. The British proudly claim that "the battles of England are won on the playing fields of Eton."

I question war as a "solution," but even if it is, what about those who don't fit? Eric Harris, co-perpetuator in the Columbine Massacre, had just been rejected by the military.

And when those who become "jocks" take their super charged testosterone off the field and denigrate non-athletes, as they reportedly did at Columbine, disaster can result.

A psychiatrist friend of mine says that rage in boys and young men is more rampant than we realize. That those who finally explode are like caged animals who are constantly poked. He warns that the fatal one last poke can come from anywhere or anybody. That's why it's simplistic to point to one culprit in the generation of a violent incident.

My husband and I did our share of "parent blaming" regarding Columbine. "How could the Harrises not have known, especially with all those bombs in their house?" we asked.

But our grown son, Scott, brought us up short. "You didn't know of the aspirin bottle/duct tape bomb we set off on the roof of the (Governor's) mansion?" he queried with a grin.

He was right. I hadn't known. And I had been there; right at home!

We don't always see what we should see or hear what we should hear. But we sure need to hang in there and try. In 1999 parents spend 40% less time with their kids than 1969. That's not enough, whether we have sons or daughters or both.

And, as my husband admonishes, "We need to keep boys busy, if not sports, something else — too exhausted with activity for trouble."

> *"If a boy cannot learn to verbally express feelings, he will quickly become that wounded, caged male animal, ready to pop at the next poke."*

Psychologist James Garbarino advises us that we — parents, teachers, clergy, mentors — must become bulwarks, a literal counter force, against the increasing toxicity of media, crass commercialism and super-inflated male images.

In short, while we try to change our culture, we need to protect our children from it.

In his book, "Lost Boys: Why Our Sons Turn Violent and How We Can Save Them," Garbarino describes himself in childhood as a "holy terror … prone to fits of intense rage" and writes of riding his bicycle around other people's neighborhoods "imagining what it would be like to commit the perfect crime." What derailed him from this potential life of "perfect crime?" He credits a world filled with people who cared about him and consistent spiritual guidance.

Garbarino also strongly recommends something that flies in the face of traditional norms: Generous doses of "androgyny." To counter the super-aggressive male genes, boys need constant permission to show and develop their softer "female" side.

If a boy cannot learn to verbally express feelings, he will quickly become that wounded, caged male animal, ready to pop at the next poke.

Much has been written about the importance of an ever present *strong* father figure in the positive development of a boy. The evidence is in. I believe it all. Just one plea to that strong father, stepfather, uncle or grandfather:

A little tenderness, too, please.

Father figures have to give it in order to permit it

All the Lonely Fathers
Ask a Man What He Fears Most in a Divorce and He Will Tell You Losing His Children

Denver Post
NOVEMBER 23, 1986

"I NEVER MISS A SUPPORT PAYMENT," SAID THE divorced father of two, who has been without permanent employment for the past 18 months.

"I will beg, borrow, or sell something before I miss that payment. It makes me feel good. I'm meeting my responsibility as a father, and I'm backing it up with the bucks."

This father and I were meeting over lunch. Although he had tried to get joint custody, he found that joint custody was not possible under Colorado law unless both parties agree to it. He didn't want to "fight" for his kids. But he did, and he lost.

What hurt the most was that his children, at first, saw his loss as their gain: "We won! We won!" shouted his 5-year-old son, jumping up and down after the court hearing.

"Mommy says 'we won!'"

This man, who has just started his own business, sympathizes with "weekend fathers." He is one.

"I get my kids one night a week for dinner, every other weekend and for a month in the summer. These times are the most important times in my life. I wouldn't give them up for anything, and neither should any father have to give them up.

"I agree, a man should be thrown in jail if he doesn't support his kids. But so should a woman who reneges on a father's visitation! Some men don't pay because they are cut out of the personal sense of fatherhood all together. And why should they?"

Other divorced fathers are rallying with the same cry.

A man who belongs to the New York League of Divorced Fathers said in an interview with CBS correspondent Bernard R. Goldberg:

"Fathers are actively discouraged in retaining an interest in their children. Why do we wonder that we have an Everest-sized problem in unpaid child support? Hasn't the obvious dawned on social workers, judges, and politicians? If you don't allow a man to feel like a father, he'll stop acting like one."

And, writes Craig Donaldson of Arvada, in a letter to the editor:

"I've been divorced for seven years and have been through torture trying to ensure visitation with my children. Despite my ex-wife's continued attempts to alienate me from my children, I stay as involved in their lives as I am allowed, and I never miss a child support payment. She's got me right where she wants me — the wallet without the face."

But the "wallet" does appear out of reach for many fathers.

Non-custodial fathers fail to pay $4 billion in child support annually. More than the millions of women owed child support do not receive it, despite court orders.

The Denver Post / Maureen Scance

Lenore Weitzman, author of "The Divorce Revolution," studied divorced persons in Los Angeles County. She found there was little variation in compliance with child-support orders by the father's ability to pay. Among those with gross incomes (after divorce) of $30,000 to $50,000, 29 percent made no payments or paid irregularly. For those with incomes of $20,000 or less, the proportion was 27 percent.

Yet a study conducted at the University of Toronto found that when fathers had joint custody and no roadblocks were put in the way of their visitation rights, the child-support default rate dropped from as high as 70 percent all the way down to 7 percent.

A tremendous emphasis has recently been put on the feminization of poverty and the fact that when a family breaks up, the custodial mother's standard of living goes down 73 percent. Conversely, the single father's standard of living goes up 42 percent.

I've seen that statistic from Weitzman's book dozens of times. On average, her statistic may be correct, but it is only a statistic. And there are hundreds of fathers out there who do not fit the mold.

In a reaction to what many men see as unfair stereotyping and the denial of any say in their children's lives, at least 200 father's rights groups have sprung up around the United States. Most are pushing for laws that would make joint custody the norm, unless it could be proven that sole custody was in the "best interest of the child."

Louisiana, Idaho and Florida have such joint-custody laws. California, Michigan and Oklahoma also have laws which favor joint custody in a variety of ways. The Colorado Legislature has twice rejected a law which would establish "mutual custody."

Some feminist groups are against the legal presumption that joint custody is best, arguing that many fathers seek joint custody primarily as a way of punishing their ex-wives. But other feminists, like Karen DeCrow, the former national president of the National Organization for Women, believes there are advantages to the establishment of joint custody as the norm:

"As long as women have the exclusive responsibility for raising children, we will never have equality in the marketplace," says DeCrow.

Other people, including myself, question the legal presumption of joint custody, because a joint custody arrangement that is resented by one partner could wreak even more destructive emotional havoc on the children of divorce. From the friends I know who have it, joint custody takes almost as much work, compatibility, and sensitivity as staying in a marriage.

But some answer must be found to the dilemma of fathers who empty their wallets regularly in support of their children and are, at the same time, denied their very fatherhood by their ex-spouses or by the system.

A psychologist who was quoted in an article by Goldberg said that if you ask a man what he fears most in divorce, the man will tell you he's afraid of losing his children.

"We read a lot about feminization of poverty," writes Goldberg. "Why have we heard virtually nothing about what we might call the 'masculinization of loneliness?'"

A Quiet Nursery No Child's Delight

Denver Post
c. 1988

THE LITTLE ROOM IS A BURST OF CLEAR, SHARP color in a classy, but otherwise subdued house. A milky way of stars arches across its bright blue ceiling; an orange sunrise replete with pink clouds adorns the east wall. The carpet is pale blue. Soft. Durable. Spotless.

Nearly half of all American marriages are believed to end in separations.

— *Parade Magazine.*

The little room holds miniature furniture. A child's piano — perhaps an antique — sits in one corner. A knee-high "work" desk rests against the west wall. An untouched pad of drawing paper and slightly used assorted crayons adorn its top.

More than a million new children each year watch their parents' marriages dissolve.

— *New York Times.*

Under the south window, which faces the bay, a square lidless toy box reveals red plastic dishes, a tiny can of Campbell's soup, a yellow Donald Duck pitcher, a rubber band, colored beads, a string and a small pack of Kleenex.

At the time of divorce, preschoolers are profoundly upset about the very logical possibility that both parents will abandon them.

— *Judith S. Wallerstein, "California Children of Divorce" study.*

A rubber ball and rolled-up kite lie nearby, the latter still in its plastic wrap. A gigantic conch shell rests on the built-in cupboard under the window and serves as a bookend for a set of child encyclopedias.

For younger children, divorce evokes strong feelings, tears and profound sadness … as they speak of their loneliness and continued sense of deprivation.

— *California study.*

Propped in the corner of the window sill is a large stuffed circus clown, smiling, one arm out-stretched. Beside it rests a furry baby seal and a small ceramic horse.

After 18 months, the children of divorce appear to be psychologically worse off. Almost half seem more troubled.

— *California study.*

The room had once been a nursery. It is *still* bravely trying to be a nursery. Forlorn but hopeful, its cleanliness a tribute to the children briefly there.

A nursery not so much outgrown, but abandoned. Perhaps suddenly, without warning.

(Most) children of divorce have the sense of (being) deprived of play time and a sense of leisure.

— *California study.*

The young Florida couple who built this nursery split in 1983. We know them only slightly. And their children, then ages 2 and 4, not at all. She has the children. He has the house. We hear he visits them frequently.

While few deny that an unhappy couple may better their own lot by divorce, there is room to doubt whether this holds true for the children.

— *Marie Winn, "Children Without Childhood."*

He is "terrific," say people in the community where they live. And she is "super-neat" also, say their friends. It's just that they are incompatible, their differences irreconcilable.

Fantasies that their natural parents will resolve their differences and remarry persist in more than half of the younger children of divorce.

— *California study.*

And the little room stands bright, expectant, waiting.

STEREOTYPES:
How Much Can We Change Them?

Camaraderie
Making Mistakes Together

Denver Post
SEPTEMBER 1, 1985

THIS SUMMER I TOOK A FOUR-DAY COLORADO Outward Bound trip down the Green River with 23 other women, only five of whom I had known before. Three inflatable rafts. Three female instructors. Eight women per boat.

One participant reported that her friends at home had been amazed when told of her upcoming venture. Why would any woman want to take such a trip with other women, they had asked.

Well, I can think of at least one reason.

I went primarily because I wanted to experience more of the action. I've been on plenty of male/female river trips. And they're great. But a predictable role division of responsibilities reigns from the moment the rafters assemble on shore.

Usually the men have more experience, so of course they will "captain" the difficult rapids. The men are stronger, so they will carry the heavy equipment; more adroit with ropes, so they will secure all dunnage to the rafts. And so on.

As joyful as these trips are, I always find myself frightened of making mistakes, so I shy away from intruding on male turf. Then I come away feeling I missed something.

This time, I missed nothing. I learned to tie three kinds of knots. I learned to call out orders in a whaleboat captain's voice. I learned to "pry" left and "draw" right and vice versa. I learned to make mistakes, unself-consciously. And then I learned to correct them. All in due time. And so did everyone else.

After three days of trial and error, the process of tying the equipment to the rafts evolved its own smooth rhythm. Our paddling became a pattern, too. Smooth, strong, determined, synchronized.

Our instructor seldom took over the command. If the person "captaining" the raft made a judgement error, or the crew's teamwork failed, so be it. We were left, sometimes frantically, to recover from our mistake, retrieve ourselves from a sand bar, push ourselves off a rock, or paddle out of a "hole."

Sometimes it was scary.

The disconcerting roar of an upcoming rapid, growing louder as we grew nearer, could set our teeth on edge.

On occasion we disembarked to look downstream and to plan our course of action. As we climbed back in the raft after scouting such rapids as "Disaster Fall's," "S.O.B." and "Hell's Half Mile," their names would echo ominously in our ears, mental maps of the river course and its obstacles glazing over our eyes.

But through doing, we learned, really learned.

And we gave full rein to our aggressive "masculine" side.

Yet, neither did we deny our feminine side. We cooked gourmet meals and lingered over them. Our instructors built a sauna, in which we sat until its heat propelled us to race naked into the dark night of the cold clear river, where the smooth undercurrent washed away the sauna's sweat, and the concentric surface ripples reflected the moon.

We took soapless showers in waterfalls, heads back, mouths laughing, eagerly engaging the rushing water as all of us were learning to engage the wilderness.

We isolated ourselves on a two-hour "solitude," sharing with each other feelings about our ambitions, our children, our careers, our frustrations and dreams. We made new friendships and strengthened old ones.

And the last day, we followed an instructor, who, suddenly with a deep-throated yell, jumped from a beached raft and dived into the deep gray-brown mud of the shore. At least 18 of us took this mud bath, wallowing and staggering and falling in the slime like a group of barking, playful baby seals.

The actual ages of the participants ranged from late 20s to early 60s. But we all *felt* the same age: young.

At the last day's debriefing, one of the oldest women and the very youngest confessed that this was the very first time they had ever set aside time just to be with other women. And eyes filled with tears at their former denial of female camaraderie.

Someone asked an instructor if the extraordinary sense of solidarity which evolved through the almost perfect four days would have been weakened if we'd had to face real hardship: equipment breakdowns, illness, overturned boats, burnt breakfasts, incessant rain.

"No," she answered with the wise smile of one who leads more than 20 such ventures per year. "That would have made your bonding even stronger."

Maybe she's right.

But it's hard to see how.

> *"Through doing, we learned, really learned. And we gave full rein to our aggressive 'masculine' side."*

Some Scenarios Don't Work Out

Unseen burdens

But what we women schlep with our arms and hands — perched on the edge of one hip, or strung over the shoulder like self-encumbering lasso — is only the visible part of the weight we pull.

Women, says a 1979 United Nations report, do two-thirds of the world's work, get paid one-tenth of the world's wages, and own 1 percent of the world's property.

Denver Post
JULY 23, 1985

I SIT AT HOME ON A FRIDAY EVENING READING AN article by Letty Cottin Pogrebin on "schlepping." Women, says Pogrebin, schlep more than men. To schlep means to carry encumbering articles.

Women not only schlep the logical things needed for their own day's activity, but various sundry things that enhance the lives of others: diapers for the baby, lunches for the kids' outing, household goods for the family.

I remember endless schlepping when our kids were small and we lived in a house with sunless, north-facing steps and the garage a half block down the street:

Schlep library books to car with one arm while guiding 3-year-old over the ice on steps with the other arm.

Schlep dog food, left in car from last grocery trip, to house.

Schlep baby and the baby seat to the car, return and schlep bag full of favorite toys for the baby's sitter.

After trip home, reverse same schleps, substituting new baby bottles for dog food. Etc.

I'll leave the "pay" and the "property" for another column, but the work issue fits here, partly because we do carry more than our share of the load. Not just grocery baggage and kid baggage, but *worry* baggage.

Let me explain: if any of our kids is really in danger, both Dick and I will worry. But once the danger is past, I will *still* worry. I won't just be thankful that everything turned out all right. I'll continue to worry — to dwell, instead, on everything that could have gone wrong.

"Schlepping" worry baggage doesn't just include the dramatic or the dangerous. Its load also encompasses the worry over hurt feelings, guilt over lousy parenting, concern over spousal relationship.

"An argument with my husband in the morning will really blow my day at work," said a close friend of mine. "Yet, I just know he turns it *off* the minute he walks out the door."

> *"What we women schlep with our arms and hands—perched on the edge of one hip, or strung over the shoulder like self-encumbering lasso—is only the visible part of the weight we pull."*

Parental example

No doubt these sex-stereotyped generalizations are unfair to certain individuals. Such strict dichotomies cannot possibly define all men and all women. There must be exceptions.

But back to worrying over potential dangers to one's kids. My mother used to laughingly tell a story about my father and how he handled his nightly "worry" about his teenage daughters. Right before his head would hit the pillow he would ask, "When will the girls get in?"

Told the bewitching hour by my mother, he would then roll over and sleep. My mother, on the other hand, would stay awake, read, until she heard us arrive.

Then, first thing in the morning, my father would say, "Did the girls get in safely?" Physically, my parents both had been at rest. But mentally, he slept while she "schlepped."

Surprise ending

This was all brought back to me tonight after we let our 14-year-old daughter and her girl friend go on a self-selected excursion about which we had very little knowledge.

Dick looked worried as he went to bed. He also looked sleepy. I give him 15 minutes of continued wakefulness, I thought smugly, as I settled down to read for the two hours we had allowed Heather and her friend to do their own thing.

But my husband surprised me and confounded the whole gist of my sex-stereotyped "schlepping" theory.

"I couldn't sleep till after the girls came in," he said in the morning, naming the exact time the door had clicked and the hushed giggles had trailed up the stairs.

It doesn't make for the neat, congruent ending I'd planned.

But some men *are* exceptions.

Sometimes.

"Can't Do" Belief Takes a Stumble

Denver Post
June 4, 1985

L AST SUMMER I WROTE A COLUMN ON LEARNING to use the word processor. I'm still learning to use the word processor. But I'm not using it right now. Right now, I'm writing these words on the old standard yellow pad.

Anything I write during the work day — usually for publication — has to be composed on yellow paper and recorded later. Yet anything purely personal, done in "off hours" — like my journals — I can compose from scratch on the processor.

Is this behavior an example of the strange relationship females have with machines? I don't know, but it seems this female can only call up her journal file and compose on the word processor in the wee hours of the morning, because at that time no one is around to laugh at her slowness, her mistakes, the tedious way she goes over the manual.

Mary Alice White, psychology professor at Columbia University, said recently to a New York Times reporter:

"A lot of men approach machines as if they know how to put them together and can control them, while women generally assume that they don't and they can't."

But why do women assume "can't do"?

Father is bothered

A father I know thinks it's biological. He is not smug about this. In fact, as the father of a daughter, he is bothered.

"I couldn't believe how the boys just took to the project and the girls just stood there," he said shaking his head, after working with a group of gifted 13-year-olds on a school project which required the construction of a self-propelled motor car. "It's got to be in the genes."

But is it in the genes?

What girls and boys do with toys is often cited as instructive "gene determined" behavior: Girls go after dolls and stuffed animals. Boys go after trucks and trains.

Yet studies of what *adults* do with toys, when they play with children, is even more instructive regarding determined behavior.

According to an experiment conducted in 1983, if a baby is dressed in pink and called a girl, "she" will be handed dolls by adults who play with her. If a baby is dressed in blue and called a boy, "he" will be handed things that can be manipulated.

Yet this "programmed indoctrination" theory of female machine-phobia seems too simplistic. My sister and I were taught to hike, to high-jump, to play tennis and to target-shoot, because these were my father's interests. And most of those interests became our interests.

Taken to hydraulics lab

However, we were never encouraged to enter engineering, his profession. And when he took us to the hydraulics laboratory at Stanford University and showed us the "water-works," he did not invite us to operate the opening and the closing of the valves, which released or restrained the rushing water.

Would our father have engaged us in the actual operation of this machinery if we had been boys? Or simply if we had *asked* him? And why didn't we ask?

Thirteen years ago, our daughter — age 1 — learned how to pull back the switch on a manually operated race-car track we had given her brother — age 4 — at Christmas. The result of this accomplishment engendered pure delight. She spent far more hours than her brother did "shooting" the cars around the track.

Is the world full of former 1-year-old girls who experience this kind of gleeful mastery only to have it "trained out" later? You bet, say psychologists, even in 1985.

Yet, as I write this, positive examples contrary to the female "can't do" attitude abound. My 41-year-old female administrative assistant has achieved total mastery over the word processor, can compose or copy on it, and talk on the phone at the same time.

And that daughter of ours, now 14, who once manipulated the race track, does all her school reports on the processor, takes computer lessons weekly, and has designed her own computer program.

Is this "can do" phenomenon rooted in her genes, inherited from her grandfather's engineering skills? Or was it exposure to the race-track toy at age 1?

Whatever its "roots," it sure skipped a generation.

Gender Differences in Kids Show Up Early with the Toys They Seek

Denver Post
FEBRUARY 10, 2013

MY 14-MONTH-OLD GRANDDAUGHTER SITS ON the floor tenderly rocking her milk bottle back and forth in her arms.

"Hmm, maybe she needs a doll?" I say, quietly wondering if such a Christmas gift would be gender stereotyping her too early.

"*Of course* she needs a doll," retorts my daughter, the toddler's mom, in a practical, post-feminist voice.

Suddenly, I am remembering my attempts at the progressive upbringing of said daughter and her brother in the 1970s.

When Scott was about 6, I gave him a book called "William's Doll," then was guiltily relieved when he totally ignored it. (Would liking dolls, or even doll books, mean he would turn out to be gay?)

But when Heather at age 1 played with her older brother's racecar track more than he did, I was overjoyed.

So did my *attitude*, perhaps unconscious, about what each would choose govern their choice of play activities? Or did my attitude even matter?

Recent brain experiments have revealed that the biggest gender differentiation in 3-year-olds is that, across human cultures, boys will quickly choose a toy gun and a girl will choose a doll. This is the age they are forming their gender identity with intensity and purpose.

"Toy preferences almost certainly have an innate basis …. One clue is that male monkeys prefer to play with trucks while females prefer dolls," write neuroscientists Sandra Aamodt and Sam Wang in their 2011 book, "Welcome to Your Child's Brain."

Of course, culture and parental attitudes have an influence. But only to a degree, and usually later on in the child's life when he or she is secure enough in his or her gender identity to branch out.

Denver Waldorf School educator Nancy Blanning, who has worked with young children ages 3 to 7 for more than 30 years, says that the big question is, "How can we offer experiences that both temper and enhance the child's natural choices?"

For example, at Waldorf, both boys and girls have been given cloth dolls that they will turn to at naptime, but often in differing ways. Last week, for example, two of the boys attached their dolls to broom handles and began swinging them around. "We see that, whatever the toy, boys need to move things and to build things," Blanning said.

"I am appalled at the gross vengeance with which stores have recently returned to promoting toys by gender. But in the long term, I'm not sure this 'super sexist marketing' makes much difference."

As a feminist, I am appalled at the gross vengeance with which stores have recently returned to promoting toys by gender. But in the long term, I'm not sure this "super sexist marketing" makes much difference.

So here's my message to parents (especially moms) who worry about the daughter who only "thinks pink" at the age of 3: Relax! Given broader opportunities, she will most likely grow out of it. And if she still likes all things pink at the age of 20, that's OK, too.

And to parents (especially dads), here's a more crucial message: "It is true that about half of the boys who prefer girl toys do grow up to be gay — and also true that many of them do not," write Aamodt and Wang.

"Playing with girl toys and adult homosexuality both result from earlier influences on some boys' brains, perhaps due to prenatal experiences or genetics," they write. "By the time you can observe the behavior, the outcome is out of your control, so you might as well get comfortable with it."

Yes, I did give my granddaughter a soft, snuggly doll named Buttercup for Christmas. Delighted, she immediately cuddled it to her neck and took it to bed for her nap.

But later, she watched her older brother's new, remote-controlled "terrain twisters" bumping and colliding, accompanied by their screams and laughter.

Then, *thwapp*! Throwing Buttercup against the wall, she scrambled toward the action.

Personal Growth:

Increasing Awareness, "Aha!" Moments

CREATING, WRITING, WORKING:
Stepping Up, Stepping Back

Conquering Those "Re-entry Fears" by Facing Up to Them

Denver Post
FEBRUARY 5, 1979

"**W**ELL, THE SECOND CAMPAIGN IS OVER; WHAT are you going to do now?" asked my friend at a crowded Christmas cocktail party.

I knew what I was going to do, but I wouldn't tell her. A feeling of panic closed off my normally spontaneous reactions to such questions. I simply couldn't say at that point I was going to do a weekly column for The Denver Post.

That panic returns at this minute, not because I don't have anything to say: I've already completed three columns to succeed this one. Nor am I frightened because I am speaking to a possible audience of 260,000-plus families; years of campaigning and public speaking almost have eliminated my stage fright. I'm not even paralyzed by deadlines; articles, like college term papers, have a way of getting done.

> "Possibly I'm frightened of failure; more likely, however, I'm afraid of totally independent success."

But, at this moment, I am trying to come to grips with what the essence of this column will be, and I'm not sure that I know how to put it into words. I've always dreamed of a professional arena where I could put my political, social work, homemaker, and motherhood experiences to work at one time. It seems I have found the ideal assignment and I am highly challenged, but I am also scared.

Possibly I'm frightened of failure; more likely, however, I'm afraid of totally independent success. I've read that many women who show amazing competence working on crusades for others have great difficulty when given the chance to say: "This is what I am all about!" Possibly this is what I now experience, but this hesitation itself is perhaps a good starting place.

This special type of fear may be related to other psychological phenomena that particularly affect women; for instance, doubts about re-entry into paid work, mental barriers concerning money, guilt about saying no. These and other conflicts that women struggle with daily are issues I hope to explore.

Rapidly changing role expectations for women and men are producing in all of us new questions and fears about how we parent our children, how we set personal and career goals, and how we view ourselves within society. Every day I have glimpses of how people (including myself and my family) deal with these challenges.

Small but dramatic incidents from my personal, professional and political journey stand out as meaningful in a larger societal sense: the anguish I felt, that moment 10 years ago, when I first left my 6-week-old newborn to return to paid work. As a social worker, I sensed the helplessness of that welfare father in a hot, steamy, tenement kitchen learning to cook for his 2 and 3-year-olds after his wife had left; the shocked and defeated expression of the unwed, pregnant 18-year-old when she realized she couldn't raise her baby and go to college. And I saw the panic in the eyes of my own 4-year-old when she moved from her small, secure bedroom to the Governor's Mansion.

Right now I am conquering my own reentry fears by stating them. Other problems have simpler solutions. Still more challenges cry out for simple recognition before they can be dealt with. To me, raising the question often seems more important than giving an answer.

If you are with me or already have been there, whether you have similar contrasting stories, stay with me.

Attention, Chauvinists! Women Not Inefficient—Just Different

Denver Post
NOVEMBER 26, 1979

WE WERE DOOMED BY ALPHABETICAL DESTINY. Robert, an "S," sat right in front of me, a "V," all three years of high school. We both were in the "top" English class.

Another test day dawned.

With a flare, our teacher yanked up the movie screen, revealing the blackboard test question. In an essay, we were to dissect and deliver the essential message of Dickens' "A Tale of Two Cities." The question was in four parts.

I was just beginning to read the second part. Already, Robert's pencil was flying. Never did he stop to think, to chew his eraser, to roll his eyes in feigned lack of knowledge or to scratch his neck. Here we go again: I groaned and caught the sympathetic glance of another classmate across the aisle.

Robert. The Flying Wedge.

He never paused. Thus, my pauses seemed interminable. His mind moved with processes full speed ahead. My mind, in contrast, seemed caught in a state of torpor, moving in alternating patterns: Think, write, recall, write, daydream, write, analyze, write.

"If we go to the same college, I'll die!" I moaned to my family.

"Don't let him get on your nerves," said my father. "You're doing great; you're just a different person." His reassurance was constant and consistent. I needed to hear it each time.

In college I found that different minds work in many contrasting ways. My freshman roommate, Kay, was so bright she never had to study in high school. She turned to me in desperation, beseeching me to help her learn, not the subject matter, but my method of studying.

But Kay didn't use my method. Slowly, she developed her own.

When overwhelmed by study demands, Kay would announce she needed to "dream on it." She then would lie down, pull a pillow over her head and sleep for 18 straight hours. Eventually rising with a defiant toss of the pillow, she would "hit" the desk for an 18-hour crack at the books. Her pages would start flying like Robert's pencil.

Kay. The dreamer.

I think of work patterns I have seen or read about more recently. Virginia Valian, psychology professor, is a procrastinator. So petrified by the writing of her doctoral thesis, she found she must force herself to begin it in five-minute segments. To ensure that each segment of work would last not a second longer she would set the alarm clock.

"I still remember that first five minutes," writes Valian in her essay, "Learning To Work."

"I worked steadily, though with difficulty and anxiety. I knew, however, that I could last out five minutes of difficulty and anxiety. So I continued. At last the bell went off and I collapsed. I went into the bedroom and threw myself on the bed, breathing hard and feeling my heart race. It really was a big deal."

Virginia. The Ph.D. with the "Sesame Street" attention span.

Artist Miriam Schapiro starts her projects in a strikingly different way. In an article of the book "Working It Out," by Pamela Daniels and Sara Ruddick, Ms. Schapiro describes herself getting into the action: "I have had to develop a way of getting down to work that is probably best thought of as a way of 'playing.' When I make up my mind to start work on a new painting, I go through what I call a 'bloodbath.' I get out all my papers, all my paints. I play with them in every way I can imagine; I smear around on the paper to get the feeling of paints on my hand. I leave my ordinary world and literally go into another house, a house of painting … at the end of the day, I may have 25 'works' all over the floor."

Miriam. The player. It is she with whom I most identify.

I don't paint, but I do go through exactly the same process when I write. It doesn't show, as I write in straight lines on a legal pad and appear very organized. But my first thoughts are mindless and childish as Ms. Schapiro's first images. I have to get "it" all out and any fantasies or daydreams related to "it" before even a short piece begins to take shape.

Miriam Schapiro's husband is an artist, too. But he has a totally different approach to his work. Linear, organized, total. No transition, no prelude necessary; like Robert, or like my husband. Three males. All forces operating full speed ahead.

And four women: each one with a work process that differs not only from that of the men but from those of each other. Doubtless, examples could be found of "linear" women and "dreaming" men!

Yet, is it possible that our society's cultural conditioning of women predestines us to use our unconscious, or sleep, or play, or our daydreams in our work? Have most men, on the other hand, been conditioned to shut out "all that" and work from the intellect alone? I don't know.

I do know we live in a society which measures speed and unit produced per moment as a supreme value. Could it be this value is so pervasive because, until recent times, the major creators, workers, teachers, and tone-setters have been men? It seems likely.

Recently, to my editor, I bemoaned the inefficiency of my process compared with that of a male colleague.

"You're doing great; you're just a different person," she replied empathetically.

Reassurance.

Again, I really needed to hear it.

Light at End of the Funnel

Denver Post
FEBRUARY 28, 1984

FIVE YEARS AGO THIS MONTH, I STARTED WRITING one column a week for the Post. In July of last year, I upped it to two. "What's it like to meet that deadline?" people ask. "How do you do it? Where do you get your ideas?" In this column, I'll try to answer those questions.

For some reason, it helps me to visualize my column process as a funnel with a large elliptical top. Experiences, thoughts, facts, dreams and inspirations tumble into the funnel competitively. But only a few make it to the bottom in the same form they entered.

Unlike the kitchen appliance by the same name, my funnel is "terraced." Some thoughts get "stuck" on these terraces permanently; others may be dislodged with a sheer force of new material or with the slight "shaking" of the funnel on a lethargic day.

Still others hide until a synchronistic idea "finds them." When this happens, "sympatico" words can roll smoothly through the narrow cylinder at the bottom, dropping to my yellow legal pad, almost writing themselves. A real inspiration is a straight shot, which doesn't even touch the sides!

Birthing of ideas

But most times the birthing of the ideas through the funnel is not that easy. The thoughts more often fall unorganized on the page, handwritten, haphazard, incomplete, too many, or too few, to fill the 64 lines allotted me on Tuesday and the 79 on Sunday. Rewriting can take anywhere from two to 20 tries.

The satisfactions of working with this funnel is that it centers and interprets my life. Everything is "grist for the mill." Column-writing lends itself to a short term, concrete sense of completion. It is a craft as well as an intellectual exercise. I not only have to "hear" what I'm writing, but I have to "see" how the sections, quotes, the one-liners fit on the page.

Are the paragraphs "too heavy" for the subject?

Is the text too chopped up by quotes and references, thus losing the reader in a disjointed scramble?

The frustrations of this funnel image, and the task of column writing in general, is that the more ideas I get, the more I know I cannot use. Not only do some ideas get lodged permanently on terraces, some fall over the sides and never enter the funnel at all.

'Touch and go'

Another frustration is the "touch and go" nature of the game. A columnist can get fully absorbed in a topic, but can almost never become an expert. One always has to move on. Now. No delaying. Ever cognizant of the next "assignment's" demands.

"I don't have any ideas that are more than 700 words long," said one columnist whom I read recently. I'm sure I don't, either. The thought of writing a lengthy article or a book intimidates

me like the thought of my twice-a-week deadline intimidates others.

Columnist Georgie Ann Geyer writes about the difference between newspaper reporting and column writing "… 'covering things' isn't always helpful in a column. Columns demand thought, meditations, judgment, original investigation; not so much running around …."

The change to two columns a week in July drastically curtailed my "running around." I've cut way back on formal "first lady" speaking engagements. I go places where I can learn; listen more, talk less. Spend more time in my Levi's, in the Denver Post library, in my study, nose in a book, feet on the desk, ear to the phone.

Geyer says that she tries to "immerse herself in her interviewees' perceptions." I try to do this, too, with my interviewees and with my correspondents. Those who drop me letters via mailboxes, drop ideas into my funnel each week. These letters are not all personally answered, but all *with a signature* are read, often reread, pondered and filed away for future use.

So thank you, letter writers, for being my link to all readers; for being "grist for my mill" or "flour, sugar, spice and bitters for my funnel." Here's to the next five years!

Women Writers

They Are Constrained by a Fear of Hurting Their Family

The Denver Post / Maureen Scance

Denver Post
OCTOBER 26, 1986

AUTHOR LOUISE BERNIKOW ONCE WROTE, "I live at a turning point. There are more books now than before in which women tell the truth."

Maybe. And maybe not.

I think of her quote as I reread "Letting Go," the Oct. 5 column where I described my "neurotic" fear about watching my 18-year-old son set out on his own.

It's not that I lied. It's just that I didn't quite tell the whole truth. I represented the "craziness" of my fears, rather than the reality of my fears.

And the reality is that *I love that strapping, unpredictable, often difficult man-child as much as I did when he was a cuddly, predictable, easy-to-handle infant.* And I want him to live to grow up!

"Yuk," he'll say if he reads this.

That's coming on too strong.

But, just suppose I didn't love him. Or suppose I didn't love my daughter, or my sister, or my mother, or my husband and all those others one is *supposed* to love. Then I wouldn't just leave out "strong" feelings when I write about family members. I wouldn't write about them at all.

Or suppose I loved them all, but not all the time. Or suppose I didn't like certain things about them. Or as much as I love my kids, I sometimes wish I didn't have them. That, although I love my husband, occasionally I wished I were single.

Would I tell you? No way.

And that's why many women still don't tell the whole truth. We are born and/or conditioned to protect our families. To trivialize or downplay our gut feelings, locking them in cellars of our preconscious like lethal gases, fearing they would annihilate our relatives if they seeped out.

And when a woman is brave enough to spill her guts and her tears, her family, indeed, may act as if it has been annihilated! A most talented young woman who recently published a book regarding the death of her infant child wrote me a letter last summer.

In it she told me how hurt she had been over her in-laws' lack of acknowledgement of the grief she and her husband had experienced, and then how further devastated she had been by their response to the book's criticism of their neglect:

"On Mother's Day, we called K.'s mother to wish her a happy day. I barely got 'Happy Moth…' out of my mouth when she began screaming at me that I was 'a despicable liar' and that everything I wrote was 'lies, lies, lies!'

"I gave the phone to K.

"She then called K. (her son — my husband) a 'spineless jellyfish' because he 'let' his wife write 'those' things. Now she couldn't give the book to any of her friends because I made her look like a 'bitch.' We were then informed that they (two sisters, one aunt and one uncle) would never forgive me as long as they lived."

Tough stuff. Especially on Mother's Day.

And yet this woman's book told a truth that other families need to hear: That *that* particular death, that *any* death is important. And that extended family members can be unknowingly brutal to a couple mourning the loss of a small infant, especially when the couple can, and probably will, have another child.

> *"It's not just that women must combine pen labor with childbirth labor, that the nurturing of our children competes with the nurturing of our creative spirit."*

A friend of mine from high school had her first book, a novel, published in the late '60s, and it was about the '60s. A contemporary of her mother wrote to my mother, horrified that M. could *do that* to her parents. How could she hurt them so badly?

Upon reading the book, I discovered that the author did not even mention her parents or her family. The book merely contained many '60s ideas, some "counterculture" characters, and a few four-letter words!

Another author I know refuses to write about a batch of old letters she just found which tells a distressing and poignant story about her father, now in a nursing home. "Not until he's dead, and everyone he knows is dead!" she says emphatically, fully resigned to the fact that by that time she may be dead too.

Throughout history, men writers outnumber women writers by at least 10 to 1. Suddenly it dawns on me why. It's not just that women must combine pen labor with childbirth labor, that the nurturing of our children competes with the nurturing of our creative spirit. Or that women's expertise has not been taken seriously.

It's not just the time split, or the credibility split. It's the loyalty split.

And even the woman writing fiction must be "careful."

The fact that, until this century, most women novelists were single and childless, and that many wrote under a man's name, says it all: The less family, or family "name," they had to protect, the more they could tell the truth as they saw it.

It's not that I urge truth for the sake of defamation. Some of the recent "Mommy Dearest" type books disgust me in their raw grab for attention and dollars.

My point is not that one should tell a story to hurt. It is simply that if one can think *only* about possible familial hurts, a person who may never "lie" may still never write a truthful word.

Years ago, when I read Nancy Friday's "My Mother, Myself," I vowed I would write the sequel — "My Daughter, Myself." Why not? There was something very much missing in Friday's book. Although Friday had a mother, she did not have a daughter. And I do have a daughter. But I never wrote the book.

The fact is, I could never expose a child of mine in such a brutally honest book, especially a still-growing child.

And more talented women writers than I will not tell their stories either. And we'll all be the poorer for not knowing that what goes on with us perhaps also goes on with others. That we are not alone in our loves, our hates, our irrationalities, and our darkest thoughts.

For most of us will elect family protection over self-publication. And maybe that's the way it is. And the way it has to be.

Unfortunately.

Balance
I Want Time to Listen

Denver Post
JANUARY 5, 1986

CUTTING BACK.

On a Thursday in early December, a group of anchorwomen from three major networks came together as panelists on the "Phil Donahue Show" to discuss the successes and the hassles of their lives.

In response to a question from the audience, one of the panelists responded: "A balanced life is not possible! Something is always out of balance. The best you can expect is to pull it back into balance, and then expect something else to go out of whack."

No kidding.

At the same time Donahue was on, I was applying makeup with one hand. With the other hand I was alternately underlining preparation material for my own local TV show interview (coming up in a half hour) and putting the finishing touches on a column (due Friday). With one ear, I was listening to the TV, and with the other ear, the school-work questions of our 15-year-old daughter who was home with a cold.

Back in July of 1983, when I started writing two columns a week, I knew my life would become more unbalanced, and it did. It also became more challenging.

With a series of stretches, pulls, yanks, tumbles and a dozen leaps of faith, I pulled things in and out of "whack" for two and a half years. Through these "gymnastics," my writing got faster, my priorities grew sharper. And I'm glad I did it.

But now it's time for a different challenge. For that reason I have decided to drop my Tuesday Living & Arts column and to only write weekly in Contemporary.

The issue is one of balance, but it is also one of pace. This Christmas we rented a video camera to record traditional family events. Every time the tape was put on "fast forward" I looked at the woman in the yellow sweater running frantically around the Christmas tree, and I saw myself the way I've really *felt* for the past two and a half years.

Maybe it's simply that middle age is catching up to me. So be it! I'm tired of seeing how much I can do just to prove that I can do it. I'm tired of reading only enough of a book for a good column quote, then moving on to another book and another column. I'm tired of always having one eye on the clock.

> "*Every time the tape was put on 'fast forward' I looked at the woman in the yellow sweater running frantically around the Christmas tree, and I saw myself the way I've* actually felt *for the past two and a half years.*"

This year I want some time to reflect on the transition that we are making from "political family" to "citizen family." I want to savor the events surrounding our son's last year in high school — not just "schedule" each one in like one more "obligation."

I want to listen to my husband's ambitions and doubts, and my daughter's excitement and insecurity about what they want in the next stage of our life together. I want to listen to myself and feel what my dreams and fears are. And when I'm writing, I'm not listening to anybody.

There are definite dangers in cutting back my professional life. My personal life could take over. I could listen too much and start taking the responsibility for balancing others' lives. I could put myself in the situation of "Well, she's not that busy now ... let her do it." I could let trivia fill former work time. I could feel guilty about having free time, so then fling it away indiscriminately.

(And I do feel somewhat guilty, because there are so many women — no, so many *people* — who do not even have the choice of cutting back their work hours at middle age — or at *any* age!)

Cutting back also is the partial loss of a platform, and of perceived professional "power." In the eyes of many it's almost "un-American" not to keep climbing, to keep adding, to keep pushing — even to the point of burnout or incompetence, or both.

I could put this all in "quantity vs. quality" terms. But that's cliche and too simplistic. Besides, it might lead me and others to assume that since I'm writing half as much, each thing I do write should be twice as good.

I don't know if the quality of this column will improve. I do know, however, that the quality of my life will improve. And perhaps, eventually, by cutting down on the number of words written, I will find more explicit, more cogent, more creative words with which to explore issues and express myself.

In the meantime, maybe I'll get my Sunday column done before my Thursday TV show. And maybe I'll even get my TV show preparation done in time to watch Donahue through the makeup mirror and listen with both ears. And just *maybe* I'll be able to turn off a stimulating "column-inspiring" TV show and listen, really *listen* to my daughter.

Cutting back will hardy produce "perfect balance."

But at least "the woman in the yellow sweater" will no longer be racing through the "balancing act" like a character on a fast-forward video tape.

And I'm glad.

Mostly.

Getting Acclimated
Reflections on a New Space and an Old Space

Denver Post
MARCH 1, 1987

A DIFFERENT SPACE.
If God had created heaven, it might resemble Hanover, N.H., after an 18-inch snowfall. That is, if you are a cross-country skier as I am. And if you don't have to drive your car to work each day, as I don't.

Hanover is a community of approximately 10,000 people, close to half of whom are students at Dartmouth College. We live almost on campus in the Montgomery House, a comfortable, somewhat-rambling, New England brick-and-frame home.

My office window overlooks the frozen ice of Occom Pond, gray as I write on a weekday but dotted brightly by ice skaters on the weekends. Outside the window, 3-foot icicles hang from the eaves, partially obscuring the still-tentative first flakes of yet another storm.

Winter in this place would not be heaven for everyone. Two decades past, driving off to work each morning at 7:30, or slightly later, bearing babies and house-bound by toddlers, it would not have been heaven for me. And two decades hence? I don't know. In my 70s decade, I might just like it even more.

Older people seem younger here. Even their voices on the phone. One woman whom I guessed to be my age turned out to be 65. Another whom I judged to be 60 is 70. But maybe it's just I'm "hearing" younger. Because I *feel* younger here.

I don't know why. "Young" is not a term I thought I'd be applying to myself as I audit courses with 18- to 22-year olds. In my

The Denver Post / Maureen Scance

Women's Studies course, "Sex, Gender and Society," the professor asked how many of the class of 28 women and two men plan to have children.

Plan to have …. Not only have I *had* my children, but I have a "child" the age of these kids. Not only is there a 30-year age gap between me and them, there is a 20-year age gap between me and the two women who teach the course.

Next term, with all that immense seniority, I will be a "resource" for another Women's Studies course. This term, I'm content to sit and listen.

Which brings me back to that different space.

For me, this New England "space" is not only one of Currier and Ives quaintness. It is not only the physical space of a small town with houses dwarfed by huge snow drifts. *That* I expected.

What I didn't expect was the new mental space. The expansion of the mind which contrasts with, but is also generated from, the compactness of the geography.

I thought that in "gearing down" from politics, I would automatically "gear up" my writing and other professional work. Not so. Instead, I find myself at a production standstill. All systems stopped.

Somehow, here, I no longer have to prove myself. I don't want to meet a weekly deadline. I want to release that inner spring that has been coiled up through 20 years of politics, professional endeavors, and being a parent. I want hours just to think, moments just to be.

I want to delve into the pictorial and intellectual intricacies of my art history course. I want to know the professors, the students, and the citizens who populate this rarefied, some would say "elitist," environment.

And, to paraphrase New York Times columnist Anna Quindlen, who wrote recently about cutting back on her work load, I find I want to be more a "person," and less of a "personage."

One weekend about three years ago, my sister called me from California just to talk. She asked me what I was doing. I thought for a moment and then answered, "Nothing." Then I gasped, realizing that, since the first year I married, that was the first weekend in which there weren't at least three crucial, mandatory things I needed to do before Monday morning.

Here, if I let myself, I can have six months of "do nothing" weekends, a chance I may never have again. A chance to kick up my heels like a colt scaling a Robert Frost fence, a chance to watch the perfect snowflake melt on my mitten.

> *"A chance to kick up my heels like a colt scaling a Robert Frost fence, a chance to watch the perfect snowflake melt on my mitten."*

This column will continue, but it will no longer follow this form. It will come out once a month instead of once a week. It may or may not be the same kind of column. It may take the voice of a New England correspondent. It may examine feminist/familial issues in more depth.

It may try to analyze the residual sexism in a "macho," formerly all-male college which is now over 40 percent female. A coeducational institution which still keeps "Men of Dartmouth" as its institutional song. A college about which a young woman student recently commented, "I went to an all-girls boarding school, and I never once felt like a second-class citizen until I came here."

It may take directions I have not yet thought of. For my new space is one of reflection, not of relentless, brain-pounding, production.

Conventional wisdom says I should keep this column space weekly. It's the prime spot in the most-read Sunday section in the Rocky Mountain West. I dreamed of this space, fought for this space. The great competitive ethic says I should hold onto this space each week. In fact, everything out there says I should hang tight to this space — Sunday after Sunday. Except my gut.

So I'm letting it go.

Thanks for your continuing feedback.

And watch for me once a month.

AGING:
I Worked Hard for That Wrinkle!

Middle Aging
A Sense of Ambivalence

Denver Post
APRIL 15, 1984

YESTERDAY I CLIPPED A WASHINGTON POST article by Myra Macpherson called, "There's Life in the Old Girls Yet." As I filed it in my folder entitled, "Aging," I noted that the yellowed clippings on the subject were doing just that — aging! Obviously for three, four, no — five, years, I've avoided writing about the topic. Enough procrastination. Today's the day. But aging is only part of the issue. If I were allowed to headline my own columns, perhaps this one would be called "The ambivalence of *middle*-aging."

The fact is I resent this "middle aging!" Resent that if I don't exercise 30 minutes every day, rain or shine, *one* day of skiing will render every muscle sore. Resent that my voice echoes my father's when he was my age and said, "Why don't they make books with big print anymore?" Resent that I can gain twice as much weight eating half as much as I did at half my age.

Resent that as I approach 47, I must keep to an almost religious regime of "moderation." One drink too many and the disposition pays. One heavily chocolated dessert or caffeinated cappuccino and the sleep pays. When the sleep pays, the face pays: Little half-moons under the eyes droop to milk-saucer size.

A friend of mine, most attractive in her late 40s, told a story of rummaging in her mirror-bottomed jewelry box for an earring: "Suddenly, I saw that my face was falling. No, *not* falling. Cheeks, chin, and forehead were actually *plunging* toward the mirror. Forget the earring! I made a vow never to lean over my desk, or anything else, if anyone was looking!"

The expense, time and effort it takes to shore up the falling face, to blush on the sunburn (which I now assiduously avoid getting from the sun), to camouflage the darkening indentations in the corners of the eyes irritate me. The whole procedure feels demeaning, anti-feminist. Worst yet, it's boring!

Most of the fraying clippings in my file suggest that the youth worshipping American culture is neurotic in its adulation of thighs without "wibble-wobbles" and unwrinkled faces with only one chin. The column I originally intended to write on aging would preach *against* the pursuit of youth and *for* the enjoyment of a mellowing middle age.

And there are distinct advantages to middle age: When my daughter says my shoes aren't "with it" and my prized designer jeans are now "out of it," only a small part of me takes offense. The other part, the mellowing part, breathes a sigh of relief. How liberating to be past the age of ever again having to compete with "teeny-boppers" or even mid-twenties boppers.

The mellowing part, at times, even yearns toward the mid-century birthday. According to author Madeleine L'Engle, a woman at 50 finally is free to be an eccentric if she pleases. Perhaps in three years I'll take to wearing wild hats with purple plumes, black leather gaucho pants and long chains of jewelry that hang to the waist. Or perhaps, I'll let all the artifice drop and just be *me*. Plain and natural. We'll see.

Journalist Barbara Varro writes: Some middle aged women "aren't secure enough to acknowledge they have a few miles on them. So what if they have wrinkles; they also have a special brand of savvy that comes from having experienced, and survived, the peaks and valleys of life."

I'd like to include myself in that savvy group, yet …

Yesterday, I got my first modest royalty check from the sale of my book, "Second Banana." When my husband asked me what I was going to do with it, I replied, "I don't know — perhaps I'll start a future face-lift fund."

Do I mean it? I don't know. "An over-40 feminist contemplates a face-lift with the same ambivalence with which an environmentalist with bugs in his garden eyes a can of DDT," writes New York Times columnist Mary-Lou Weisman. "Such embarrassing encounters with hypocrisy, such uncomfortable moments of truth are visited upon the passionately committed with awful frequency." She is speaking right to me.

"The more I age, the more sights I want to see, the more articles I want to write, the more mountains I want to climb. Clearly, there's life in this old girl yet!"

Another author writes a descriptive paragraph about a social gathering of variously aged females: "The really older women were more attractive than the middle-aged ones. The older women weren't trying so hard to look young and had the sense to finally accept themselves."

The more I age, the more sights I want to see, the more articles I want to write, the more mountains I want to climb.

Clearly, there's life in this old girl yet!

Life, yes. *Sense?* I'm not so sure.

Minding Elders
With Luck, We'll All Grow Old

Denver Post
MAY 27, 1984

TODAY IS THE DAY OF THE OLDER AMERICAN'S Day parade. I'm glad the organizers are calling themselves Older Americans!

As the sheer number of the old grows larger — 13 percent of the population will be over 65 in the year 2000 — the cult of youth is dissipating.

Some oldsters are ahead of the demographic curve in their upbeat attitudes. They reveal both acceptance and pride in their age. In a Rocky Mountain News article, Alfred R. Zipster, retired newspaper reporter and public relations executive, disdains his contemporaries who downplay their years.

"What baffles me is the oldster who states triumphantly:

'You're only as old as you feel.'

Nonsense!

You are, of course, as old as you are. And one of the tricks of old age is to face it squarely. Few of us have mastered that trick. Instead, we indulge ourselves in dreams and delusions."

Zipster, 63, castigates those who resort to the euphemism "senior citizen."

"I have yet to see people under 55 referred to as 'junior citizens,'" he writes.

He also takes a swipe at those junior citizens nearing 50, who call themselves "middle-aged,"

rather than "older-aged," when the actual mid-life point is now 35 for men and 39 for women. "It's comforting to know they will live to be 100," he writes.

Another oldster, a Denver woman of 87, sends a letter that gently chides me for the column in which I expressed my ambivalence about "middle aging." After outlining her day's activities, which begin at 5:30 a.m. with 20 minutes of exercise, she closes:

"So I say to you, stiffen your courage. Life is not over at 50, but challenging and interesting, even though at times tiring."

A quick look at the history books reveals that for certain oldsters, age, experience and energy combine to make old age not only challenging and interesting, but productive and awe inspiring. For example:

Winston Churchill, at 65, became prime minister of Great Britain and inspired that country to victory in World War II.

Cervantes, at 68, completed what many believe to be the greatest novel of all time, "Don Quixote."

Galileo did his most important work in his 70s.

Clara Barton, founder of the Red Cross, continued to work 14 hours a day until the age of 90.

Suddenly it occurs to me why the word "old" is pejorative. It's not the fact that one is *old* that's the problem, but the insinuation that "one is old, *therefore* …

Therefore, one is senile.

Therefore, one is deteriorated.

Therefore, one is incompetent.

Therefore, one is out of touch.

Therefore, one has no contribution to make."

Zipster admits that a "tiny minority" of old people may exhibit some parts or all of this sad profile, but the "vast majority" do not. Growing old means slowing down, mentally and physically, but slowing down is not stopping.

Yet, those stereotypical "therefores" do exist!

A few weeks ago, I personally experienced this stereotyping when, for the first time, that syrupy condescending voice that the very young reserve for the old was applied to *me*!

Out to dinner at a ski area restaurant with seven women, all but one my age (47) or older, the waitress — who looked 17, but was probably 27 — approached our table, gushing sweetly, "Oh — ladies' night out?" She didn't add "How quaint," but she might have. The back of my neck prickled. Her attitude clearly said, "you are old …."

Therefore, you shall be treated gently and probably served slowly.

Therefore, this must be your one night a year of innocent and genteel fun; life away from equally aging husbands.

I wanted to tell her the truth — that some of us could have skied circles around her that day; that all of us were engaged in a much more active social life than this "genteel" dinner represented.

I wanted to tell her a lie — that the *real* purpose of our outing was to pick up younger men; that we would drink ourselves under the table, and that if she didn't watch out, she'd still be waiting on us at 2 in the morning. Anything to wipe that condescending smile off her face!

I'll be only 63 by the year 2000 but, in spite of the pejorative "therefores," I'm clearly beginning to identify with the oldsters.

Perhaps, by then, being old will be so "in," I'll lie about my age — *upward*! In the meantime, a word of advice for all you junior citizens.

Call old people what they are: older Americans.

And treat them with what they deserve: individuality and respect.

The Big Five-O
New Sense of Power Defeats Depression

Denver Post
JUNE 7, 1987

BY THE TIME THIS COLUMN APPEARS I WILL HAVE hit the big "Five O." Today, reaching the half-century mark feels OK, even liberating. A month ago it didn't.

I had just had my hair frosted but somehow, on a visit to the West Coast, the California air turned the blonde gray. At first I didn't feel any older, but to others, it was clear that I had aged:

"I used to know you when you were young," said the friend of my mother's at the church in which I grew up.

Young? I thought, puzzled. I don't know this person from my childhood. I probably first met him 10 years ago … but, of course! I realized with a sense of shock. That's exactly what this man of indeterminate age and questionable manners meant:

Forty equals "Young."

Fifty equals "No-Longer-Young."

A cloud of depression hung over my head for the rest of the day. Dumb! I chastised myself: You are being childishly trivial. Overly sensitive. Vain. And stupid. Where, in heaven's name, are the seeds of that serene, unflappable woman you hope to become? Can one unflattering comment disperse them to the Bay-area winds?

Self-berating did nothing to budge me from my mood. So I tried self-encouragement: What's the matter with you anyway? Don't you still have the slim body of an athletic 39-year-old? Isn't your metabolism more resilient than most people your age? So, bug off, Father Time!

But none of it worked. What I later realized was that I was coming up against my own prejudice about aging. For years, when I met an older friend who suddenly appeared *much* older than the last time I had seen her, I would feel sad, slightly repelled. I would mourn for her youth.

I might even discount her wisdom.

"What can she know about people 'my age,'" I would wonder. And then be ashamed of myself for being "ageist," for playing right into the hands of the media-inspired youth cult.

During the next two days, I found myself being discounted as I had discounted others. It seemed that my "gray" hair was rendering me invisible, at least to strangers. Overnight, I was more likely to be spoken of as if I weren't there.

Was I becoming paranoid? Was my own feeling of decreased worth promoting the discounting reaction? I don't know. I do know that Gloria Steinem once said that "man-power," both real and perceived, increased with age. "Woman-power," on the other hand, decreases with age.

But all of that is only one side of the aging coin.

For this week the coin flipped over and I don't experience that loss of power. Instead I experience

> *"It seemed that my 'gray' hair was rendering me invisible."*

a special growing, integrated, distinctly feminine power. So much so that when a Dartmouth student told me she was glad I had led their women's club discussion group because "an older woman can really help us focus on our lives," I didn't feel depressed, I felt proud.

That's the good news about aging, at least my aging.

The other good news is ENERGY. I may get longer jet lag than I did as a flight attendant, but my day-to-day energy level is three times what it was when I was young and my kids were younger. "Ankle-biters" take bigger chunks out of maternal "energy banks" than they ever did out of anyone's ankles.

The further good news is **assertiveness**. As I turn 50 I speak my mind with fewer self-effacing gestures. I care less what people think. And although my body has not yet taken to wearing weird hats and walking barefoot in the rain, my spirit is doing just that.

Barbara Lazear Ascher writes that as you approach middle age, you "become the person you always were" and that the person you always were, if you are female, is likely to resemble your mother.

Some women would scream and run at the thought of "becoming like their mothers." Yet to me, the thought comforts. My mother is one whose deep caring and sensitivity continue to affect the hundreds of lives close to her in nourishing, positive ways. At 78 she is a role model for aging gracefully.

The Denver Post / Maureen Scance

And I have other inspiring models I will try to incorporate into my own old age: cross-country skiers in their 70s, political activists in their 80s, great thinkers in their 90s.

"You have to decide early on what kind of older woman you want to be," said my friend, the late Jessica Luna, who died of cancer in her early 40s.

And I'm deciding, and its exhilarating! God willing, and health holding, I am lucky to be growing old in 1980s America. For if I had contracted breast cancer a generation ago, I, too, might have been dead in my early 40s.

In short, as George Burns once said, "Getting older ain't all that bad when you look at the alternative."

So, yes I like growing older.

Even though I'd still like to *look* younger.

Does this duality of feeling signal an irreconcilable personality split?

Nope. As a Gemini, I've been reconciling a "split personality" for 50 years.

Midlife
Women Feel Joy at Accomplishments

Denver Post
AUGUST 6, 1989

O N A WARM DAY LAST SPRING I FOUND MYSELF, car window rolled down, singing at the top of voice to the tune of some ditsy 1950s song, playing full blast on the radio.

It was a joyous day, but a perfectly normal day. Nothing to be particularly thrilled about, nothing to be down about. Yet I was inexplicably "up."

This wind of well-being blows more and more lately. Now, age 52, I compare this gentle breeze with the unkind winds of youth.

In the old days, when I was "thirtysomething" — raising young children and trying to make political and career ends meet — then, given a day in which there was nothing tangible to rejoice about, a dulled angst would push against my precarious state of well-being and an ache would rise in my throat.

"This wind of well-being blows more and more lately."

Today, in the absence of anything specific to depress or worry, a joy rushes in instead.

New York Times columnist Margaret Morganroth Gullette calls this phenomenon "midlife exhilaration." She sees it all around her. And I see it all around me, despite the practical problems of being a member of the "sandwich generation."

Women friends of mine, saddled with tuition for their college kids or almost homebound by an aging parent, don't call to complain. They call in excitement about some new project they are starting, some weekend off they are going to take. There is little angst and even less guilt. They are not neglecting their "duties" or their loved ones, but neither are they going to neglect themselves.

Gullette feels feminism has something to do with this womanly feeling of radiance in midlife: "As young women, many of us were underemployed in one way of another: dithering or uncertain, punching our time cards until midlife self-discovery … feminism … like Mother Time, lured us forward, cajoling, 'Have patience, it will come.'"

By our society's standards, we women have more power in our youth than we do at any other time. And this power is measured by our beauty and our ability (and willingness) to reproduce.

We lose that youthful beauty and that reproductive capacity as we age. And there's not a thing we can do about it!

I know, I know. Some of us have our first child at 43. Others of us, with the help of an exercise class here, a cosmetic tuck there, and the new heartily heralded Retin-A, can manage to pass for 39 when we're 49, etc.

But look up close. The bad news is that real youth has fled, whether the tummy is ballooned by pregnancy or "tucked" by surgery.

The good news is that it doesn't matter as much as we thought it would.

Since we have lost the "power" assigned to us, we can at last become what we want. And as we

The Denver Post / Maureen Scance

become what we want, we become truly powerful. Like a kid we have nurtured, we have to let it go to let it grow.

Not all middle-aged women attain this peace and confidence, of course. Some are so bogged down with the nitty gritty of poverty or day-to-day survival that they could never think of themselves as "dithering" when young or "radiant" when older.

But those of us who have the luxury of introspection can use this luxury to understand more about other women, not less. And to give them a boost.

"I knew well enough I was counted among the lucky ones," writes Gullette about her young motherhood days — middle class, married, white, one child, working on an advanced degree with a husband who "helped" — "But then, why did I feel so little and mean and finished?"

Why?

Perhaps because "happiness" was "assigned" to her as a status symbol along with beauty and marriage and motherhood. Any woman who, in her youth, exhibited even *some* of these "power achievements" was considered "crazy" if she was not happy all the time. (Was this designation of "craziness" a prefeminist way to keep her quiet and "in her place"?)

But who, in any stage of life, is happy all the time? The Declaration of Independence guarantees us the *pursuit* of happiness, not its constant presence.

Conversely, at middle age, since we no longer feel failed and freakish if we are not happy all the time, we are happy. And what about this new-found exhilaration? What can we do with its energy?

First, as Gullette suggests, we can change the strong countercurrents in our culture that still deplore aging, especially in women:

"We look good to one another. We earned these wise smiles, these capable hands, this air of competence … we're admiring our age because it's a part of us, whom we like so much better than we ever thought possible in the bad old days."

Sooner or later we'll persuade the world to view us in this new high-powered way we view ourselves.

This doesn't mean we become superpositive Pollyannas. Or that we spend the rest of our lives driving around town singing at the top of our voices and embarrassing any adolescents who have not yet voided the nest.

No ma'am! The World awaits our joy and our talents. As Gullette writes: "Our youth was pinned down by too many minute strings. Now that we're out of the house and standing up to the world, the world looks interesting, lousy and challenging, all at once. For people who think like this, what's the next task we are going to take on together?"

Should we start with the ozone layer?

Coming to Terms with 80

Aurora Sentinel
June 16, 2017

I approach my 80th birthday as I write.

Yet, when I try to come to terms with this event — How did I get here? What have I accomplished and what have I lost? What do I do with the time I have left? — the lives and losses of others keep intruding.

For example, Denver Holocaust survivor Jack Adler. I stand in awe as I listen to Adler's CPR interview with Ryan Warner: Adler, 88, celebrates two birthdays, the first in 1929 when he was born, the second in 1945, when he was liberated from Dachau by the United States Army. The only Holocaust survivor of his family, Adler spends much of his life educating others about the Holocaust at schools and military bases.

Then I am reminded of the personal friend whose adult son just died in a foreign country. An unspeakable horror. And, of course, there are the ever-presenting sorrows of compatriots my own age whose spouses are declining or dying, their own heath and abilities fading.

One woman, age 90, recently moved to assisted living with her husband, age 91. She could have stayed in their Senior Center apartment and simply visited him there, but she did not. "I have slept with this man for 60 years," she says with fierce loyalty and determination. "I'm not going to stop now!"

Just today, Denver artist and tennis champion Mark Luna honored me with a painting of his, paying tribute to his mother, the late Jessica Martinez Luna, a feminist "sister" of mine in the mid-1970s.

I visited Jessica regularly in 1982 when I was recovering from breast cancer and she was dying of another cancer at age 46. Her favorite topics: Sex, power and politics. What would Jessica's life have been like if she had lived? Somehow I see her marching with me in the Washington D.C. Women's March Jan. 21. No doubt she would be waving a colorful "anti-Trump" sign, yelling unprintable epithets, but laughing while doing it.

How do I dare compare my 80-year-old life and challenges with any of these who now parade before me, some facing new issues as they age? Others living, or having lived, lives full of loss or trauma, or not lived at all?

"You live a charmed life," said my best Colorado friend when we were still in our late 40s. She said it kindly, but I became defensive. After all, I had been devastated by the sudden death of my 60-year-old father, laid low by post partum depression, both when in my 30s, then scared witless by breast cancer when I was 44. Didn't sound "charmed" to me.

But more than 30 years later, I do live a charmed — perhaps blessed — life. And I am grateful, knowing full well that trauma, loss and heartbreak could come at any moment. So, why does it matter if only half of my political and professional goals have been realized? That creaky knees and minor ailments increasingly assault my flexibility and energy?

Being a Gemini, will my dominant Type-A "twin" call me toward continued engagement to make the world a better place, or will the recessive, pleasure seeking "twin" simply tell me to enjoy the world as it is?

Suddenly, another late, great friend pops up in my mind. It's Sue O'Brien, my former editor and mentor at the *Denver Post*, who died at age 64, in 2003, of colon cancer. "Get your butt in gear, Lamm!" O'Brien says. "You're lucky to have more healthy years, so use them!" Yup, that's the way I was leaning, but I needed a shove.

At least for a while, however, I will indulge in my blessings — my partner in a 54-year marriage still filled with love and laughter, a sister to whom I am as close as our late mother could have dreamed, two grown children and their spouses all of whom are better parents than we were, four "perfect" grandkids — and just "kick back" with that fabulous family.

And with my friends! Friends, always there for me, whom I neglected dreadfully through the intense years of political strivings and career yearnings. Friends, some of whom presently need me more than the world does; others whom I just want to grab a lunch, a beer, or a coffee with — right now, while there's still time.

> *"I do live a charmed— perhaps blessed—life. And I am grateful, knowing full well that trauma, loss and heartbreak could come at any moment."*

LOOKING BACK, MOVING FORWARD:
Thriving and Surviving Right through to the Wedding

Class of '59
The Best of Times and the Worst of Times

Denver Post
JULY 15, 1984

THE SILENT GENERATION. THE PASSIVE generation. My generation.

Ever since I returned from my class of '59 college reunion, I've been consuming literature on the 1950s, hungry to absorb what passed me by at the time. For at Occidental College, in the years of '55 to '59, my class, indeed, lived up to its stereotype of silence.

Yet, what astounds me as I read is not so much how we failed to make ourselves heard, but that we also failed to hear. Not everything, of course. The big events did penetrate the collegiate aura of self-absorption. I do recall being aware of:

- President Eisenhower's heart attack, September, 1955.
- Grace Kelly's wedding, April, 1956.
- Eisenhower's resounding re-election, November, 1956.
- The ordering of the National Guard to Little Rock, Ark., September, 1957.
- The Soviet launching of the space satellite, Sputnik, October, 1957.
- Angry Venezuelan mobs attacking Vice President Nixon's car in Caracas, May, 1958.
- Castro's takeover of Cuba, January, 1959.

Though each of these events roused me and my classmates momentarily from our pursuit of the good grades and the good life, none, with the exception of Grace Kelly's wedding, generated any heated discussion that I can remember.

And other significant events evaded us completely:

When, in December of 1955, a 42-year-old black woman named Rosa Parks refused to give up her bus seat to a white man in Montgomery, Ala., Eldridge Cleaver wrote: "Somewhere in the universe a gear in the machinery had shifted." But no one I knew felt the shift.

When Occidental guest anthropology lecturer Margaret Mead cautioned the women of our generation that "eternal happiness could not be found through piling five kids into a station wagon," she was ignored.

And when Redbook magazine published an article in 1956 entitled, "Why Young Mothers Feel Trapped," no one I knew read it (although 24,000 young 1950s mothers, only slightly older than ourselves, responded in letters to Redbook

194

with their own "trapped" feelings). The tiny seeds of the women's movement were being sown, but not in the dry Southern California soil that my friends and I trod.

The seeds of the anti-nuclear movement also were being sown. In August of 1958, a group of scientists debating the threat of nuclear fallout agreed that the bones of all Americans could be affected to some extent by any nuclear explosion anywhere on earth. Historian William Manchester wrote of that meeting, yet no one I knew was aware of its significance.

"Other directed Americans" is what sociologist David Reisman called us, meaning not that we were directed charitably *toward* others, but that we were directed *by* others and their opinions of us. The supreme accolade of the '50s was to be called "well-adjusted." And well-adjusted was not to question too loudly or even to perceive too sharply.

Economist John Kenneth Galbraith chastised the whole adult establishment for its conformity:

"… these are the days when men of all social disciplines and all political faiths seek the comfortable and the accepted; when controversy is looked upon as a disturbing influence; when originality is taken to be a mark of instability; and when, in minor modification of the scriptural parable, the bland lead the bland."

The bland are no longer bland. The '50s passed. Our generation came of age. Some of us were radicalized, and all of us were modified, by the revolutionary '60s, the introspective '70s; our individual consciousness further raised by employment, sex discrimination, marriage, children, careers, divorce, remarriage, the no longer expanding economy, the empty nest and midlife reevaluation.

Yet, when those 130 class-of-'59 adults came together at our reunion, most of us took on the characteristics of our old selves. We were languid, laid back, unintense, and for a full two-and-a-half days did not read the paper or discuss world events.

"What astounds … is not so much how we failed to make ourselves heard, but that we also failed to hear."

And in view of the case I've built in this column, I suppose I should say it was boring, degenerate, even immoral to regress to such a stage. But, it wasn't. For 60 hours, it was *wonderful!*

Quote: *"… I cannot wish I had been nurtured in a different place. It was the only garden I knew."*

— Susan Allen Toth

20 Years of Growth Pains
Haven't Dulled the Luster

Denver Post
AUGUST 20, 1979

AUGUST 20, 1959. I SIT UPRIGHT, WIDE AWAKE 15 minutes before the alarm goes off. I hug my knees, think of my good fortune, and look out the window of the small motel near Stapleton Airport. No smog obstructs the front range; Pikes Peak to the south and Longs Peak to the north are equally as visible as Mount Evans in the center. Denver, Colorado! And I expected to have been sent to some obscure, humid city in the East.

August 20, 1959. Today our small class of United stewardesses, trained in the old World War II barracks in Cheyenne, Wyo., will be graduated in a ceremony at the Brown Palace Hotel. We will receive our wings, kiss our fathers (the only man a stewardess in uniform was then allowed to kiss) and have our pictures taken in the arcade that connects the new Brown to the old Brown.

Twenty years ago. What else was different beside the continual abundance of clean air? The memories of that August have inspired me to look for comparisons, think about the city and do a little research.

I start in the archives of The Denver Post. Twenty years ago, I must have searched the classified sections of those same August papers, looking for apartments in east Denver. Yet, today I discover that the most impressive local news items of 20 years ago had eluded my attention completely.

For instance: 1959 was another "Centennial" year. Downtown, much of Denver's citizenry had dressed in clothes typical of the Gold Rush era and celebrated the 1859 "Rush to the Rockies." On the eve of Colorado Day, to initiate the monthlong series of events, every light in the downtown office buildings had been turned on. No one had protested.

Smog, energy crisis, and auto congestion were uncoined thoughts. By September 1959, I cheerfully had helped keep up the one car per two persons ratio, as I borrowed $300 from my parents and bought a 1949 Chevy.

Twenty years ago, the Eastern Slope and the Western Slope were continuing their historic wrangling over Colorado's scarce water. Yet, circles, triangles, and squares still were only geometric forms. They had yet to become the symbols which now govern the lawns, lives, and vacation plans of every Denver homeowner.

August 1959. It had been less than a year since social leader Edna Boettcher had given her last dinner party at 400 E. Eighth Avenue and succumbed to a stroke. Yet, the process already had begun to raze the Boettcher Mansion and auction its historic contents.

The Boettcher Foundation had generously offered the property to the state for a governor's residence, but the Legislature balked. Gov. Steve McNichols was yet to save the mansion on the last day of 1959 with his famous statement, "Not to accept it violates my good sense of business. It's a good deal."

Secure in my own "traditional woman's job" and feeling lucky to be earning $290 per month plus travel benefits, I must have missed or passed over the following Post item:

"Woman Police Detective Demoted" read the headline. The story concerned Det. Doris Shelley, divorced mother of an 8-year-old daughter. Mrs. Shelley was described by male detectives as an "able investigator and an outstanding interrogator," yet she was demoted back to the rank of policewoman. Reason: The City Attorney's office claimed that "the charter makes no provision for women detectives."

Twenty years later, touched and curious, I locate Mrs. Shelley (now retired) by phone. She is pleasant and philosophical:

"I was re-promoted in 1963, but the demotion was still a sore point then. Of course, I felt the same way any woman would today. But in those days there wasn't much you could do. After all, it was 1959."

1959. Denver University still had a football team, but the word bronco referred only to a bucking horse. The population of the entire metro area was still under 1 million. One could ski at Loveland Basin for $3.50 a day and at city-owned Winter Park for even less. The tallest structure in downtown Denver was the First National Bank building. The average home sold for $13,000, fresh cantaloupe for 10 cents a pound, and gas for 33 cents a gallon.

1959. Denver worried about how to become bigger and better. By 1969, its residents were worrying about whether it would suffer as the suburbs grew in comparison. Yet, recent statistics have shown that the white flight was slight; that it was more likely the declining birthrate which lowered the enrollment in the Denver Public Schools.

1979. Denver no longer faces the fear that the city will become old, poor and underpopulated. Instead, its residents worry about whether the poor and even the middle-class can afford to live in the inner city. Can Denver survive with its historic integrity the money and people that the energy boom is expected to bring?

1979. The Denver Police Department, like most public agencies and private businesses, has at least a few women at every level. Although the car per capita is up to two cars per three people, ridership on public transportation multiplies monthly, and bicycles are everywhere.

1979. A suburban man writes the Rocky Mountain News with vitriolic hatred of the core city. He owes Denver nothing, he claims, and as far as he is concerned it can "fold up and fall into the Platte." He owes it nothing except his suburban existence. Without Denver, he wouldn't even have the choice of living in a surrounding area.

August 20, 1979. Denver with all its problems. Yet, I still hug my knees and think of my good fortune. One might say of the city of Denver what has been said of the system of democracy. "It's not a perfect city, just the best one we've got."

Joy at Existence of Other People

Denver Post
November 2, 1981

I WAS EIGHT THE YEAR MY FATHER AND I WENT TO climb the cliffs of the New Jersey Palisades across the Hudson River from our apartment in Riverdale, New York. We carried a small metal camping mirror. At exactly noon we would shine the mirror back over the Hudson River and my mother and sister would signal us back with another mirror from the fourth floor window of our apartment.

As their tiny mirror twinkled across the miles in the Hudson haze, my imagination ran wild! Suppose everyone in every apartment window had shined a mirror? I could visualize the sultry day lit up in a horizontal stream of stars along the river. Every apartment window! Think how many families lived in those apartments thinking their thoughts and living their lives. And if there were that many families along the Hudson, how many in New York? In the United States? In the world?

"What are you daydreaming about?" my father asked as I stood there staring, even though the twinkle had long since disappeared.

"Nothing," I said, as I usually did when asked about daydreams. Besides, how could I explain my sudden insight — that I was a part of all people — even people I would never know, and perhaps wouldn't like — and that this belonging made me feel warm and closer to God than anything I had ever heard in Sunday School?

The humanity insight. The person awareness — that part of a whole. The simple joy at the mere existence of other people. Since that year of my awakening, I've found many others who share the same awareness. "Ontology" is what Madeleine L'Engle terms it, as she describes the moment from her own childhood:

"... I was seven or eight years old. We lived in an apartment on East 82nd Street in New York. My bedroom window looked out on the court, and I could see into the apartments across the way. One evening when I was looking out I saw a woman undressing by her open window. She took off her dress, stretched, stood there in her slip, not moving, not doing anything, just standing there being.

"And that was my moment of awareness; that woman across the court who did not know me, and whom I did not know, was a person. She had thoughts of her own. She *was*. Our lives would never touch. I would never know her name. And, yet, it was she who revealed to me my first glimpse of personhood."

I find myself experiencing this sense of ontology when I look upon a city from afar; I feel it when I watch a happy family that does not know it is being watched in a restaurant; I sense it on the trails of the Rockies, on the bustling streets of New York, the public school yards of Denver at lunch time.

But there are times when I lose it. Once was in India in 1967. The pavement swelled and seemed to rise with the stifling heat. The beggars, the sellers, the tourists swarmed among the bodies — some sleeping, some sick — that lay on the streets of Calcutta.

The suffering was appalling. Every afternoon a shade of weariness lowered my eyelids, and I would almost run back to the hotel room, not having the energy to come out and deal with the "sights" again 'til the next day.

Aghast at the way the upper caste Indians would simply step over the bodies of the ill and dying, my husband and I were unkind and cutting about those who would approach him as a public official, mistaking him for congressman, hoping he would find a way for them to emigrate to the United States.

Yet, as we extended our stay there, we became more aghast at something else: Ourselves. Slowly, we, too, were becoming like the upper caste Indians — stepping over the dying and the ill, deftly, swiftly, as we proceeded on our way to view market places and historical monuments.

How quickly we learned to divorce ourselves from their misery. One hungry person is possible to help; a hungry society is beyond individual efforts, and the mind numbs to the enormity of the suffering. The scene was so overwhelming — one had to divorce one's self in order to survive, to stay psychologically intact.

It is this self-protective reaction that comes back to me when I read of the burgeoning populations in undeveloped countries — the 600 million of India, the billion plus in China, the 3 percent a year increase in Latin America. When I hear on the national news that Mexico alone will double from 70 million to 140 million shortly after the year 2000, I worry about the starving poor, the infant mortality rate, and the potential revolution of the "have-not's."

But I worry also about the "haves." All people need counterpoint: a balance between closeness and space to appreciate humanity. The ying and yang of existence is both embracing and standing apart.

"Once we lose that childlike awe in the mere existence of other people—the easier it becomes to 'step over the bodies.'"

As crowds increase on any continent, it's not just the bodies of the dying, but the souls of the living that may wither. Once we lose that childlike awe in the mere existence of other people — the easier it becomes to "step over the bodies." And once we shut our eyes to take that first step, the chasm between compassion and crass disregard yawns irretrievably. Thus, all humanity is threatened.

Visualization Aids Recovery

Denver Post
NOVEMBER 1, 1983

ONE OF THE BOOKS I READ IN THE HOSPITAL while recovering from breast cancer surgery was "Getting Well Again," by Carl and Stephanie Simonton. The book convinced me that the process of "visualization" was a technique I could incorporate in my recovery.

According to the Simontons, the patient should visualize an animal: a tiger, a wolf, a piranha, anything capable of viciousness. The imagined animal then is mentally engaged into service as a health-aid and a friend. When the person meditates, the animal (or a swarm of them) is visualized charging through the bloodstream, gobbling up, tearing apart, and destroying the cancer cells.

Stimulated by the thought of engaging in such a process for my own healing, my imagination ran wild. But what animal to choose? For two nights I considered and rejected various animals for various reasons — too large, too ugly, too lumpy, etc. None seemed to suit me, until finally, out of the forest of my thoughts sprang a silver fox. I slept.

A surprising gift

The next day I had an unannounced visit from an old friend I had seen only rarely since my flight attendant days. He came early and did not

> *"Finally, out of the forest of my thoughts sprang a silver fox."*

stay long. We did not talk of illness or visualizations. On departing, he left me a small gift. "Just something I wanted you to have," he said as he disappeared down the corridor.

I reclined on the hospital bed and gingerly took off the wrapping. There in my hand was a small pewter box with a slender fox carved delicately on the cover.

Stunned at the seeming coincidence of my unspoken choice and my friend's gift, I called my sister to reflect.

"That's the outward confirmation of an inner symbol," she said excitedly. "You've clearly found your animal!"

"It's what Jungians call an irrational or a casual synchronicity," said a Jungian therapist, who visited me the next day.

Later that week I had a long phone conversation with Marilyn Ferguson, author of "The Aquarian Conspiracy."

"You'll find you will have more of those synchronistic experiences as you open yourself to them," she said. Hmmmm. Did I need to get sick to open my spirit to such phenomena? Maybe. Yet, they have happened with more frequency as I have become well.

"These synchronicity things will come up in clusters," said Dr. Martin Rossman, a physician-lecturer at a health-wellness conference I attended last fall. And that very weekend I was presented with three seemingly "coincidental" pairs of happenings.

One speaker, Dr. Ashley Montague, noted anthropologist and social biologist spoke of the significance of human touch, particularly skin stimulation, in human development. He emphasized the need of children for such physical nurturing. I believed him; I'd read the infant studies before. But for older children? Mine, if anything, were physically avoiding me, in fact, pulling away.

Unexpected welcome

I was pondering this as I came home and climbed the stairs when the door of my daughter's room flew open. "Mom," she yelled. "I'm glad you're home — I really need a backrub!"

Saturday, I went to the conference grumbling. My husband and I growled at each other that morning and I was still tense. Tense, but right, I told myself. Right! Now if only he could see how right I was.

"Some people would rather be right than happy," said the first speaker, Dr. Gerald Piaget. "If we are always so invested in being right, we may even modify data to fit our own perceptions. Thus, we never get beyond the fray." Yes.

Sunday, my conference workshop was titled, "Enhancing Self-confidence, Self-knowledge and Individual Choice." That night, my husband and I went out to dinner at a small Oriental restaurant. As we discussed the synchronicity phenomena and their possible implications, I broke open my fortune cookie. Its message read: "Reaffirm belief in yourself — know your own feelings, and do as you want."

"Having It All" in a New Light

Denver Post
OCTOBER 9, 1984

LAST SPRING I WROTE A COLUMN ENCOURAGING young people, particularly young women, to assume they "could have it all" — love, marriage, children, career success — at least over the process of a lifetime.

"Maybe you can't have it all, *all at once*," I wrote.

But you can "have it all" — eventually — if you make certain priorities at certain life periods, plan efficiently and work hard.

A month later my message was validated by a graduation speech by Joan Bennett Kennedy, in which she told the seniors at Manhattanville College in Purchase, N.Y.:

"The most important thing I can share with you is the personal knowledge that decisions are not irrevocable, that choices do come back, sometimes in different forms and different ways, but they can be remade. And there is time, time to shape a balance between family and friends, work and career …."

Then a friend came to visit. This friend is a soulmate, a person often on my "wave length," supportive of my work. But with this column, she disagreed strongly. Or, at least, she disagreed with the Pollyanna tone of my injunctive.

Never again

"Sometimes we have to make painful choices — not just priorities," she said. "And sometimes, those choices exclude whole areas of potential. And for some of them, there will be no second chance."

This friend — a teacher, counselor, and theology school student — cited her own decision not to bear children. "That is something one cannot go back to and rethink after a certain age. The reproductive cycle doesn't come around again."

She also pointed to the career-ambitious "Kramer vs. Kramer"-type father who decides to take custody and full charge of his children, without relying on a housekeeper or other surrogate. When this man climbs off the fast track at work, he may not be able to climb back on it later. And he knows it.

"There are *some* positives about all this," continued my friend. "I can't tell you the other possibilities that were freed up once I made the painful but irrevocable choice not to have children. Suddenly, all energy tied up in keeping that option open, and in balancing the other potential options, was free to go somewhere else!

"Getting older means saying no to some choices, grieving for them, and going on. It means going deeper instead of broader. It means — instead of panic about not doing it all — the realization and acceptance that you're not going to do it all, and that's OK."

> *"In saying 'no' to that career choice at that age, I shut the door that would not open again."*

Redirected

Another friend tells of two major childhood ambitions which were thwarted: to swim the English Channel and to ride in the Kentucky Derby. She did neither, but instead went into tennis "with a vengeance," winning all the trophies she needed to indulge her competitive spirit and release her enormous physical energy.

And maybe this is what Kennedy means when she says the decisions are "not irrevocable, that choices do come back, sometimes in different forms and different ways." In short, one puts that specific goal energy into a different area of achievement.

But perhaps I become Pollyanna again. Some choices *are* painfully permanent. I made one myself in graduate school when, at the age of 30, I decided not to pursue a career in child psychoanalysis because of the time the intensive training would take away from my family. In retrospect, I'm glad that "analytical" energy went elsewhere. But, in saying "no" to that career choice at that age, I shut the door that would not open again. And I knew it.

And perhaps the very young are aware at some subconscious level that the wide-open fling of one door may shut another with a bang. That's why they want to "have it all" — right now, quickly — before age closes in and opportunity narrows. That's why they anguish over each choice. That's why each decision can seem so crucial, so irrevocable.

It just might be.

Prejudice
A Slap in Anyone's Face

Denver Post
August 25, 1985

WHEN I RETURNED FROM A TRIP TO ISRAEL in 1979, a friend asked me if I had felt "different" there. I thought a minute, answered in the negative, then asked her why she'd asked.

"Because everyone is Jewish!" laughed my friend, who is Jewish. She then explained how wonderfully ordinary she had felt when she was in Israel, for the first time in her life part of a country's majority rather than part of a minority.

Black writer Nell Ervin Painter expresses the same sense of reclaimed majority and ordinariness in an article she wrote about living in Ghana in the mid-'60s:

"In Ghana, I became just a woman. I let down my burden of responsibility to the 400 million people of African descent …. I was free to enjoy myself and become something I have often missed intensely in the years since I came home — ordinary."

Many of us American White Anglo-Saxon Protestants carry the delusion of our majority status with us, even though we WASPs are in fact less than 5 percent of the world's population. We don't feel different, even when we are different. We think we fit because we always have fit.

Sometimes we think we know what minority status feels like. But we can't really know. Or can we?

Once I attempted to "know" vicariously. In graduate school in 1965, I wrote an in-depth report on the book, "Black Like Me," by John Griffin, the white journalist who disguised himself as a black and traveled in the South.

I tried to put myself in Griffin's shoes.

As he slipped into his black skin, I slipped into that same black skin. As he experienced rejection, abuse and violence, I "experienced" rejection, abuse and violence.

Attempting to absorb and integrate the indignation I felt in Griffin's shoes, I wrote what I thought was an accurate portrayal of the terror of a Southern black living in an oppressive white power structure.

My paper came back. The only comment under the B- was "Aren't you a little emotional about this?"

My white instructor's fine-lined, haughty handwriting dripped icicles on my passionate indignation. Her tone seemed a racial slap, for at the moment I felt black.

Yet, perhaps her criticism was valid. Perhaps she objected not so much to my emotionalism as my attempt to over-identify with, even to claim, black suffering as my own.

A friend I saw just last week tells another story. At a certain women's organization meeting a few years back, the members began discussing a controversial agenda item: Should the group make a public commitment to lesbian rights? A woman who had accompanied my friend to the meeting became so distraught over the subject that she retired to the restroom in tears.

"I just don't belong here!" she sobbed to my friend who followed her.

"Yes," responded my friend sympathetically. "Now you know how *they* feel."

There was a time in 1967 when I experienced discrimination firsthand. No, that's not quite true; it was my husband who did.

We were traveling on isolated Hokkaido, the northern island of Japan, which before the 1972 Winter Olympics was infrequently visited by Westerners.

After settling ourselves in the sparse room of a small Japanese inn, Dick and I each headed for the separate communal bath appropriate for our sex. I had the women's baths to myself, and after taking an extra-long soak, came back to our room and found Dick sitting cross-legged on his floor mat, reading and scowling. His dry hair told me he had been out of the bath for some time.

"It made me so mad," he said through clenched teeth.

"What?" I asked.

"They stopped all conversation when I got in the water," he said, shaking his head. "Though I couldn't have understood a word they said, they didn't even look at me, but slowly, one by one — all four of them — got up and left the baths."

We stared at each other with instant recognition of what neither of us wanted to admit. In that part of Japan, at that time, we were the Occidental "barbarians." The unwashed, the unwanted, the untouchable, the "un-ordinary" no matter how clean or how friendly.

Simply because of the roundness of our eyes and the color of our skin, we were rejected.

And for that one brief moment, we experienced prejudice; a moment that pales beside the persecution other minorities have suffered. But, nevertheless, a moment we have not forgotten.

"In that part of Japan, at that time, we were the Occidental 'barbarians.' The unwashed, the unwanted, the untouchable."

Taking Big Risks — Living with Triumph & Failure

Colorado Woman News
DECEMBER 2000

ELEANOR ROOSEVELT ONCE SAID, "FIND THE one thing you think you cannot do, and do it." In other words, take big risks!

For the past two years I have been developing and teaching seminars and courses on Risk Taking — when you do, when you don't, how to decide, how to live with triumph and "recover" from failure. In the process, some of my own pre-conceptions and the standard clichés about risk have been subjected to deeper scrutiny. For example:

• *Women will take the risk of emotional sharing more often than men.*

Not always. In an intensive five day course which advertised that a major requirement would be to share personal risks in class, I had expected more women than men to sign up. Instead I got 17 males and five females. The men revealed their hopes, fears and traumas every bit as much as the women. Some males did disclose, however, that they had difficulty sharing intimately with their "significant other." In short, "class talk" was safer than "pillow talk."

• *Men are naturally bigger risk takers than women.*

Depends on the risk. In the intensely physical areas of sky diving, bungee jumping and extreme skiing, young males prevail. But in the willingness to "lose face," or in the taking of years off to raise children — knowing their careers can be slowed or derailed — women are more likely to risk.

American culture defines risk in a male "go-for-it" way. Even Eleanor Roosevelt did. As one young man in the intensive class said about "finding the one thing you think you can't do and doing it," "It depends on your motivation."

He had been challenged by a friend to jump off a 40' cliff into a lake of undetermined depth. He refused and felt awful — like he'd denied himself, diminished his friendship and totally lost his "macho" image. Later he found that his friend, who did take the leap, had been motivated by proving something to his father. "I didn't need to prove anything like that to his father or to mine," he mused later. "I could have risked my life over someone else's family psycho-drama!"

• *Young people don't think about the upsides and downsides of taking risks — they just do it.*

Not true!

Young people worry, in fact agonize, over risks as "regular" as whether to break family ties and go away to school, whether they should transfer to a less expensive school than D.U. (for example — many have to work two jobs to cover expenses), whether to drop out for a time, change majors, whether to end a long-term relationship and whether to marry across cultures.

Moreover, many of these University of Denver students — often unfairly characterized as "spoiled and rich" — have confronted crucial, sometimes life-threatening decisions, which required the taking of big risks.

— A very young woman faced breast cancer in high school. Because of poor family history, she had to decide whether to risk having a double mastectomy at the age of 18.

— A sophomore male athlete took the risk of quitting his gang and making his church friends his peer group. He became a "born again" Christian and withstood the derision from his former "friends."

— A junior has returned to D.U. after flunking out due to poor grades and drug addiction. In the interim, this young man went to New Zealand, worked on a farm and slept in his tent, crying himself to sleep each night for a month. After a year, he is drug free and determined to make it through school.

— Another junior finds the social pressures at D.U. difficult. He is an alcoholic, but has not had a drink in a year. He attends Alcoholics Anonymous meetings regularly, and feels that every day might be a "risk."

— A young single woman, unexpectedly pregnant, risks the decision to have an abortion.

— Another, in the same situation, takes the risk of becoming a single mother. She now works and attends school while raising her two-year-old son.

• *A successful risk outcome guarantees "happiness ever after."*

> *"If you carry the project successfully to term, no one wants to hear the downsides. There are few support groups for the 'sorrows' of victory."*

Actually, I was "on to" the defects in this cliché a long time ago, partly through experiencing first child birth. In short: The pregnancy goes well, the delivery is on time and the baby is perfect. So why are you depressed?

Yes, there are hormonal factors in the "baby blues," but I dare say that it is also that parenthood changes your life forever. Your former life is over and your "old self" gone for good.

Winning an election or getting a big promotion can produce "post partum depression" too. As in "baby bearing," if you carry the project successfully to term, no one wants to hear the downsides. There are few support groups for the "sorrows" of victory.

When, in 1974, my husband took a "long shot" chance at the Colorado Governor's race and won, he was mildly depressed for two years. His opposition hated him and his supporters gave him no quarter when their issues weren't moving fast enough. Even at moments of triumph, he longed for his former life.

However, taking a big political risk and losing is even tougher. When I lost my race for the U.S. Senate in 1998, it felt as though someone had died. Sometimes I would wake up at night petrified, asking: "Who is it? Who is it?" Then I would fall back asleep, relieved but still saddened. The "death" was not of a person, but of a dream.

All Alone
When Well of Self-Assurance Runs Dry

Denver Post
SEPTEMBER 9, 1984

THIS COLUMN HAS BEEN A LONG TIME GROWING. It started, soft and unformed, somewhere in my gut when I began my month's leave from The Post in late July.

It took shape three weeks later when I began writing again and all my family members were gone on their own vacations. A perfect time to be alone and work or not work as I pleased, I thought. No interruptions, no meal planning, no chauffeuring, no scheduling, no interactions.

No feedback. None. Nothing on my column, since there had been no column. No letters. No phone calls. No passing comments.

No flack. No kudos. Nothing from my family, since there was no family. No hugs. No tantrums. No tears. No sharing. No laughter.

As a person who has privately touted "self-sufficiency," I pride myself on not needing much succor. I could do "my thing" in isolation, I thought. And I can. But "my thing" has always been more outwardly confirmed than I realized. Just *being* in print is a confirmation. Just having family *around* is an affirmation.

Once I envied writers like May Sarton or Annie Dillard, who could have a whole season alone and write. After my time alone, my envy has dissipated, and I stand in awe.

If an author is working on a book, and her work is not currently in print, how does she know her words, her phrases are real? If she doesn't have people around, how does she know how she exists? Does such a person sing loudly in the shower? Pinch herself occasionally just to make sure she is really there? I did. And I was only alone for a week! I also called friends.

But, mostly I worked. And I worked out. And I sat and thought. And I felt. I let myself feel whatever came to me: Joy over my good health, guilt over a commitment not kept. Sorrow over the glitch in a friendship. Recrimination over a parental lapse in sensitivity. Pride in a child's accomplishment.

And I learned. I learned why more people who could well afford it don't take more time off alone and schedule nothing. Or when they do, they immediately begin to fill up their unscheduled hours as if they were running for president.

I gained a fresh insight into why lawyers don't take sabbaticals; why fathers don't take paternity leaves; and why full-time homemaking is a psychological impossibility for some women, once their children are in school; why people who have worked hard all their lives dread each tick of the clock that brings them closer to retirement.

For when we let ourselves and our schedules go, which is supposed to be good for us (and probably is), we can "go" anywhere. When I got on a "high" I was energized and expanded. I danced through the routine jobs: fall closet clearing, record and tape sorting, photograph pasting, clothes mending — quickly, gracefully — as if all were choreographed parts of a ballet where I was center stage.

When, on the other hand, I felt sorrow or guilt, there was no scheduled "must" to break the feelings. The obsessive agonizing just went deeper and deeper, until it bottomed out.

No schedule. No feedback.

The week alone reminded me of another time I felt out of touch. About four years ago, I wrote a column which solicited information. All readers had to do was check their responses on an accompanying form, clip, and mail it to me.

My column came out on Monday. By the following Monday, I had received only four responses. My first reaction was anger. Even my "blankety-blank" women's group didn't bother to write!

Then depression. With such miniscule response, of course I would be fired. I didn't just feel I was losing my job, but that I was losing me.

Actually, more than 700 responses were arriving at The Post mailroom, but since my mail usually

> *"It's the existential condition of humankind to be insecure.' Without stimulation, without feedback, even a seemingly full well of self-assurance can run dry."*

came to the house, I hadn't even thought to check at the paper. The week of isolation and rejection, which felt very real, turned out to be a sham.

In relating this episode later to my sister, I laughed at myself for my stupidity in not checking the mailroom, and then chastised myself for being so depressed. Even had the response been low, I, in my wisdom and maturity, should be beyond that need for validation, I said.

"But you won't get beyond it," she said. "We never do. It's not YOU. It's US. It's the existential condition of humankind to be insecure." Without stimulation, without feedback, even a seemingly full well of self-assurance can run dry.

Suddenly, I have a flash of insight into the reason children who feel neglected will do anything to gain attention. And as adults, when starved of feedback, we don't really change. We only develop more sophisticated versions of the child who runs in circles chanting: "Look at me! Look at me!"

20 Years of Surviving

Denver Post
OCTOBER 7, 2001

IT WAS ON LABOR DAY OF 1981 THAT I WAS diagnosed with breast cancer. No one but the doctors, my husband and I knew how bad it was.

I wasn't supposed to make it.

With 15 lymph nodes positive of the 25 removed, my survival odds were 40 percent. When my estrogen receptor test showed I might respond to the relatively new drug, tamoxifen, my odds increased to just over 50 percent.

I'll take it, I thought, at first grudgingly. Then with quick resolve. Fifty-one percent? That's all I need — I'll beat this.

I also got mad. When my husband's press secretary said the "East Coast press" had determined that the Colorado governor's wife was a "goner" and I'd better be prepared for tough questions, I nodded. But inwardly, I seethed.

What do *they* know?

I'll show them!

When certain friends approached me with a look that signaled they were not only sympathetic but almost in "pre-mourning," I looked them straight in the eye and, with a bright smile, disarmed them. Why should they worry? I wasn't.

At first it was an act. But later I believed it. Two weeks after surgery I went to visit my mother in California. A mother myself, I knew she needed reassurance more than I did.

Sitting in the same Palo Alto park in which I had strolled my kids when they were infants, the September sun radiated through my navy blouse to salve my wounded chest.

The soft smells of the fall air mingled with my sweat and the unique odor of sun-drenched dark cotton. A train whistle sounded, and suddenly, deep within my being, I knew. I would live to watch my teenage son and pre-teen daughter grow up, to graduate, to marry. And like most of the women on my family tree, I would become an old lady. At only 44, never had the prospect of "old" looked so good.

I don't mean to sound Pollyannaish or to offer oversimplified advice. Attitude is not everything. I had friends with better prognoses and heartier attitudes than mine, also with kids to nurture to adulthood, who did not survive breast cancer.

But attitude is *something*. And if it does not ensure your survival, it enables you to live better while you live.

My confidence did not cause me to shun treatment. I took my full 13 months of chemotherapy, and my body showed it. My hair thinned, dark circles appeared under my eyes and my cheeks puffed up from prednisone. I did my medications, my visualizations and my water exercises. I napped, gave up caffeine, changed my diet, took vitamins, developed my spiritual life.

In fact I did every sensible thing, and some not so sensible, suggested in behalf of my own healing. I worked hard. And, let's face it, I was lucky.

There are no simple cures to complex diseases. But there are always those to suggest them.

"Just get with God, and you'll make it."

"Accept Jesus as your savior, and he'll save you."

"Your mind caused your illness; get your mind right and you'll cure yourself."

Each mandate took its turn buzzing about my brain like an annoying insect, then I shook my head and cast them off one by one. I just didn't believe in the "magic bullet" theory of life or death. Never had. Still don't.

The local press never asked those "tough questions," which is why no one knew until now about my poor prognosis. Did they not know what to ask? Even after the honest revelations of women like first lady Betty Ford, was there still too much embarrassment about intrusive, personal, "breast-type" questions put to a woman? Perhaps.

Or did I eventually bore them with my daily press releases from the hospital, and a major press conference when I arrived home at the Governor's Mansion? For one thing, I had learned as a political spouse who came of age in the Watergate era that a good offense is the best defense.

Answer all. Hide nothing. Stay positive. And eventually the story becomes a nonstory.

That was then. Now is 20 years later.

And two very common questions still surprise me:

First, "How *are* you?" asked with that very solicitous and concerned look, usually from people who haven't seen me for over a decade. Do I look sick? That much older? Their tone makes me want to turn and look defensively over my shoulder. Is the grim reaper on his way and I don't know it?

Then I realize. They are remembering the cancer that I have (almost) forgotten. "Fine." I smile. "No recurrences." And they relax.

Second, "I read your book 'Second Banana.' How did you possibly manage in the glare of all that publicity?"

The truth is, the publicity made it easier. Because of my public platform as Colorado's first lady, I was able to turn a personal trauma into a public crusade: Examine your breasts! Get that mammogram! Don't delay! The dozens of women I

Photo, Sept. 1981 / Dottie Lamm

Special to the Denver Post, Sept. 2001 / Ed Komicki

might have helped as a private citizen turned into hundreds.

I also had a support system that wouldn't stop. And late at night, I mourned for the women who had breast cancer but no loving families, no caring doctors, no staff, few friends and no press to give their disease "significance."

Medical science has progressed to the point that I now know next to nothing about the intricacies of breast cancer and survival tips. But I still give psychological support to those in need, including that former gubernatorial press secretary, Sue O'Brien (who is now The Denver Post editorial page editor), my dear friend and former sister-in-law, Barbara Lamm (who this summer completed the Avon Breast Cancer 3-day walk), and a woman facing a double mastectomy who phoned me from the Western Slope at the exact moment I began this article.

> *"In retrospect, I think I was not only lucky to survive breast cancer, but maybe even lucky to get it."*

Twenty years out, my life goes on stronger, not despite the disease, but because of it. When you beat the odds, your life attains more purpose. So you were "saved"? Saved to do what? To take more risks!

Recent risks include running for the U.S. Senate in 1998 at the age of 61 and embarking on a 16,000-foot Himalayan trek in Tibet and Pakistan at age 63.

What's next? I'll report back after we return next year from a sabbatical in New Zealand.

In retrospect, I think I was not only lucky to survive breast cancer, but maybe even lucky to get it.

And yes, I did live long enough to see children grow up. On Sept. 29 — 20 years to the month from my diagnosis and surgery — Heather got married in Aspen, and Scott was the usher who walked me down the aisle.

I didn't just "watch" Heather's radiance and joy as she descended the stairs on the arm of her father to wed fellow business school graduate Alexander Ooms. After the couple were presented to those gathered as "husband and wife" by my sister, the Rev. Jane E. Vennard, I danced past midnight to celebrate it!

No, there is no such thing as a "magic bullet."

But each day I thank God for my life.

ENCOUNTERS WITH NATURE:
Inspiring and Intimidating

Treasures That Need Not Be Gathered

Denver Post
JULY 2, 1983

A LITTLE OVER A YEAR AGO WE WERE PRIVILEGED to enjoy a four-day retreat at a friend's home on the Oregon coast. In celebration of summer with its sense of renewal, I share a page from my journal of that retreat:

The little shells, sand dollars and black shiny rocks lie in sparsely scattered streaks on the Oregon beach. Because the treasures are spread wide apart, the beach walker is beckoned seductively by each unique jewel. I pick up two perfect sand dollars and then four glinting flat rocks.

I feel like a trespasser. This is a public beach, yet on this June afternoon it occurs to me that in my 4-mile walk I've seen two other beachhikers, three cars, one truck and a piece of litter — a bleach bottle stuck upright almost defiantly in the sand.

"The eyes and lids of the weathered summer homes remain shut as if each residence is grabbing one more wink."

Otherwise, my company has been one jackrabbit, two caterpillars and a multitude of sea gulls. The road along the beach is strewn with wild iris and bright gold Scotch broom. The eyes and lids of the weathered summer homes remain shut as if each residence is grabbing one more wink before the onslaught of its summer family.

The beach stretches miles ahead like woven beige fibers of the finest cloth; the surf laps gently at its edges, lying flat. Cold water splashes ankle high. Hawkeyed, I'm almost oblivious to the chill. Suddenly, the sand dollars, the four stones do not seem enough.

I pick up a jagged brown rock that I think I shall use as a paperweight, then a third sand dollar, then a black stone encircled with an unbroken white line (the kind we used to call "lucky stones" when we were children). Let's see; the sand dollars for my kids, the stones for me; and any others at home I could go to, bearing gifts?

My beachbag is heavy.

Reluctantly, I turn from the ocean to search for the place where I left my shoes and socks.

I sit a minute on a large driftwood log. Between my feet a special variety of sprawling blue-green beachgrass makes a delicate pattern on the white sand.

My hand pauses as it drops my dark glasses in the wide beachbag. My treasures lumped together at the bottom of the bag have lost their luster. I think of my drawer at home where other such gifts from nature lie dull and listless among castoff pieces of jewelry.

Trespasser. The word comes back to me. At first reluctantly, but with satisfaction increasing, I take out each rock and sand dollar and lay them back on the sand. I turn to go, relieved. I have been there. But I have not trespassed.

A Quiet Haven For the Mind

Denver Post
AUGUST 9, 1983

WE SIT ON THE SMOOTH GRANITE ROCKS AND say nothing.

I count the sounds. The gentle wind whistles in the trees. The nearby stream crackles. The distant waterfall rumbles. The crickets chirp. No other sound. Nothing. And we sit here 45 minutes.

The 9 o'clock sun of the Aspen wilderness area penetrates the body without burning the skin. In front of us is Maroon Pass. At the right are the towering, treacherous Maroon peaks. Behind us the valley is framed by the wide arc of jagged black promontories thrust into the bright blue sky.

We are not mountain climbing today, just hiking. This meadow is our destination. No need to hurry. Sit and enjoy the soundlessness.

It's seldom so quiet

Mentally I compare it to the buzz of the city. Even on languorous summer days, hums and screeches penetrate our ears. If it isn't rush hour, some huge mechanical lawnmower screamingly ravages the earth in the name of trimness.

As August Heckscher says about city life:

"We may turn off the television, resist the temptation of high-fi, close the windows and double lock the door — still the vibrations of the world penetrate our consciousness … the murmur of traffic is everywhere, insistent and continuous …."

I try to hold the silence of this moment in my hand — take it home in my brain or my backpack. If, in the hectic pressured noisy times to come as we return to civilization, I could just sit still each day for a moment and remember this silence, this centered feeling which reminds us that so much of what bombards us with urgency and noise is unimportant.

We had not sought silence today as much as exercise; we had not sought solitude as much as release. But it is the silence and the solitude that we will remember.

Others go after their silence more directly. Like David Mazel as he approaches a state park in northern California:

"Somehow I knew that I wouldn't see or hear any other person. I wouldn't even sense the lingering presence of hikers who had gone before me. I was entering a singular and unused-seeming place, as right for soul as for body …. The quiet sound in me like a secret promise."

Alpine inspiration

Or like Pierre Tradervand who spent a summer in a Swiss chalet 7,000 feet high in the Alps:

> *"I try to hold the silence of this moment in my hand."*

"The silence here … why it is the universe echoing the music of the spheres, the music of life and love. But we must listen and learn. And then we hear it. Imperceptibly at first, then louder — and everywhere — as the inner ear is attuned."

Or like Rushworth Kidder on a cold winter night in Maine:

"… the stars hung frozen in the winter night, and even the wind had grumbled off to bed. Here and there a branch snapped with the cold, and now and then the ice on the lake, shifting and cracking, spoke dark syllables into the pines. But otherwise, silence, a vast, refreshing, wholly uplifting quietness."

For us, silence comes not on a breath-freezing winter night in Maine, but on a sunbaked day near Aspen. It finds us, we do not find it; and, it finds us partly because we do not find it necessary to talk.

"… what a release from the friction of the world, what a legitimate refuge, what a privilege … to be able to sit with another human being in complete and comfortable silence."

— Barbara Cook

Touch the Undershirt

Denver Post
MARCH 13, 2011

N O, I CANNOT WALK ONE BIT FASTER! I'VE TRIED. Lord, I've tried, especially on those few straight stretches of groomed path. No matter. The trekking group of 10 is always ahead of me. Out of reach.

We are on the famous Patagonian "W" Trek in Torres del Paine National Park. Our dream vacation, to hike and sightsee in Chile.

Occasionally my husband — tired, too, yet faster than me — drops back to see if I am "OK." I nod.

But I am *not* "OK." I want to yell, scream and swear. No, I won't faint, won't fall, probably won't even stumble, but my knee twitches, my varicose veins swell and pulse, the backpack's straps dig into my shoulders.

Mostly it's my pride that hurts. As a child, I was often the first to reach the mountaintop. I remember climbing Mount Tallac in the California Sierras and being the first of my Scout troop to touch the undershirt someone had tied to the summit post.

In later years, I've been content to be in the middle group. But I have never been — constantly, perpetually and devastatingly — last, no matter my effort, day after day after day.

You might ask what we two septuagenarians were thinking when we signed up for this 40-mile,

four-day backpacking trek. I guess we were not thinking that we would be 25 years older than the next-oldest in the group and 50 years older than the youngest. And if we had "thought," we would probably have gone anyway.

After all, we did fine on the equally challenging Milford Trek in New Zealand a decade ago. Clearly that decade made the difference.

How did we become so arrogant as to think that just because we work out regularly we would go on with the speed and strength of our youth forever? Has our basic (and lucky) overall health heightened our arrogance, and lessened the wisdom age is supposed to bestow? Perhaps. But to heck with that wisdom right now!

It is the fourth and final day of the trek. It is raining hard and the Patagonian wind is gusting with a vengeance. Today the whole group must make this 8-mile trip over rocky terrain in five hours to catch the 1 p.m. ferry that will take us back to our bus. If we miss the ferry, we must walk back the 8 miles, take a slower boat and not reach our last *refugio* (glorified dormitory) until midnight.

I am panicked I will delay the group. Dick worries, too.

> *"I am panicked I will delay the group. Dick worries, too."*

As the two *viejos* on the trip, we have felt somewhat marginalized from the gang that bonded mostly without us. Yet, one by one, we have made friends.

Suddenly, I am buoyed by a scene from my youth, when my pride and sense of inclusion were on the line. At the age of 9, I was commanded by a physical education teacher to play softball on an all-boy team. I had never played softball.

Stuck out in center field by the team captain, I fidgeted. Until, of course, that inevitable fly ball came down toward me in a slow but terrifying arch. "I will catch the ball. I will catch the ball. I will catch the ball," I repeated. And I did.

Now, 64 years later, the mantra changes: "I will catch the boat. I will catch the boat. I will catch the boat." Somehow my step gets lighter and a little faster. I did catch the boat. And so did the group.

Exhausted on the ferry, I am both thrilled with my accomplishment and cognizant of the fact that the right "mantra" will not always pull me through the encroachments of age. Part of me is ready to accept that.

But another small side of me still whispers, "Go, girl! Touch that undershirt. Be first."

Touching the Cosmos:

Philosophy, Psychology, and Ethics

END OF LIFE:
How Do We Prepare? How Do We Grieve?

Willpower
What If You Die Anyway?

Denver Post
C. MID-1980S

DON'T YOU DARE GET SICK WITHOUT IT. Willpower, that is. It's the latest thing in health care — a miraculous source of power that supposedly can separate the living from the dead, literally.

In recent newspaper and magazine articles, we are being told that willpower can make the difference between surviving a catastrophic illness or not making it.

For people who believe that, and, in fact, are recovering and doing well, I cheer their survival. More than that, I admire their resolve.

But what about the people who exhibit the same amount of willpower but don't make it? What about the cancer patient who says, "I'm going to beat *this* thing," *but* doesn't. Or the AIDS patient who shows uncommon willpower, faith and grit — but dies anyway?

Does death from a terminal disease now mean that you didn't try hard enough?

What's evolving here is a blame-the-victim mentality, and we're all vulnerable to it. I know I used to be, until I got seriously ill.

When, seven years ago this fall, after my modified radical mastectomy, I went to my first chemotherapy treatment, the very dear friend who picked me up said something that at first heartened me but later was disturbing.

As I got in the car and reported that aside from the nauseous smell of the chemicals the whole thing really wasn't so bad, she grabbed my hand and said, "You did so well! I'm so proud of you!"

As this ritual exchange continued after each treatment, I began to wonder: Would she *not* be proud of me if I passed out on the floor or threw up in the car?

Many chemotherapy patients do pass out or throw up. Indeed, as determined as I was to get well, it wasn't my willpower but my basic good health — and just pure luck — which determined that my own body chemicals didn't react to those toxic chemicals in a more severe way.

I think of my friend Linda who had a mastectomy almost the same time I did. Linda and I went to lunch to buoy up each other's willpower. And Linda had as much or more of it than I.

A proponent of healthy eating who consumed only the most nutritious foods, she was younger

218

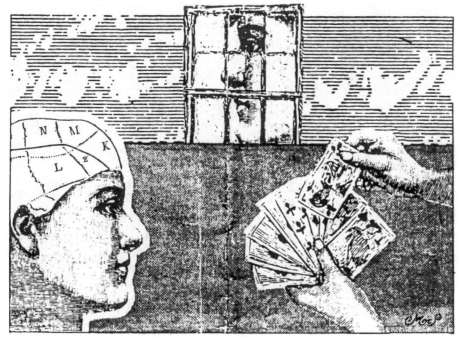

The Denver Post / Maureen Scance

for their tragedies. Therefore, the person who doesn't "make it" can be subtly blamed and shamed as well as mourned.

"He just didn't try hard enough … she just didn't have enough faith …," we think secretly, telling ourselves that *our* willpower would have pulled us through.

And if willpower is treated as the only factor in success or cure, it can lead us to bizarre psychological readings.

During my hospitalization, another dear friend, a strong believer in the omnipotent will, said to me, "You made yourself sick, Dottie. So you can make yourself well."

He meant it as a pep talk, as a faith investment in my personal power. But instead, it evoked worry and self-recrimination. Yes, my stress level and certain anxieties might have contributed to my illness. But, "made myself ill"? Hardly!

Wasn't it enough to have cancer? Did I have to have guilt, too?

Another strange psychological pronouncement came after the 1982 death of my friend Jessica — artist, feminist, intellectual gadfly and Hispanic activist.

and better fit than I — a serious five-mile-a-day runner as opposed to my meager two. In addition, Linda exhibited a deep spirituality, a faith which motivated her to travel far and wide in search of healing techniques which would augment her conventional radiation and chemotherapy.

But within a year of our lunch, Linda was dead, leaving a husband and two young daughters. Yet, there is no way Linda did not "try hard enough." She wanted to live to see her kids grow up as desperately as I wanted to see mine.

In Rabbi Harold Kushner's book "When Bad Things Happen to Good People," the author emphasizes that even for the "moral," the "fit," and the "faithful," there is a certain cruel randomness to life.

But most of us don't buy this randomness. People want to find reasons for the triumph and reasons

Following the memorial service, I mused with a mutual friend of hers about why Jessica had not sought a certain type of cancer treatment.

"But, Dottie," exclaimed the friend, "didn't you know? Jessica *wanted* to die."

I was too stunned to respond.

Jessie had her masochistic streaks, but "wanted to die"? Never! Not even middle-aged when she succumbed, Jessie loved growing older, more powerful. I remember her drawing vivid verbal pictures of the kind of dynamic, eccentric older woman she would become. And as she painted these pictures, she would throw back her head and laugh a throaty, triumphant laugh.

It's not that I deny the enormous force of will-power. In fact, I believe some seriously ill people die because they don't have it and that those of us who succeed, at *anything*, almost always exhibit it.

But those who do not succeed don't necessarily lack it.

For life is not just willpower, work, faith and positive thinking. It is knowledge, luck, miracle, whimsy, serendipity and timing. And sometimes it's even tragedy, despite our "will" to think otherwise.

The Many Faces of Bereavement

Denver Post
FEBRUARY 28, 1983

DENIAL. IMMOBILIZATION. ANGER. GUILT. Depression. These were the agonies most frequently expressed by readers who shared their personal bereavement experiences in response to my Jan. 24 column on the grief process.

LaVerne Skunberg, whose 24-year-old son died in an accident six years ago, writes: "No matter how one handles it, there will always be times when nothing helps. When the 'no help' (stage) happens to me, I am totally immobilized. For a space in time I feel that if I move I will shatter. Thankfully, the feeling soon passes and is overcome by the raw pain of loss. I am better able to deal with the pain."

The discharge of anger frequently helps a grieving person out of the helplessness and immobilization described by Mrs. Skunberg. Some bereaved rage against the deceased or against the circumstances which caused or surrounded the death. Others direct their anger against the "pettiness" of the everyday problems of associates when such "trivia" is compared with the devastation of their own loss. One takes out her fury on the sunshine: When a day dawns bright and clear, she wants to "scream out that the sun has no right to keep shining brightly as though nothing had happened."

Guilt accompanies anger in some cases, especially when grief results from death by suicide or the loss of a young child. A Denver area woman writes: "It took several years after (my son's suicide) to forgive myself: If I had done this ... or maybe this ... or this ... If ... If ... If ... If — STOP!"

Another respondent details the suicide of her 28-year-old brother: "Besides sorrow, my primary feeling since his death has been guilt. I have thought that I should have spent more time with him, should have called him more often when he was in emotional pain."

The parent of a 3-year-old who died after a short illness writes: "The most difficult part of coping with his death are the feelings of guilt. Quite often when my living child (age 5) gets sick, I relive the death, and my ministrations which were not quite right or enough to help my first child get well."

The "Why?" or the "Why me?" questions often dominate the grief process of those whose bereavement is the result of an accident or is otherwise premature. A 40-year-old minister whose wife was killed in a boating accident while saving their youngest child feels that it is only natural to scream "Why?"

"The soul's primary hunger is not for pleasure or for power, but rather for meaning," he writes 16 months after the tragedy. "It is meaning which makes our lives worth living and it is meaninglessness which moves the soul in the direction of death ... somehow this field must be plowed so that some good fruit may be reproduced."

Yet, it usually will be months, even years, before "good fruit" will be recognized as resulting from the loss of a loved one. Mourners cannot be hurried through this process by well-meaning friends, but must be allowed to experience their loss, anger, guilt and pain.

The Reverend Stuart Haskins writes of a parishioner who said, "My neighbor tells me I should not grieve, because my husband is with God, but, God help me, I want him to be with me!"

After a period of months or years, when what psychologists call the "grief work" is done, most mourners experience what the Rev. Mr. Haskins terms "a return to hope and effective reality." Some are even able to "plow the field so some good fruit is produced."

A Denver widower who had considered suicide after losing his wife is finally able to write: "I reflect no longer on the thoughts. Those thoughts are exterminators of the good life."

LaVerne Skunberg expresses her determination to keep going in the last stanza of a poem written by her son's grave:
The towering peaks wait silently, their hope to give
The pain wracked mind tries reaching out
For promise, seen but hardly understood

> *"My neighbor tells me I should not grieve, because my husband is with God, but, God help me, I want him to be with me!"*

Resigns, itself, accepts as positive, the will to live.

A Denver mother tells of the spiritual growth she has attained in the painful years she spent coming to terms with both the death of her daughter in a car accident and the suicide of her son.

"Life is a gift … even if children die before parents. Let me share with you … I'm overwhelmed. When I think that my two children could have come into this manifestation for my soul's growth … not theirs … mine … what love! I'm in awe, as I have grown spiritually and I say, humbly, 'Thank you, God.'"

Books recommended by readers: "When Bad Things Happen to Good People" by Harold S. Kushner; "To Live Again" by Catherine Marshall; "Death Be Not Proud" by John Gunther; "To Live Until We Say Goodbye" by Elisabeth Kubler-Ross and M. Warshaw; "If I Die and When I Do" by Franki and Barbara Sternberg; "A Grief Observed" by C.S. Lewis.

Distancing Ourselves from Others

Denver Post
APRIL 25, 1983

A COUPLE WE KNEW WERE INITIATING A TRIAL separation. Later, after they reconciled, the woman wrote to me in response to a message I had sent them during the time they were apart.

"You were so thoughtful to show you cared," she wrote. "It was a shame that many people were so threatened by 'another going-under' that they couldn't respond at all."

"Another going-under." Whether it's a marriage deteriorating, an illness that could prove fatal, or the death of someone else's loved one, how quick we are to distance ourselves from acquaintances' trauma.

If a couple is divorcing we may think: But that couple seems so much like us! We thought they had worked out their problems. Have we worked out ours? Fear. We should call, but which one do we contact? Him? Her? Both? Threatened and confused, we do nothing.

If an illness strikes, we are even quicker to disassociate. That business acquaintance who just had a heart attack. He seemed so healthy. As we push off the descending cloud of fear, what do we do for the heart attack patient? Often nothing.

Tragedy, or just plain difficulty, hits people we know; instead of responding, we wrap ourselves

> *"Instead of responding, we wrap ourselves tightly in cloaks of denial."*

tightly in cloaks of denial. We act as if we see no evil, hear no evil and ignore all evil, it won't happen to us. My friend's note reminded me how appropriately I responded this time; it also reminded me of the many other times I had not responded to acquaintances in distress.

Sometimes our denial is compounded by truly not knowing what to say. And, until we experience trauma ourselves, we haven't yet learned that the form of the message or the choice of words doesn't matter as much as the fact that we send them.

Readers who responded to my February series on grief wrote of how crucially important friends were to them in their mourning process. Some respondents gave advice to potential friends of others in grief or in trouble.

A Colorado Springs woman who lost her 37-year-old sister to a brain tumor wrote: "The most important thing to do is something rather than nothing at all. Most people do not realize how desperately you need to hear from them, and it is never too late to respond ... take the initiative to take food, send cards, or flowers, run errands, and care for children ...."

Other readers sent words of caution and advice which could best be summed up by the phrase, "Try to walk in the moccasins of the traumatized person before you speak."

Do not tell a grieving person, particularly a grieving child, not to cry. A young woman writes, "My grandfather died in my home when I was 15. I went alone to sit and cry. My uncle, unfeeling, walked over to me and said I must not cry. To stop … I decided then I would never tell someone not to cry. It is the most healing way to deal with grief."

Do not say, "It's for the best," even if in your opinion the demise of the deceased person was timely, or ended suffering. If it is for the best, the grieving person will eventually see that, after he or she has had time to mourn. A person in grief must not be hurried.

If you have neglected to write that note, make that phone call, or send those flowers, and then unexpectedly meet up with an acquaintance in grief or illness, simply extend your condolences on the spot. Don't recount the reasons why you didn't respond earlier: a sufferer should not have to add your guilt to his or her burdens.

Do not falsely encourage the dying patient: "For the dying patient to *listen* in a non-judgmental manner is difficult at best, yet in a patient's case almost imperative," writes the woman who lost her sister. "Well-meaning suggestions of thinking positively, increased physical exercise, miracle healing, or ideas for 'getting well' may not enhance the patient's acceptance of their circumstances and impending death."

On the other hand, do not inadvertently discourage the recovering patient. At my first public appearance after my mastectomy in 1981, a well-meaning woman rushed up to me and said, "I'm so sorry about your surgery. I just had a friend die of breast cancer. Here is her husband's phone number, in case your husband needs it."

Yet, with a little tact and foresight, almost anything one says or does for a troubled friend will be taken kindly and appreciatively.

A Denver woman who lost her son in an accident writes: "Friends don't have to be strong, just present, and willing to listen. One wonderful neighbor came immediately and said, 'At times like this I have the strength of warm Jello, so I just came to cry with you.'"

"Human beings are God's language," said Rabbi Harold S. Kushner, author of "When Bad Things Happen to Good People," in a recent Denver address. Whether it is a marriage going under, a friend succumbing to a dread disease, or an associate grieving the loss of a loved one, let's not be afraid to speak.

Doctors Need Sympathy Rx

Denver Post
DECEMBER 3, 1985

HUMANISM.

Not "secular humanism."

Just plain humanism. The School of Medicine at the University of Rochester in Rochester, N.Y., has begun a two-year course on the subject. In this course, patients teach the doctors the human/psychological aspect of being a patient.

According to Art Ulene, the "Today" show's in-house doctor, physicians can become "calloused" to patients' feelings. They need to learn to approach patients as total human beings.

Not a bad idea, I thought, as my mind clicked back over a series of medical episodes told to me just over the past summer. "Callous" might be too strong a word, but "casual" surely would fit. So would "insensitive" and "flip" and "unprofessional."

A friend of mine took her 19-year-old daughter-in-law to a local hospital for an abortion. The young woman, barely out of high school and married with one child, had decided on an abortion so that she could continue to support her family while her husband was in school. Although this young woman was firm in her decision, she also was distraught.

Emotional state

"The hospital staff treated her as if she were simply having a tooth removed," my friend said. "Her emotional state was totally ignored. No nurse, no social worker, *nobody* to listen to her cry, to hold her hand, to say a kind word. It's like they thought of her as just another dumb pregnancy to be terminated!"

Another friend broke her arm in an accident, and after a series of appointments with a compassionate and gentle M.D., she went to a physical therapist. My friend removed her blouse and bra so that she could do the arm exercises more freely. The therapist was so freaked out by the sight of bare breasts he started chiding her as if she were a child and made her put her blouse back on. In short, he completely failed to help her.

A well-known political figure in his late 60s had eye surgery. In relating this experience he said, "The docs just went cut, cut, cut — all the while, they never missed a stroke of last week's golf game." He laughed heartily, but then stopped and admitted, "I suppose (their conversation) should have made me think, 'They damn well know what they're doing, or they wouldn't be talking so much,' but it didn't. It scared the hell out of me!"

Special treatment

This man's experience reminded me of an experience of my own 18 years ago. I was in intensive labor for 12 hours with our first child. The nurses who massaged my stomach talked about their boyfriends over my sheeted body and acted as if I were just one big contracting uterus. I know nurses help deliver hundreds of babies a year, but this was my first baby, and I wanted to be treated as if I were special.

And that's the point of the class in humanism. Every patient is special. I personally have not had one negative experience with medical people since the nurses babbled over my belly 18 years ago. But as Art Ulene says, "Doctors are people. The pressure they are under sometimes counteracts their common sense."

Perhaps this course on humanism should be required not just for doctors, but for all medical personnel. Not just in medical schools, but perhaps a mini-course every five years.

Just as a reminder that patients are people, too.

Is It a Fetus or a Baby?

Denver Post
JULY 18, 2012

OK, I'M GOING TO BE EMOTIONAL ABOUT THIS one.

My heart goes out to Heather Surovik of Longmont, who lost her fetus in an automobile accident on July 5. It is a tragedy when pregnant women are the victims of crime, heartbreaking and sad for the family and the community. Heather Surovik was due to deliver any day when the accident occurred.

Yet my compassion for the Surovik family quickly turns to anger. Head-swelling anger at the perpetrator of this grievous loss, Gary Sheats.

Sheats, 52, who slammed into Surovik's car injuring her and killing her fetus, had a blood alcohol level of 0.292, three times the legal limit.

And this was his *fifth* DUI offense. Yet the "system" never allowed him to be jailed long enough to keep the public safe, or to be treated for his alcoholism intensely enough to cure him.

Since this latest offense caused "bodily harm," Sheats has been charged with several felony counts involving DUI and leaving the scene of an accident. Yet, the maximum sentence on one of these counts is only 12 years. And should he be charged with only a DUI misdemeanor, his maximum jail time is 60 days.

Sheats cannot be charged with murder or even vehicular homicide. Why? Because in Colorado, a fetus does not become a "person" until he or she is born. And only the killing of a "person" is considered a murder or homicide.

That infuriates Surovik's grandfather, Tim Onley. "Our biggest issue is that they are not calling it a baby," Onley told Denver Post reporter Jessica Fender, adding that he hoped to do something to legally designate an unborn fetus a person.

If I were in Onley's shoes, perhaps that is what I would want to do, too.

And yet, "personhood" measures are dangerous and could lead to the government and politicians intruding in our personal lives, such as getting into our medical records to investigate miscarriages, dictating the birth control we use, and interfering with private medical decisions that should only be made by a woman with her doctor.

In short, under a "personhood" law (supposedly designed to pro-tect the fetus), it is actually the pregnant woman who could be evaluated for possible murder charges if she suffered a miscarriage. It is the woman who

could be charged with vehicular homicide if she, even sober, caused an accident that killed her fetus.

It is the woman and her doctor who could be charged with murder if she elected an abortion even if medical complications threatened her health.

It is the woman who, if she became pregnant as a result of rape or incest, would be forced to carry her pregnancy to term, taking away her ability to make her own decisions in a difficult situation.

No, the "personhood" trade-off is too harmful to women and families. "Personhood" for the fetus, as appealing as it sounds in this heartbreaking case, could actually bring more heartbreak to more mothers and potential mothers in the long run.

Let's try instead for stricter punishment, longer sentences and long-term treatment when indi-cated for DUI offenders on the second — not the fifth — offense.

"This was his fifth DUI offense. Yet the 'system' never allowed him to be jailed long enough to keep the public safe."

Colorado is one of only five states that does not have a felony charge for repeat DUI offenders. Let's change that, too.

Why Should Terminal Patients Have to Leave Colorado to Seek a Peaceful Death?

Denver Post
OCTOBER 9, 2016

PATTI JAMES, AN 80-YEAR-OLD RETIRED NURSE from Littleton with stage 4 lung cancer, recently told me, "I am living with cancer. Having the option of medical aid in dying would provide me with tremendous peace of mind."

If the Colorado End-of-Life Options Act, Proposition 106, succeeds this November, James will be guaranteed that peace of mind.

Proposition 106, known in other states as "Death with Dignity," and submitted for the ballot by Yes on Colorado End-of-Life Options, allows a terminally ill, mentally capable person (over the age of 18) to request a prescription from a physician, obtain medication, and — if his or her suffering becomes unbearable — to *self-administer* that medication to shorten the dying process and bring about a peaceful death.

This law would not be compulsory in any way. Its safeguards include:

- A diagnosis of six months or less to live must be confirmed by two physicians, independently.
- If either of these physicians suspects that a patient does not have the ability to make a rational, informed decision, a psychological or psychiatric examination is required.
- The patient *himself or herself* must make two verbal requests 15 days apart, and a third written request must be made in front of two witnesses, one of whom must have no familial or financial connection to the patient.
- Health care provider participation is voluntary. However, insurance companies cannot deny payment on a health, life or annuity policy because someone used the law.
- Anyone who coerces a patient or tampers with their documents commits a felony. (Numerous examinations of Oregon's nearly 20-year-old Death with Dignity law have revealed no proven incidents of coercion or abuse.)

Sadly, the young, as well as the old, can face terminal illness.

Matt Larson, a Denver attorney and Colorado native, was diagnosed with brain cancer in the spring of 2015 at the age of 35. Last month he wrote in a Denver Post op-ed supporting Proposition 106:

"I personally don't know whether I would take the option to exercise medical aid in dying, but … simply having the option would bring me a tremendous amount of peace and comfort now, while I continue my fight."

Brittany Maynard, a 29-year-old healthy, vibrant, just-married Californian, was diagnosed with brain cancer in early 2014.

After going through various aggressive treatments to no medical avail, Maynard, knowing

Brittany Maynard died in Oregon in 2014 using that state's Death with Dignity law. Her husband, Dan Diaz, is campaigning in Colorado in favor of Proposition 106, the End-of-Life Options Act, which is based on Oregon's law. / Photo Dan Diaz

dying for their terminally ill patients who qualified for it.

Maynard's death on Nov. 1, 2014, became an international story of bravery, determination and devotion.

And for her husband, it began a national campaign to get such laws passed in other states. (Maynard had initiated this campaign three days before her death during a phone conversation with Gov. Jerry Brown of California, urging him to sign an "End-of-Life Options" bill if passed by the Legislature.)

The bill did pass, and on Oct. 5, 2015, Brown signed it into law, making California the fifth state to enact such compassionate legislation.

Hoping Colorado will be the sixth, Diaz has come to Colorado three times to campaign for Proposition 106.

"Why should anyone facing a terminal illness have to move away from family, friends and familiar comforts to another state to have a peaceful and compassionate death?" asked Diaz in an interview last month.

Indeed, many cannot. And why should we?

that in dying she could face excruciating pain and torture that would devastate her and her loved ones, decided she wanted to be able to take control.

Her husband, Dan Diaz, was fully supportive. But the couple faced a huge impediment: California did not allow the medical practice of aid in dying.

So in a move, followed aggressively by press, they relocated to Oregon, where, under the Death with Dignity Act, they found a supportive environment where physicians could prescribe medical aid in

Animals Give Humans a Lesson in How to Die with Dignity

Denver Post
SEPTEMBER 24, 1985

CHARLIE, MY FRIEND'S 12-YEAR-OLD POODLE, died last week.

"We could tell he was going, so we carried him out and laid him in his spot under his favorite tree and I just sat with him," said my friend.

"At noon I went inside for a while and when I came back he was gone. I covered him with a canvas until we could bury him, as we'd agreed …

"When we lifted the canvas that evening, there was our cat snuggled up against his still body, waiting for him to wake up and play. She didn't even know he was dead. But Charlie seemed to know he was dying."

In condolence, I told her of the death in 1976 of our beagle/basset hound, Peter. Peter ran into a car while chasing a squirrel in Cheesman Park. Gently, we lifted him to the car seat and drove him to our veterinarian in south Denver.

"We'll do what we can," said the vet — kind, but non-committal. Peter lay on the table, his huge brown eyes sad and trusting.

Departing, my husband and I exchanged tearful glances.

> *"Funny that I should be measuring the segments of my own life by the potential life span of a dog."*

"Pete's not going to make it," he said.

"I know," I said, choking on the words. "And I think he knows it, too, but he's so calm."

Another friend recently told me of the death of her family's spaniel during the December 1982 Christmas storm. "The most agonizing thing was that Lady really wanted to be outside to die alone, but the weather was so bad we just couldn't let her go. She knew it was her time … maybe we should have let her go out … freezing to death would have been quicker … preserved her dignity …."

I am thinking about all these pet deaths now as I run our 2-year-old Labrador/mutt, Moki, in the park on a crisp fall morning. How long will Moki be with us? I wonder.

When she dies, will she leave her two "empty-nester" owners reminiscing about the night their 12-year-old daughter picked her out from a litter of 10, way back in 1983? Will they then ruminate, as they have done increasingly of late, about "how time flies"?

I don't know. Where will we be at that time, anyway? Funny that I should be measuring the segments of my own life by the potential life span of a dog.

Moki and I stop briefly as we pass an elderly gentleman walking his white poodle — the same poodle he has been walking for seven years. When our family first knew this gentleman, he was spry enough to help us chase our basset hound, Travis.

Now the gentleman is an amputee. He walks slowly, cane in one hand, dog leash in the other. His face heavily lined, his manner still courtly, he touches his hat and asks politely, "And how have you been, Mrs. Lamm?"

How have I been? Something catches in my throat as I answer, smile, and sprint away with Moki. Will this old man outlast his dog — his one companion left to him in his old age? Part of me hopes not.

Yet when his dog does die, when our dog dies, they will be much more accepting of their dying than we humans are of ours.

As Anne Morrow Lindbergh wrote of the death of her beloved dog, Thor: "He is giving up life as nobly — as he lived — not clinging to it. Animals show no fear of death — of pain, yes, but not of death — and so it is very moving. He makes no effort to live; his body accepts death with a kind of grace."

CHARACTER, BEHAVIOR, RELIGION:
So, Why Should I Believe What You Believe?

The Right to Quit Must Be Earned

Denver Post
FEBRUARY 14, 1983

THE STORY BOOK CHARACTER I REMEMBER MOST fondly from the time I read to our small children is "Zooey Katz." The littlest and lowliest of the cats in the Kingdom of Katzenville, Zooey is last in the long chain of Katzenville cats which parade in circles all day holding up each others' tails.

Finally realizing that no one would ever hold up his tail, Zooey revolts. He drops the tail of the second-to-the-last cat, causing him to do the same to the third-to-last cat, and so on up the line.

My children and I would howl and applaud, lauding the smarts of little Zooey Katz, the follower who became a leader by breaking the Kingdom's useless protocol. "He did a far, far braver thing; he simply said 'I quit!'" reads the story line.

It's one thing to applaud a storybook character who quits. It's quite another to quit ourselves. Our Horatio Alger hang-ups often condition us to stress perseverance

> *"Our Horatio Alger hang-ups often condition us to stress perseverance no matter the cost."*

no matter the cost. Lacking the bravery of a Zooey Katz, we are likely to go round and round in our own orbits, even at the price of a miserable life or a potential coronary. "He worked himself to death, finally and precisely, at 3 a.m. Sunday morning," writes Ellen Goodman of a six-day-a-week, 8 a.m. to 8 p.m., 51-year-old corporation vice-president.

A couple of years ago, the Phil Donahue show featured a panel of three middle-aged male executives. Two had just quit their six-figured salaries, one to become a social worker, the other to try his hand at freelance writing.

The audience applauded the two mid-life career changes. But the third panelist did not cheer his contemporaries. Still reaching to attain his own six-figured salary, he branded the other men as not only foolish, but somewhat immoral.

"What if everyone quit like you did?" he asked. "What would happen to society?"

At the personal level, whether or not to quit depends on variable and often conflicting circumstances. On the same day I validate a friend's quitting a hated job, or a college student's "stopping out," I will pepper my own children with the usual pontifications on perseverance: "What? Kids in our family don't quit soccer in the middle of the season!"

Fifteen years ago I had a friend who had borne four children before I even had one. Through her birthing, nursing, diapering stages, she also had managed to achieve a doctorate in physics. Now, at the young age of 35, she was becoming well known in her field. Struggling with career/child-rearing decisions myself, I asked her how she did it all, especially with four.

"Not too well," she answered. "Sometimes I would get so exhausted I would start hallucinating." Did she ever think of quitting? Never.

Silently, I vowed if my career ever became so demanding that I started hallucinating, I would quit. Three years later, I did quit. Though the decision was right for me, something in me still recoils at the sound of the word.

Another friend recently was outraged when her grown son, home over the holidays, announced that he really didn't find his new job fulfilling and was going to quit. "In this economy? No, you're not!" his mother said.

"Craig Morton just quit!" he answered in defense.

"When you've worked at a job or at a goal as long and hard as Craig Morton you will have earned the right to quit!" she replied.

On the public and societal level, "quitting" can take on strong symbolic proportions:

When Sen. Ted Kennedy last year announced he would not seek the 1984 presidential nomination, much of America breathed a collective sigh of relief. The fact that Kennedy was facing ridicule and potential violence that would wreak havoc on his family, his party and his country made his decision seem palatable — even heroic.

But when a person quits for a reason that challenges dearly held traditional or societal values, he or she is often viewed with disdain. Thus the reaction of the third panelist on the Donahue show when he saw the likes of himself rejecting the socially sanctified pursuit of the almighty dollar.

When in the 1960s, masses of youth "dropped out," the adult establishment was outraged. These youngsters had clearly not "earned the right to quit." How could they simply give up the educational and material goals their parents had sacrificed so much to attain?

Whatever our philosophical view of quitting, it's easier to applaud a "Zooey Katz" when he's challenging someone else's kingdom.

Insults
Some Can't Be Ignored

Denver Post
JANUARY 26, 1986

AT A RECEPTION HELD FOR US DURING DICK'S first gubernatorial campaign, a woman came up to me and gushed, "My husband says you don't dress well enough to ever be a first lady, but I want you to know that *I* think you look just fine."

I stared at her in total silence. But I give myself no credit for trying to be polite. It's simply that I was floored speechless.

Joanne Davidson's column "Insults: Not Worth a Scene" (*Contemporary, Jan. 5*) brought many a similar encounter back with sharp feeling. It also elicited such a rush of jumbled thoughts on the subject I could barely sort them out. But now I'm ready to try:

First, I agree with the consensus of Davidson's column that "scenes should be avoided at all costs," at least when the insult is a personal one that deals with no bigger issue than dress or image.

But what about an insult that puts down a valued idea, degrades a cherished tradition, or stereotypes a whole group of people? I soon "wrote off" the woman at the campaign reception with good humor. Her insult, after all, was intended as a compliment. Another insult, delivered during the 1978 campaign, was not:

An angry woman holding a beautiful Oriental baby girl approached me in a crowd after a parade.

"See what we had to get!" she screamed, shaking the baby at me. "Because you and your husband let Americans have abortions, we had to adopt one of *these*."

The brilliant autumn day suddenly seemed to grow cold; a sour taste rose in my mouth that did not abate for hours. Again, I was speechless, but this time not because I had been hurt, but because I saw how that lovely child eventually would be hurt by her adoptive mother's hateful attitude.

Yet nothing I, whom she hated, could have said could have assuaged her. Anything but my silence would simply have increased her venom. So again, a "no scene" was the best scene.

But there are times when at least a "mini" scene is called for. One of them is in dealing with sexual harassment.

Feminist author Barbara Ehrenreich writes: "After more than a decade of consciousness raising, assertiveness training, and hand-to-hand combat in the battle of the sexes, we're still too ladylike. Let me try that again — we're just too *damn* ladylike."

Ehrenreich, in a recent Ms. Magazine article, goes on to describe how she handled a recent unwanted sexual advance: very poorly.

"I, a full-grown feminist," writes Ehrenreich, "had behaved like a ninny — or, as I now understand it, like a lady."

Sometimes if we don't deal straight, at least with the important things in our lives, we can drown

> *"But there are times when at least a 'mini' scene is called for."*

in our own niceties. But to always express our pique is as non-productive as to never express it.

Carol Tavris, in her 1983 book "Anger," resoundingly debunks the 1960s "Let-it-all-hang-out" ethic. According to Tavris, constantly venting anger merely keeps one rehearsing one's feelings, makes one more angry, and solves nothing. The purpose of anger is not to express it for the sake of expressing it, but to motivate the person experiencing it to make a change.

I loved Davidson's example of the socialite who, when insulted, stays calm and collected, but then goes home, screams angry X-rated rejoinders into her tape recorder, tosses the cassette into the trash compactor, and flips the switch.

But when more than your image is trashed, then perhaps your anger should be spared the trash and directed at the trasher.

One woman I know, when faced with a sexist comment, stared down her antagonist with an icy stare and, "ladylike" but firmly, said: "I'm sure you didn't mean to put down all women with that remark, but your attitude is most offensive."

Whether the rejoinder changed her antagonist's attitude, who knows? At least she tried.

Ehrenreich believes one of the reasons women love to watch "macho" movie stars is because we revel in getting out of our "ladylike selves" and identifying with a toughness we lack.

My latest "macho" movie favorite is a female: big strapping Sofia in "The Color Purple."

When you see this movie, watch how men and women flee for cover when Sofia's fist starts to curl. Eventually, and tragically, this curled fist lands Sofia 12 years in jail. But until it leads to her downfall, the audience, male and female, loves it: Pow! Anytime she gets mad.

It's not that I'd recommend that any of us women simply deck someone over a mere verbal insult.

But Sofia sure was fun to watch.

Pow!

Apologies
Sometimes They're Necessary

Denver Post
NOVEMBER 27, 1983

ONE OF THE THINGS THAT STRUCK ME WHILE reading the various Kennedy analyses and anecdotes last week was the late president's almost total lack of defensiveness.

Time magazine reports that after the Bay of Pigs fiasco, "President Kennedy made no effort to escape blame for the folly, to cover it up or excuse it. We made a terrible mistake, he said, let's go on from here."

Political pundits have suggested, only half facetiously, that President Nixon could have avoided the Watergate fiasco if, instead of condoning the cover-up, he simply had gone on network television and — to the background strains of "Stars and Stripes Forever" — grinned broadly and announced, "Ladies and gentlemen, I screwed up!"

Kennedy apologized and the nation forgave. Nixon did not, and he was disgraced. These two historical examples brought into focus what a confused and sometimes convoluted value our society places in the act of apologizing, whether it be in the political realm or the personal.

Let's take the personal:

On the two extremes most people would agree: A person who *never* apologizes is rigid, self-righteous, and impossible to live with. You know the kind of person: someone who accidentally steps on another's toes, ventures not even a perfunctory, "I'm sorry," but withers the "stepee" with a glance that asks, what the "h" that toe was doing there in the first place!

At the other extreme is the wimp: the person who minces around, phrases of "Excuse me," "I'm sorry," "Please forgive me," perpetually rolling off the tip of the tongue. The kind of person who acts guilty for taking up space, who knows that *everything* — including the weather — is his or her fault. This individual is also impossible to live with — unless your ego craves a doormat.

But in the middle, the message is more mixed. I'm not an expert on etiquette; I'm a slightly out-of-practice social worker who, without researching the experts, will try to unmix these messages, at least on the personal level. Here goes:

First. Somewhere we have picked up the idea that apologizing means weakness. It doesn't. It's the truly strong person who can say, "I'm sorry. I blew it!" The secure person's self-image is high enough so that one admission of error does not bring it tumbling down in a psychological slag heap.

Second. An apology is not always an admission of wrongdoing. You can be "sorry" even if you are "right." For instance, a spouse may say to a spouse, "I'm sorry that the business trip I must

> *"Somewhere we have picked up the idea that apologizing means weakness. It doesn't."*

take at this time makes you so unhappy." But still go on the trip.

Or, a parent may say to a child, "I'm sorry that our family plans won't allow you to go skiing with your friend. I know how much that trip would have meant to you." But still stick to the family plans.

More perplexing is the situation in which you feel partial guilt: you contributed to an argument with friends, but you didn't cause it. A possible apology might be, "I'm sorry for my part in what happened last night." This is what could be termed an "enabling apology." It enables others to follow suit.

Tougher yet is when you *aren't* sorry, but propriety, politics or your own prosperity demands that you say you are. You gave the "blankety-blank so and so" just what was deserved. In this scenario you have to measure your "survival" needs against your "integrity" needs. Unfortunately, I have no answers. Either choice is painful. I have made them both.

In the service of parental pride, or the development of "character," parents sometimes *demand* that their child apologize for an act over which the child feels no remorse whatsoever. Part of me views such a demand as correct training for the "real" world. Another part of me recoils from it as a wretched assault on a child's integrity which causes him or her to *never/ever* want to apologize. Besides, it can backfire.

My grandmother used to tell a story of my uncle, who at age 5 was rude to an elderly lady he didn't "cotton" to. When my grandmother insisted he apologize, he said, "But she's just an old lionface!"

Whereupon my grandmother sat him down and explained to him the necessity of respecting adults even if you didn't like them. My uncle nodded solemnly. So together they paid a visit to the lady.

When the aged "apologee" opened the door and frowned, my uncle blurted out, "I'm sorry! Mrs. Lionface!" and bolted, leaving "Lionface" still frowning and his mother "blushing purple."

So I did call on one "expert" — my grandmother. If I should have called on more, I apologize.

Conversion
Dangers of Disparaging Non-Believers

Denver Post
OCTOBER 14, 1984

As I PERUSE THE VARIOUS EDITORIALS WHICH explore the religious fervor infusing politics this year, I am reminded of a personal encounter with a woman who tried to convert me to born again Christianity.

This attempt at conversion was not an unfriendly one. It occurred shortly after my breast cancer surgery in 1981. And the woman, whom I had known since 1968, was genuinely concerned for my health. Furthermore, I like this woman — whom I'll call Linda — and I still like her.

When Linda called me in early 1982 and said she was worried about me and wanted to come by and talk to me, I knew she had conversion in mind. As an ecumenical Christian who believes no religion has a monopoly on truth, I was relatively sure I was "unconvertible." Yet I met with her because I was drawn to her spirituality and I wanted to hear, first hand, of her own religious experience.

An hour and a half conversation ensued; a conversation which, although totally amicable, became increasingly frustrating for both of us.

Linda told me the history of her own conversion. She explained how receiving Jesus and being born again had allowed her to forgive a certain family member who had hurt her terribly as a child; how only the total acceptance of Christ could allow her to purge herself of a 30-year hatred, which was poisoning her life. Linda, indeed, seemed "born again," in the best sense of the phrase; and I exulted with her in her new found peace.

The frustration began when I tried to tell her my story — that when I was in the hospital, I, too, had had a religious transformation. That facing possible death had strengthened my belief in God. That there was a whole level of trivial concern that just dropped from my being. That I had become more forgiving of those from whom I had received mental and/or emotional injury.

And the frustration grew when I was hit with a simple realization: I could rejoice with Linda over her spiritual journey, but she could not rejoice with me over mine. She could not accept my transformation as real: since *my* transformation was not *her* transformation. And *her* transformation was the only "right" one.

And although she did not say this directly, Linda's frustration and sadness implied that without my being "saved" by personally accepting Christ in the exact way she did, I might not recover from my illness.

Now, how does this very personal attempt at the conversion of another individual relate to the institutional attempt of some churches to impose their religious beliefs on society at large?

It relates because, whether the arena is personal or political, the process of dismissing and/or disregarding the religious orientation of the "infidel" is the same.

I do not denounce the fact that religious beliefs affect one's political associations and political actions. Of course, they do. And that is natural.

Neither do I denounce a church which tries to persuade its members to vote a certain way, and even asks them to influence *others* to vote a certain way — whether this church be the church of Jesse Jackson or the church of Jesse Helms.

In politics, it's not the attempt to influence that is frightening. What is frightening, and what I do denounce, is the "writing off" of those who refuse to be influenced; the moralistic categorization of the non "true believers" as some kind of forever damned sub-species.

In Newsweek (Sept. 17), Rabbi Alexander Schindler, president of the Union of American Hebrew Congregations, wrote:

"The members of the radical Christian right violate the bounds of reasonable democratic discourse when they say that those who oppose them are not misguided or wrong, but sinful, intolerant, and unpatriotic." I agree.

And, Sen. Barry Goldwater — an outspoken advocate of Americans' traditional values — has said it more bluntly:

"I'm frankly sick and tired of the political preachers across the country telling me as a citizen that, if I want to be a moral person, I must believe in A, B, C, or D ...."

In the personal arena, when one group of religious institutions disparages the moral framework, the intentions, and the very character of those who differ from them, this disparagement becomes prejudicial, exclusionary and elitist.

Even more frightening, it threatens to demolish the very cornerstone of America's democratic tradition — the ethic of free dissent.

Amen.

> *"What is frightening, and what I do denounce, is the 'writing off' of those who refuse to be influenced; the moralistic categorization of the non 'true believers' as some kind of forever damned sub-species."*

Belief in God and Human Potential Aren't Mutually Exclusive

Denver Post
OCTOBER 29, 1985

WHEN FEMINIST GLORIA STEINEM WAS invited by the Denver Women's Partnership to address the "Women Who Work" conference in June last year, a hue and cry arose from a small group of conservative Christian women.

Not so much because Steinem was a feminist.

But because she was a "secular humanist."

Letters of complaint received by sponsoring organizations claimed that in the Saturday Review of Education (March, 1973) Steinem had written, "By the year 2000 we will, I hope, raise our children to believe in human potential, not God."

I looked up Steinem's article. Indeed, she did say exactly that. And although I'm usually "sympatico" with Steinem, I find I agree only with the first half of her statement.

"What does that make me? A non-secular humanist?"

Maybe I'm missing the essence of the "Divine Power vs. Human Power" debate of the decade, but I never have understood why children can't be raised to believe in both human potential *and* God.

What does that make me?

A *non-secular* humanist?

Whether it is 1985 or the year 2000, secular institutions should teach our children respect for human potential. Religious institutions should teach them belief in God. At home, parents should remain free to teach them either, neither, or both.

This freedom, and other freedoms, are drastically curtailed when, as in the communist U.S.S.R., the secular institution of government denies its citizens their right to worship God and to participate in religious rites.

But freedom is even more drastically curtailed when religious institutions dictate to the secular, as does the Ayatollah Khomeini's Muslim Fundamentalist government in Iran.

There are those in this country who would advocate a Christian fundamentalist government. One sees this advocacy in the claims of the Christian fundamentalists that this a "Christian nation," that non-believers are "non-American," that a certain percentage of all public officeholders should be avowed Christians, that organized prayer should be returned to the public schools.

All this brings me to an interesting comparison of Christian and Muslim fundamentalists, which I read recently in the Secular Humanist Bulletin.

I don't identify with the "secular humanist" label. But I do think the following comparison raises a valid concern:

"Christian and Muslim fundamentalists believe their scriptures are the divine inerrant word of God/Allah."

"Both assert that governments should be run according to their Scriptures and decry the separation of church and state as an infidel's concoction."

"Both rationalize, or are blind to, the barbarity in their scriptures."

"Both think that all education should teach *their* religious values."

"Neither accepts a diversity of religious and non-religious views."

"Both would exclude the non-believer from political and social positions."

"Both think their values are the only ones acceptable in society."

"Both insist that women must be submissive to men."

"Both believe that the secular view is an evil device of the devil which should be eliminated."

"There is one important difference. The Muslim fundamentalists control at least one country's government: Iran. The Christian fundamentalists do not control any country's government. At least, not yet."

Let the Prayer Be for Humanity, Despite Belief

Denver Post
MAY 28, 1985

"IN JESUS' NAME WE PRAY."
I would like to have been the first one to bring this issue to the public's attention, but, although it has long been a gripe of mine, I was "scooped" by King Features columnist Vicki Williams.

In her May 4 newspaper column, Williams wrote of attending three banquets — all for secular causes, all in a rural area of the Midwest — and then complained:

"At all three dinners, the prayer before the meal ended with: 'In Jesus' name we pray.'

"Though I was raised a Christian," she wrote, "I'm not what one would call devout. But I couldn't help but wonder how those Christians who do consider themselves devout would have reacted if the prayer had unexpectedly ended: 'In Buddha's name we pray.'

"Would they have been indignant? Insulted? Would they have resented being forced in public to thank the god of another? And if so, do they think non-Christians don't feel the same way?"

Williams goes on to say that maybe it's different in the large cities of the coasts "where diversity of religion is a matter of fact."

But often it is not different. Just as it is not different in the Queen City of the Plains.

It happens often

For I have attended not three, but hundreds of banquets where the person who gave the invocation or benediction either didn't assume, or didn't care, that a certain percentage of the attendees might not have been Christians.

I even attended a predominantly Jewish benefit one time where the Mormon bishop, invited by the Mormon honoree to give the benediction, mentioned Christ three times in a closing prayer which lasted less than a minute!

Now before I am labeled as the "anti-Christ," let me say that I, too, was raised a Christian. I have been a Christian since I attended Sunday School at the age of 5 and expect to be one till the age of 95, or till my death, whichever comes first.

I have repeated, "In Jesus' name," hundreds of times — in church, at church conferences and other strictly religious functions, at family dinners, even at some weddings and funerals. And that is fitting and proper.

'Higher spirit'

But it is not fitting and proper when one publicly invokes the "higher spirit" to assume that each person's "higher spirit" is Christ. Or Buddha. Or Mohammed. Or any prophet specific to, or treasured by, one religion.

Supreme Court Justice Robert Jackson wrote in 1943:

"If there is any fixed star in our constitutional constellation, it is that no official, high or petty, can prescribe what shall be orthodox in politics, nationalism, religion, or other matters of opinion, or force citizens to confess by word or act their faith therein. If there are any circumstances which permit an exception, they do not now occur to us."

True, a benefit or a celebratory dinner is not an "official prescription of orthodoxy." But it is a quasi endorsement. Enough of a validation to make disbelievers feel uncomfortable.

Bothersome trend

Williams writes, "America seems to be trending more and more toward an aggressively Christian view of itself and that trend is worrisome. To me, the strength and magnificence of the American way lies not in its commitment to Christianity, but in its commitment to religious tolerance — in its respect for the beliefs of the individual, whatever those beliefs may be."

The more I think about this, the more I wonder. At a secular event, should there even be an assumption of a belief in God? Perhaps invocations should be worded to invoke, not God, but each individual's higher sense of purpose, creativity, willingness to sacrifice, and elevated sense of humanity.

Williams said it first, in a different paper, to a different audience. But to her ideas, I say, amen.

To whatever God you choose.

If you choose.

Musings and Memories:
Fleeing the Frenzy

On Vacation
A Time to Clarify and Simplify

Denver Post
JUNE 1, 1986

A DIFFERENT SPACE.

The plane hadn't even taken off before that special feeling lifted me up. I was still sitting in a seminar in Denver, but my bags were packed, my instructions left, my checklist of cares dropping one by one.

Is this why I travel? Is this why I throw my schedule of "have-tos" and "shoulds" into chaos, condensing days of duties into three, arising before 6, finishing up after midnight, packing in snatches of time, wondering if I'll collapse before I go? All for a four-day vacation?

I think so. This time we are going to Expo in Vancouver — business for my husband, but vacation for me. Yet it doesn't really matter where I go — Europe, Mexico, or the sand dunes of Colorado. That feeling comes, as I walk out the door.

> "Out of the blue, the solution to a problem I've been struggling with comes. The last line of a column simply appears."

The different space is not one of "mind-drain," but of mental clarity. Before I take off on a trip, I visualize my mind emptying itself of thoughts and perceptions. My brain will lie on a beach, only taking in impressions of the wind, sun and surf. Even if the body will be touring London or climbing a peak in the San Juans.

But that isn't what happens. My thoughts don't disappear. They increase. And the perceptions are not of a vacationing fuzziness, but a new-found precision. All of a sudden, I can sit in seminar and listen. Really *listen*. Without taking a note, I can remember and process each thing that is said. I can't seem to do this when I am "home."

Out of the blue, the solution to a problem I've been struggling with comes. The last line of a column simply appears.

I don't think of my daily life as a struggle or a burden. I'm privileged to be able to choose most of the things I do. But even choices can become entrapments by their never-ending demands. Our children were choices. So are my deadlines. So are my political tasks, volunteer roles, mansion projects and personal friends.

Often I don't even know that all these choices and their subsequent commitments are closing in on me till I leave. Especially now with our upcoming move. Rooms in which I used to take "mini-vacations" are scanned with an anxious eye. What goes with us? What stays? What is given away? What is stored? What is needed? What is not?

But picking and choosing among personal belongings in a huge home with its own gift of space is only symbolic of more important picking and choosing. Every few months, I need to pick, choose, throw out and store. Clarify and simplify. And going on vacation seems to be the only way.

Sometimes the ideas that come to a freshly liberated mind turn out to be useful; others hair-brained. It was while climbing mountains in South America I decided to become a social worker; while probing the underwater reefs in Grand Cayman, I thought of writing a column.

But it was also on a vacation that I decided to go back to work as a flight attendant for United at age 40, take a 10-week "women's trek" in Nepal during an election year, become a professional photographer, enter theological school.

These ideas dissolved in the jet stream the minute the shift in cabin pressure told me we were descending to Stapleton. And so have others. But at least the ideas come. At home I can plod, scramble or careen around for weeks, sometimes months, without an original thought.

I use to over-prepare for vacation trips. Read everything I could. Know all my brain could hold

to make the trip more meaningful. But I gave that up. It is too much like how I must work at my desk. Knowledge for a column or a speech has to be gained before one completes it or delivers it. On a vacation, one can experience first and learn later.

Away, the mind can pursue its fancy, not limited by what one needs to know, do, perform or communicate by this Friday, or next month. In London, once, I spent a whole day talking to bobbies about crime statistics. Not because I'd use them, but because I wouldn't.

In New York, I took a nostalgia trip on the train up the Hudson to Riverdale and tried to follow a favorite walk I took as a child. It was gone, and it didn't matter. For vacations are the process of doing, not the goal.

John Gardner once said that human beings, like plants, should be "permanently" moved and repotted every seven years. I would add that they ought to be temporarily repotted perhaps every seven weeks.

In Victoria, British Columbia, our guides were a married couple who had never been to San Francisco. We told them maybe they didn't need to go, that Victoria and Vancouver have so much comparable beauty and charm. But that was a dumb, pandering thing to say.

Of course they should go to San Francisco.

Or somewhere else.

We all should go somewhere else.

Life's "Moments" Kept in Memories

Denver Post
SEPTEMBER 15, 1980

SUMMER IN NEW HAMPSHIRE, 1940. THE sprinkler spins round and round. Absorbing the rays of the morning sun, its spray forms a pale rainbow on the white slats of the garage door. The pebbles of the gravel driveway press hot against my palms leaving a spattering of indentations which, to my wonderment, fades away. I press again.

Enchanted and wonder-filled — that early morning; the smell of clean, soft earth wafting upward; the sunshine washing my back with a sense of well-being. Summer at my grandparents' home. The dew in the grass would still be cool. I knew that by moving a few yards I could trade the hot pebbles under my hands for the lawn's cool, damp lushness on my feet. I choose. I would do that in a minute.

Choosing, knowing, wondering, well-being — my first conscious memory of the wonderment of the world and a sense of myself as an actor in it. I couldn't have been more than 3 years old.

As an adult I have wondered if my memory of that moment would be any more clearly enhanced with a photograph. Doubtful. A photograph may bring back in vivid detail moments we have half-forgotten. But one's most joyous,

> *"The generative origins of such events inevitably lie elsewhere—vivid but unphotographed—where memory alone is possession."*

spontaneous, euphoric moments that feel like "just yesterday" are more clearly etched on the brain alone — or perhaps on the soul. "Memory is possession," writes the poet Jean Ingelow.

Winter in Colorado, 1967. In a trance, I enter the back door of our new home. The Christmas tree bulbs blink with welcome, and the particles of melting snow outside the picture window dance with the intensity of the noonday sun. No music plays, but the combined blinking and sparkling seem a cacophony of song. I sit on the window bench. Home from the hospital with our first born child.

We do have a photograph of that moment, but it does nothing to evoke the intensity of feeling; just a typical young woman in a typical black turtleneck and green miniskirt, smiling at a typical tiny bundle of baby, wrapped in blue.

Winter in California, 1969. The upward-licking flames of the robust fire in the fireplace frame the strands of my mother's gold-silver hair, as she hugs me in a farewell at the door. I am crying slightly, but she is not. A week after my father's funeral, her faith, serenity and warmth flow as intensely as the flames. The shock was before; the real sadness would come later. But that moment is neither; instead it captures an isolated episode of tenderness, joy and reaffirmation. Memory is possession.

Briefer moments flash into consciousness. I cannot go to the Colorado mountains in the summer without recalling my first sunset drive to South Park on a rare evening when the vast range of mountaintops turned purple simultaneously. Nor can I visit the sea without recalling one special bright noontime when the gulls swooped by the open balcony of the San Francisco Cliffhouse. The gulls, white and sleek as their wings reflected the sun, caught my bread crusts in midair as they dove round and round in a hypnotic circle.

Such moments can be connected with love — romantic, and familial. But they do not have to be. Love does not make them, though they often illuminate love. "There is no one and only," writes Anne Morrow Lindbergh, in her immortal "Gift from the Sea." "There are just one and only moments."

Often such moments are connected to pure solitude. None can be planned; and few come from the Big Events in life which are organized well in advance and over-invested with meaning. Weddings, promotions, inaugurals and anniversaries aren't likely generators of pure unadulterated joy. For although they herald personal change and progress, their spontaneity can be killed by obsessiveness with detail; their deepest meaning sacrificed to their form, their "noteworthiness," or social significance.

From those events, photographs abound; but the generative origins of such events inevitably lie elsewhere — vivid but unphotographed — where memory alone is possession.

Human Cycles, Clearly Visible on a Train

Denver Post
JULY 20, 1981

THE LINE IS LONG ON THE UNION STATION platform from which we board the Rio Grande. We are too late to obtain seats in the famed Vista Dome, but as the train makes its first lurch forward, the children's downcast faces light up with fresh anticipation of our round-trip holiday to Glenwood Springs.

An elderly woman traveling alone joins us at a dining car table for breakfast. Her husband, she tells us, worked for the Rio Grande for 54 years. He began as a waterboy at age 16, worked up to the engine shop and eventually became an engineer. They were married in 1920.

"I buried my husband two years ago, at the age of 86, and I just buried my daughter's 65-year-old husband last week. I'm now on my way to Salt Lake City to take care of a sister who needs surgery," adds the spry, 85-year-old woman.

"And where are you going?" I ask the young couple across the table from us. The couple responded excitedly about their Grand Junction journey to the wedding of the woman's younger sister. The older woman smiles sentimentally. "We, too, were married in Grand Junction," she says.

On the way back from the dining car, we pass a family with four children. Three are healthy, vibrant and assertive. One sits listlessly, resting against a pillow. His eyes are half shut; his head bobs with the rhythm of the train. They take the train once a month round trip to Denver for treatment of her son's illness, I overhear the mother say. She does not elaborate.

Cycles.

Large cycles, one begun decades ago with a marriage in Grand Junction, regenerated by an unrelated marriage, taking its first steps from the same town.

Narrower, regular cycles like the one which encompasses a sick child going to a hospital.

Short, relatively insignificant cycles like my daughter, her friend and myself, taking a Glenwood Springs pleasure trip, up one day and back the next.

A young couple with huge backpacks starting out for a train and bus trek around the West.

All different in scope and significance. But cycles just the same.

Cycles of train passengers can't vary much from those of car or plane travelers.

Yet, as the metal wheels clack onward over the dry, hard-rock valleys and rolling hills not quite ready to burst into summer color, the train itself seems to throb with the rhythm of life's cycles.

In a car, direction can be changed instantly on the whim of driver or passenger. On a plane,

"The train itself seems to throb with the rhythm of life's cycles."

one must make the commitment to a specified destination as one boards; yet, a plane does not allow one the luxury of observing and feeling the changes close up.

On a train, the singular commitment to destination must be made, but even as telephone poles whiz by at maximum speed, one cannot obliterate details of the journey.

I wonder about the tracks running through the fields that just passed by. Are they recent scars from last summer's off-road vehicle? Or the remains of a wagon trail of a hundred years ago?

Gray, weathered shacks with doors wide open, like yawning mouths, dot the landscape, then disappear. To think that, at one time, that one shack might have been a home, that other a general store, another a stagecoach inn to host weary travelers who journeyed a week to reach the destination we will attain in one day.

As we approach Glenwood Canyon, the rocks and cliffs turn reddish orange, striking a brilliant backdrop to the gold-maze color of the underbrush. The tops of the hills turn black as the clouds creep over.

Human Cycles.

Nature's Cycles.

So clearly visible on the train.

Walls: Paths to Freedom, or Obstacles?

Denver Post
MAY 29, 1984

THE BRICK WALL STRETCHES DOWN THE EAST side of the Governor's Mansion. Like most walls of its height it is designed to divide, to keep people out. My houseguest's daughters don't see it that way. To them it is a path — a road infinitely more fun than taking the paved walk from the garage to the house.

Part of me shudders as I watch the girls, 7 and 9, prance back and forth atop the irregular wall, which sometimes tops a 10-foot drop. Will they stumble as they whisper and giggle? Will their untied shoelaces catch on the spikes? They don't watch where they are stepping, but with two days of practice, their feet seem to have learned each crack, each irregularity that could plummet them down to the ground.

Walls of my youth

Part of me shudders, but another part wants to shuck my high heels, donned for an indoor reception, and join them on their elevated path. My "parent" personality turns to "child." Maybe it's spring fever, but I start recalling the walls of my youth.

> *"For me ... 'climbing a wall' and then walking it ... is a way to pretend that for a while at least, I am slightly more 'elevated,' purposeful, and in touch with the universe than I am on the ground."*

The earliest was a long low curb in New York's Central Park Zoo. I couldn't have been much more than 3. A lion's roar scared me; I fell off, but bounced up on the curb in less than a second. "My wall" was more fascinating than any animal I had been brought to see.

Then there was a three-foot wall that wound its way down a little street in Portsmouth, N.H. The wall that hugged the sidewalk appeared designed to keep each 18th century Victorian house from crumbling to the street. Atop it was the only way I ever walked to town with my grandmother.

Maybe for children, walking a wall is the means of going one's own way without going too much against parental restrictions. Maybe, like a jungle gym or a dirt pile or a roof, it is a way to make oneself bigger — bigger than life — or at least bigger than adults. Maybe it's just a way of testing and mastering balancing skills.

Walls as barriers

For most adults, a wall usually means "keep off" or "keep out" — "you are not invited." Psychologically, a "wall" is something your mind or emotions smack up against and cannot climb over. For a marathon runner, the "wall" is the force that "hits" and makes you stagger around at the 18th mile. "Climbing the walls" is a negative expression, meaning something is bugging you or that you are wanting out.

But for me, even as an adult, "climbing a wall" and then walking it is an invitation — a way to pretend that for a while at least, I am slightly more "elevated," purposeful, and in touch with the universe than I am on the ground.

The Great Wall

On a tour of China, my most memorable excursion was the day we climbed the steps of the Great Wall. Part of me wanted to keep going — even on the part that had not been restored; to walk infinitely atop broken stones and weeds on the one man-made structure that astronauts can see from outer space.

But my favorite wall was another one from my childhood: an ivy-infiltrated, partially crumbling, stone structure that was companion to the wooded pathway my mother, sister and I used to walk to the neighborhood swimming pool on those hot, sultry, July days in Riverdale, N.Y. One day I fell off the wall and as I tried to get up, I fainted. Despite maternal discouragement, the next day I was back. I still see this wall when I read the first lines of a poem by Edna St. Vincent Millay:

Look how the bittersweet with lazy muscle moves
aside
Great stones placed here by planning men not with-
out sweat and pride.
And yet how beautiful this broken wall applied
Not more to its first duty; to keep sheep or cattle in;
Bought up by Beauty now, with the whole calm
abandoned countryside …

Mini-Vacation

Denver Post
March 1, 1982

Arizona sunshine through the palms
The day snuggles in like a babe in arms
The one-eyed morning expands
I'm away
Nothing presses this minuscule day
No Saturday cartoons bombard my dreams
Do the children have bread, cereal, cream?
No puppy at 6 a.m. can bark
Will the people complain across the park?
My space is empty
Palettes and tables bare
Pings of homebound concern dissipate quickly
to the air.
At home I shun such vacuums
A day dawning unstructured clear
Time too short to waste a minute!
What to do to add my bit!
Nothingness?? A creeping fear —
Action above all, don't slow down —
Keep yourself in a twit.
Homebound days do not allow
The vacuum to surround
Which I feel now.
The hole and the whole wrap me in cotton
gossamer wings
I take you total nothingness
And my heart sings.
I don't have to jog — but I may.

I don't have to write — but I can.
I don't have to read — but I probably will.
This minute I just luxuriate in the quiet; the still.
Nature abhors a vacuum
Not me.
Today I love nothingness
Passionately.

ETHICS AND MORALITY:
From Consciousness *Raising to* Conscience *Raising*

Parents' Rights
To Decide Their Child's Fate

Denver Post
FEBRUARY 2, 1986

"HIS NAME IS JIMMY. SHOULD HE HAVE BEEN Allowed to Live?"

This question topped a November 1985 McCall's magazine story about Jimmy Barash, a baby born in 1974 two months premature, deaf, hydrocephalic, brain-damaged, retarded, and blind. Now 11 years old, Jimmy weighs 26 pounds and has no measurable IQ.

Jimmy almost died three times before he was 4 months old. But each time, hospital machinery pulled him through.

Once, when Jimmy's father, Paul Barash, said that he wanted Jimmy removed from all the equipment so that God could decide whether he should live, the doctor shook his head.

"Our job is to save lives," he said.

When Paul pleaded that he was not telling the doctor to destroy him, but just to let nature take its course, the nurse glared at him.

> "The key question in the McCall's article is not 'Should Jimmy have been allowed to live?' but 'Who decides?'"

"Look how beautiful he is," she said. "How could you want to kill him?"

Intimidated, Paul Barash gave up.

The story of Jimmy and his family, retold in November McCall's, is a modern American Tragedy. After Jimmy's release from the hospital at the age of 4½ months, Paul Barash, an employee with a Wall Street brokerage house, and his wife, Seraphene, a bank teller, went from solid middle-class status to bankruptcy, welfare, food stamps, and total poverty in three short years.

Presently, the Barashes, who have developed health problems of their own, owe $18,000 in medical bills and $12,000 in other bills and loans. Paul has gotten off welfare, but he can't make too much money, or Jimmy's Social Security disability benefits will be cut.

Trying to hold the family together, keep Jimmy at home, and tend their other two children, they feel cheated by the government since, says Paul, "It would cost the taxpayers $30,000 to $40,000 a year if we put Jimmy in an institution."

But I digress. This is not a "cost to the taxpayers" column. This is a "parents' rights" column.

The key question in the McCall's article is not "Should Jimmy have been allowed to live?" but "Who decides?"

251

And it seems to me that, when the life to be lived is to be no life at all, it is the parents who should decide whether their severely disabled newborn should be taken off hospital machinery, or should be given life-lengthening surgery.

For it is the parents who will care for the child, perhaps for as long as they live. It is the parents who are likely to be impoverished emotionally and financially. It is the parents who may have to deny their other children a normal life. It is the parents whose own health is at risk. Not the doctor's. Not the hospital's. Not the government's. Not the clergy's.

Conversely, if the parents want everything done to save an infant with a poor prognosis, that too is their right, whatever the cost. And society should find a way to treat the family humanely and compassionately.

Many other "Jimmys" have been born since 1974.

One, of course, was the highly publicized "Baby Jane Doe" of New York — the 1983 case in which the federal government intervened to "save" Baby Jane when her parents considered the possibility of not having life-lengthening surgery for their daughter who was born with an exposed spine and less than half a brain.

And just last month, Lynn and Jack Bellingham of Boston (after 13 surgical procedures at a cost of $1 million on their deformed, brain-damaged, severely ill, newborn son Ricky) threatened to sue Children's Hospital in Boston if the medical personnel continued to prolong their child's life with machinery. This time, the doctors concurred that "enough was enough." Ricky died a painless death Jan. 20.

But powerful spokespersons would disagree with these doctors' decision. Surgeon General Dr. C. Everett Koop is one. In a speech last spring he stated, "In all my years (in pediatrics) I never had a child come to me later and say, 'Why did you try so hard to save my life?'"

With due respect to the eminent physician, of course he didn't! How many "Jimmys" can get out of their adult-sized cribs and come to him and say anything at all?

So *should* Jimmy have been allowed to live? Yes — if, after he was taken off the life-sustaining machinery at his parents' request, he was able to live without it.

But the Barashes should have been allowed to decide to withdraw the equipment. Instead, they were denied this right to decide, and then denied the right to decent aid by the same society that denied them their right to decide!

And Jimmy, at age 11, lies on a beach towel moaning each time the radio is turned off or he loses his pacifier. Paul looks a decade older than his 39 years. Seraphene talks wistfully of "just once" being able to sneak off to a movie with her other two children.

And the bill collectors call on the phone.

Suicide
Who Makes the Decision?

Denver Post
SEPTEMBER 8, 1985

ALL SUMMER I HAVE BEEN HAUNTED BY A column that Jim Sanderson wrote for Contemporary on June 9.

It concerns a 58-year-old woman, named Marilyn, who had just been diagnosed to have Alzheimer's disease. This woman wrote a letter to Sanderson, explaining that, because her debilitating illness would leave her husband with horrible memories of her and very few financial resources, she was considering suicide.

She followed by asking Sanderson to "help other people to understand that there are times when ending one's life is one acceptable solution."

I'm even more haunted by Sanderson's column now. For last month I received disturbing news. An old friend of mine, also in his 50s, is said to have been diagnosed as having the same disease.

For the purpose of confidentiality, I'll call my friend Hugh. And as I think of Hugh, 25 years slip by. Teased, envied and admired in his youth for his "Charles Atlas" build, Hugh was a physical fitness nut long before it became fashionable.

"I had to become a muscle man!" he told me once. "I was a tall, skinny, acne-infested kid with no friends. I decided to build my body and I did. And I know now I can build my life, in any direction that I want."

And Hugh did build his life the way he wanted, believing totally that a person is the author of his own existence. Last year I learned from mutual friends that Hugh was planning to take time off from two pressure-filled and success-filled jobs to organize a mountain-climbing expedition to Europe, continued evidence of this "take charge" approach.

Now, instead, he's wandering around Asia looking for a cure. At least that's what these same friends say. Nobody knows for sure. Only that he is gone.

Jim Sanderson, in printing Marilyn's letter, seems to build a credible case for suicide, but then, in his response, suddenly turns away from her plea to justify it "as one solution."

Instead he offers some fatherly advice about seeking every possible chance for the cure of her disease. In addition he gently chides her for underestimating her husband's love for her. Letters from readers which were reprinted in his July 28th column overwhelmingly supported both his advice and his chiding.

My own opinion on this subject was suddenly crystallized on Aug. 27 when side by side in the Denver Post appeared the following two stories:

"Ex TV reporter writes of role in mom's suicide."

"Wife slayer loses his bid for freedom."

The first story highlights excerpts from Betty Rollin's new book, "Last Wish." Rollins', after hearing her terminally ill, 75-year-old mother's plea, "This isn't life … I want to die more than anything else in the world," reports she conducted research that helped her mother commit suicide.

The second story discloses the latest verdict in the appeal process of a 76-year-old Florida man, Roswell Gilbert, who was convicted of murder in the "mercy" shooting of his 73-year-old wife who had Alzheimer's disease.

So, a woman gives her mother, at her mother's request, the information by which she can take her own life.

And an elderly man kills his wife, not at her request, but because of his own feelings of love and mercy. If all the facts be known.

Yet, all the facts are not known, in either case. They probably never will be. And questions remain that blur the lines of distinction between the two cases.

Couldn't Rollins's "giving information" in some ways be seen as "murderous" as pulling the trigger? And wasn't Gilbert, in a sense, justified in acting on what he perceived would be his wife's

request if she were still in a mental state capable of making it?

"Blurs" to the side for a moment, my answer to each of these questions is "No."

For if suicide is indeed ever justified, it is only so when it is the expressed wish of the terminally ill person. Not when this wish is "assumed," even out of love, by someone else.

So, my crystallized intellectual stand is that, yes, there may be times "when ending one's life is one acceptable solution," so long as this solution is initiated by the ailing person who seeks it.

"For if suicide is indeed ever justified, it is only so when it is the expressed wish of the terminally ill person."

But an intellectual stand is light years away from the giving of personal advice.

It would be hard, if not impossible, to give such "advice" to a person who is (or might be) actually considering suicide. Sanderson couldn't give it to Marilyn, a stranger, even in a letter. And I couldn't give it to Hugh, a friend, even if he asked.

Morality
Young Girls' Approach

Denver Post
FEBRUARY 19, 1984

HARVARD PROFESSOR CAROL GILLIGAN HAS written a book, "In A Different Voice," in which she analyzes the special moral development of girls and women. In the January issue of Ms. magazine, Gilligan says:

"Something happens to girls when they're about 12. In some ways, a crucial question for the future will be 'How do we get females not to abandon what they know at 11?'"

What could an 11-year-old girl know that could possibly hold a key to the future? According to Gilligan, a lot:

For example, she knows that moral dilemmas sometimes offer courses of action other than strictly "right" or "wrong" solutions. Gilligan cites a study in which two bright sixth-graders, Jake and Amy, were asked the following hypothetical question: A man's wife is dying and he cannot afford the drug that would save her life. Should he then steal it?

Jake responded with a logical "yes." Life is more valuable than property. If he were arrested and brought to trial, the judge would understand this and be lenient.

Amy, however, refused to accept the problem as it was asked: She saw it as less of a question of legality and more as one of relationships. Maybe he could borrow the money, she ventured. Or why couldn't he "talk it out" with the druggist to get a better price? For if he stole the drug and went to jail, and then his wife got sick again, his wife could be abandoned anyway.

Both Jake and Amy wrestled intelligently with the moral dilemma. Yet, since Amy's responses were concerned less with law and logic and more with relationships and "connectedness," she was scored a full stage lower in maturity and judgment than Jake.

According to Gilligan, this adherence to an ethic of relationship and connectedness is the reason young girls are less likely to play games in which there will be defined winners and losers. Instead, they prefer games where everyone can walk away with pride: A win/win situation.

Yet, as a young girl approaches adolescence, she finds herself in a lose/lose situation. Why?

Because she senses that her special type of morality is viewed as inferior by the male-oriented dominant culture. Her ethic is not "logical." It is sometimes circular. It does not answer questions directly. It brings in "extraneous" facts. And the example of Amy shows that her senses are right! Her special sensitivity has taught her to read the reactions of others very accurately. Thus, the innate wisdom she possesses serves to stunt its own growth.

> *"Yet, as a young girl approaches adolescence, she finds herself in a lose/lose situation."*

As a young girl grows up, she finds her special ethic useful in the subculture of the home. But, she doesn't dare bring it to the "big world" of work or politics for fear of rejection. She senses, again accurately, that she will be disregarded — not only by boys and men, but by all the adult women who have abandoned what they knew at 11 and, in Gilligan's words, have gone "ethically underground."

Gilligan maintains that a basic fault of the dominant society is that it views unconstructed female wisdom as "troublesome." (Amy lost points partly because her answers didn't fit the male-developmental model.) A major reason Gilligan wrote "A Different Voice" was to convince the academic establishment that this "different voice" should be welcomed openly as "research, creativity, progress or knowledge." Something that is separate from, but equal to, the "dominant voice."

The paradox here is that just as the growing female must take on some of the dominant culture's rationality in order to *voice* her different knowledge, the dominant society must adapt some of her relationship-connected sensitivity before it can *hear* what she's saying.

But, why should we be concerned with all this? Why should we encourage young girls to stay "above ground" with their special morality and continue to speak in their "different voice?" Why is this 11-year-old female morality of connectedness a crucial key to the future? Gilligan gives one answer in a succinct sentence:

"Our notions of winning and losing have been rendered obsolete by nuclear technology, so we need a new set of rules."

Women who have retained some of their pre-adolescent wisdom, and men who have absorbed it, know that war is a lose/lose situation. They evaluate victories and losses in battle not with isolated body counts, but with how each body *counted* to the family who lost it.

They see even in "enemy" nations how each family of "theirs" is connected to each family of "ours." And how all families' life lines are connected to the ozone layer, which could be destroyed in the next war, with the resulting destruction of all families. In short, the continued abandonment of that "different voice" could spell the abandonment of *any* future.

Another Mommy
The Child's Welfare Should Come First

Denver Post
JULY 20, 1986

O NE DAY WHEN OUR SON WAS ABOUT 2½, AND I was working part-time, my regular baby sitter got sick. It took me about two hours to find a substitute sitter. By the time I finally walked Scott up the steps to her home, I was frantic and frazzled.

But Scott was unperturbed. "'Nother sitter, 'Nother sitter, 'Nother sitter," he chanted gaily as he climbed the steps. Because he liked his regular sitter, even the word "sitter" had positive connotations to him.

I thought of this rather minor episode last month when I read the heartbreaking story of the Wyoming couple who had to give up custody of their 3-year-old adopted daughter.

In a 4-to-1 decision, the Wyoming Supreme Court instructed Mary and Lonnie Penney to return Elizabeth Sarah, whom they had adopted at birth, to her unwed biological mother, 19-year-old Tammy Doyle.

Doyle, who had petitioned for custody of Elizabeth Sarah, won her case on a technicality; at age 16 when she relinquished Elizabeth Sarah she had not signed the post-birth adoption agreement, required by Wyoming law.

Devastated, the Penneys nevertheless tried to ease the transition for Elizabeth Sarah as gently as they could.

"… I started telling Liz she had another mommy," said Mary Penney to Post reporter Dana Parsons in a front page story June 22. "It was the first time I'd ever told her. I just thought one way or the other, it would be best if she had a little forewarning.

"'Mommy' has a good connotation to her. So she was excited about meeting another one."

Another mommy. Another mommy. Another mommy. I could almost hear Elizabeth Sarah chanting these words as easily as our Scott had talked about another sitter. But there is no way that Elizabeth Sarah's transition will be easy.

In this case, the birth mother "won."

The adoptive parents "lost."

But did anyone consider the best interests of the child?

Clearly, four out of five justices did not.

Yet how much blame can one lay on the justices? Their job is to interpret the law. And, although most child adoption and custody laws include clauses that refer to the "best interests of the child," too often the laws subordinate the child's "best interests" to an adult's "selfish interests." They also tend to favor the biological parent even when best interest of the child almost always lies in remaining with the "psychological parent."

The "psychological parent," according to child development experts Joseph Goldstein, Anna Freud and Albert J. Solnit, is the parent who has performed the day-to-day, nitty-gritty duties that add up to the nurturance of the child — the one to whom the child has bonded, physically, mentally and emotionally.

In their book, "Beyond the Best Interests of the Child," these authors take the controversial position that it doesn't matter whether the psychological parent is a biological parent, an adoptive parent or any other caring adult. But that, for the future emotional health of the child, the child's earliest, most consistent parental relationship should take precedence. They further suggest that the *only* exception to this precedence would be the proof of gross negligence or abuse.

In other words, parents' rights should be secondary to the child's welfare even if a petitioning parent is technically or legally "correct," as Tammy Doyle was.

Such cases are not simple.

Perhaps the most difficult type of case is one in which a very young child is "stolen" by a non-custodial parent, and then is found three or four years later. Obviously the abducting parent *did* wrong. And the custodial parent was wronged.

But if the abducting parent has raised the child well and has become the "psychological parent,"

"For the future emotional health of the child, the child's earliest, most consistent parental relationship should take precedence."

should the child then go back to the original custodial parent in order to right that parent's wrong or to compensate for the parent's past suffering? I think not.

The authors of "Beyond the Best Interests of the Child" maintain that although we can "feel" for everyone in such cases, it is the child's right to continuity that should prevail.

In addition the authors recommend that, in an adoption case, "the adoption decree be made final the moment a child is actually placed with the adopting family. (And that) the period for appeal should be drastically shortened …."

I agree. And so, I believe, would one of the justices in the case of Elizabeth Sarah. The lone dissenter, Chief Justice Richard J. Thomas, wrote:

"I cannot perceive how it would serve the best interests of this little girl to be separated at this time from the only parents she has ever known … I cannot avoid a clear perception that psychologically this court is cutting this baby girl in half."

Bad Humor
Cruel Jokes Cross the Line

Denver Post
MAY 5, 1985

BACK WHEN I WAS A FLIGHT ATTENDANT, A passenger introduced herself as a graphologist and "just for fun" asked to analyze a sample of my handwriting.

"No sense of humor," the graphologist said after a cursory look at my scribble. "People who leave a small left hand margin generally lack a sense of humor."

I was devastated. I couldn't have been more upset if she had found some great moral weakness or a total absence of rational intelligence.

This was supposed to be "just for fun" and I couldn't find it funny, an uncomfortable paradox that only complicated my devastation! Was my sour reaction just proof of the pudding?

I have thought about the incident over the years each time I hear a racist or sexist joke I don't think is funny. I don't want to laugh. Sometimes I succeed in showing my distaste. But at the same time I worry, "Maybe it's just me. Is there something wrong with my sense of humor?"

"Men (and, I presume, women) will confess to treason, false deeds, arson, murder, or a wig. How many will own up to a lack of humor?" wrote essayist and humorist Frank Moore Colby.

But I'm tougher now. And more self-confident about what is funny and what is not.

Columnist Joe Bob Briggs was recently fired from the L.A. Times Syndicate for cruelly making fun of the poor and black of the world.

Since The Denver Post had the decency not to print this particular column, neither will I directly quote him. Suffice it to say that how anyone could be amused at his "humor" — which also stereotyped the handicapped, Orientals, and "stupid" whites — is utterly incomprehensible to me. But it shouldn't be.

Humor as a weapon has been around for a long time. And those who use it seem to be desperately clutching to their own status needs.

Betty Swords, professional cartoonist and teacher of "humor power" at University of Colorado at Denver, in a book she is writing points out that historically humor has solidified and continues to solidify the power of the white male majority by poking cruel fun at those who differ: minorities, women, the handicapped, homosexuals, the poor. Each barb of cruel humor commits a "little murder," Swords maintains.

> *"Humor as a weapon has been around for a long time. And those who use it seem to be desperately clutching to their own status needs."*

Let's look at two jokes about women:

"I owe everything I have to my wife: headaches, ulcers, ticks!"

"Women shouldn't be out working and taking away a man's pay — they should stay home and steal it from his pockets like other wives."

When one of these jokes is told at a banquet, does a woman laugh? If she does, is she just being a good sport? Is she trying to please her husband or her boss? Or is she actually buying that negative, "murdered," image of herself, and perpetuating it for other women?

If she does not laugh, does she lack a sense of humor? Will she be labeled as one of those "dour feminists"? And will she eventually band together with her sisters to develop a special inbred women's humor — as minorities have done? A "victim" humor, a private humor, that allows the powerless to transcend the pain imposed.

She may. But the problem with victim humor is that, although it may help the individual transcend the pain, it does not help the group transform the society which stereotypes it.

As Swords points out, laughter on both sides tends to keep the power structure firmly entrenched and its subgroups securely in "their places":

"Civil rights activists were never known for their humor. Blacks were not giggling gaily on their march to Selma, Ala. Nor were women liberationists yucking it up while struggling for their constitutional rights as citizens." No wonder the status quo got nervous.

Ridicule more tightly binds the disparaged to their own sense of powerlessness and sometimes influences them to act out a societally prescribed stereotype: If told enough times that, as a woman, I am weak, silly, conniving, thieving, and frivolous, I may become weak, silly, conniving, thieving, and frivolous.

Even more dangerous to the ridiculed group is the fact that an object of laughter in a "good" psychological and economic climate can become an object of hatred when the times turn sour. As humorist Sam Lebanon wrote of the Jews in Nazi Germany:

"'Their' old eccentricities were now declared menacing vices no longer to be laughed at, but to be obliterated by destroying 'them' down to the last 'him.' Humor becomes homicidal, even genocidal."

Joe Bob Briggs' column committed a "little murder" in each sentence.

Joe Bob Briggs' column was potentially genocidal.

Joe Bob Briggs deserved to go.

Conflict of Courage vs. Loyalty Often Involves Searing Decisions

Denver Post
AUGUST 11, 1980

THE ELEMENTARY-SCHOOL STUDENTS WERE discussing citizenship. Loyalty and courage were two of the most often mentioned words.

"But sometimes loyalty and courage fight each other," said a sixth-grade girl. "What do you do then?"

The bell rang. The mood changed, and the children filed out.

"'Courage' is a word too freely thrown around," said John France, head of the Colorado National Guard, at a dinner party the same evening. "Take a fighter pilot. We feel he is courageous to the extreme because most of us cannot imagine ourselves in his situation. But to him, his achievements are just a logical extension of what he and his peers have expected him to do."

A logical extension of peers' expectations. To act on such would be to perform in a loyal manner. To act against such peer expectations could be courageous. Or it could be traitorous, depending on who is judging.

A person of the opposite political party who votes often with one's own is a hero, a statesperson to the nth degree. A person of one's own party who does the same is described in words too strong for print.

That politicians lack courage to go against "the moneyed interests" is a widely accepted cliche. Yet, in actual political life, it is vastly more difficult to go against one's own philosophical and emotional supporters than against some distant and impersonal "establishment."

Saying "no" or publicly disagreeing with the person who spent Saturdays and Sundays pushing a baby carriage door to door canvassing for your cause pits courage and loyalty on a stomach-sinking collision course.

For we all build our communities of support. The community may be the political party we have chosen, a strong centralized church into which we are born, or a loosely knit, spreadout group of friends who think the way we do and share our experiences.

Yet, whatever our community, its hold on us is strong and going against its tide is painful.

Sonia Johnson was excommunicated from the Mormon Church for criticizing its position against the Equal Rights Amendment and for beginning a countermovement: Mormons for the ERA. She was willing to give up the cherished religious affiliation central to her life, and to alienate members of her family, because she believed in something deeply.

That the church is still part of her resonates in her conversation with columnist Ellen Goodman.

> *"In actual political life, it is vastly more difficult to go against one's own philosophical and emotional supporters than against some distant and impersonal 'establishment.'"*

"Ironically I am what they made me. I'm strong because the church makes strong women. There is a song in the church: 'Do What Is Right and Let the Consequences Follow.' I took them at their word."

When one is faced with two equally strong and meaningful values, what does one do? Most of us will sidestep those head-on situations if we see them coming, but sometimes we find ourselves mired in a courage-testing dichotomy inadvertently. And many of us who appear courageous have never really been tested against the mores of our own reference group.

In 1978, local writer and Democratic activist Patricia Gilmore displayed courage when she published her well-written articles against the Equal Rights Amendment. She was not only going against popular Colorado sentiments, but more difficult, against the views of those in her own intellectual community whom she deeply respected.

"If I had been younger and more impressionable I would have been intimidated by those friends who not only disagreed with my stand but seemed to be questioning my right to take such a position," states Ms. Gilmore two years later.

A more recent and very vivid national example of a woman in the courage vs. loyalty conflict

is former vice chairwoman of the Republican National Committee, Mary Crisp.

Mary Crisp, to most of us, appears comfortably and conventionally in the mainstream. A dynamic, sensitive and attractive political activist, Ms. Crisp is effective with groups of both men and women. Like 55 to 65 percent of Americans, she favors the national Equal Rights Amendment.

So, in Detroit last month she scrapped her original speech on "Party Out-Reach." Instead, she reminded the Republican National Committee of its 40 year commitment to the ERA and chided the platform committee for dropping this commitment:

"Now, we are reversing our position and are about to bury the rights of 100 million American women under a heap of platitudes," said Ms. Crisp with indignation.

Mary Crisp took a majority opinion to a minority-opinion group. Not so difficult, we are tempted to think. Yet people in that small group were lifelong friends with a premium on unity and loyalty. Other people in that small group had the power to break her future political career.

Said Ms. Crisp to me in a recent phone conversation: "Though I'm now completely cut off from a viable political future, I did not feel courageous at the time. I was simply swept away by the moral obligation of doing what I thought was right."

Trimming the "Horns" of Health Care

Denver Post
OCTOBER 3, 1993

THERE WAS ONCE AN ELK THAT ROAMED THE green hills and forests of Ireland. As this elk evolved, his horns became more and more magnificent.

First adapted for fighting other males and attracting females, the branching grandeur of his headdress eventually became entangled in the trees. Stuck there, an easy mark for predators, the Irish elk became extinct.

Psychology professor Willard Gaylin, president and co-founder of the Hastings Center for Bioethics, likens this Irish elk to the American Health Care System.

The "horns" of the nation's health care dilemma, says Gaylin, are: 1) Technology; 2) Autonomy.

According to Gaylin, it was not until the 1930s that medical technology, in fact even medical *intervention,* was any more likely to do good than harm. But now technology can do anything from the sublime to the ridiculous.

Two examples of the sublime might be: cataract surgery for the old and testicular cancer treatment for the young. The first procedure enhances old age. The second ensures old age to young men who just a generation ago would have died.

> *"Yet, to become unhooked from the twin horns of Technology and Autonomy, we cannot continue to offer futile or marginal care to everyone."*

Two examples of the ridiculous could be: Spending $1 million to separate Siamese twins at birth, one of whom will die, the other of whom has a 1 percent chance of survival; and the keeping on life support systems a 90-year-old man who is dying of four, yes *four*, terminal illnesses.

"Autonomy" demands we do everything medically possible, no matter the degree of hope or futility.

Yet, to become unhooked from the twin horns of Technology and Autonomy, we cannot continue to offer futile or marginal care to everyone.

I fully realize that I am preaching a doctrine by which I will have to live.

I already live with it via my 85-year-old mother who just had a knee replacement. Medicare paid for the procedure.

Would I deny her, or any other healthy senior, this? No. But should "autonomy" for my mother stretch to her having a heart/lung transplant? No. Those precious transplant parts should be reserved for those further down the age line.

Same with breast cancer, my own disease. Twelve years ago insurance paid for my mastectomy and extensive chemotherapy. Yet if cancer should hit me again, should my "autonomy" demand coverage for some new experimental drug which has no track record? No.

On Sept. 22, the president and Hillary Clinton announced their new comprehensive health-care package. That night, Americans polled on television responded overwhelmingly to the Clintons' leadership with a willingness to give.

The next day, Jean Hummel, co-owner with her husband Gordon of Hummel's Delicatessen in Cherry Creek North, told me that they expected to pay more for their employees' insurance.

"But if that means prescription medicines and all people will be covered, it's worth it," she quickly added. And her response is only one example of our local willingness to give.

Being willing to give, however, is only half the challenge.

Being willing to *give up*, especially those treatments at the margin, will be our second test.

Our giant health-care system stands before us like the great American elk. Its two horns, technology and autonomy, tower dangerously toward the trees. We don't want to get rid of this grand headdress, just clip it and keep it adaptive.

Because the predators are out there. So are what Dr. Gaylin would call "our raging medical appetites."

Can we rein in our appetites and clip our own horns? Each person, just a little?

If we can't, despite reforms, our great American health-care system, which rockets toward 20 percent of our GDP, may topple of its own weight.

Extinction by bankruptcy.

Bad Things Still Happen to Good People

Denver Post
FEBRUARY 18, 1996

IT'S EASIER IF YOU CAN BLAME SOMEONE.

When five members of a rural Colorado community were killed in the head-on collision of two pickup trucks early this month, my first reaction was horror and revulsion. My second reaction was rage.

Why weren't the victims — four of them children — wearing seat belts?

My third response was that of total helplessness.

Why? *Why* do such tragedies have to happen?

I do not know the two families involved in this accident, but my heart reaches out to them, partly because of another fatal crash, the week previous, which hit close to home.

Natalie Bond — the 10-year-old killed in that collision (of a Subaru and a tractor-trailer) on Interstate 25 near Castle Rock — was the granddaughter of a member of my women's group, a friend of mine since high-school.

Stupefied when I got the phone call, I tried frantically to find "fault" — or at least a "reason" — for this horrendous catastrophe. But to no avail. Seat belts were worn by all — the two who died, the three who survived. Drugs and alcohol were not a factor. Neither was bad weather.

The 19-year old driver of the Subaru, Natalie's baby-sitter, was not irresponsible, just inexperienced. As a driver in training, she had her aunt, a licensed adult driver, sitting next to her as the law requires. The aunt was killed; but her two daughters in the back seat, sitting on either side of Natalie, were spared.

An accident. Pure and simple. Yet so complex.

"There is no reason. It was not caused by God. It is not God's will," said one of the ministers at Natalie's memorial service. "But God abides with us through our sorrow."

Randomness exists. As Rabbi Harold Kushner said, bad things happen to good people.

There are no answers. But when such horrific cruelty strikes close to us, we continue to search. We must. We have to. Not only because "meaning" could ease our sorrow. But because finding "fault" in others might "protect" us and ours from such a fate.

> *"If God is really present in our pain when random disaster strikes, even in our anger we would be less judgmental."*

If we can blame a drunken driver. Or a negligent parent. Or a daredevil teenager. Then we can say: That won't happen to *me*. I and mine don't drink and drive. *We* parents would never let our kids do that. *My* kid wouldn't speed.

Which brings me to another kind of tragedy. When 14-year-old Gina Bernard was shot to death by two teen boys last month, I instantly became enraged at the father, who gave the boys access to the guns.

But when Chuck Green, in his Jan. 17 column, and his respondents who wrote to The Post on Jan. 19, came down so hard on Gina's mother,

Mary Ann Romero, for not knowing where her daughter was so late at night, I became suspicious of their anger, and even of my own.

It's not that I don't think those writers to the editor, mostly parents, are not good parents. Or that I approve of teenagers being out at 3:00 a.m.

But are those parents so sure they *always* know where their children are? That their teens *never* lie? Are they certain that their kids' friends don't have access to guns, or booze or drugs?

The best parent in the world can make a fatal mistake. And that's exactly what terrifies us.

Subsequent reports indicate that Mary Ann Romero got off welfare eight years ago and was providing for Gina by working three jobs. Isn't this what we are saying welfare mothers should do? Yet, if they are at work when a tragedy occurs, are we then saying they should be home?

Do we somehow subtly delude ourselves into thinking that if we parents, especially we mothers, are always home, our children will always be safe?

I don't know.

But I do know this: If God is really present in our pain when random disaster strikes, even in our anger we would be less judgmental.

We should never stop searching for causes that will enable us to prevent tragedy when we can.

But we are fools to think that finding the faults in others' actions can keep *us* eternally secure.

Reaching Outward and Inward:
Touching Others, Searching Self

A Very Busy Man Who Took Time to Aid a Stranger in Distress

Denver Post
JUNE 25, 1983

Very busy man, VBM. Three and one-half years ago I wrote of a VBM friend of mine who took 90 minutes to help a stranger. The stranger, a lost, retarded adult, attracted the VBM's attention in a supermarket parking lot one cold winter evening. The VBM, sensing the man's confusion, spent from 7:20 to 8:50 p.m. driving the man around Denver to connect him with the van which had dropped him off for a group recycling project.

Last week the VBM did it again. This time the man he helped was not retarded, but was handicapped by the loss of a leg.

The VBM had left his downtown office around 9 p.m., when he was approached by the neatly dressed young man on crutches. The man asked the VBM directions to 20th and Glenarm. The answer the VBM gave seemed to confuse rather than help the young man. So the VBM offered to take him to the address, in his Volkswagen parked nearby.

At first the young man was reticent.

"Have you been drinking?" he asked of the VBM as he peered into the Volkswagen.

"No."

"Well, I lost my leg in a VW accident …. I don't know if I should …."

"I haven't been drinking. You'll be safe."

The young man got in. The address at 20th and Glenarm turned out to be St. Andrews Abby Transient Shelter. The young man, it seems, had been treated earlier in the day at Colorado General for a problem related to the loss of his leg. As he was from out of the city and knew no one in Denver, the hospital personnel had suggested the shelter as a place for him to spend the night.

But he arrived too late. He was told by the woman in charge that no new residents could be admitted after 8 p.m. All the beds were taken, and his admittance would be against sanitation rules. She advised him that with so many people out of work he would have to come early in the morning to be assured of a place for the next night.

The VBM then drove the young man to the Samaritan Shelter at 18th and Logan. Same story. No room. Too late. Line up in the morning.

As the young man was in considerable pain and appeared to be either slightly emotionally disturbed or affected mentally by the painkillers given him earlier in the hospital, the VBM suggested going back to Colorado General. The man agreed reluctantly, saying he was sure he wouldn't be accepted for the night.

He wasn't. The admitting nurse said that she couldn't give him a hospital bed without the doctor's orders, and the doctor's orders clearly said the patient needed outpatient treatment only.

The VBM then suggested he drive the young man to a motel. The man accepted, saying he had friends in Fort Collins and Boulder who might be able to come for him the next day. He also had a small disability check that would probably arrive at a local bank the next day.

On the way to the motel on Santa Fe Drive, the VBM bought the stranger two tacos and a pack of cigarettes. Upon arrival, he paid $7 of the charge for the $11 motel room: the man, who had $5, paid the balance of the bill, retaining $1 for bus fare to the bank and phone calls.

The purpose of telling this story isn't to lament the lack of facilities for the homeless, jobless and disabled in Denver, although clearly there is a lack. It isn't to chastise shelter personnel who didn't accept the man for the night. "They were very nice and only doing their jobs," said the VBM. Neither is it to criticize the admission nurse at Colorado General. The man's medical problems, likely, didn't merit a hospital bed at taxpayers' expense.

The purpose, instead, is to point out that personal charity isn't dead. Stories abound about man's inhumanity to man, woman's inhumanity to woman, bystanders who fear "involvement," and people who go back to sleep instead of dialing 911 to report screams in the night.

The VBM had worked a 12-hour-day, but added another hour and a half to take a young stranger's plight personally. He was not too important, too busy, too uncaring or too frightened to help another human in distress.

I'd like to reveal his name, but he's too self-effacing.

"It wasn't any big deal," he said two or three times while relating the story to me. Maybe not, but it was a "little deal" that counted. And it's good to know people like him are out there.

Helping Muslims Feel at Home

Denver Post
SEPTEMBER 8, 2001

"NO, NO, NOT NOW!" EXCLAIMED THE YOUNG Somali mother as she jumped up from her prayer rug.

"Not now. We are praying!"

Red-faced, I apologized profusely, quickly shutting the door to the small room. Clearly, I was too early. Yet, no sooner had I sat down to wait for her, she opened the door and reappeared.

"I am ready now," she said, her smile radiating eagerness, her arms hugging a copy of the U.S. Constitution that I had promised to help her review.

Many Somali moms are studying to become U.S. citizens. While all of them want to keep their religious traditions, they still aspire for their children to become fully American, succeed at school and in life, and strive for college.

For two years, I have volunteered at the Somali Community Center of Colorado, tutoring children in the After School Program. Once, a friend asked me if the children were "becoming acculturated to America."

"Yes," I answered with a laugh.

The children, most of whom were born here or came when very young, speak unaccented English, are bright, energetic and eager to learn. They also compete, play foot games under the table, grab each other's pencils, and use American slang. Too acculturated, I sometimes think.

However, this acculturation process is not so easy, especially for the adult Somali refugees who have fled their chaotic homeland. And yet how much should America's secular culture accommodate Islamic religious and cultural needs?

What is to be done, for example, when Muslim employees request time off and designated places to pray at work?

Should public swimming pools be closed to men at certain hours so Muslim women will feel assured that no men outside their families see them uncovered? More urgent than workplace issues or social conflict are the instances where Muslim Shariah law might conflict with U.S. secular law.

I found it shocking when, in 2008, a New Jersey judge ruled that Shariah law permitted a Muslim immigrant from Morocco to rape his Muslim wife, despite the fact that marital rape is illegal in New Jersey. (Fortunately, the decision was overturned on appeal.)

We cannot out of religious "tolerance" or cultural sensitivity ever allow any religious law to supersede our secular ones.

Omar Nur, program director of the center and an American citizen since 1993, conducts a fatherhood program to help Somali men adjust to American life and customs.

"In Somalia, the father is seen as the sole provider, protector and 'discipliner' in the family," says Nur. "Once in the U.S.,

> *"We cannot out of religious 'tolerance' or cultural sensitivity ever allow any religious law to supersede our secular ones."*

particularly if the father arrives here after the family,

the mother has been the provider, whether she is working or receiving state aid for refugees.

"This is a complete role reversal. And fathers need to learn that physical discipline of children and wives is not OK in the U.S. In fact, here it is called 'domestic abuse,' and they can go to jail for it."

By October 2011, the center will have graduated 29 dads from its classes, in one of 76 such programs in Colorado. Funded by the Colorado Department of Human Services, it has been recognized as the state's Fatherhood Program of the Year.

Volunteers at the Center all initiated a women's commercial sewing program, a women's English literacy/conversation class, and sessions to provide help in obtaining citizenship.

A Gallup poll shows that 60 percent of Muslims feel that they are "thriving in America," second only to Jews at 62 percent. Yet, unsurprisingly, 48 percent of Muslims also cite instances of discrimination.

According to the Pew Research Center, Muslim population growth in America is expected to grow from 2.6 million in 2010 to 6.2 million in 2030.

No matter how one might feel about this expansion, couldn't we agree that places like the Somali Community Center can only raise the "thriving" statistic to new heights and reduce the "discrimination" statistic considerably?

In a nation where all of us — newcomers and old-timers alike — worry about both our personal and national security, wouldn't the success of such endeavors improve the likelihood of both kinds of security and diminish our distrust and fear of each other?

Helping Your Fellow Man

Denver Post
August 8, 2013

ONE DAY BACK IN THE 1980S, I WALKED THE hills in San Francisco with author Tillie Olsen.

Perplexed by the plethora of panhandlers in various garbs and degrees of destitution, I asked Olsen, "How do you tell which ones are deserving? Who really needs help?"

"Dottie!" exclaimed this mother of four, who, to support her children, stuck with menial jobs for 20 years without writing a word. "Begging is *hard* work!" End of conversation.

Last winter in Morocco, I witnessed begging in a different cultural context. A little old woman with wizened face and humble posture stood at the main gate to the Medina, rattling her cup and mumbling her pleas.

One day we went through the gate with a young American friend, Mary, who had lived in Essaouira for a year. They exchanged a few words in the local dialect, then the old woman looked close to tears. Mary hugged her and said "thank you."

Mary explained that this woman always greeted her and her dog with a smile and gave the dog a treat. "But I had to put Ruffo down last week, and she was expressing her sorrow."

Mutual sorrow and mutual respect.

When I told this story to two Denver friends, they each commented that people begging anywhere need respect and recognition as much as they do money.

One, a minister, wrote in an e-mail, "(I know) a woman through a lunch program at our church, and when I see her on the corner with her sign, I open the window and wave and call her by name …. I do not give her anything but my recognition of her as a person."

Panhandlers in Denver can range from the sympathetic to the scam artist. Bennie Milliner, executive director of Denver's Road Home, gave me examples of the two extremes:

One, an older, disabled man who solicits on a thoroughfare near the airport, plants himself on his corner every day. As soon as he makes the $32 to cover his motel stay, he packs up and heads "home." The other, a middle-aged man, picks a favorite spot downtown, makes his haul, then goes to an alley where he has parked his car, sheds his begging garb, and drives off.

Denver officials I spoke with reminded me that panhandling, covered by the First Amendment, is a legal activity. It cannot be banned, but it can be regulated. For example, under a variety of Denver ordinances, panhandlers cannot approach or verbally harass a passerby; cannot block vehicle or pedestrian traffic; and cannot solicit within 100 yards of an ATM machine.

However, the best way to help the homeless, say the officials, is to put change into one of the 55 blue smart meters stationed around Denver. There are plans for 30 more of the newly refurbished meters (which all take credit cards) in the near future. There are hopes the meters will generate up to $100,000, all of which goes into programs directly benefiting the homeless.

I just dropped $5 into the meter on Sixth and Broadway, but I also have recently given to a woman holding a "single mom needs Rent" sign, and to a man claiming to be an Iraq war vet. Then, just last week, I approached a young panhandler on the corner of 15th and Larimer streets. Although I intended to simply hear his story, it was so compelling that l ended up parting with $2.

Call me gullible. Call me a bleeding heart. And call me if you know of a 12-step recovery program for those addicted to giving to people instead of machines.

> *"Call me gullible. Call me a bleeding heart. And call me if you know of a 12-step recovery program for those addicted to giving to people instead of machines."*

Finding Compassion at Our Borders

Denver Post
SEPTEMBER 13, 2015

THEY BRAVE DISASTER, DESTRUCTION AND potential death. Yet the refugees from the war-torn Middle East and Africa still come, fleeing war and persecution to seek safety in the Northern European countries — which, with few exceptions, do not want them.

In early September, a Care International plea for funds popped up on my computer: "Refugee Crises; humanity washed ashore." We were sickened by the photo of a dead 3-year-old Syrian boy on a Turkish beach, his father in tears.

In late August, the refugee calamity unfolding was that the estimated number of dead bodies, abandoned by smugglers in a truck on a major Austrian highway, had risen from 50 to 71.

The deaths by suffocation of these men, women and children, mostly Syrian, trying to cross from Hungary into Austria cast a pall on the nearby Regional Conference on Refugees being held in Vienna. German Chancellor Angela Merkel, "shaken by the awful news," addressed the conferees:

"This reminds us that we in Europe need to tackle the problem quickly and find solutions in the spirit of solidarity."

But can they, and will they?

"We were sickened by the photo of a dead 3-year-old Syrian boy on a Turkish beach, his father in tears."

Germany, with the strongest economy in Europe, has been the most generous in accepting refugees, accounting for 40 percent of the 334,080 asylum applications to the EU in the first five months of 2015. As many as 800,000 are expected to apply for asylum this year. That is nearly 1 percent of Germany's population.

Nevertheless, other European countries are balking, and I can understand their resistance as much as I can identify with and sympathize with the refugees. Even if the current numbers of desperate people fleeing war diminish, what will happen when migration inevitably ratchets up again due to economic collapse, over-population and global warming in the Middle East and Africa?

All the values of my youth taught by my church, by the civil rights movement, by my education in social work emphasize the rights of all people, no matter where they reside.

Then, as an older adult striving for, though not attaining, public office, I was taught that tough, sometimes agonizing, choices have to be made.

A liberal friend at a dinner party shocked me when she said, "Europe has to draw the line. Set a date and say, 'Here is when you go back, even if it means you die.'"

I shudder, yet fear she may be prescient. Whatever decisions are reached on the immediate crisis at the meeting of the European Interior Ministers scheduled for Sept. 13, they are bound to be short-term.

The population of sub-Saharan Africa alone is expected to quadruple from 1.1 billion to 4.2

billion by the end of this century. Can all the disenfranchised or climate-threatened people from the Middle East and the southern hemisphere move to Northern Europe? Hardly.

Despite all my liberal teachings, I am still a nationalist. I feel a nation's boundaries should be as sacred and self-determined as a person's boundaries.

Yet, I hope never to lose my sense of identity with, and compassion for, people fleeing war, persecution, rising sea levels or those simply trying to better the economic situation for their families. I hope never to start branding them as "inferior," or as "the other," or to turn away from their suffering simply to justify my nationalistic instincts. May we find a way to help them where they are.

Visions of my own grandchildren rise before me. I look once more at the body of that little boy, and I cry.

MODERN DILEMMAS, EVOLVING RESPONSES:
Where Do We Go from Here?

Times Change, Fear of Being Victim Grows

Denver Post
APRIL 6, 1981

South Denver, 1972.

AN OLD MAN WAS CRAWLING UP THE STREET — the gutter to be exact, east from South Broadway in Englewood. Obviously inebriated, possibly injured, he was clearly in danger of being hit by a car.

I slowed down my Volvo station wagon, glanced at my 1½-year-old daughter strapped into the baby seat in the back, and hesitated — only for a moment. Of course, I had to pick him up and try to get him home. He certainly was in no shape to be threatening.

As I struggled to help him in the car, he mumbled his address; within minutes I had deposited him on the neatly trimmed lawn of his home in a modest southeast Denver neighborhood, waiting only long enough to see his scowling wife open the door.

> *"I can't remember how many times our house became a lighthouse of assistance for human vessels in distress."*

Our house in southeast Denver was not large, but its location on a raised corner lot near Harvard Gulch gave it visibility and an air of prominence. The tricycles and toys that cluttered the front yard no doubt served as a beacon of accessibility.

At any rate, I can't remember how many times our house became a lighthouse of assistance for human vessels in distress. Strangers, all. Strangers, welcome.

Capitol Hill, 1979.

From the back seat of another station wagon, our daughter, 8, pointed to a shirtless young man lying at an awkward angle over a low wall surrounding the entrance to a neighboring high-rise apartment.

"What's wrong with him?" she asked excitedly.

"I don't know," I said, "but let's see if we can help."

I circled the block, parked and locked the car and told my daughter and her friend to honk the horn like crazy if he gave me any trouble.

He didn't.

"Thanks," he groaned, as I poked his shoulder and advised him that if he wasn't sick he'd better get moving before the July sun charred his back.

"Quite a party," he mumbled sleepily as he ambled up the street, donning the T-shirt he had used as a pillow.

"Our" prominent Capitol Hill home attracts strangers in distress, too. But they are helped by guards. I seldom see or hear of them. That, of course, is safer.

But precisely when did the weight of my thinking shift from helpfulness first to safety first? Perhaps it shifted last year with the nationally publicized shooting of Dr. Michael J. Halberstam and the murder of John Lennon.

Or perhaps this year when I read in The Denver Post that Colorado stands sixth in the country in serious crimes committed and 16th in violent crimes.

Perhaps three weeks ago as I read of the child molester, still not apprehended, who has sexually assaulted 23 children in their own homes, almost all between Capitol Hill and south Denver.

Or possibly last night, as my young friend relates with terror how just that afternoon she and her daughter were accosted in their own apartment by a thief who somehow had obtained a key to their suite.

Perhaps now, March 30th. My pencil freezes rigid in mid-air as the chilling news of the assassination attempt on the president interrupts the soft music on the radio.

Columnist Ellen Goodman writes:

"It isn't just the criminal offense that affects our lives; it is our own growing defensive. When we learn to turn on the alarm, put the jewelry in the refrigerator, push down the buttons in the car, think twice about walking down the street, our lives are diminished. Our lives are diminished not only because we fear violation, but because we fear our own good instincts. Daily we become less free to be good neighbors. Potential acts of charity, which in previous days allowed us to be kind, if hardly heroic, we now view with painful, paranoid ambivalence."

South Denver, 1981.

Might the drunk, so classically positioned in the gutter, be but a lure, an entrapment for an unaware young mother and child, set up by potential kidnappers hiding in the bushes? Better drive by.

Capitol Hill, 1981.

Might the young man with the sunburn be hiding not only his face, but a crazed or violent personality? Perhaps a gun? Serious crimes do occur in midday. Beware. Better drive by.

We better drive by. Don't open the door. Don't get involved. It's safer for us not to take even a tiny chance.

Safer, that is, until the person in distress is "us."

Episodes Make You Search for Own Moment of Truth

Denver Post
MARCH 10, 1982

ITEM — PAGE 1. THE DENVER POST: BYSTANDERS ignore a young mother's plea for help as a naked man harasses her in a residential area in broad daylight. Babbling incoherently, the man attempts to wrest away the stroller in which she is pushing her 8-month-old daughter.

Item — Editorial page, The Denver Post: Several customers wait on the sidewalk until they can find a waitress to pay for their lunches after being evacuated from a burning restaurant in downtown Denver.

Ironically these two stories appear in the Post on the same day.

In the words of the editorial writer: "Those (restaurant) customers left a 'tip' for the public — an unexpected reaffirmation that our basic values aren't as decayed as often assumed."

At another time, those words could ring more true. We would welcome them anyway and hope that they were a sign, a mark of one-upsmanship for humanity's basis goodness.

But the observers who ignored the woman in trouble left no "tip" for the public. And some did far worse than to just drive by or to sit passively in their parked, locked cars.

One bystander, when approached for help on his doorstep by the desperately frightened woman, simply mumbled something about how much he was enjoying the show!

A report of the same incident by another newspaper mentioned how another man merely stood back and said, "It's your problem, baby."

It's perhaps too simplistic and too obvious to suggest that the nobility of the persons willing to pay for lunches they can well afford pales beside the dishonor of other persons who apparently are afraid to risk potential minor injury for what might have been a major catastrophe for a terrified woman or even a fatal injury to an 8-month-old baby.

The naked man wasn't armed, and in time was subdued by the temerity of a newspaper reporter (Brad Martisius of The Post) who approached the deranged man screaming menacingly.

Yet, the stark feelings evoked in us by the harassment incident go deeper than contempt for the passive bystanders or identification with the victims. For, eventually, each of us, upon reading either story, has to ask himself what he would have done. Many of us, I dare say, would have stood by to pay our lunch bills.

But, probing one's own depths on our potential reaction to the naked man can be more wrenching. What would we each be like in our "moment of truth"? Is one of the reasons we become so

> *"Is one of the reasons we become so disgusted by passive bystanders that we fear, deep down, that we might react as they did?"*

disgusted by passive bystanders that we fear, deep down, that we might react as they did?

I am reminded of another incident in a Los Angeles supermarket in which a friend of mine was involved a few months ago.

While my friend was standing second in line at a checkout counter, a woman immediately ahead of her collapsed with a heart attack. My friend, completely untrained in first aid, instinctively, immediately, loosened the woman's collar and began mouth-to-mouth resuscitation.

"While we were engaged in this life or death struggle," my friend angrily related later, "the people far back in line became so damned impatient. Some were even complaining about their melting ice cream or their missed television shows!"

Then she stopped, mused a moment and added: "But, honestly, I don't know, I was so close I had to be involved; but if I had been more distant, perhaps 10th in line instead of second, would I have been grumbling about my ice cream?"

None of us really knows what he/she would do in such instances.

Hemingway said, "Courage is grace under pressure." Will one of us exhibit this grace out of an innate goodness of soul? Will another of us exhibit courage in one instance and pettiness or cowardice in another, our choice of action depending completely on our mood of the moment or our distance from the incident?

Stories such as these make us search nervously, tentatively, for clues to our own character. Yet, no one of us is truly tested until we are in such a spot, physically and mentally "on the line." And maybe that, more than the horror of a victimized person, is what is most frightening.

Think Young
Generation Faces Huge Costs Caring for Aged

The Denver Post / Cindy Enright

Denver Post
OCTOBER 6, 1990

NO WONDER THE YOUNG WOMAN NEXT TO ME on the plane flipped over the feature story on the Daughter Track to the hard news section of Newsweek.

She can avoid it now, but eventually the Daughter Track could become her "hard news."

Let's say this woman is 25. That means that her middle age would come between the years 2010 and 2030.

Her "baby bust" generation is the smallest to hit the scene since the Great Depression. Yet its future responsibilities loom awesome, partly because of its small size.

Newsweek reports that today the average American daughter spends 17 years raising children and then turns around and spends *18 years* caring for an aging parent or in-law. With the way we "oldsters" are living longer, and the sheer number of the aging Baby Boomers right behind us, this woman's "parent caring" time could stretch to 20 or 25 years.

Additional worrisome statistics:

- In the 1940s, a plethora of 13 workers was available to support one retiree. By the early 2000s, only 2½ workers will be available to support one retiree.

- Right now 12 percent of the U.S. population is over 65. By 2030, 21 percent of the U.S. population will be over 65.

- By 2030, the population of the *old* old — those over 85 — will have skyrocketed from 4 million to 10 million.

These are not depersonalized numbers. Not for this young woman. And not for our family. My husband and I easily could be two of those *really* old old — 90 plus — in the year 2030. And our two "baby bust" kids could just be easing toward their own retirement.

A paraphrase of that old Beatles' song keeps running through my head as I write this: "Will you still neeeed me, will you still feeeed me — when I'm 94?"

But seriously, what kind of sacrifice and goodwill can we expect from this new generation?

Remember, these are the young people already predicted to be the first generation in America that won't "do better" financially than their parents did. These are the young people already saddled with housing costs, child-care costs and increasing transportation costs astronomically higher than any preceding generation faced.

A Time cover story on the "twentysomething" generation suggests that today's young adults may feel no obligation whatever to care for their parents, as they do not feel their parents cared much for them.

These young adults are angry, says Time. Angry about their parents' divorces. Angry about "being left to raise themselves." If there is one commitment these young adults will make it will be to their own kids, not to their parents.

In short, the seeds of a strong resentment factor have been sown. Add to this resentment factor an even more ominous one: Many of this new tax-paying generation will be made up of minorities and new immigrants who will feel even less obligation to the huge groups of retired, wealthy, white elderly.

And, on average, the elderly *are* wealthy. They have more disposable income than any other age group. Furthermore, they pay far fewer taxes.

In fact, says the Congressional Joint Committee on Taxation, in 1990 a typical young worker with a spouse, a child and a $30,000 salary paid up to five times the federal taxes paid by a typical retired elderly couple with a $30,000 income.

So, what's the solution for that huge group of us who are aging and that far smaller group that will be supporting us?

First, the easy ones:

We need immediately many more home health-care programs, home-visitor programs, elderly day-care programs, respite-care programs, hospice programs, mandated dependent leave legislation that will allow daughters and sons to take time off to help elderly relatives. In fact, *anything* that can help the multigenerational family cope and allow seniors to stay in their own homes or in a family environment.

In addition, we need a variety of retirement living facilities to meet the needs of both the well and ill elderly. We also need massive education on "living wills" and the laws that affect them.

Second, the harder solutions:

- A requirement that admission to nursing homes will be contingent upon the prospective resident signing a "living will."

- A tax shift that would allow full taxes on the 85 percent of Social Security received that is an income transfer. Right now, our entitlement programs transfer $270 billion a year to all the elderly regardless of need, when we could lift the poor elderly out of poverty for $5 billion.

- A long-term care program financed by the wealthier elderly for the poorer elderly. I know! I know! The attempt to do this in catastrophic care was, indeed, a catastrophe. The rich elderly don't want to pay for the poor.

But do they — do we — really want our kids to have to pay for this? When I say we, I mean exactly that. As an aging American, I expect to have to live by the rules I recommend.

Give me a robust early retirement, a legally guaranteed living will, a comfortable nursing home or hospice, and when diagnosed comatose, demented or terminally ill, a quick exit.

In short, let my kids spend their limited resources on their kids!

Students Can Be "Dumbed" Up or Down

Denver Post
DECEMBER 4, 1994

CLASS DUMMY.

At the 10-day "Total Immersion" Spanish course I took last July at Dartmouth College, I was assigned to a too-high-level class, and I became the worst student in a group of nine.

This "class dummy" identification was a totally new experience for me. My generally high level of self-esteem plummeted. Consequently, new fears of inadequacy kept my anxiety level skyrocketing and my learning curve absolutely flat. One hot New Hampshire night I woke up in a cold sweat. I had dreamt that I was plotting to *kill* one of my instructors.

This experience replays itself now because of the controversy raging around Charles Murray's and Richard Herrnstein's new book, "The Bell Curve: Intelligence and Class Structure in American Life."

The book — which maintains that at least 60 percent of intelligence is genetic, that IQ is a reliable measure of that intelligence, that blacks as a group consistently score 15 points lower than whites, that psychological factors are relatively unimportant, and IQ is unchangeable through environmental forces — is heralded by some and scorned and feared by others.

Although I welcome the dialogue, my own fears are very specific and center around two questions. One has been echoed by many commentators — from liberal-leaning Carl Rowan to conservative-leaning Joan Beck: If up to 40 percent of IQ is not genetic, why do the authors give such short shrift to that 40 percent?

The second fear springs more from my own instincts. Let's say that IQ scores *are* a fixed phenomenon. What happened to the old-fashioned adage that success is due 10 percent to inspiration and 90 percent to perspiration, and that even if IQ cannot be changed, performance certainly can. My low self-esteem in that Spanish class had me so "dumbed down" I couldn't think rationally — I was even dreaming of murder!

> *"If dumbing down can happen so quickly to a middle-class, middle-aged, white person with a generally high self-confidence level, won't it happen even faster to a black ghetto teenager with no self-esteem, a 'zip' accomplishment record, and a teacher who writes him or her off at first glance?"*

If dumbing down can happen so quickly to a middle-class, middle-aged, white person with a generally high self-confidence level, won't it happen even faster to a black ghetto teenager with no self-esteem, a "zip" accomplishment record, and a teacher who writes him or her off at first glance?

Conversely, if people can be dumbed down, can't they also be "brightened up"? Of course. Examples of the latter are:

- In "Summer Scholarship," a Northeast Denver drop-out prevention project, 511 academically "at risk" elementary school pupils entered small-group summer reading programs. In the first year, 61 percent of those improved both their reading skills and their attitudes. And almost one third rose a whole grade level. I don't know what the IQ level of those children is, or if it changed. But if performance and attitude improved, does it matter?

- The Hostos high school for at-risk teenagers in the South Bronx is having similar results. After four years, 80 percent of these originally designated "probable dropouts" are headed for college.

Black conservatives are writing that, yes, environment is important in raising moral, successful children, but environmental changes have to be made earlier and the responsibility rests with the black community itself to lower illegitimacy rates and increase parental responsibility.

Fine. Whatever works!

That's the point. Some things do work. And whatever doesn't will get routed out in this ever more conservative political climate. As a taxpayer, I worry that some "environmental" attempts to raise IQ and/or performance may *do* nothing.

But as a social worker and as an American, I worry far more that the Murray/Herrnstein emphasis on group averages and "static" IQ scores may give us all a convenient excuse to *try* nothing.

The Earth
We Must Understand Our Responsibilities

Denver Post
SEPTEMBER 2, 1990

TODAY 5.3 BILLION PEOPLE INHABIT THE EARTH. By the year 2030 that number will double.

During this week alone, another 1.7 million people will be added to the world.

At the same time, 100 animal species become extinct each day.

Every 10 minutes a square mile of rain forest is destroyed.

Every five minutes 9,000 gallons of oil are spewed into our seas.

Scientists debate the speed and effects of human-induced global warming. But no one debates its existence.

The above statistics and scenarios are not natural disasters.

They are human-made tragedies, created by ignorance and/or greed, girded and rationalized by worn out principles and biblical injunctions, wise in their day but disastrous in ours.

Genesis condemns humankind to a perpetual state of ignorance and travail because Adam and Eve committed the "original sin" of eating the fruit of the knowledge tree. Yet, despite our sin and our ignorance, Genesis commands us to be fruitful and multiply and to assert dominion over the earth, the sea and all its species.

We have obeyed all too well.

And if we continue to obey we will doom ourselves and our planet.

In 1854, Chief Seattle of the Puget Sound Indians was asked to sell a large area of land in what is now Washington state. In a letter to President Franklin Pierce, pleading that the white man continue the red man's stewardship of this land, Chief Seattle wrote: "We are a part of the earth and it is a part of us. The perfumed flowers are our sisters; the deer, the horse, the great eagle, these are our brothers …

"We know that the white man does not understand our ways. One portion of land is the same to him as the next, for he is a stranger who comes in the night and takes from the land whatever he needs.

"The earth is not his brother but his enemy, and when he has conquered it, he moves on … his appetite will devour the earth and leave behind only desert …

"I have seen a thousand rotting buffaloes on the prairie, left by the white man who shot them from a passing train …

"The earth is our mother. Whatever befalls the earth befalls the sons of the earth. Man did not weave the web of life, he is merely a strand in it. Whatever he does to the web he does to himself."

Almost 150 years later the developed nations continue to exercise "dominion" to plunder, while

> *"They are human-made tragedies, created by ignorance and/or greed, girded and rationalized by worn out principles and biblical injunctions, wise in their day but disastrous in ours."*

the underdeveloped nations continue to overpopulate. Not all of our present ignorance and evil stems from the injunctions of the original Genesis, by any means. The majority of the world's people have never even read it!

But just suppose a few key phrases of Genesis, written originally between 900 and 600 B.C., were rewritten or "updated," say 200 or 300 years ago. And suppose its

The Denver Post / Maureen Scance

modernized tenets had become known throughout the world. And suppose the revised passages looked something like this:

"So God created Man and Woman in his own image, in the image of God created he them; male and female created he them, and named them Adam and Eve; and made them husband and wife.

"And God blessed them, and God said unto them, be fruitful and multiple, and replenish the earth, but multiply carefully lest ye usurp the grass and the water and the air and the fruit of the trees and leave naught for your grandchildren and other species of the earth over which ye shall have stewardship.

"And the Lord God planted a garden eastward in Eden; and there he put the man and the woman whom he had formed.

"And the Lord God commanded the man and the woman, saying of every tree of the garden thou may freely eat: especially that of the tree of the knowledge of Good and Evil, for you of all the

earth's species shall have the gift of free will, and if your free will is not informed by the knowledge of good and evil thou shalt surely die.

"And the woman saw that the tree was good for food and that it was pleasant to the eyes, and a tree to be desired to make one wise. She took the fruit thereof, and did eat, and gave also unto her husband with her; and he did eat.

"And the eyes of them both were opened, and they knew that they were now wise; and they were afraid because they knew that they could no longer obey God blindly, but must use their newborn knowledge intentionally for the sake of themselves, their descendants, and the animal kingdom and the earth over which God had given them stewardship.

"And the Lord God said, Do not be afraid. Behold, the man and the woman have become as one of us, to know good and evil: and now he and she are worthy of their stewardship of the earth and all its creatures. Let us celebrate in the name of woman and of man and of God."

Would God be pleased with this re-writing and with those who followed his tenets?

The God that I know would.

And *would* we follow them?

Perhaps. If we are deemed wise instead of ignorant and sinful, maybe, just maybe, we would behave as such.

Chief Seattle said:

"One thing we know, which the White man may one day discover — our God is the same God .... The earth is precious to him, and to harm the earth is to heap contempt upon its Creator."

And upon ourselves.

And upon all other species of the earth.

And upon life itself.

An Agonizing "Scruples" Game about a Real-Life Tragedy

Denver Post
JUNE 1987

SCRUPLES.

Last month on a sailing vacation, our family of four (son, 20, daughter, 17) played the game Scruples. Here's a sample question from the game:

You work at a bank. Another employee is blamed for your error, involving thousands of dollars. It cannot be traced. Do you own up?

It's a tough game for parents to play with their kids. You would like simply to enter into the spirit of the contest. Instead, you get caught up in hoping your kids will give the "right" answer, hoping, too, that you, as parents, will come across as "scrupulous."

I continued to think about this game long after the vacation ended. Then I read a tragic Denver Post story, which prompted a real-life "scruples" question that made my hair stand on end.

You will remember the story. It involved a young couple killed when their car hit another vehicle broadside at a rural intersection in Adams County. Before the accident, a stop sign at the intersection had been removed, presumably by teenage vandals.

So, there's the Scruples question:

Let's say, as a parent, you read about this incident. Then, the next morning, you discover a stop sign under the bed of your 18-year-old son.

You confront your son and find to your horror that *his* sign is *the* sign.

What do you do?

Your son has caused two deaths. You are sickened, conflicted and terror-stricken. If the "death weapon" had been a gun or a knife, the police would be seeking it as evidence in a murder case. But there is no search for a stop sign.

You call your lawyer, and he advises you to do nothing.

It was an accident, your lawyer emphasizes. The couple was partly to blame. They were not wearing seat belts. Their 11-month-old infant, fastened securely in his baby seat, was unhurt. The county was partly to blame. When the accident occurred, the stop sign had been missing for longer than 24 hours.

If you take your son in to the authorities, with the idea of making him responsible for his actions, he could be charged with criminally negligent homicide and could spend from one to four years in prison. He could even be charged with manslaughter, which mandates a two-to-eight-year prison sentence.

Felonies! Prison! But your son is not a criminal!

He needs four years in college, not four years in the "pen." Your fingers grasp the bookcase by the phone for support. You inhale sharply and watch your knuckles turn white.

Parents should bring up their kids to be responsible for their actions. You've tried to do just that. But your son didn't understand the possible consequences of his actions. Though no longer a juvenile, he is young. Boys will be boys. And aren't parents supposed to protect their kids?

The family of the dead couple could sue for reparation. God knows they deserve reparation. But from your son? From you? Your son has never even gotten a speeding ticket. He's a congenial B-plus high school senior with a part-time job. To your knowledge, he has never stolen anything before except a "Corona St." sign, a couple of years back.

The thought strikes you hard. That's the sign you should have made him return. Instead, you wrote off the incident as a gag, a prank. Perhaps you didn't bring up your kids to be "as responsible for their actions" as you thought.

Oh God, is all this your fault?

Maybe. But you still don't deserve it.

But what did that young couple do to "deserve" death?

What did that baby boy do to "deserve" losing his parents?

You understand from the newspaper account that the father's mother will raise her grandson. If she should sue under the wrongful-death statute for the cost of his upbringing, she could take all your son's college savings and most of what you own.

"Two people are dead. Your son has lost his innocence. And you have lost yours."

Stay quiet, you will tell your son. This episode must not go outside the family. The guilt he must bear overwhelms you.

But suppose he doesn't show guilt? What would absence of remorse say about him? About you? Either way, he should have professional psychological help. You will get it for him. You will also get it for yourself.

Yet, deep in your gut, you know nothing will ever again be the same. A certain "lightness" has gone out of your family forever.

It would not be "right," nor loving nor smart for you as a parent to turn your son in. You know that. But in the greater, cosmic, moral sense of the word "right," you have failed.

Two people are dead. Your son has lost his innocence. And you have lost yours.

You have not lived up to your scruples.

Politics:

Pronouncements, Process, and Politicians

The Personal *Is* Political and Vice Versa:
So Speak Up!

Our Military "Emperors" Are Naked

Denver Post
JANUARY 31, 1983

A COUPLE OF YEARS AGO MY DAUGHTER AND I had the following conversation:

Heather: "Why are we building nuclear bombs?"

Mom: "I guess because the Russians are."

Heather: "But couldn't they mean the end of the world no matter who sets them off?"

Mom: "Yes."

Heather: "Then why don't we just stop?"

Mom: "It's not that simple. We have to negotiate …."

Heather: "I don't understand. Why don't we just stop — all of us — the Russians, us, everybody! Why don't we just stop!?"

My daughter's outburst reminded me of the child in the parable of "The Emperor's New Clothes."

The emperor and his court had been duped by the royal tailors into believing that anyone who could not see the non-existent clothes they had "tailored" was hopelessly stupid.

"Children can expose a basic truth with one comment because they have little investment in the established order."

When the emperor paraded through the streets to show off his "finery," it took an innocent child to declare, "But the emperor is naked!"

Children can expose a basic truth with one comment because they have little investment in the established order. For adults to see truth as clearly takes a leap of faith, a letting-go of old mind-sets, a process that historian and philosopher Thomas Kuhn calls "paradigm shift."

According to Kuhn, and to Marilyn Ferguson who expands on his thesis in "The Aquarian Conspiracy," "A paradigm shift is a distinctly new way of thinking about old problems." It is not a gradual process. It occurs all at once. The new paradigm is not "figured out" but suddenly seen.

Children see because they are not encumbered by old paradigms. The child in the parable saw that the emperor was naked because the child's livelihood, prestige, belief system did not yet count on the emperor presenting himself in a splendorous manner. The child's truth did not depend upon the emperor seeing the truth.

The modern child can see the futility of the nuclear arms race because she or he has not yet been brain-washed by generals who, since the invention of the bow and arrow, have preached that the side with the most weapons wins.

The child can see that if one lad has seven matches and the other nine, they are equally capable of burning down a barn filled with hay.

During the Vietnam war, thinking adults began to see the paradox, the hypocrisy of another military paradigm. When military defenders said, "We had to destroy the village to save it," these adults did not nod their heads in a stupor. Instead they challenged the old mind-set: Destroy? Save? How are these words possibly compatible?

Just this Christmas a friend sent me a message that was a new paradigm view of a military invention.

The message began with a headline from the New York Times of Aug. 9, 1981:

"Reagan orders production of two types of neutron arms for stockpiling."

"These weapons are designed to produce far more radiation and far less blast and heat than other tactical nuclear weapons so that they kill people without severe damage to their surroundings."

The message ends with a poem the author conceived after pondering the New York Times story.

The house still stands.
Bookcases along the wall replete with volumes.
Poetry, music, art, some mysteries, some fiction.
The desk holds stationery, pens and stamps,
Unfinished letters, notes reminding someone to pay bills.
Collect the laundry.
Get the children shoes for school.
Outside the garden flowers in the sun.
Roses and peonies go unpicked,
Bicycles lean against the wall.
Tennis racquets sprawl across the court.
Somewhere the bell of a Good Humor Truck rings idly.
Propelled by the wind, and clocks strike hours.
A cat, perhaps a dog, a mouse, moves shakily, sniffs for food.
And listens.

— Eugenia Rawls

An Open Letter to the Pope

Denver Post
AUGUST 1, 1993

DEAR JOHN PAUL II:
    Welcome to Colorado. We of the Rocky Mountain West are honored by your eminent and gracious presence.

Although not of the Catholic faith, I admire your outspoken stand against war, discrimination and intolerance, and your promotion of the fact that a more equitable distribution of material resources would make a better world.

On July 5, I read that the goal of your visit will be an "Embrace of Humanity." I applaud. If there is any time humanity has needed such a powerful, inclusive embrace it is now.

I then read on July 9 that the Papal Encyclical "Veritatis Splendor" (translated "Splendor of Truth") will continue the Catholic Church's ancient ban on all artificial birth control, on the grounds that contraception "blocks the transmission of life."

Respectfully, I must ask you:

- Does the transmission of life, no matter the quality of that life, or the health of the mother, who could die from giving birth to one more life, exemplify the Splendor of Truth?

> *"The Old Testament command, 'Be fruitful and multiply,' made sense at the time of Christ, when the world population totaled 250 million—less than the U.S. population today."*

Where is the "splendor" of a mother dying in childbirth?

- Does your Embrace of Humanity not include those women who, when they are able to space their children by at least two years, will have healthier, happier children who will be more likely to grow into productive, tolerant adults who exhibit the very humanitarian qualities you extol?

- How can your denial of contraception be expected to bring to an end the tragedy (and in your eyes, the sin) of unsafe, illegal abortion which kills close to 200,000 women a year?

- Can even your powerful, encompassing Embrace of Humanity include not only the present world's population of 5.4 billion, but the more than 10 billion the population could reach by 2030? That doubling of the population, 97 percent of which will occur in the developing world, cannot help but bring more war, more violence, more starvation, more discrimination — the very terrors against which you so boldly stand.

It is true that, up until now, it has been political and social inequities which have contributed more to world hunger and environmental degradation than the population explosion. But only up until now!

For even as the developing countries stabilize their politics, and the developed nations reduce their consumption levels, no "distribution plan" can be expected to reach more than twice the population the world carries today.

No technological breakthrough will arrive fast enough to ease such enormous human pressure on the Earth's fragile ecosystem.

In short, the world needs, and women want, contraceptive technology.

More than 140 governments now support family planning programs.

Still, according to a World Bank report, 40 percent of the world's married women wish to avoid further births, but do not possess the contraceptive technology to do so.

The Old Testament command, "Be fruitful and multiply," made sense at the time of Christ, when the world population totaled 250 million — less than the U.S. population today.

It makes sense no longer.

In 1992, on the 350th anniversary of the death of Galileo, the Catholic Church offered a posthumous apology to this great scientist for its persecution of him and its rejection of his Solar Centered theory of the universe.

I have read that when the officials acting for Pope Urban VIII initiated their arrest of Galileo, he implored them: "But, look into the telescope! Look into space!" They refused to do so.

Today, I implore you. It is not space with its potential that needs your powerful gaze. It is the Earth with its limitations.

Please. Don't refuse to look.

In 350 years, it will be far too late for a papal apology.

If You're Not Worried, Get Worried — And Vote!

Colorado Woman News
October 2000

WHEN JANE FONDA SPOKE TO SUPPORTERS of Rocky Mountain Planned Parenthood last spring, she began by quoting an anti-choice view of sex from 1873.

"Sexual intercourse, unhallowed by the creation of a child, is lust. A wife without children is a mere sewer to pass off the unfruitful and degraded passions and lusts of one man."

But just in case you think such views are dated, listen to a recent *Denver Rocky Mountain News* Letter to the Editor.

In response to an Ellen Goodman column, which chastised insurance companies that covered Viagra for men, but not contraception for women, Matt McGuinnes from Sterling writes:

"Viagra, it is claimed, helps men to (let us put this delicately) function fully. The Pill does just the opposite: It takes an otherwise healthy (fertile) woman and makes her unhealthy (infertile). Goodman is not concerned with health, but with frolicking — making it possible for women to act in a sexually irresponsible way, just like men."

In short: Sex is dirty. "Un-pregnant" is unhealthy. Women who do not want to become mothers are moral derelicts. All men are lustful louts.

These may not be the actual words of the anti-choice radical right, but they do express its sentiments. Add to it the fact that their ultimate goal, just as it was at the beginning of the modern women's movement in 1873, is the curtailment of the power of women.

I will not try to be objective about the upcoming election. For if George W. Bush and Dick Cheney are not card carrying members of the "radical right," they give every indication they will let its leaders sit at their table — perhaps at its head.

George W. Bush has said, "I do not like abortions. I will do everything in my power to restrict abortions." And in Texas, he already has — signing 18 anti-choice provisions into law in three legislative sessions.

The Republican Party Platform still calls for a ban on abortion with no exceptions.

And, as *New York Times* columnist Gail Collins warns: *"When it comes to abortion, George W. Bush's move to the center consists solely of his willingness to accept the votes of people who disagree with him. The tent is huge, but the ring master is only listening to the folks who entered from the right."*

Much has been written about the hazards to Roe v. Wade of the Supreme Court appointments that could be made by such an administration. And they are real.

But there are other dangers to choice from presidential powers, dangers that could manifest themselves much more quickly:

Power Number One: All the other appointments the President must make immediately — Federal judges at the district level, the Attorney General, the Secretary of Health and Human Services, the commissioner of the Food and Drug Administration, the Surgeon General.

These appointments could drastically affect access to abortion, the approval and distribution of RU-486, the availability of emergency contraception, and insurance coverage of contraceptives.

Power Number Two: Issuing executive orders — Like the international "gag rule" which would deny funds to foreign agencies and governments that even discuss abortion as an option.

Power Number Three: Utilizing veto power (and withholding it). Clearly a President Bush, unlike President Clinton, would SIGN, not veto:

— A ban on late term abortions with no exception for the health of the mother;

— Amendments to bar the FDA from using funds for testing, developing, and manufacturing RU-486;

— Acts declaring the fetus a child with full rights, like the "Unborn Victims of Violence" Act;

— The bill to ban anyone but parents from the "interstate transportation" of minors for the purpose of obtaining an abortion. (This latter piece of legislation caused pro-choice and pro-gun safety California U.S. Senator Dianne Feinstein to remark, "I could transport an AK-47 across the state line into Nevada, but not my pregnant granddaughter!")

Power Number Four: Influencing appropriations.

Appropriations, both for domestic and for international family planning programs, are the preventive arm of the pro-choice movement.

Teen pregnancy has fallen to its lowest point in 60 years! But a Bush administration could curtail this fortuitous fact by funding exclusively programs that push abstinence only — which is exactly what he did do in Texas — or programs that require parental consent even for contraception.

As Jennifer L. Pozner, women's desk director at FAIR (Fairness and Accuracy in Reporting), writes: "Bush ratified parental notification restrictions (in Texas), but he has offered no initiatives to reduce unintended pregnancies, no expansion of family planning funding of services, no comprehensive sex-education programs and no insurance coverage of contraceptives."

Is that "Compassionate Conservatism"?

A Planned Parenthood Federation of America poll taken last winter found that only 18% of the electorate said they would be "very worried" if Roe v. Wade were overturned.

And women, especially white married women in the suburbs, the "soccer moms" that have supported Democrats in the recent years, are still leaning towards George Bush.

HELLO!!

Don't they realize their daughters' very lives and futures could be at stake? And that far more than abortion rights are threatened?

Who can deny in a day of AIDS that their daughters and sons will need good quality sex education, taught by qualified people? Or, as Jane Fonda said in her speech, at least not by people "who think that the vulva is a Swedish automobile."

Who can deny, in an age of sharply rising health care costs, that women will need accessible, affordable family planning covered by insurance?

Fonda weighed in on the Viagra vs. Contraceptive debate, too. Chastising the members of the South Carolina House of Representatives — who just voted not to add prescription contraceptives to their state employees health care plan (which also covers legislators), but included $200,000 to cover Viagra, she quipped: "Guess who's running for 're-erection'?"

But let's get serious, very serious.

If you are one of the 18% that's "very worried" about choice, take your message to others. And get them to vote.

If you are not worried, get worried.

And vote, vote, VOTE!

Gun Control: Walk the Walk — With Petitions

Colorado Woman News
FEBRUARY 16, 2000

RIGHT NOW, AS I TYPE THIS ARTICLE, A SPECIAL CBS National News report reveals that in the month before the Colorado Legislature convened, the National Rifle Association gave to certain members of that body a total of $16,950 in political contributions.

That's more in one month than the NRA had contributed to Colorado legislators over the past three years!

Is it any wonder, then, that of the five modest bi-partisan gun safety measures proposed by the Governor and the Attorney General, the only two that passed were those two favored by the NRA?

Even the bill to mandate criminal background checks on gun purchasers at gun shows was shot down in the House Appropriations Committee despite the fact that a full 94% of Coloradans strongly support the measure.

Clearly, when NRA dollars flow, common sense flees.

And by the time the 2000 Legislature adjourns, the conservative Republican majority most likely will have forbidden municipalities to:

1. Set their own standards for issuing concealed weapons permits.

2. Release names of those issued concealed weapons permits.

3. Sue gun manufacturers for damages.

Conservatives love to talk about "local control": But what kind of local control is not allowing a city like Denver, with a higher crime rate than others, to set its own standards?

The NRA and other gun groups speak of the sanctified right to bear arms.

But what about the right of parents not to have their infants snatched from their arms by fire power?

The NRA speaks of the right to go anywhere with a gun.

But what about the right of children to go to school and to grow to adulthood in safety?

Nationwide, as many children are killed each day by gun injuries — homicide, suicide, and accidents combined — as were killed that one fateful, tragic day at Columbine last spring.

In 1998 the United States suffered more firearm deaths (35,563) than the top eight other industrialized countries combined. And in 1999, just since Columbine, another 3,094 Americans were murdered with guns.

In Colorado the suicide rate is higher than the homicide rate. The number of children killed accidently while playing with guns is also high. Yet the Legislature "shot down" a very reasonable Safe Storage Bill which would have simply required adults to keep their guns in a place unreachable by children.

I do not advocate denying adult, responsible, non-criminal, non-spouse abusing citizens to own guns and to use them, for hunting, for sport, and in self defense when necessary. I was taught to target shoot at age nine and, as the elder of two daughters, I knew that this trust my father invested in me was a privilege not granted to many young females in the 1940's.

My father collected guns and was a member of the NRA. Yet, if he were alive today he would be appalled by their "shtick."

As a social worker and as the mother of two grown children, I understand that violence is not "caused" by guns any more than it is by any other weapons. The causes of violence are complex. And it is urgent that we deal responsibly with the root of violence as well as its result.

In the meantime, however, we can render violence much less lethal simply by keeping guns out of the hands of the people who should not have them — namely criminals and kids. As Denver Mayor Wellington Webb once said: "I've never seen a drive-by knifing."

NRA, take notice!

The citizen battle against your power has just begun and we citizens will eventually prevail. We are on the cusp of a tidal wave that will eventually wash anti gun safety politicians out of office.

Every single one of the Governor's and Attorney General's five initiatives are favored by more than 79% of Coloradans. And in every single category, women favor gun safety measures at a higher percentage than men.

So what do we women do with this new, post Columbine, power and passion? We reflect the state of our numbers. We talk the talk. We walk the walk. We march the march. In short we get busy. When the challenge gets tough, the tough get challenged.

First: We join the efforts of SAFE Colorado, the bi-partisan PAC promoting gun safety, in its goal to put the law to mandate criminal background checks on all purchasers of guns at gun shows, on the Nov. 2000 ballot.

We will not let one small committee of the Legislature deny 94% of our populace its common sense wish for more security.

Second: We join the "Million Mom March." No, I'm not kidding. On Mother's Day, May 14, 2000, one million mothers, grandmothers, step mothers, foster mothers, Godmothers, future mothers and honorary mothers (which includes fathers and men) will march on our nation's Capitol to petition our federal officials to pass stronger gun safety legislation.

The "Million Mom March" advocacy group originated with a group of women in New Jersey who were tired of watching school shooting after school shooting on their television sets. The movement has now spread to almost 50 states.

In an article about the families of gun violence victims, columnist Anna Quindlen wrote: "The bereaved have done their work .… It's time the great complacent majority, the 70 or 80 percent of us who think that guns should be available within reason but regulated within reason, too, began to do ours. Public policy ought not to be made one bullet wound at a time."

So walk the walk — with petitions.

And march the march — with a message for your congressperson.

Do your share.

I'll see you there.

So We're Not to Blame?
We Could Still Do Better!

Colorado Woman News
DECEMBER 2001

I AM WRITING THIS ON THE CUSP OF OUR FIRST victory in Afghanistan. Routing the Taliban from Kabul is no small matter; albeit, it was the Northern Alliance who did the routing and we don't know how, or even IF, this fragile "coalition" will govern after the war.

And the morning dawns with yet another victory. Eight foreign aid workers held hostage by the Taliban, including two young American women whose parents have been praying for their safety for four months, have been released and are on their way home.

As an American and as a mother, my heart rejoices with the families of these young women.

But I curb my euphoria.

In last month's column I wrote the following about the September 11 Terrorist Attack: "There is nothing any of us have done as individuals or as a country to 'deserve' such vile retribution." And I don't back down from that statement one iota.

Yet, in the last 30 days I have read, attended seminars and "soul searched" in the attempt to better understand both the "climate" of the world

> *"Not only does America 'set the world's temperature,' but through its language, it determines the very tone and volume of its intense storms."*

in which we live and the way in which America "governs its thermostat."

For not only does America "set the world's temperature," but through its language, it determines the very tone and volume of its intense storms.

In an article titled "Phantom Towers" (*Women's Review of Books*, Nov. 2001), feminist author Rosalind P. Petchesky points out the strikingly similar "twin towers" of religious arrogance exhibited by Osama Bin Laden and George W. Bush:

Bin Laden declares a jihad, or holy war against the U.S., its civilians as well as its soldiers.

Bush declares a crusade against the terrorists and all who harbor or support them.

Bin Laden declares himself the "servant of Allah fighting for the sake of the religion of Allah" and to protect Islam's holy mosques.

Bush declares Washington the promoter of "infinite justice" and predicts certain victory, because "God is not neutral."

Don't get me wrong. I'll pick Bush's Holy War over Bin Laden's any day! But the sameness of the rhetoric reminds me how any fervent cause can use the "pseudo holy" to justify its goals. It also throws me back to some simple and not so simple truths about us as a nation.

If we are so "holy," why, way before terrorism struck on American soil, has our Congress catered to the insatiable desires of the Defense Industry, particularly in projects as outdated and useless as the Missile Defense Shield?

Why, indeed? Profits, of course.

The following scenario is instructive:

During my 1998 U.S. Senate campaign, I approached a wealthy Defense Industry "giant," a charming gentleman of the "old school" who also turned out to be a liberal of the "new school." He said he would support me financially for my civil rights, women's rights, human rights stands and even thanked me for running.

"Of course," he added as I exited his plush office, "I will expect to visit you when my defense appropriations are up."

I read recently that even Democrats had supported Bush's restoring 1.3 billion dollars in spending authority for the misconceived "missile shield." Why should we be surprised?

If we are so "holy," why have we created decades of world resentment by supporting such coups as Pinochet's against the democratically elected Allende in Chile and helped prop up such authoritarian regimes as the Shah of Iran and the Saudi Dynasty — the latter two mainly to keep secure our own oil interests?

And why, with all our wealth and its resulting consumer products, which we love so much yet denounce so frequently, are we not more generous?

As our national wealth expands and towers over other nations, our non military foreign aid shrinks and almost slithers away. We, the richest country in the world, don't even meet the U.N. Standard of 7% of GDP!

If we are so "holy," couldn't we at least become members of the U.N. human rights coalition by ratifying The U.N. Convention on the Elimination of All Forms of Discrimination Against Women (CEDAW)? Afghanistan is the only other nation who has not ratified CEDAW. And we are the ONLY nation not to have ratified the Convention on the Rights of the Child.

True, we treat both women and children with more equity and humanity than do many countries who have ratified these treaties. But signing on the ratification dotted line would put our face in the world; our feet walking the walk as we continue to talk the talk.

I don't believe for a minute that becoming less "consumer oriented," spreading more of our wealth, or defending true democracy rather than greed would guarantee that all the world's people would love us and that we would be forever safe from American targeted terrorism.

We are the world's only Superpower so there are always going to be those who hate us purely for who we are no matter what we do. And there will always be corrupt leaders of destitute countries who will be happy to ship up their populace's anger and deflect it toward us to save their own skins.

I don't feel I'm part of a "holy war," but as a patriotic American I feel I live in the best, if not the "holiest," country in the world. In short we have the power, the potential, and yes, the obligation to do more good than any other country on earth. And we do "do good." Especially as individuals.

It's just that as a nation, however, we could do SO MUCH BETTER.

Our Boys Are Falling Behind in Education

Denver Post
APRIL 18, 2010

WHAT'S THE NEXT BATTLE FOR AN AGING feminist?

Boys.

Granted, the battle for women's rights and equality has not been completely won, but the new reality is that in the future, it will be males who are most endangered.

Currently, up to 60 percent of the students at an average co-educational college or university are female. The majority of bachelor's degrees are now awarded to females in every racial and ethnic group. By 2017, the ratio of female to male college graduates will be 1½ to 1. One demographer calls that prediction "staggering and transformational."

Feminists have lobbied for a societal transformation where the rights and talents of women are fully recognized. But is *this* the kind of transformation we want? A "role reversal," where women will reign supreme in all fields but the sciences?

Is it healthy that even those men who do stay in college seek fewer student leadership positions and perform worse academically than women do? Won't these factors, combined with the lower graduation rate, promote a "marriage gap"?

How many college-educated women today would want to marry a man with such low educational achievement, skills or ambition that he would be permanently relegated to the role of full-time "homemaker" — not by choice, but by default?

How did this educational gender gap happen?

Over the past 30 years, the world has become more verbal. Yet, on average, the verbal parts of boys' brains do not develop to capacity until fourth or fifth grade.

The acceleration of formal academic learning has been pushed back earlier in the school curriculum. Reading was once a first-grade challenge; now some schools expect to see beginning reading skills when a child enters kindergarten.

This push has hurt boys far more than girls. Anyone who has watched pre-schoolers interact knows that the typical girl's verbal acuity develops far sooner than that of her male playmates. One brain scan study revealed that the language areas of brains in 3½-year-old girls mirror those of 5-year-old boys.

Well-meaning parents and teachers who push boys to read and write too early may see their efforts backfire. Feeling a keen sense of failure, some boys lose interest in learning, an apathy that lasts and limits their efforts later, when their brains catch up with their bodies.

For example, boys are far more likely to be held back a grade in fourth grade and then again in ninth grade, an action that promotes a suspension rate for boys that is twice as high as that of girls. This in turn leads to a male dropout rate of 32 percent compared to 25 percent for females.

To some, this boy crisis is difficult to accept. "Boys will be just fine … it's girls and women we still have to concentrate on," a feminist colleague said recently during a rather heated "boy gap" discussion.

"Look around," say others. "How can we worry about boys when men still rule the world?"

That's true — for now.

Because of this oft-cited factor, it is easy to ignore statistics or to "forget" to put them out there.

In test score achievement accounts reported in the mainstream media, one will find an analysis of racial gaps, income-level gaps, rural/urban gaps, and private school/public school gaps, but seldom evaluation of gender gaps.

So what do we do? First, we need to find out what works. In "Why Boys Fail: Saving Our Sons from an Educational System That's Leaving Them Behind" (AMACOM BOOMS, January 2010), author Richard Whitmire bemoans the widespread indifference to the issue. The U.S. Department of Education, for example, has yet to launch a single probe into gender gap, says Whitmire.

> *"If a men's movement develops for boys, I'll join it. And, as an aging feminist, I'll still fight to take big chunks out of that glass ceiling for women."*

We need to be practical and proactive, not "politically correct." After all, if the advocacy efforts to move middle-school and high-school girls into math and sciences taken on by feminists and educators in the 1980s and 90s paid off, why wouldn't a similar effort work on behalf of boys' literacy in elementary school?

Do boys need a "men's movement?" If so, maybe it could rally around some of the successes already achieved at the primary level of boys' education.

Here are three examples, two from Whitmire's book, one from Colorado:

- An all-boys charter elementary school in New York has lengthened the day, including 50 minutes of physical fitness along with art and music, and providing each student 2½ hours of literacy instruction each day with reading programs that range from poetry to phonics. One class raised its "reading at or above grade level" score from 37 percent to 77 percent in three years.

- At an urban, co-ed (half black, half white) public elementary school in Delaware, a program of concentrated tutoring is flourishing. The tutors may spend three, half-hour sessions with a child each week. This program has moved the school's ranking from near bottom to the sixth-highest in the state. Last year, 100 percent of the boys and 98 percent of the girls passed the state mandated fifth-grade reading test.

- In Colorado, Audra Philippon, principal of AXL, a public elementary charter school in Aurora, divides her boys and girls into same-sex classes from kindergarten on. "They love being alone for learning," says Philippon. Both genders are taught with similar "active-learning" methods. This school is only 18 months old, but because of teaching methods learned in the first year, the 2009-10 kindergarten boys are doing just as well as the girls.

Note that the schools differ in many ways, yet the common factors are engaged learning, physical action, strict discipline and caring adults.

If a men's movement develops for boys, I'll join it. And, as an aging feminist, I'll still fight to take big chunks out of that glass ceiling for women. But as a grandmother of three young boys, I'm going to do my darnedest to keep young boys from sinking into that academic mud floor.

Kudos, Planned Parenthood

Denver Post
May 8, 2011

Happy Mother's Day, Planned Parenthood! You deserve some hard-earned recognition for all you do, especially for mothers.

Your services and your clients have been characterized recently by some outrageous statements. Bad enough was the charge by Sen. Jon Kyl, R-Ariz., that "90 percent of what Planned Parenthood does is provide abortions." In fact, the opposite is true. Ninety percent of the care Planned Parenthood provides is preventive care, such as annual exams, birth control and cancer screenings.

Even worse was Glenn Beck's declaration on Fox News that "only hookers use Planned Parenthood." That's not only wrong, but insultingly so.

In a recent online article, Clare Coleman, former head of the Planned Parenthood network in New York's Hudson Valley, asks us to picture a typical Planned Parenthood patient: "You're a working woman between 20 and 24 with a job you don't love, a toddler you'd die for, and no health insurance. You live paycheck to paycheck, and you know penny to penny how much cash you've got until the end of the month. You're rushing home on Route 9 to relieve your mom who's with the kid, and the engine light on the car comes on. You feel a wave of panic. You know you're always one emergency away [from] everything falling apart."

Hardly a "hooker." This young mom could be you, your sister, your daughter, your friend.

On this Mother's Day, it is important to remember that a considerable number of Planned Parenthood clients are already mothers. They include a mom on the brink of financial uncertainty; a mom trying to leave an abusive partner; a mom suffering with a serious health condition; a mom who has found that her two children have a genetic disorder that she does not want to risk passing on to a third child. The majority of these women will be seeking contraceptive services, not abortions.

Some of the special services that our Colorado Planned Parenthood affiliate (Planned Parenthood of the Rocky Mountains, or PPRM) offers mothers or soon-to-be mothers:

- Contraception: Children spaced at least two years apart are more likely to be healthy — and so are their moms. Affordable birth control empowers women to plan their families.
- Prenatal programs: Through a partnership with the Rose Hospital Midwifery Program, PPRM offers case management for at-risk pregnancies. One goal is to reduce low birth weight. Others include healthy habits during and after pregnancy, like good diet and tobacco cessation.
- Childbirth classes: PPRM recently began offering childbirth classes, which are designed to help a woman, and often her partner, feel comfortable and confident about her impending birth.
- Midlife services: These include gynecological exams, cancer screenings and menopause evaluation and monitoring. Mothers are still mothers, even when they are no longer fertile.

Last month I was privileged to tour the new Planned Parenthood Health and Education center in Colorado Springs. According to the center manager, Madonna Huntingford, a full 91 percent of clients have no form of health insurance to pay for their visits.

To deny public funding to such mothers, prospective mothers, and fathers is perhaps the most anti-motherhood, anti-family action politicians could take.

Yet, those who claim to be "pro-family" regularly do exactly that. Just prior to this Mother's Day, the Indiana Legislature voted to cut the entire $3 million in federal money that previously had gone to the state's Planned Parenthood clinics. Shame on them! What a slap in the face to the mothers and prospective mothers of Indiana.

So, thank you, Planned Parenthood of the Rocky Mountains, not only for your services but for your advocacy. So far you have not only helped keep such dire anti-choice, anti-family measures out of Colorado, but you also have supported pro-motherhood legislation like House Bill 1021 (passed in 2010), which mandates the inclusion of pregnancy in health insurance plans.

Special kudos to you on Mother's Day.

> *"On this Mother's Day, it is important to remember that a considerable number of Planned Parenthood clients are already mothers."*

Labeling of Edibles Is Too Lax

Denver Post
APRIL 12, 2015

A S A GRANDMOTHER AND LONGTIME CHILD advocate, I am appalled by the increasing availability of edible marijuana products to children.

Why? Because it is so easy for kids to ingest them accidentally.

Unmarked marijuana edibles are showing up everywhere, warns Smart Colorado, a youth advocacy group focused on protecting kids from marijuana.

Colorado citizens voted to legalize recreational marijuana in 2012. Stores licensed to sell pot officially opened on Jan. 1, 2014. In the first nine months of that year, 14 children affected by edible marijuana were admitted to Children's Hospital Colorado. This compares to the 14 total cases admitted in the previous two years *combined.*

Some courageous legislators are stepping up to the plate. Last month, when a bill to delay the process of labeling edible pot was introduced, the measure was struck down by a 5-0 vote in the Senate Health and Human Services Committee. Kudos go to Kevin Lundberg, R-Berthoud, chair of the committee, who said, "Legal edible marijuana products need to be clearly identifiable, packaged and labeled. If it's not identifiable, it's not legal."

> *"Unfortunately, our kids are serving as guinea pigs in a highly risky experiment,' said Carlson."*

Diane Carlson, co-founder of Smart Colorado — which was recently endorsed by all four of Colorado's living ex-governors — notes that outside packaging of marijuana edibles can be indistinguishable from everyday non-marijuana foods, candies and beverages. This is dangerous and confusing for kids and adults alike.

Clearly the industry, which cannot sell directly to anyone under 21, is preparing our kids to be the consumers of tomorrow. Remember when smoking was made "cool" by ads attractive to teenagers?

Christian Thurstone, director of the STEP Program at Denver Health — one of Colorado's largest youth substance-abuse treatment programs — has conducted extensive research regarding marijuana and the developing brain. His research shows:

- Youth exposed to marijuana in utero have a 5-point decrease in IQ at age 6; a greater chance of depression, hyperactivity and impulsivity at age 10; and lower school achievement at age 14.
- At least one in six adolescents who experiment with marijuana will develop an addiction to the drug.
- Heavy use starting in adolescents who experiment with marijuana will develop an addiction to the drug.
- Heavy use starting in adolescence predicts up to an 8-point drop in IQ from ages 13 to 39. It also predicts a two-fold risk of psychosis in adulthood.

Lakewood High School Principal Lisa Ritchey is outraged. In a December 2014 CNBC segment, "Kids and Pot: What's the Harm?" Ritchey told correspondent Harry Smith: "Legalization has been bad for kids …. They don't get it!

"Marijuana is so easy to get. Their parents have it, their brothers have it …. They do not believe it is bad for them."

Education groups, in addition to Smart Colorado, are springing up. One is SAM, the Colorado affiliate of the national group Smart Approaches to Marijuana.

Lisa Young, mother of a Lakewood High freshman who campaigned to keep retail pot out of Lakewood, said "at every turn, activists are being bamboozled by paid pot lobbyists at public meetings. The marijuana industry is only interested in profit; romancing kids with tempting edibles, and convenient vape pens to hide their use …."

"Unfortunately, our kids are serving as guinea pigs in a highly risky experiment," said Carlson. "It is critical that Colorado starts putting the health, safety and future of its kids first."

Shamed into Protecting Women

Denver Post
SEPTEMBER 14, 2014

L AST MONDAY A COLLEAGUE WHIPPED OUT HIS iPhone and showed those at our dinner table the now infamous video of Ray Rice, the Baltimore Ravens' star running back, brutally knocking out his fiancée (now wife) in an Atlantic City elevator in February.

Shocking? Yes. But perhaps even more shocking was the fact that Rice was finally dealt a blow in return: banned indefinitely from the NFL.

According to an Associated Press report, NFL officials may have received and viewed the video earlier than NFL Commissioner Roger Goodell originally claimed. If so, he should have banned Rice sooner. But he didn't. A ban came only after public shame.

Shame. It's the same word that appears repeatedly in many recent articles on sexual assault on our college campuses. Sexual assaults are too often treated as pesky PR problems, not serious crimes. The institution is to be protected first and foremost, the victims secondarily, if at all. Only with public shaming does the institution change its ways.

Perhaps the most dramatic story was that of a freshman at Hobart and William Smith Colleges in Geneva, N.Y. According to a July 12 story in The New York Times, "Anna" was sexually assaulted and forcibly raped after a party by three football players. After the assault, Anna took her complaint to the college authorities.

Although the accused men changed their stories twice, first denying any sexual contact, then admitting only to oral sex, the school's disciplinary panel quickly cleared the athletes without further investigation, even though lab tests taken at the police station revealed forcible penetration which left seminal fluid. The district attorney dismissed the case without even taking DNA samples from the accused.

As William Boardman wrote in an online essay, "Hobart has shown little capacity for shame, except perhaps for trying to shame the victim."

Anna, however, would not be shamed. Although she dropped out of school for a semester, she has now returned to help organize an anti-sexual assault student group. And Hobart is finally taking some proactive measures.

Hobart's is only one of the dozens of activist rape awareness groups on college campuses. A particularly controversial campaign, which operates nationally, is the gender equity group UltraViolet, which warns students who are accepted at colleges with reputations of sexual assault.

For example, to those students considering Dartmouth College in New Hampshire last year, the following message was delivered to them by UltraViolet as an online ad: "Dartmouth has a rape problem. Find out more before you decide."

"It's a shame it takes shame to make those in power do the right thing."

Karin Roland, the group's organizing director, says, "Universities can either take student safety seriously, or we'll bring grass-roots pressure to push them over the edge to do it." In other words, it's the power of shame.

This year's college applications to Dartmouth dropped 14 percent. Although no solid evidence exists that UltraViolet's campaign was a cause of this drop, Dartmouth is now taking a zero-tolerance stand on sexual assault and has implemented a mandatory expulsion policy for those proven guilty of rape.

Pressure on colleges is also being felt by the fact that 55 of them are presently under federal investigation for possible violations of Title IX for ignoring reports of sexual abuse.

In addition, a bipartisan group of U.S. senators has just introduced a bill which would hold schools accountable for how they handle sexual assault allegations.

I salute all the above actions against the sexual abuse of college women. At the same time, I desperately wish they had not been necessary.

And I wish the NFL's Goodell had immediately banned Rice *before* a viral video made him do it.

It's a shame it takes *shame* to make those in power do the right thing. Rice should have been dumped a long time ago. And it's time to dump Goodell, too.

Making the Case against Trump

Denver Post
JULY 10, 2016

TEN YEARS AGO MY HUSBAND, FORMER Colorado Gov. Dick Lamm, and I wrote an op-ed for The Denver Post asking this question: Is Democracy really up to the task of solving the myriad of challenges we are facing?

As I review our question a decade later, I would reverse it to ask: Are *we* up to the task of saving democracy?

As a progressive Democrat and a Hillary Clinton supporter, I find myself in good conservative company — such as that of New York Times columnists Ross Douthat and David Brooks and author Andrew Sullivan — when I warn that the 2016 election is more than a game changer. It could be a disastrous *direction* changer if Donald Trump is elected president.

The possibility of electing such an egotistical, autocratic, violence-inspiring, gun-promoting, crude, boastful, know-nothing, xenophobic, racist and sexist candidate to the highest office in the land would be a tragedy, not just to the Republican Party, but to democracy itself.

> *"The possibility of electing such an egotistical, autocratic, violence-inspiring, gun-promoting, crude, boastful, know-nothing, xenophobic, racist and sexist candidate to the highest office in the land would be a tragedy, not just to the Republican Party, but to democracy itself."*

But to defeat this self-promoting bully, we have to better understand the forces that propelled him to become the Republican Party standard-bearer.

One reason is that people — including some middle-class working and educated people — are angry. Their jobs are going overseas, their real wages have not been raised in 40 years, they do not see their children going to college or rising above them in economic status.

They resent undocumented workers taking their jobs and crowding their children's schools. They are angry at the factories that have closed down and closed them out, and that government has done almost nothing to train them for new positions.

They feel downtrodden and immobilized by their, or their children's, enormous student debts. They are frightened of terrorism and do not feel it is prejudicial to worry about Muslim immigration.

And none of this necessarily makes these Trump supporters racist xenophobes.

But politics, like nature, abhors a vacuum, and what a potential disaster that such an autocrat as Trump might move into this leadership vacuum. History — particularly the rise of fascism in Europe only 80 years ago — has shown that when political vacuum occurs, an autocrat *will* move in.

Pollsters have found that the theme running through all the issues that voters are angry about is the feeling that "People like me don't have any say." They feel they are disenfranchised.

So for those of us who fear a Trump presidency, our job is to listen to, empathize with, then proselytize the disenfranchised.

Trump's excesses can prevent discussion of the many nuances of the issues he raises. For example, many progressives are not "open-border liberals." We worry about the effects of overpopulation in our own country, and the fact that immigrants sometimes take the jobs of our own poor and unemployed at the time that so many U.S. jobs are simply disappearing. Yet we are stymied from expressing these views as they may line us up with Trump's anti-Hispanic, anti-Muslim views, which we strongly disavow.

Clearly, this is crisis time in America. We may have to stretch well outside our comfort zones — to listen more intently and then to engage those who confront us even when we fear them.

As Eleanor Roosevelt once said, "You gain strength, courage and confidence by every experience in which you really stop to look fear in the face. You must do the thing which you think you cannot do."

It Will Take All of Us to Overcome

Denver Post
AUGUST 11, 2016

"AMERICA IS WEEPING," SAID CONGRESSIONAL Black Caucus chairman G.K. Butterfield on July 8. He was referring to the racial violence and bloodshed that had spilled over into the consciousness of all America.

That week, two defenseless black men had been killed by police officers — one in Louisiana and one in Minnesota. Then came the "retaliatory" assassinations, by angry black men, of five Dallas police officers and, a week later, three officers in Baton Rouge, La.

Though I was horrified by all the accounts I read about these incidents, it was an editorial cartoon in the Denver Post on July 10 that hit me the hardest. "WE HAD BETTER OVERCOME" pleaded the caption above Jim Morin's drawing of an African-American man and a white police officer, facing forward together, arms around each other's backs, and a lone tear falling from an eye of each.

Suddenly I was catapulted back 51 years, when I, along with a plane load of other white and black Coloradans, flew to Alabama to march from Selma to Montgomery, demanding voting rights for black Americans.

Our marching song, of course, was "We Shall Overcome."

Sadly, we have not overcome.

In all fairness we *have* progressed in some ways. Fifty years ago, the articulate and brave Dallas police chief, David Brown, who is black; the African-American surgeon, Dr. Brian Williams, who at Dallas Parkland hospital worked frantically to save the white police officers; and Tim Scott, the first African-American U.S. senator from South Carolina, who gave a passionate speech about being black on the Senate floor, would never have been in those esteemed positions.

Yet the average black man has not "overcome" prejudicial and structural barriers that we whites do not suffer. It is a nationally known fact that black men and boys are more likely to be arrested, charged, searched, mishandled and even killed by police, for the same minor traffic offense or petty crime for which white men and boys are not. It's a burden that each black male shares by the factor of his black skin.

(The Denver Police Department, responding to citizen demands, will begin collecting its own racial data on arrests soon.)

"The average black man has not 'overcome' prejudicial and structural barriers that we whites do not suffer. It is a nationally known fact that black men and boys are more likely to be arrested, charged, searched, mishandled and even killed by police, for the same minor traffic offense or petty crime for which white men and boys are not."

It is also true that the vast majority of police officers, still mostly white males, do not abuse people of color. The fact that they are blamed for the actions of a very few is their burden, one which each shares by the factor of his blue uniform.

Let's recall that Dallas police officers who were killed on July 7 were actually marching in unison with Black Lives Matter demonstrators, some of whom were even taking selfies with the officers. The tragic irony is that a lone black crazy man with no connection to the group, who simply wanted to "kill white policemen," could end the peace and the genuine attempt to "overcome."

When a white politician answers the chant of "Black Lives Matter" with the phrase "*All* lives matter," he or she is met with fury.

And I'll admit that at first I didn't understand why that was.

But when I try to stand in the shoes of a black person, and recall our country's 200-year history of violence to that person's ancestors, I finally get it. The collective cultural memory of those lives not mattering feeds the imperative that *their* lives, and the lives of their children, must matter now. And they must.

On July 12, nearly 500 white people attended a public Showing up for Racial Justice meeting in Denver to protest the violence.

The Rev. Anne Dunlap, an organizer with the group, says it is *urgent* that white people show up. "As long as white people are silent, the killings will continue," she says.

She's right.

It's time to stop the weeping, and, once again, get out the marching shoes.

Are Hate Crimes and Fear the New Normal? They Don't Have to Be

Denver Post
DECEMBER 22, 2016

I FEAR I HAVE BEEN SLEEPING. ALTHOUGH THE election of Donald Trump is only six weeks past, I seem to be adjusting to the "new normal."

I watch the nightly news for the president-elect's latest Cabinet choice, sigh, then turn my attention elsewhere, as if I were watching events in another country.

Then a person *from* another country, Nigerian writer Chimamanda Ngozi Adichie, publishes an article in The New Yorker that wakes me up from my post-election slumber. The article is titled "Now Is the Time to Talk About What We Are Actually Talking About." Here are just a few of her salient wake-up points:

- "[I]n response to this [election] there are people living in visceral fear, people anxiously trying to discern policy from bluster …."
- "Things that were recently pushed to the corners of America's political space — overt racism, glaring misogyny, anti-intellectualism — are once again creeping to the center."

- "'Identity politics' has come to be associated with minorities, and often with a patronizing under current…. [Yet] White Americans have practiced identity politics since the inception of America, but it is now laid bare, impossible to evade."

Why have I, at least partially, evaded the increased venality of some in my "tribe"?

After all, I have *read* that nationally, hate crimes against Muslim Americans have grown to the highest number since right after the 9/11 attack, and that locally, the Aurora police have reported at least nine hate-inspired incidents against African-Americans in the first weeks since the election. "People are scared," one resident told The Denver Post after her door had been sprayed with racial slurs.

And I *heard* Denise Maes, public policy director of the Colorado ACLU, say at a Nov. 29 town hall meeting in Denver that more than 500 people called the ACLU in the two days after the election fearing for their civil rights or with offers to help protect the rights of others.

"There is an inherent danger in just the rhetorical tone of the new administration … that tone frees people up to act on their worst instincts."

So even before the Inauguration of Donald Trump, I am learning that there is an inherent danger in just the rhetorical tone of the new administration. And that that tone frees people up to act on their worst instincts.

Yet, I am heartened to read some of the reassurances from activists and public officials that came out of the Nov. 29 town hall meeting, as summarized by Denver District Attorney-elect Beth McCann:

- Maes, from the ACLU, said that regardless of what the federal government does or does not do on immigration, we must make sure that Colorado remains a safe place for all of us to live. There will be no walls and no one should live in the shadows.
- Laura Reinsch, political director for One Colorado, said, "Colorado's laws are stronger — or offer greater protections for LGBTQ Coloradans — than on the federal level. Our state's anti-bullying and non-discrimination laws cover sexual orientation and gender identity."
- And Scott Levin, regional director of the Anti-Defamation League, said: "The ADL fights to stop defamation and to secure justice and fair treatment to all." Levin spoke particularly to the efforts of No Place for Hate, an ADL sponsored K-12 initiative to create a community of inclusion and respect in schools.

Almost 200 people attended this meeting. Capitalizing on the crowd's concerns and its eagerness for action, Maes, Reinsch and Levin encouraged all to get involved with civil rights organizations.

In her New Yorker article, Adichie closed with this plea: "Every precious [American] ideal must be reiterated, every obvious argument made, because an ugly idea left unchallenged begins to turn the color of normal. It does not have to be like this."

No, it does not.

Now fully awake, I vow to do all I can to see that such ugly ideas and the attacks they generate do not become the "new normal."

Elections, Transitions, Deflations:
All Part of the Process

You Ask What Are the Real Agonies of Political Life? Hold on and Listen

Denver Post
October 13, 1980

A young man with an unmistakable political gleam in his eye recently asked me about "the political life."

"But I don't want to hear just the good things," he explained. "Tell me what the agonies are."

Obligingly, I gave him my standard spiel. For a conscientious full-time politician, the agonies are these:

You are in it for the long-term success of the society; but you are reminded more frequently of your short-term failures — especially by those who love you the most.

Even when a triumph is hailed, no one but you will really know the volume of sweat, blood and tears it took to make it work. And if you publicly enumerate the gallons it cost you, you will be labeled an egoist, a martyr, a braggart or worse.

You start out in your role with the illusion of dictating events — but you soon find events are dictating you.

When a daring or creative project turns out well, all involved will get the credit; when it flops, the "buck" stops with you.

Every person who wants something feels he or she owns a "piece" of you; no matter how you scatter your "pieces," you'll find you simply can't be everywhere you are needed at once.

The day-to-day frenzy can swallow up your long-term dreams and immobilize your creative energy until your eyes glaze over.

No one with a plain eight to five job can understand the speed, scope and intensity of the demands that come at you all hours of the day and night. And the little demands will sap your stamina more than the big.

"The more expert you become at the day-to-day give and take, the more you are expected to give and take it."

The more expert you become at the day-to-day give and take, the more you are expected to give and take it.

Some days your hard work will go unnoticed by everyone; unless you make a mistake.

You alone will decide whether the ailment in the system requires a sympathetic ear, light bandaging, or whether the ailment is symptomatic of a deeper ruse requiring strong medication and maybe surgery. Much will ride on your diagnosis. And sometimes you will be wrong.

So many good people and good causes will plead for your ear, your time, your blessing and your feedback. You won't have time to think, plan or prioritize; and you wonder whatever tempted you into your chosen role in the first place.

You have precious little privacy, and occasionally you will want to just quit — take your backpack, your bike, or your sports car and trek to a distant horizon where no one will recognize you. But you won't, you know intuitively what job is cut out for you, although the results of your efforts may not be seen for years — even by yourself.

The young man was silent; the gleam in his eyes a little duller though by no means extinguished.

"There must be no other job quite like it," he commented, slowly recovering.

"Well … there's one that comes close …."

"What?"

"That of a full-time parent-homemaker," I said.

Even the Governor's Family Faces the Nitty Gritty of Everyday Life

Colorado Statesman
November 26, 1982

T HE NIGHT I LEARNED I MIGHT HAVE TO HAVE breast surgery, my son proclaimed that he would not go to the orthodontist and would never wear braces. My daughter announced she had an earache and would need a doctor's appointment in the morning instead of her diving lesson. A family of four expressed their intention to spend the following night with us. My sister called to say my mother had broken her foot. And a bat flew down the chimney of the master bedroom, driving my husband and me to sleep in the guest room, temporarily filled with our son's scuba diving equipment.

Worried about my medical state, annoyed by the domestic turmoil that seems to arrive on the heels of any trauma, I reached for happier thoughts that might bring some much-needed sleep.

Staring at the guest room ceiling, I remembered the first time I had entered that room to store my coat for Governor Love's Christmas party in 1966.

"Great place to visit …," I had thought as I took in the palatial mansion. "But who'd want to live here!?"

"Be it every so humble, there's no place like home" has now become a family joke that someone repeats each time we turn into the spacious driveway after a vacation.

Special Memories:

— Our first official party when our daughter and her friend, ages 3 and 4, entertained guests by stripping nude and washing their underwear in the Italian marble fountain.

— The day we worked so hard to scrub and shine the mansion office for visiting Presidential candidate Ted Kennedy to use for his early morning phone calls, only to find later that our still untrained basset hound had slipped in ahead of the Senator and left his "calling card" right at the foot of the chair.

> *"High-sculptured ceilings, plush carpets, security guards, and iron gates don't begin to protect one from nitty-gritty."*

— The day I was showering for my first "official luncheon" and plumbers in the basement turned off the hot water mid-shower. Out I came, wrapped in a long towel, screaming indelicately. That became known as the First Lady's "first official tantrum."

— The day the Governor opened the coat closet to find a new Historical Society volunteer standing among the coats, solemnly rehearsing her presentation for tour day. She was mortified. He was amused. Later, to the delight of all the Historical Society guides, he sent her the standard blue proclamation naming her "Official Governor's Mansion Closet Inspector."

And there were less happy times: The day our beagle-basset was hit by a car and died. The day our son threw a snowball and hit a Denver police car; the night he shot a B.B. gun into the air and hit an apartment house window. The day our daughter and a friend jumped out of the bushes and scared some tourists so badly we received a complaint letter from Nebraska.

Why all this reminiscing? I'm not sure. Perhaps I just want you all to know that high-sculptured ceilings, plush carpets, security guards, and iron gates don't begin to protect one from nitty-gritty.

But, would I have missed the past eight year? Never!

And, am I happy to be here another four years? You bet!

Transition
It's a Many Splendored, Multi-frustrating Thing

Denver Post
DECEMBER 28, 1986

"Hოw's THE TRANSITION GOING?" PEOPLE ASK. "I don't know," I usually answer.

And I don't. It depends on the day.

Some days I wake up wild with enthusiasm for our new beginning. So excited about becoming a middle-aged student in the hallowed ivy halls of Dartmouth College, I want to "space" all this transition stuff and simply be there right now.

But this particular day, I woke up with a migraine headache, dropped an open bottle of 150 Anacin all over the bathroom counter, and burst into tears over the view of the sunrise from the leaded glass windows of "my" dressing room, a view which will be "mine" only two weeks longer.

The night of the election, as the spotlight shifted, I stood in the audience, just one of the hundreds of ecstatic Democrats. As I watched the spotlight follow the Romer family to the podium, I felt a huge sense of relief — a lightness, an almost giddiness, as if an unacknowledged, but ever-present, weight was being lifted from my shoulders. As if I would rise out of my shoes and float 12 inches off the ground.

I hadn't known I'd had a 12-year weight on me. I've loved living in the historic, spacious Governor's Mansion. I've loved having a platform and political influence. I've loved the National Governor's Association meetings, the friendship with other political spouses. I've loved being the wife of the governor of the state to which we both migrated out of choice over 25 years ago.

The pressures were intense the first two years of "our" term. But after those two years, a piece of cake, I thought.

The weight that remained was unfelt, invisible, until it started to lift. The shock on Nov. 4 was not that the pressure was lifting but that it had been there at all.

Then there are other days.

Typical moving days.

Days in which a docile room which I have resolved to "totally clean out" stands up and defies me. And I spend four hours on the four drawers of just one desk, filled with letters, memorabilia and just plain junk I didn't even know was there, junk which multiples as I work.

Humor columnist Dave Barry, who recently moved from Philadelphia to Miami, writes that when you move it's as if "all of your possessions, possessions you threw away years and years ago, rise up and come limping back to your house and nestle in the backs of closets, waiting to spring out at you ...."

He's right. They do.

Some days the enormity of the project becomes so defeating, I enter a defensive sort of stupor and find myself sorting the big paper clips from the small paper clips or performing some other meaningless, repetitive task.

And then there are the days of anxiousness and self-absorbed worry: The weight *is* lifting.

Dick and I both agree. We check out our mental temperatures and take our emotional pulse, regularly. Together, and alone. But will it continue to lift? Or will it descend like a leaden boomerang — the day, the moment — we are shorn of the position, the power, and all the subtle support services we may have become more accustomed to than we know.

It's not just that no State Patrol person will drive us, and no cook will fix our dinner, but will *any* person even return our phone calls?

We elected to get out. But that doesn't mean it's all smooth sailing. For I have found that the adage, "There's no big loss without some little gain" has a flip side. "There's no big gain without some big loss."

When we gained this position, the big loss was personal freedom.

When we regain our "freedom," the big loss will be political power. And power may be passed willingly and graciously, but never easily.

The stress experts say that even a positive change will produce stress. And the problem with the positive change is that you don't know you're stressed, and you don't think you ought to be stressed, so you don't understand what crazy thing is going on with you.

So I worry about what two people "be-knighted" by titles and surrounded by sound and fury will do when the cheering and booing stops, when the drumbeat of constant feedback fades.

Will the silence be sweet or nerve shattering? Will we bask in its blessedness, or rush toward its echoes, needing its acclaim, creating new noises, too soon, in order to again feel "real"?

I don't know.

In fact, as many books and articles as I've read on change and transition, I still don't know very much.

I simply don't know how to deal with the emotional roller coaster, the need to gear up to get the columns done before I take my "moving break" on Jan. 4. The need to gear up to finish other certain crucial projects before my platform lowers to ground level like a stage set at the Country Dinner Playhouse.

And how at the same time to "gear down," to break off, to pull away, to disengage from all the other activities that no longer really matter. To sit, Buddha-like, amid the wrappings and the Christmas trappings, to savor both the moment and the decade, the promise and the losses.

We are leaving a historical property, which has indeed been our home, a way of life, and 12 years of growing and growing up. We are leaving our son, a dog, our furniture, our mementos, and our files.

We are taking our daughter, another dog, down parkas, cross-country skis, and a word processor. Our family is splitting up as all families do. Not breaking up, but splitting up.

So to tell you the truth, I have no idea how the transition is going.

Writing and even thinking about a major "transition" when you are in its midst is like reading a book on natural childbirth when you are in the throes of intensive labor.

This transition is hard and painful and joyous and exhilarating. It feels like heaven. It feels like hell. And, like intensive labor, it feels as if it will never end.

Goodbye to the Mansion
But Never to All the Wonderful Memories

Denver Post
JANUARY 4, 1987

"MEMORIES."
That's what was playing on the radio as I walked into my husband's study on the third floor of the governor's mansion.

I expected to find my husband. He was not there. I was greeted only by memories — hundreds of them.

How long had it been since I'd really looked at the things in that study? Was it 1975, when we moved in Claude Boettcher's desk from the store room? Or 1986, when we hung the old llama rug we had bought on our honeymoon in Peru? I don't know.

Predating the rug is the gray driftwood fish that hung over the fireplace in Dick's bachelor pad.

Then there's the picture of Dick and Gerry Ford — his favorite living president — relaxing comfortably at Vail.

A collection of political cartoons, most funny to us — all, I'm sure, funny to some. A self-framed Picasso print, "Guernica," from the old days. A professionally framed Remington print, "Return of a Black Foot War Party," from newer days.

A wooden oxen with a sleepy rider, hand-carved, from our 1967 trip to Thailand and other points east.

A ceramic duck from Mexico.

A wooden duck from Taiwan.

A brass duck from San Francisco.

A "silver" spike.

A miner's helmet from old Colorado City, adorned with hand-painted columbines.

And at least 300 books, ranging from John Dos Passos' "The Men Who Made the Nation" to "Podium Humor" by James C. Humes.

But the memories don't stop at the study door.

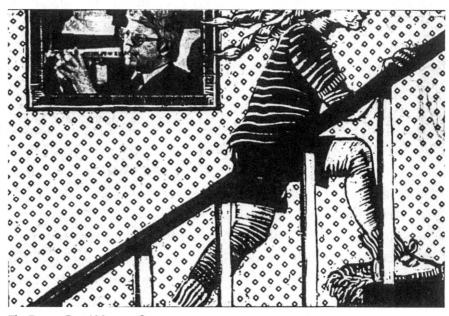

The Denver Post / Maureen Scance

The mansion staircase is filled with memories, too. No mementos here — just the backdrop for living memories, some photographed, some not:

Of Brownie troops and giggling girls bouncing up the stairs.

Of spilled soda pop, crushed Girl Scout cookies and scowls from Mom.

Of 9-year-old Heather taking three steps at a time, rushing, eyes gleaming, pigtails flying, anticipating the delivery of her new canopy bed.

Of 11-year-old Scott and buddy, Bill Plock, thundering up the stairs, laughing and gasping for breath, chubby cheeks flushed with the victory of a "won" football game.

Suddenly the pigtails and the Brownie uniforms turn to stacked heels and hose, and five 13-year-old young ladies pose for a picture before going off to a friend's bar mitzvah.

And rosy cheeks and baby fat turn to beards, sprouting from faces atop gangling, rangy athletic frames struggling under the weight of electronic amplifiers. Little Leaguers turned rockers, never destined to play anything as soothing as "Memories."

And as I write, a full-blown, live "memory" trudges up the stairs, asking for her phone messages, carrying her lacrosse stick, school pack on her back.

I smile, then frown slightly, joyful to see her, yet somewhat annoyed to have my reverie interrupted. Which brings me to another memory: Sometimes I am better at romanticizing motherhood than I am at practicing it.

A few months later, I reel with disbelief at the passage of time when our son, who was rocked as an infant in the old green La-Z-Boy chair, carries the same chair single-handedly down the stairs and out the door to his new apartment.

Then there are the political memories:

Jimmy Carter seeking the Democratic nomination for president. He and my husband standing at the foot of the stairs, conversing intently, both in their blue jeans. "Will *he* be president," Scott asks, whispering. "He looks like a cowboy!"

Teddy Kennedy, flushed, smiling, pursuing the same nomination, ascending the stairs with Kennedy "vig-ah," preceded and followed by a least three aides and six Secret Service men.

And the historical memories:

The late John Evans III, then in his 90s, standing at the foot of the staircase reminiscing about his wedding day, Nov. 11, 1908, when he married Gladys Cheesman. "I can still see my bride descending these stairs in her wedding gown," he says, stroking the bannister, overcome with emotion.

And Heather greeting Princess Anne with a slight incline of her head, dutifully, solemnly, just as she had been instructed.

"Memories."

When we first heard that song in 1984, my husband was awe stuck. "I'd give up my 12 years as governor to have written that song," he exclaimed.

"No, you wouldn't," I said.

"You're right," he laughed.

But now he is ending his 12 years of governorship and we're giving up the study, the staircase, the mansion, but never, *ever*, the memories.

Thank you, Colorado.

Putting the Campaign in Perspective

Denver Post
MAY 10, 1992

YOU DIDN'T EXPECT ME TO BECOME A campaigning spouse again? We're even. Neither did I.

But this time, as my husband makes his bid for the U.S. Senate, things will be different from when he ran for his third term as governor 10 years ago.

In short, I will not give up this column.

Writing, combined with public speaking, has become my profession. It is no longer just a First Lady "side job" as viewed by some when I began it in 1979.

This newspaper has changed with the times. Whereas once my column was considered by the management as "too political" to run during campaign times, it is now considered as a column in its own right.

Whereas once I was "benched" during election years, I will now continue as a player in my chosen profession. Wouldn't a doctor or a lawyer or a schoolteacher who was a political spouse do the same?

My only restriction is that I may not tout my husband or trounce his political opponents in print. That's fine.

Out there in the political arena, I'll hurl enough political hardballs to last a lifetime. In this space, I will dwell on softer, more personal matters.

Josie Heath, one of the three Democratic contenders for the Senate nomination, has been my close friend for almost 20 years. As I write this, it feels far more important that we remain friends for the next 20 years than that she wins or he wins.

Betsy Considine, wife of the most probable Republican contender, and I had lunch about a year ago. None of the political wags I know could believe we didn't talk politics. But we didn't. We talked about the true nature of the feminine ethic. I hope we'll get back to that conversation one day.

In fact, it often has occurred to me that perhaps the softer, relationship-oriented issues *are* the ones that really matter.

It's like the metaphor of the river and the banks. The river's rushing torrent — like wars and political battles — gets all the attention. And well it should. The torrent, at its height of power, can carve new canyons, tumble over precipices, and sometimes flood the banks. In short, the river makes history.

Yet, through the ages, it has been and continues to be the everyday minutiae of activity on the banks — the birthing and building, the marrying and dying, the nurturing and loving — that sustain life, no matter the twists, turns and floods of the river.

Since my second child left home in 1989. I find I have drifted from the banks and jumped full force into the river. Now, in the midst of a torrent that feels like a burst fire hydrant, I may use this space as a reprieve — a place to "bank" and reflect.

On the banks, we try to put things into context, not to take them out to score a political point.

On the banks, we try to grasp complexity in all its fullness, not to simplify in the quest for a sound bite.

Suddenly, and maybe *because* of the intensity of the campaign, I realize I miss my "banks" activities; not only the nurturing of my kids, but the other generative capacities I have dropped, like helping at the local school or serving as a board member of the Women's Foundation of Colorado.

Ideas for this softer, gentler column keep bubbling up as I write:

- What it sounded like to hear two young macho-looking men on a Vail chairlift last winter discussing their love lives, not in terms of sex and conquest but in words of tenderness, conflict and respect.
- What it feels like to campaign with my young children no longer grasping my skirts, but now, both young adults, grasping the issues as clearly as we do, and sometimes more so. When we began our first campaign for the governorship, our son was in kindergarten and our daughter barely 2. Now she is almost 22 and may come home for the summer to campaign with us.

So stay tuned. Out there you will see a fighter, hair afire, charging for one goal and one goal only. Here you will see a thinker, a reflector trying to integrate conflicting strands and keeping it all together.

(Unless, of course, something of such immense societal import hits me that I just *have* to write about it!)

In the meantime, I must respond to two questions that people keep asking me since Dick and I made this joint decision to jump back into elective politics.

The first question: "After spending half your life trying to get women more involved in everything, don't you wish *you* were running?"

No. I've got the dedication, but not the stamina. I *need* to climb up on the banks for a few gasps of air every once in a while. Elected office at such a high level would submerge me in the river to the point of drowning.

The second question: "Isn't it painful for you to be campaigning against a qualified woman, and a friend at that?"

Yes.

No elaboration needed.

Loss Felt Like Death, but Now a Vision Heals

Denver Post
AUGUST 30, 1992

"I'VE BEEN RICH AND I'VE BEEN POOR," SAID Sophie Tucker about wealth. "Rich is better."

Same with politics. We've won and we've lost; winning's better.

The day after the Aug. 11 Democratic senatorial primary, our loss felt to me like a death in the family.

No one had died. My husband, the defeated candidate, sat reading the papers, solemn, pensive. I stood, sipping my coffee and looking out at the rain. Our daughter slept. Our son had just called from Oregon with condolences.

A pall hung over the house.

When was the "service"?

How do we get past this first election defeat?

Later I try to explain to our daughter:

There are political tides we have ridden to success. Your dad rode — No, he led! — a populist, environmental tidal wave to the governorship in 1974. His opponent — a decent, capable Republican with no ties to Nixonian Washington — was washed out in the anti-Watergate tide.

Elections are not civics classes where the best orator gets the blue ribbon.

This year we thought we were leading a second reformist tide. Did our "ocean" roar a song no one wanted to hear? Or were we just too far ahead of the wave's crest?

No matter. Someone who rides the tide successfully for 20 years picks up a lot of debris. Some of it sticks. And wham! A new, 1990s-style populist tidal wave slammed us good.

Flash back: Election night. Everyone all smiles on the stage. Democratic Unity Party. Campbell wins. Lamm and Heath join hands with the victor. Someone from the Heath campaign whispers, "When do we just get to say 'Oh s——!'" I laugh. "Tomorrow, when the mic is off."

It's now the end of August. And the pall has lifted. I'm not going to spend the rest of my life crying, "Oh s——!" or spewing other four-letter words. Yet, a new critical edge enters my perceptions.

An enticing freedom resounds as we are bounced, unceremoniously, back to the private sector. Freedom in not having to hound reporters to cover our cause. Freedom in not measuring every word for its political effect. In thumbing our noses as the newspapers splat on the door step. In not grabbing, half asleep, for the radio or TV dial at 6 a.m. to see how our latest issue has been interpreted, misinterpreted, slaughtered or ignored.

So. Up one day. Down the next.

We don't throw everything we've got into a dream, a mission for this state and country, a campaign battle for four months, and then decompress that easily. We don't put the rest of our lives

> *"Did our 'ocean' roar a song no one wanted to hear? Or were we just too far ahead of the wave's crest?"*

"on hold" for an entire summer and then pick up the pieces as casually as we pick up the green and white Lamm signs from our supporters' lawns.

LOSE *is* a four-letter word.

But lose is *not* a death in the family.

And lose is also LIBERATION!

It's now September. There has been no "service." We found we didn't need one.

We just need to hold this vision in our hearts:

Our East Colfax office. The last week of the campaign. Even the walls buzz with energy, as the metropolitan areas surge our way. Staff and volunteers — close to 50 of them — phoning the counties, organizing the final mailings, the last literature drops. The younger staffers rushing in at 6 a.m., gluttons for more work, after spending all night putting up signs.

The next generation — our reason for entering the race — working for us as we work for them.

As these 20- to 30-year-olds move to other campaigns and other causes, we need to remember that our message, *their* message, will not be diverted or deluged by cross-currents. That these young adults, with their unbounded vitality, will never drown in the undertow.

We hold tight to this vision, as we let go of the campaign.

FIERCE FEMALES:
Challenging the World

Steinem Speaks
A Visit with America's Foremost Feminist

Denver Post
November 20, 1983

GLORIA STEINEM WAS AUTOGRAPHING HER book, "Outrageous Acts and Everyday Rebellions," at the Tattered Cover book store in Denver last month, when a woman with a nervous giggle approached.

"I don't agree with half of what you say," ventured the woman in a high-pitched voice, "but you have done so much for women, I just had to meet you."

The leader of America's feminist movement and founder of *Ms.* Magazine smiled. "I know you are doing things for women, too," she said softly.

I had heard Gloria Steinem talk about the "Empowerment of Women" before. Now I was seeing her put this empowerment into action. Later, in personal conversation, she expanded on the empowerment theme:

"Women get more radical with age. It makes a certain anthropological sense. Because to the extent we have power, we have it when we are young, as childbearers, energetic workers, etc. So the average 40- or 50-year-old woman probably has less power and social value than she did when she was 18.

"For men, it's the other way around. The average 18-year-old guy has less power and social value than he will when he is 40 or 50. This radicalization with age holds true for women in public office, too. The longer they are in office, the more 'feminist' they get."

I was curious how Steinem saw feminism as a force for solving world problems — for example, the population explosion:

"For over-population, feminism is the *only* answer," she replied with vehemence. "When women are given the means to decide whether they have children or not, the population goes down. When women can control their fertility, they do. Most of the population experts, unfortunately, don't view it that way. They fear in giving women the power that we will either breed like rabbits, or that we won't have any children at all, or that we will be sexually promiscuous.

"Also, the experts say that Third World women have to be able to read first. There they are,

> *"I had heard Gloria Steinem talk about the 'Empowerment of Women' before. Now I was seeing her put this empowerment into action."*

crawling on their hands and knees in the jungle, or walking 15 miles for contraceptive help, and the experts say they have to read first! They may not be literate, but they are smart. It's logical for us to want to control our own bodies. It just makes sense."

And what about war? Can the application of feminist principles reduce its likelihood?

"Women in Congress have always voted less for war and for military spending — except for true self-defense, like during World War II when we were attacked — than men have. It used to be called 'conservative' (isolationist) to vote against military spending; now it's called 'radical.' But women of both parties tend to vote that way."

What are Steinem's goals for the 1984 election?

"Working for — just trying to get women out to vote! If 60 percent of us turned out to vote, there would be no more Ronald Reagan."

Steinem also is working for a group called "Voters for Choice." She feels that "pro-choice" voters can now be mobilized around "pro-choice" candidates — as "anti-abortion" voters historically have been mobilized around their candidates. "We have had 80 percent public approval on reproductive freedom issues through the last decade. Now we, too, are willing to vote on that issue alone."

Did Steinem ever wish she had married and had children?

"No. I tried to talk myself into it. I always assumed I would because *everyone* got married. But when I thought of it, it was like a wall came down in front of me; I felt I'd have to give up my name, give up my work … when I realized one day I was happy the way I was."

Is it even *possible* for high-impact, feminist women to be married and have a family?

"Oh, of course! Most feminist are married — just like most women are married. Robin Morgan is married with one son. Bella Abzug is married, has grown daughters who are just fabulous and Bella practiced law through all her pregnancies. Her husband is funny, terrific. Letty (Cottin) Pogrebin is probably the happiest married person I know."

And this column is only part of what Gloria Steinem reflected upon in our hour-and-a-quarter conversation. As I play back the tape, I am surprised at how much of it deals with personal and professional concerns, the feminist nuances of our own lives.

I don't think I had approached Steinem with a nervous giggle, but as I left her, my step was lighter and my head a little higher. It's clear that to Gloria Steinem, the "Empowerment of Women" is more than an intellectual phrase.

Women Reaching the Top

Denver Post
APRIL 22, 2012

A S COURAGEOUS AS OUR EARLY FEMALE PIONEERS, they are, indeed, women to match our mountains.

Out of the thousands of women who have influence in Colorado, I set out to choose the top five. It was a daunting task. Therefore, I kept to those women who have influence outside of Colorado's borders as well. Here are my selections:

Marilyn Van Derbur became "Colorado's own Miss America" while a student at the University of Colorado at Boulder in 1957. The two decades of motivational speaking that followed won her another title: Outstanding Woman Speaker in America.

However, Marilyn's real work began at age 39, when her personal life began to implode. As her daughter, Jennifer, turned 5, the birthday triggered long-buried memories of incest perpetrated by her father, the socially prominent and wealthy Francis Van Derbur, from the time Marilyn turned 5 until the age of 18.

Suddenly, her body went into long spells of paralysis, as her conscious mind struggled to keep those memories down.

Her story was never supposed to become public. But, of course, it did.

When, at 53, Marilyn's picture appeared on the cover of People magazine with the headline "Miss America Overcomes Shame," there was an outpouring of support. She was shocked when 900 people showed up at a congressional hearing on sexual abuse to hear her presentation.

But that was only the beginning of her passionate new mission: Speak to all who would listen about the horror of incest and the trauma of other types of sexual abuse; listen to the victims and their stories; and, armed with her self-authored book, the prize-winning "Miss America by Day," give seminars on preventing abuse.

Over the past 21 years, Marilyn has spoken in more than 500 cities and has been in contact with more adult survivors of incest than anyone in America.

Now approaching 75, Marilyn still spends up to six hours each day on the phone and answering e-mails, counseling the hundreds of abuse survivors — female, male, young and old — who contact her from all over the globe.

Marilyn Van Derbur Atler: Saving the world — one speech, one survivor at a time.

"Heeeeere's Elbra!" That was how I heard **Elbra Wedgeworth** introduced to an ecstatic crowd in 2007 after she had helped secure the 2008 Democratic National Convention in Denver.

It was her dream, an epiphany she had in early 2005. As president of the convention host committee, she is the first to give credit to the many others involved, but it simply wouldn't have happened without her.

No one who has watched Elbra's diligence over the years would have been surprised at her success. After she was elected to the Denver City Council in 1999 and became its president in 2003, her "can-do" attitude was duly noticed by other council members and the public: She not only oversaw the multimillion-dollar budget, but also revised the council rules and completely restructured the council committees.

Armed with the values that her parents, Walter and Castella Wedgeworth, had instilled — "serve your community," and "do not let others define you; always define yourself" — Elbra was ready to take on the world.

And she did. As an African-American and the first black female to ever head a convention host committee in either party, Elbra's proudest moment was watching Barack Obama walk across a stage to deliver his acceptance speech at the convention she had helped to bring to her hometown.

Now, at age 54, she serves as a member of the Denver Exploratory Committee for the 2022 Winter Olympics, a position that makes her eyes sparkle.

Not in favor of the Olympics coming here? Watch out, because what Elbra wants (and works hard for), Elbra usually gets.

Elbra Wedgeworth: If you dream it big, it will come.

Urban preservationist and developer **Dana Crawford** has been a civic and business leader in Denver for more than 40 years. But it was even earlier than that — in the 1960s — when Dana realized that much of Denver's original downtown was about to be demolished as part of an urban renewal project.

Especially captivated by the historic 1400 block of Larimer Street, Dana's instincts said, "No."

"I literally felt the hand of fate," she wrote in an e-mail.

"I became very motivated, almost obsessed, with a need to figure out a way to save at least [this] one block from demolition." Thus "sprung" Larimer Square, the first Lower Downtown development that daily attracts Coloradans and tourists from all over the world.

But Dana didn't stop there. A few of her other accomplishments:

- The renovation of various "skid row" warehouses into livable condominium structures, including the Flour Mill Lofts, where Dana, now 80, resides today.
- The redevelopment of the historic (but run-down) Oxford Hotel.
- The foundation (with others) of the Urban Land Institute, a national organization that has had a substantial impact on preservation in cities all over the U.S. (In fact, Dana has personally consulted on urban planning in 60 cities.)

Back in Colorado, she was instrumental in saving the Brown Palace Hotel, the Navarre Building, and the Equitable Building, and has consulted with at least 10 cities outside of Denver.

Collectively, Dana has developed more than 800,000 square feet of historic properties valued at $100 million.

Dana now serves as president of Urban Neighborhoods, Inc. Just last month, she received the 2012 LoDo District's Limelight Legacy award for her leading role in the Union Station redevelopment.

This is only the latest of the many tributes she has accrued over the years for her amazing work.

Dana Crawford: Her visions then; our quality of life now.

Former six-term Denver Congress-woman **Patricia Schroeder**, an unabashed Democratic liberal, entered Congress in 1972 as the first female congressperson elected from the 1st Congressional District, and the first ever to arrive with a 6-year-old and a 2-year-old in tow.

Pat, then 32, immediately ran into a sexist firestorm. Famous among her persecutors was Armed Services Committee chair F. Edward Hebert, D-Ala., who resented the assignment of "Little Patsy" to his committee.

As "punishment," he made her and newly elected Ron Dellums, an African-American from California, share a seat. According to Pat, Hebert actually said that "women and blacks were only worth one-half of a regular member," and thus deserved only half a seat.

Pat, however, persevered. Her efforts on behalf of women's rights and those of other marginalized groups are legion, ranging from pro-choice advocacy to the securing of benefits for the spouses of Foreign Service officers.

Many consider the passage of the 1993 Family and Medical Leave Act to be Pat's biggest accomplishment.

In 1987, Pat raised supporters' hopes and dreams when she considered a run for the presidency. But she eventually decided against it.

Her "Schroederisms" (one-liners) became famous.

When asked if she could serve as a congresswoman and a mommy at the same time, she once told an all-male group: "Yes! I have a brain and a uterus and I use them both."

Today, Pat, now 70, pursues her goals of good government and equality by serving on several national non-profit boards.

The late writer and political consultant Ted Sorenson once described Pat as "a politician who could draft a bill, stir a crowd, fly a plane, bake a cake, pass a law, coin a phrase — and run for president."

And many are still sorry she didn't take on that last challenge.

Pat Schroeder: There for us yesterday; still here for us today.

Katherine Archuleta may never run for president, but she surely is an asset to the one in power now. As the political director for President Obama's re-election campaign, Katherine, 64, is the first female and first Latina of either party to fill this position.

The appointment of Katherine did not surprise me. I had witnessed firsthand her extremely effective political organizing in Colorado.

And in 1987, I worked with her (and others) in establishing the Women's Foundation of Colorado.

Of course, Katherine's résumé abounds with high-level paid professional positions, too: top aide to Mayor Federico Peña; Peña's chief of staff when he was secretary of Transportation; senior adviser to then-Mayor John Hickenlooper; and most recently, chief of staff to Hilda L. Solis, secretary of the Department of Labor.

Katherine is thrilled and energized by her new position. She writes: "My role in the campaign will forever change how presidential campaigns will be organized. Women and especially women of color will stand with other political leaders in helping to shape elections that are the very core of who we are as a democratic society."

Katherine is sensitive, but also tough. I was there, and part of the "accused," when she took on her "sisters" of the Women's Foundation founding committee for not being inclusive enough. "You are going against everything you are supposed to stand for!" she admonished us. And she was right.

Katherine should soar in the position she holds now, working 14 hours a day. She is currently in Texas, organizing Latino voters.

And if President Obama wins, who knows? She may rise to even greater heights.

Katherine Archuleta: Diversity, drive, determination and so much more.

40 Years after I Met Hillary Clinton, I'm Still with Her

Denver Post
NOVEMBER 13, 2016

WHILE OTHERS ARE ANALYZING WHY SO MUCH of the election polling was wrong, agonizing or pontificating on the new direction of the nation, today I simply pay homage to Hillary Clinton — the Hillary I have known since the late 1970s when my husband was governor of Colorado and her husband was governor of Arkansas.

In 1976, Clinton entered the Wives Association "training session" for new governors with energy and confidence. Her trademark wonky glasses and bright-colored headband firmly in place, she evidenced no makeup, only a bright, friendly smile. We immediately clicked.

White House Photo

Wow! I thought. This woman needs no "training." I noted how she listened to everyone's name and repeated it, how she attended all the governors' sessions — many of us did — but *she* took notes.

Throughout the following months we worked together with other spouses (our titles finally updated when Dr. Arthur Kunin, husband of Vermont Gov. Madeleine Kunin, joined our ranks) to get our agenda *off* the traditional track of "mansion management," and to bring speakers on substantive issues to the Spouses Association. Carl Sagan was the first one.

Years later, in the summer of 1990, Hillary and I met again for breakfast at the Brown Palace in Denver.

She was blunt and to the point. "I'm meeting with all the former and present Democratic governors' spouses to get support for Bill for president in 1992. Will you be one of them?" I demurred.

After she rattled off *his* qualifications, I had what was then a subversive thought: Why don't *you* run?

And in 2008, she did. But not until after she had:

- Withstood a tumultuous political and personal time in the White House, all the while fighting for families, especially children and their health care.
- Declared that "women's rights are human rights are women's rights" at the 1995 United Nations Fourth Conference on Women in Beijing, despite objections from the Chinese government and that of her own White House policy staff.

- Worked across party lines quietly and diligently in the U.S. Senate after her election in New York in 2000, winning the respect of many Republicans.

But 2008 was not her time. A new, younger, charismatic African-American was to make history instead. She fought hard for that nomination. Yet, after conceding, she worked graciously and tirelessly to get Barack Obama elected.

Almost immediately, Hillary answered Obama's call to become his secretary of state. In that position — yes, amid some serious misjudgments for which she has apologized — she performed loyally and brilliantly, travelling a total 956,733 miles and winning the respect of foreign leaders.

During her 2016 campaign she was heralded by husband Bill and President Obama (men not without their own egos) as the *most* qualified person to ever run for the presidency.

> *"I mourn today ... because of all the little girls out there who will have to wait for a female president as a role model."*

But this year, being "qualified" didn't matter. Throughout the race both candidates were perceived negatively by the voters — Hillary a little more so. (Although she did win the popular vote.)

Again, I will not pontificate on the reasons for her loss except to say it is clear that most voters wanted massive change, and that misogyny is alive and well.

I mourn today not only because our divided nation and the world will be deprived of Hillary's compassionate, strong and smart leadership, but because of all the little girls out there who will have to wait for a female president as a role model.

"You can't be what you can't see," said a feminist friend of mine. Sadly we have lost that "seeing" opportunity for our daughters and granddaughters.

AND A FEW GOOD MEN …

JFK's Death Only Part of His Memory

Denver Post
NOVEMBER 22, 1983

EVERYONE REMEMBERS WHAT HE OR SHE WAS doing exactly 20 years ago today — at the moment news was received that President John F. Kennedy had been shot. Yet, I remember almost as clearly what I was doing the day the new president was inaugurated on January 20, 1961. I was going skiing.

It was one of those crystal cold days when fine, white, sugar snow danced on the windshield. The sun broke bright through the clouds, only to recede again, leaving the world in swirling grayness.

That clipped speech

As we approached Berthoud Pass for Winter Park, my companion flipped on the radio. The newly inaugurated president's clipped, New England accent broke through the static:

"… and so my fellow Americans, ask not what your country can do for you, ask what you can do for your country …

"Hey, not bad!" exclaimed my friend, slapping his knee. "Not bad for a Democrat!" Although all first-time voters were supposed to have been smitten with the youthful vigor of the former PT boat hero, my friend had not voted for President Kennedy. In fact, neither had I.

I had seen him only once: a thoughtful, solitary figure, shoulders hunched against the wind as he walked toward Stapleton Airport's farthest gate on an early Colorado campaign trip. His "presence," then, did not particularly impress me, but his words, now, hooked me with their charisma, their idealism.

Not all mourned

Two years and 10 months later, I received the assassination news by telephone, then sat stupefied in front of the radio. It is said "that the whole world stopped dead in its tracks," "that all of America mourned." But some in my world did not:

Two women in the apartment next door to Dick's and mine came giggling and chatting down the hall. I jumped to the door defensively. "Sshhh! Haven't you heard?" I asked. "Yes," they said. And babbled on their way.

A member of the extended family passed through town and called to talk trivia: "What was the Denver weather forecast? How long would we live in an apartment before buying a house? Would we be going 'home' for Christmas …." Gripping the phone, I stood frozen, shocked out of even perfunctory pleasantness.

But most of America did, indeed, mourn.

Eloquent eulogy

The Rev. Richard Henry, former minister of Denver's First Unitarian Church, spoke eloquently to a quietly tearful congregation, the Sunday after the assassination:

Was he a great president? We don't know. He didn't have the time to act and we didn't have the time to evaluate. But this we do know; he was a great motivator. By the mere force of his personality, he convinced others that their acts could make a difference ….

Was he a great president? I don't know. Time magazine asks only: How *good* a president? But, I do know the difference his presidency made in my life:

First, he made the art of politics appealing and respectable. I knew, as an adult, it was my responsibility to vote and did so; yet, I had disdained politics itself, haughtily characterizing those who actually *practiced* it as either "ideologues" or "idiots."

I could care, too

Second, he solidified my ambition to become a social worker. If someone that rich and powerful could care about the poor and downtrodden, certainly I could, too.

Third, he made excellence a virtue and promoted it wherever he found it, even if he didn't understand it. He brought Pablo Casals and Igor Stravinsky to the White House even though, as Time magazine suggests, "his own taste may have run more towards Sinatra …. At least he brought them." The high intellectual goals he set for himself raised the mental goals I set for myself.

Did John F. Kennedy accomplish more in death than he did in life? On the large political scene, most likely.

But on the smaller personal scene, no. To those of us who came of political age during his presidency, our transformation was inspired not by news bulletins from Dallas on Nov. 22, 1963, but by the electric, vigorous inaugural words from Washington Jan. 20, 1961.

> *"To those of us who came of political age during his presidency, our transformation was inspired not by news bulletins from Dallas on Nov. 22, 1963, but by the electric, vigorous inaugural words from Washington Jan. 20, 1961."*

He's the Only "Good Guy" They've Got
I'm Supporting Obama, but If I Were a Republican, Huntsman Would Be My Choice

Colorado Statesman
DECEMBER 9, 2011

JON HUNTSMAN WOULD BE MY "NON MITT." That is if I were a Republican. And if I lived in New Hampshire. Here's why:

Though basically too conservative for me, he has a brain, and perhaps more important, the guts to stay independent of the "pack."

He is the only one of the Republican candidates who will admit to believing in evolution and global warming.

Though strongly anti abortion, he does not support the current array of "Personhood" Amendments, one of which is inching its way toward the ballot in Colorado for the third time. He has publicly stated that such measures, which would designate full rights to a fertilized egg, and deny women the choice of certain contraceptive methods, "go too far."

He has refused to sign Grover Norquist's pledge to never raise taxes under any circumstances.

As a fluent Mandarin speaker and a former Mormon Missionary to China, he had the guts to accept the position of President Obama's Ambassador to China, answering the "call of his country" despite partisan differences.

Although against gay marriage, he supports Civil Unions.

He defends the "Dream Act" which allows college tuition assistance and a path to U.S. citizenship for children of illegal immigrants who have maintained good moral character and who have been here at least five years.

And according to *TIME* writer Joe Klein, he is the only candidate to propose a detailed plan to break up the big banks.

I'm also impressed with his basic character: A strong family man, father of seven children, two of whom are adopted. A devout Mormon who truly lives his faith and resists preaching it to others.

A disclaimer here. I have never met Jon Huntsman Jr., but I do know his father, Jon Huntsman Sr. who was president of the student body in my Palo Alto, CA high school class of 1955.

Now known as one of the world's richest self-made men, reportedly with a net worth of more than $1 billion, Huntsman Sr. was then simply known as one of the nicest guys in the school. And the "niceness" has followed his financial success. Of the more than 1,200 living billionaires in the world, he's one of only 19 who have donated at least $1 billion to charities over his lifetime.

He and his wife Karen, also a Paly High grad, raised nine children, of which Jon is the eldest.

Reconnecting at a memorial service for a classmate last month, Jon Sr. gave me a big hug and asked about my health, as we are both cancer survivors. It's good, I assured him and then added, "and your son is the best of the Republican lot." He grinned.

Back to Jon Junior. I don't mean to overdo the character issue, but I simply can't grasp why the same Republicans who tout "moral values" want to support: A guy with Perry's memory lapses, a guy with Romney's consistency lapses, or a guy with Gingrich's outrageous moral lapses in every arena of life, from marital to academic to financial. (And before he suspended his campaign, a guy with Cain's behavioral lapses.)

Go figure!

Huntsman also seems prone to limit the "dirt" in one of the nastiest, venal campaigns ever. He clearly inherits his father's "niceness." At this writing, the worst thing I've ever heard him say about another candidate is that "Romney is equipped with a well oiled weather vane."

Well, yes.

Right now Huntsman is at about 11 percent in New Hampshire polls. The highest he has ever been nationally is 4 percent. Too bad for him and too bad for his party.

Do nice guys in politics always finish last? Seems so in Republican primaries. Will he mount a campaign as an Independent? Is his real plan to finish first in 2016?

Who knows?

But this I do know. I'm a Colorado Democrat who will support President Obama next November. But if I were a New Hampshire Republican, Huntsman would get my vote in the Primary on Jan. 10. He's the only "good guy" they've got.

Kudos to Johnston for Speech

Denver Post
June 8, 2014

Kudos to State Sen. Michael Johnston, who faced down "political correctness" at Harvard.

Johnston courageously insisted that he would honor his May 28 commitment to speak at the Harvard Graduate School of Education's commencement, despite the fact that approximately 130 students, alums and faculty had demanded that his invitation be withdrawn.

The protesters' reason: Johnston's advocacy of "test-based accountability" in Colorado schools, which they claimed "weakens the due process for the protection of teachers."

I have been appalled this year at the shocking number of prestigious commencement speakers invited to elite colleges who, after initially accepting, backed out in the face of student protest.

First, former Secretary of State Condoleezza Rice withdrew as the commencement speaker at Rutgers in New Jersey. Rice should not have been selected as the speaker because of her involvement in the Iraq war during the Bush administration, claimed the protesters.

Rutgers president Robert L. Barchi held firm and defended Rice's selection, saying it was important for Rutgers to protect free speech and academic freedom. But Rice did not reconsider.

Next was the current head of the International Monetary Fund, Christine Lagarde, who seemed a perfect fit to address the 2,500 undergraduates who attend all-female Smith College in Massachusetts. Not so perfect, claimed a group of 500 students, faculty and alums who protested online, calling the IMF "a corrupt system which fuels the oppression of women and girls worldwide."

Lagarde backed out despite the fact that Smith's president, Kathleen McCartney, and 133 faculty members stuck by the invitation, and many students supported her, too. Senior Cassandra Brazile wrote on Facebook: "I'm so disappointed …. Because we do not agree with someone, does it mean we cannot listen to them?"

And finally, when renowned progressive Robert Birgeneau, former chancellor of the University of California Berkeley, accepted the invitation to deliver the graduation address at Haverford College in Pennsylvania, he was hit with a barrage of complaints from 46 liberal students.

"What insults me is not that students protest—that, after all, is their right—but that prestigious invited speakers 'chicken out' in face of protest even when administrators and other students encourage them to come."

Why? Because he had not apologized profusely enough about his failure to control police officers' use of force on the campus during the Occupy Wall Street demonstration on Nov. 9, 2011. When Birgeneau pulled out, Haverford president Daniel H. Weiss found his choice "deeply regrettable."

So why would Johnston step up to the plate rather than step back to safety? There are likely many reasons. But perhaps the most important is his investment in true leadership. As a major sponsor of Colorado Senate Bill 191, which seeks ways to evaluate teachers and principals, he believes it is crucial that he not back down from these goals.

Ever the idealist, he arranged with the dean of the school at Harvard to have a point-counterpoint session with his detractors the day before his formal address. Twenty-five students and one faculty member showed up.

"I've found that when you meet with dissenters face-to-face, there is often more agreement than you expect," Johnston said. "They learned something about how we are improving instructional support for teachers, and I learned from them, too."

The most significant result: Johnston is now in e-mail dialogue with two of his most strident protesters, "working jointly on ideas to improve teacher satisfaction and retention."

What insults me is not that students protest — that, after all, is their right — but that prestigious invited speakers "chicken out" in face of protest even when administrators and other students encourage them to come.

"To reach out first to those who disagree is a rule I have always kept, whether on this trip to Harvard or in my work in Colorado," Johnston said in his speech. "And in every one of those hard conversations, I have learned more, grown more, changed more …. The sound of the choir makes us dance, but the words of the critic make us grow."

He received a standing ovation.

Smitten with Pope Francis

Denver Post
DECEMBER 1, 2013

I CAME BACK FROM ROME AFTER AN OCTOBER visit smitten.

Not with the ancient glories of that historic city, but with the modern "glories" of the new Pope.

No, I did not meet Pope Francis.

No, I am not Catholic.

And, yes, I will continue to protest against some of the church dogma that I think does harm to people, especially women.

Yet, how can one rail against a pope who, dwelling near Vatican splendor, comes across less like a pontiff and more like a servant of the world?

Who lives in a small apartment in San Marco rather than the traditional and spacious Papal suite in the Apostolic Palace?

Who walks, or drives a modest car, while bishops and cardinals pass him by in limousines?

Who puts together a new council of diverse cardinals from eight different countries to help him reform and restructure the church?

Who makes his own phone calls, even to the outspoken atheist journalist Eugenio Scalfari, whom he actually *agrees* to let interview him. Here are some direct quotes from that interview:

> *"How can one rail against a pope who, dwelling near Vatican splendor, comes across less like a pontiff and more like a servant of the world?"*

On evil: "The most serious of the evils that afflict the world these days are youth unemployment and the loneliness of the old."

On proselytism: "Proselytism is solemn nonsense. We need to get to know each other, listen to each other ...."

On autonomy and conscience: "Everyone has his own idea of good and evil and must choose to follow the good and fight evil as he conceives them."

On church narcissism: "The heads of the church have been narcissists, flattered and thrilled by their courtiers. The court is the leprosy of the papacy. I do not share this (Vatican-centered) view of the world and I'll do everything I can to change it."

On women in the church: "(Next time) we will also discuss the role of women in the church," says the pope to Scalfari as they part. "Remember, the church is feminine."

My Sister of Loretto friend Lydia Peña, who admires Pope Francis (especially for his "generous, inclusive, open heart"), is hopeful and patient about what will change for women. "He has said that the feminine genius is needed wherever the church makes important decisions. True, presently, he is not promoting female ordination to the priesthood. He is listening, and I remind myself that he has only been serving as pope for nine months."

Some Catholics are appalled that Pope Francis seems to be marginalizing core Catholic positions such as the censure of abortion and homosexuality, and that he has publicly said things like, "If a homosexual person is of goodwill and is in search of God, I am no one to judge."

Yet, most accounts reveal that he is *not* reversing the church position on these issues. He simply does not want to become "obsessed" with such matters to the detriment of other missions.

One specifically mentioned in the Scalfari interview: "We must restore hope to young people, help the old, spread love. Be poor among the poor. We need to include the excluded and preach peace."

Then, last Thursday, in his first Papal Document, Pope Francis expanded the economic aspect of this mission, sharply challenging those people who "continue to defend trickle-down theories which assume that economic growth, encouraged by a free market, will inevitably succeed in bringing about greater justice and inclusiveness in the world …. Meanwhile, the excluded are still waiting ….

"I prefer a church which is bruised, hurting and dirty because it has been out on the streets rather than a church which is unhealthy … from clinging to its own security."

Clearly, the pope's Jesuit roots of men and women in the service of others, and his identity with St. Francis' mission of ministering to the poor, are shining through.

I applaud!

A Talk with Obama

Denver Post
AUGUST 10, 2012

SO WHAT DOES ONE DO WHEN, ON SHORT notice, one has the opportunity to interview the president of the United States?

First, thank the powers that be. Second, panic. Third, remember that he is a human being, just like anyone else. Fourth, prepare — quickly!

The round-table discussion was set for moments after the president had delivered his appeal to women voters during a rally at the Auraria Events Center in Denver Wednesday. It would be attended only by myself and Durango Herald columnist Megan Graham.

Women's health is not only a women's issue or a health issue, but an economic issue, President Obama stressed at the rally.

True, but the loudest cheer from the mostly female audience came when Obama declared that decisions affecting a woman's health are "not up to politicians, they're not up to insurance companies, they're up to you."

So I asked the president: What, for example, in the reproductive health area, would be the long-term differences for your daughters as they enter adulthood between four more years of your presidency and a four-year term of a Romney presidency?

His response was both passionate and articulate:

"All the steps we have taken in the Affordable Care Act are going to have a direct impact on women of every age, certainly on young women …. Women are much more likely to drop out of the workforce temporarily for child rearing. Then it becomes more difficult for them to get health insurance when they get back in …. So being able to keep or get insurance is going to make an enormous difference for generations to come.

"Mr. Romney has been very clear that he will repeal the Affordable Care Act, despite the fact it's working very well in Massachusetts. And he has not at all been clear as to how he would replace it.

"It is not an understatement that Mr. Romney's judicial philosophy and mine are quite different. He has pledged to appoint judges whom he is confident will overturn Roe vs. Wade, which will obviously have a big impact."

The president said Romney has endorsed amendments in state constitutions that not only deny abortion in all cases, but also curtail the use of some kinds of contraception. "I think this takes us backwards instead of forwards," he said.

Graham asked about the conflict between individual health rights and religious liberty.

"Religious liberty is one of the essential tenets of this country. In designing the Affordable Care Act, we thought long and hard about how we accommodate religious institutions, but also (how

we) make sure that individual women are being treated fairly. I think the balance we struck was the right one.

"Essentially every woman should have contraception as part of her insurance package …. This was not something we initiated just for ideological reasons. This was a recommendation by the Institute of Medicine and doctors.

"Then what we said is that … we will have an accommodation for religiously affiliated institutions so that they don't have to pay for contraception, they don't have to promote contraception. All they have to do is to just let the insurance company provide it as part of a package.

"I continue to be a strong believer in conscience clauses, so that employees in Catholic hospitals should not have to engage in providing services that would be a violation of their religion.

"But I also think that large institutions that employ an awful lot of folks that are of different faiths and who receive a lot of public dollars have to take into account as well the interests of their employees."

Then, wishing (silently) that the president had been a little more specific about how a Romney presidency as opposed to his own would affect the future lives of his daughters, I thanked him for his time. So did Graham.

> *"The loudest cheer … came when Obama declared that decisions affecting a woman's health are 'not up to politicians, they're not up to insurance companies. They're up to you.'"*

ACKNOWLEDGMENTS

I N COMPILING THIS BOOK, I DREW INSPIRATION AND ENCOURAGEMENT FROM MANY people. In particular, I am deeply indebted to the following individuals:

Shawn Boyd, curator of archives at History Colorado, and her entire team, who helped me forage through twenty-five years of columns to find just the right ones for this collection.

My editor, Joan Sherman, my book designer, Sue Campbell, and my OCR/data input specialist, Denise Geddis, who shared their expertise and creativity to transform a rough draft into a professional, accessible, and appealing volume, as well as my photographer, Katy Tartakoff, who took the cover photo.

The many friends—some of whom will recognize themselves in these writings—who encouraged me to keep going even when the task seemed overwhelming.

And finally, my family: my husband, Dick Lamm, who offered his love and intellectual wisdom; my sister, Jane Vennard, who offered her love and spiritual wisdom; my grown children, Scott Lamm and Heather Lamm (who appear in this book probably more than they would have wished), and their spouses, Cindy Lamm and Alex Ooms, all of whom gave unconditional support and showed enormous patience; and of course, my four grandchildren—Jasper Lamm Ooms, Kennon Hunter Lamm, Tobias Vennard Ooms, and Tessa Elliot Ooms—who inspire me each day just by being who they are.

About the Author

Dottie Lamm, Colorado's first lady from 1975 to 1987 and newspaper columnist from 1979 to 2017, has worked as a flight attendant, a psychiatric social worker, a college instructor, a public speaker, and a political activist. In 1998, as a self-proclaimed feminist and environmentalist, she won the Colorado Democratic Party nomination for the United States Senate.

Now "retired," she lives in Denver with her husband of 57 years, former Colorado Governor Dick Lamm. She enjoys time with her four grandchildren—ages 15 to 8— (whenever she can catch them!), volunteers for various projects that serve refugees, mentors young people with political ambitions, and jumps in to champion candidates (especially Democratic pro-choice women) every election cycle. This year (2020), she celebrates 39 years as a breast cancer survivor. An avid outdoorswoman, in her "spare time" Dottie hikes, swims, and cross-country skis. In her youth, she climbed 34 of Colorado's 54 mountains over 14,000 feet.

This is Lamm's third published collection of columns. It is distinguished from the others, *Second Banana* (1983) and *Choice Concerns* (1996), by its emphasis on the heart over the head, the personal over the political, and the psychological over the polemical.

CPSIA information can be obtained
at www.ICGtesting.com
Printed in the USA
LVHW060520230622
721880LV00006B/362